Living with the
Rubbish Queen

Telenovelas, culture
and modernity in Brazil

Thomas Tufte

UNIVERSITY
OF LUTON

press

British Library Cataloguing in Publication Data

A catalogue record for this book is available from the British Library

ISBN: 1 86020 541 0

Published by
University of Luton Press
University of Luton
75 Castle Street
Luton
Bedfordshire LU1 3AJ
United Kingdom

Tel: +44 (0)1582 743297; Fax: +44 (0)1582 743298
e-mail: ulp@luton.ac.uk
www.ulp.org.uk

Cover Design by Gary Gravatt
Typeset in Helvetica and Times
Printed in Great Britain by Thanet Press, Margate, Kent

iv

Contents

Acknowledgements

This book project has been underway every since the idea to it was conceived a decade ago, in a bus between Salvador, Bahia and Belo Horizonte, Minas Gerais. Sitting there for many hours, reflecting upon the country I was driving through, a country I had lived, studied and worked in, listening to fellow passengers discussing telenovelas, and wondering about the role of telenovelas - that was the beginning to what in 1995 became a Ph.D and now, 5 years later, has resulted in this book.

There are many people I wish to thank for having encouraged and supported the process leading to this book. Valuable criticisms and suggestions in regard to various parts and versions of the chapters in this book have been received from Kirsten Drotner, Valerio Fuenzalida, Morten Giersing, Klaus Bruhn Jensen, Bent Steeg Larsen, Camilla Nielsson, Kristian Paludan, Finn Rasmussen, Seija Ridell, Rikke Schubart and Birgitte Tufte. I have shared the fascination for the world of telenovelas and had numerous and very engaged, both serious and joyful discussions with Ana Maria Fadul, Maria Immacolata de Lopes, Nora Maziotti and Ana Uribe. As to insight into the telenovela culture industry, into the production process and in particular into the creative process of making many people interact in telling a good story, Paulo Grizolli has been very inspiring and an important source during our pleasurable meetings both in Denmark, Rio and in Portugal.

Jose Marques de Melo deserves a special thanks, believing in the project all the way and by providing valuable support, access and relevant contacts whereever needed. A person who has been a fundamental support and challenging discussant since the very beginning has been Joao Luiz van Tilburg in Rio. He provided me with a harsh critical analysis on telenovelas during our very first encounter in Rio, back in 1991, but also provided the video recordings I needed on the Rubbish Queen. It was the beginning to a fruitful and on-going dialogue. Tilburg's personal news-clip database on Brazilian television, and telenovelas in particular, has been of utmost importance for my project. This database has finally obtained an institutional basis at the PUC University in Rio and an Internet linkage which it deserves, making it accesible to everybody. It is a unique historical archive with newspapers clippings covering more than 30 years of television in Brazil. Visit it at www.tv-pesquisa.com.puc-rio.br

Ever since the World Congress of IAMCR in Guaruja, Brazil, in August 1992 and until the Second 'Crossroads of Cultural Studies' in Tampere, Finland in July 1998, many eye-opening and thought-provoking comments have reached me from audience and discussants during my presentation of working papers. Among the most important encounters have been: Ph.D-seminar in Vipperød, Denmark, October 1992, UNESCO/IMS Conference in São Paulo, Brazil 1995, Intercom Annual Congresses 1993, 1995 and 1997 in Brazil, Congress on Media and Politics, Brussels, March 1997, BRASA-IV in Washington in November 1997 and the TV Reception Seminar at University of Copenhagen in April 1998. Thanks to all who have given feedback at these opportunities.

In the phase of writing the book manuscript on the basis of my Ph.D, three people have been most valuable: Sergio Caparelli, Jorge Gonzalez and James Lull. They have given substantial response, provided constructive critique and many good ideas. Furthermore, at University of Luton Press, I am very grateful to Manuel Alvarado for his patience and for his continuous belief in the book project. Thanks also to the rest of the team at University of Luton Press who helped this book materialize.

A particular thanks must go the the Gurvitz family in Rio Grande do Sul who, ever since I watched my first telenovelas with them, back in 1983, have made their Brazilian home mine, and engaged in my telenovela research. A very special thanks goes to Pernille for tolerating me all the way, and supporting me in the book project, throughout all phases. The largest debt of all, however, is owed to the women of Vila Nitro Operaria, Calabar and Santa Operaria who allowed me to share their time, insights and opinions in regard to living with telenovelas in everyday life.

Thomas Tufte
Copenhagen, April 2000

Introduction

On 27 December 1992 the top story in the morning news in Brazil was the death of Daniella Perez, one of the main actors in the eight o'clock telenovela *From Body and Soul* (De Corpo e Alma). Daniella had been murdered in the middle of the night on a dark highway in Rio. Initially, when the rumour spread, people were confused, because the telenovela, where she played the heroine Yasmin, was nearing its climax and end, so the question was: did the character Yasmin die or did Daniella Perez really die? Was this fiction or reality? It was the real death of the actress, and that was not all: the main suspects for the murder were her partner in the telenovela, Guilherme de Padua, and his wife in real life, Paula Thomaz.

The Brazilian telenovela audience was shocked, and many were outraged by the fact that the prime suspect in the killing Daniella, Guilherme de Padua, had not been jailed. This started a social movement, led by the mother of the victim, Glória Perez, a writer of telenovelas, demanding a total revision of the Penal Code in Brazil. The peak of this social movement came on 19 September 1993, when 70 thousand people gathered at a football stadium in São Paulo to see Glória Perez hand over 1.3 million signatures supporting the revision of the law. These signatures had been gathered on squares and streets throughout the country, in the nine months that had passed since Daniella Perez' tragic death. Shortly after the handing over of the signatures, the organizer of the event asked for one minute of silence in memory of the murdered Daniella. This silence was broken by the musical theme of the telenovela character Yasmin, Daniella's last role. Not an eye was dry and the whole event at the stadium was transmitted live on radio and television! Four years later, in 1997, Guilherme de Padua was finally sentenced to 19 years in prison, and his wife received 18 years in prison, in what in Brazil had come to be known as the trial of the decade.

This dramatic story indicates how telenovelas can articulate mass emotional involvement, stimulate national unity and also political or civic action. In the above case, para-social emotional relations had been established between an actress, her telenovela character and the mass audience. Once this relation was broken, the reaction from the audience was strong, and even had political implications. All the way, the telenovela-universe remained part of the setting, even at the stadium where Daniella was remembered with Yasmin's musical theme. Fiction and reality united into a metaphysical discourse, a discourse which is not so unusual in Brazil.

The point here is that telenovelas have a massive presence in many people's everyday lives, and that many links grow up between the telenovela and everyday life. This is the case not only in Brazil, but in most of Latin America. Telenovelas are the most watched television programmes in Latin America, with the Brazilians in this case-study watching an average of three to four a day, mainly in prime time. Telenovelas are screened six days a week, a typical telenovela having 150-200 chapters and thus running for six to seven months. In order to better understand the fascinating and at times incomprehensible relationship between fiction and reality - between telenovelas and everyday life - this book will try to answer questions such as: What cultural and generic elements characterize a telenovela? How is their massive presence in everyday life experienced, understood and used by the viewers? What constitutes the relation between telenovelas, culture and everyday life, and how does this relate to the development process in Brazil?

Telenovelas in Brazil and Television in Latin America

Brazilian telenovelas have had an overwhelming success in the ratings throughout the past 30-35 years. They are screened six days a week, four to five hours a day, mainly in prime time. Ratings reached an average of 60-70 in the 1970s and were still, in the late 1990s maintaining average ratings of 40-50 in prime time! What explains this success and this massive presence in everyday life? And how do telenovelas articulate the production of meaning and social action among people, and ultimately influence the development of society?

Telenovelas enter into the time and space of households mostly at night, during the evenings when families are most often together, occasionally with friends and relatives. In order to grasp the totality of the relations between this massive daily flow of telenovelas and the constitution of everyday life, it is imperative to apply a broad perspective in one's analysis. Instead of focusing specifically on telenovelas as media texts, I am interested in them as cultural expressions which have an active part in the everyday lives of their viewers. Understanding telenovelas as cultural expressions requires an analysis of the socio-cultural and political-economic context from which they spring.

The telenovela genre has developed as a complex cultural product with generic, social and cultural roots far back in Latin American history. One of the macro elements determining the generic development and also influencing the concrete spread of the telenovela is the institutional development of television, although the genre has much older cultural roots. Television in Latin America and not least in Brazil, is a very strong industry: older, bigger and stronger than in many European countries. Consumption of television in Brazil is very high, comparable with North American levels of media consumption rather than with the lower European levels.

Television appeared in Latin America in 1950, first in Brazil, swiftly followed by Mexico. Today, there is one television set for every seven Latin Americans (World Culture Report, UNESCO 1998: 419), and television continues to expand on the continent. In Brazil there one television for every 4.5 people (ibid).

The media industry in Latin America is expanding generally. Production is growing and the number of channels that are accessible is rising dramatically. In the 1980s the television networks of Brazil, Mexico and Venezuela increased their exports rapidly, particularly of telenovelas (Marques de Melo 1988, 1992). In the 1980s Brazil's leading television network, Rede Globo, was the fourth largest commercial network in the world, only surpassed by ABC, CBS and NBC, all from USA (Lins Da Silva, 1985 and Pumarejo, 1989). In the 1990s the scenario has become more complex, with Globo continuing to maintain a leading position which now includes cable and satellite channels. Cable television and satellite television became widespread in the 1990s among the wealthier social strata in Latin America, constituting a challenge to the traditional dominance of national broadcast television networks in countries like Brazil, Mexico and Venezuela. However, there is not yet a substantial demand for it among low-income groups in Latin America, although the tendency points in that direction.

A last characteristic I will highlight is that the television industry in Latin America is generally privately owned. State channels exist but they are insignificant in terms of size, ratings and programme production. Their programmes generally appeal to only very narrow target groups. Public service is likewise insignificant and there is practically no legal requirement for it. The result is a strong, predominantly commercial sector, reflected in the massive presence of advertising and a determined orientation towards programme policies that attract viewers and thus advertisers. Brazil's more than 110 million television viewers (out of a population of 160 million) with their 32 million television sets, constitute a huge market, and telenovelas are an important instrument in reaching this potential market.

In Brazil, the television industry grew rapidly in the period of military dictatorship, a period characterized both by heavy investments in infrastructure, industry and urban development, with growth rates among the largest in the world, and simultaneously characterized by severe political repression. Massive internal migration and profound changes in the everyday lives of many people were also part of this process.

It was in this context that television and telenovelas gained a larger outreach and higher ratings. The forms of cultural expression and storytelling changed during the process of modernization in the 1960s and 1970s and with the gradual integration of millions of migrants into urban life in the rapidly growing metropolitan centres of Brazil. Telenovelas were - and continue to be - important mediators in these processes of development. This book will illustrate how.

Telenovelas, culture and everyday life

The focus of this book is precisely on these processes of mediation, analysing how telenovelas take part in everyday life, as cultural expressions reflecting and interpreting issues of common concern, and taking account of the fact that they are cultural products guided by commercial incentives. I deconstruct the complex relationship between telenovelas, culture and everyday life.

For my definition of culture I have opted for that provided by the Swedish anthropologist Ulf Hannerz who describes it as "the meanings which people create, and which create people, as members of societies. Culture is in some way collective" (Hannerz, 1992: 3). It is a dynamic understanding of culture, focusing on the circulation and production of meanings in society, and emphasizing the social.

I also have to define the type of society at which my cultural analysis is aimed. Empirically, I focus on low-income women in three urban settings in Brazil. Again, I find Hannerz's concept for society useful. He speaks about "complex, contemporary societies" (Hannerz, 1992), referring in particular to urban settings. In this book, I have not chosen an Amazonian village or a rural area, but have deliberately focused on three contemporary urban settings in Brazil because they reflect the livelihoods and socio-economic conditions of more than two thirds of all Latin Americans.

3

As I have chosen to focus my analysis on the socio-cultural role of telenovelas in everyday life, the scale of analysis is relevant. Cultural studies, not least ethnographic work carried out by anthropologists, tend to be conducted on the micro level of society. However, I have aimed at combining a field-work study, mainly focusing at a micro level on the everyday lives of a number of selected individuals, with a comprehensive analysis of the institutional structures, political-economic trends, and the dominant ideological discourses that influence the everyday lives of people like them. Finally, I have found it pertinent to maintain a perspective on social change in my analysis, deliberately seeking to identify the ways in which the flow of telenovelas into everyday life may articulate processes of social change.

Summing up, my focus on the relation between telenovelas, culture and everyday life will be based on two general working theses which will serve as guidelines throughout the book. They are to be considered as general assumptions which I would like to analyse in depth in the course of this study:

(a) Telenovelas, like many other cultural products, respond to some of the continuous changes occurring in the everyday life of the viewers. In this way telenovelas become more than mere consumer items produced for commercial reasons. They reflect the cultural characteristics of, and concerns arising from the disruptions present in the complex societies of today.

(b) The reception of television and the production of meaning entailed in watching telenovelas have an ambivalent relationship to social change. On the one hand, watching telenovelas confirms viewers' position in a social hierarchy, thus contributing to the maintainance of the status quo. Commercial exploitation, ideological "guidance" and social integration all occur to some extent. On the other hand, the viewing of telenovelas liberates social energy and tension through an active and multi-facetted use of the television flow. This can lead both to enrichment of the lives of the television viewers as well as to social indignation and thus to social and perhaps even political action.

About this book

This book is a contribution to the current debate within the growing tradition of media ethnography. It is my explicit aim to introduce to the Anglo-Saxon audience some of the Latin American scholars who are widely unknown to them, despite the fact that they have produced advanced and important theoretical and methodological contributions to what is becoming a global concern. This concern involves finding an empirical approach to the complex relations between media, culture and everyday life. The opening chapter thus introduces the historical matrices, the socio-political context and the relevant current discussions within Latin American media and cultural studies.

Chapter 2 provides the theoretical background to media ethnography and proposes an analytic framework for putting media ethnography into operation. As is well known, media ethnography has been a contested concept in qualitative media studies over the past 10-15 years. Many media researchers, especially in Western countries, have in recent years talked about a qualitative change in media studies: an "ethnographic slant". They have looked to ethnography for help in gaining a better understanding of the media reception process. These media researchers, who mainly originate from disciplines like literature and languages as well as from sociology and institutes of mass communication research, have thus acquired a considerable interest in anthropology.

The recognition of how complex processes of communication are, and how intimately they are related to the broader social and cultural contexts in which they occur, has in recent years had theoretical and methodological consequences, the essential being the increased sensitivity of media researchers to the complexities of communication and the degree to which it is embedded in the practices of everyday life. The weakest aspect continues to be empirical studies. Very few scholars have carried out comprehensive media ethnographic studies, Mary Gillespie's 1995 study being one of the few major exceptions.

Despite the limitations of my study, it has from the outset been inspired by the ambition to apply an analytical framework founded in media ethnography, as proposed in Chapter 2. The rest of the book - chapters 3-9 - constitute my media ethnographical case study. Chapter 10 draws up conclusions and perspectives.

Chapters 3, 4, 5 and 6 aim to introduce the reader to the historical and institutional contexts from which the telenovela springs. In order to provide the non-Brazilian reader with a more global scenario within which to understand the operation of the telenovela, this part is deliberately wide-ranging and includes a great deal of factual information about the Brazilian development process, the history of television and the historical development of the telenovela. The point of these detailed analyses and presentations is to help the reader to understand the characteristics of the overall context and thus the general success of telenovelas.

Since in Chapter 2, I argue for the necessity of placing media studies in a context of culture analysis, Chapter 3 seeks to deconstruct what constitutes Brazilian culture. This is an almost impossible task given the cultural complexity and geographical extent of the country, and the multiple origins of the inhabitants. There is one point, however, which I consider it particularly important to analyse: the development of an ideologically-constructed national discourse of culture and cultural identity, promoted by the dominant class and the state and heavily supported by the media industry (which I study in more detail in chapter 4).

Chapter 4 analyses the relation between the process of modernization and the rise and development of the television industry. I analyse the strong interest taken by the military regime in obtaining a national communication network as an instrument of national control via national integration. The mass media became of strategic concern in this context and led to active support by the regime in establishing Rede Globo. It was in these same years that the telenovela experienced generic innovation and that the social routine of watching telenovelas became rooted in the practices of everyday life of the majority of Brazilians.

Chapter 5 traces the historical and cultural matrices of the telenovela, entering into the history of storytelling in Brazil, passing through cordel literature, feuilletons, radionovelas, the theatre and the circus. All these cultural expressions have in one way or another influenced the development of the telenovela as a genre and thus helped me to understand how telenovelas are related to the national and regional cultures of Brazil. Thereafter, I analyse the narrative and dramaturgical characteristics of the telenovela. One of my points is to clarify the differences between telenovelas and American soap operas. Very often, telenovelas are called Latin American soap operas. However, despite similarities in the format, I emphasize the substantially different ways in which soap operas and telenovelas take part in the everyday lives of the viewers. I continue by analysing the main phases of the development of the genre, reflecting to a large extent the processes of development in Brazilian society. Chapter 5 concludes with a thorough introduction to *Rubbish Queen*, placing it within the comedy subgenre of telenovelas and introducing the characters of the telenovela.

The production process of a telenovela, analysed in Chapter 6, is also related to the everyday life of the viewers. The ratings play a significant role in the programme policy of the television networks and influence the production process. However, the production process is complex, based on a dynamic interaction between creative processes and commercial constraints. Furthermore, the relation between viewers and the producers of telenovelas is much more nuanced than just being a question of ratings. In particular, Chapter 6 describes the production process of the telenovela *Rubbish Queen*, including how the audience influences the production process. The theme of the telenovela is further analysed in terms of the current socio-economic situation in Brazil, in that this specific theme of gathering rubbish is topical, relating to a familiar aspect of class conflict in São Paulo. To sum up, Chapters 3-6 provide a series of general analyses that in themselves give some overall explanations as to the relation between telenovelas, culture and the process of development in Brazil.

Chapters 7, 8 and 9 constitute the micro-sociological part of this case study. Here I enter into a qualitative study focusing on the everyday lives of 13 women, backed up by quantitative information about 105 women in the same neighbourhoods. This part falls into three chapters. Chapter 7 introduces the 13 women of this study, aiming to give a picture of them and their everyday lives. My purpose is to compare their characters and socio-economic situations in order to be able to define some, if any, mutual concerns in everyday life. The next step is to analyse the women's social uses of television, according to structural and relational elements. The main conclusion here is my discovery of a culture-specific sphere of signification which influences the organization of time, space and social relations *vis-à-vis* the use of telenovelas. This is Chapter 8. Finally, Chapter 9 is my reception analysis of the womens' talk about telenovelas. It springs from my focus on *Rubbish Queen* but develops into a discussion of the general socio-cultural role of telenovelas in their everyday lives. The analysis is structured along two main discourses, a personal discourse and a class discourse. Chapter 10 summarizes the main conclusions of the book, emphasizing in particular the role television fiction should have in the construction and articulation of cultural citizenship.

Finally let me clarify that all quotations that were not originally in English have been translated by myself either from Spanish, Portuguese or Danish - the original languages figure in the bibliography. A couple of French quotations have been left in French.

1. Getting into the Latin rhythm: A research field on the move

Whether it takes form of a tango, a soap opera, a Mexican film or a cheap crime story, the melodrama taps into and stirs up a deep vein of collective cultural imagination. And there is no access to historical memory or projection of dreams into the future which does not pass through this cultural imagination

Jesús Martín-Barbero, Colombia, 1993a

We know that struggles through the medium of culture do not yield immediate or spectacular results. But, it is the only way to ensure we do not go from the sham of hegemony to the sham of democracy: to block the reappearance of a defeated domination installed by hegemony in the complicity of our thoughts and relationships

N. García Canclini, Mexico, 1995a

Latin American societies are fundamentally different from the"overdeveloped" societies (Gilroy, 1993: 2) of the Western world, both in their historical development and in their contemporary social, cultural and economic characteristics. Canclini speaks of *another* modernity existing in Latin America (Canclini, 1995a). Consequently, the questions asked and the epistemological aims formulated by Latin American scholars often *differ* substantially from the ones known in for example Europe or USA. Latin American cultural studies – largely unknown outside the continent – do have strong links both to North American and European academic traditions, as will be described in this book. However, both the scholars quoted above plead for a more locally grounded cultural research in Latin America. They both emphasize that cultural studies must necessarily be grounded in and upon genuine social reality in order to produce deeper insight into the particularities of Latin American modernity. This chapter gives a brief historical background to the field of Latin American cultural studies, emphasizing the relations between media, culture and development and giving particular emphasis to the growing attention being devoted to telenovelas as a popular cultural phenomenon.

1. Development theory and media studies

Seen from a European perspective, Latin American cultural studies -and in particular media studies – are best understood when set in relation to the main phases of development theory over the past two or three decades. In this way Latin American reality and the cultural studies reflecting upon it, become easier to comprehend. The point is that many Latin American scholars, especially those rooted in the tradition of Critical Theory, approach media and cultural studies within this broader perspective of development.

Some non-Latin American analysts have argued that Latin American cultural studies seems to be less politically committed than the critical theory scholars of the region, as for example Alan O'Connor in his introduction to the field (O'Connor, 1991). I wish to argue in this chapter that the emerging Latin American cultural studies tradition contains some of the same basic epistemological, social and political concerns as the critical media research of the 1970s and 1980s, although these concerns are approached from a different notion of politics, with different objects of study and put into operation through a plan of research that is very different both theoretically and methodologically. However, to clarify the links between the varying research traditions in media and cultural studies, let me first outline the trajectory of development theory within which they can be placed.

The three major trends within the history of development theory are: modernization theory, dependency theory and the theory of popular participation. Generally speaking, these correspond to the three major trends within the history of media studies in Latin America: the functionalist theories, the structuralist and critical theories and finally the more recent development of cultural studies.

The *theory of modernization* springs from 18h century European development optimism. Among the most prominent modernization theorists is Walt Rostow and his *phase theory* (Rostow, 1960). He considered modernization as a very simple, ideal and mechanical development strategy. The development of society was in his eyes a linear process, where any country must pass through five distinct phases to become a fully developed modern society. It is a very behaviouristic understanding of development, where the aim of modernization is understood to be the production of fully developed societies of mass consumption. The function of the media is to serve and support the development process in the best possible way, and functionalist media research seeks to analyse how this occurs . Functionalist media research orients itself towards North American empirical media research, examines the technical and concrete functions of the media within society and accepts the structure and role of the media as something given. It is largely linked to market research. Critics call functionalist media research positivist, reductionist and supportive of the status quo.

The *theory of dependency* emerged as a rupture with the modernization theorists' development optimism. It developed in the late 1960s, evolving into a substantial and widespread critique of the general modernization process. It was chiefly theorists from the developing countries, not least from Latin America, who did not believe that the problems of their countries would disappear as soon as "development" occurred in the form of economic growth and industrialisation. The dependency theorists believed that international capitalism was the root of the problems of the developing countries. They spoke of unequal exchange and developed theories about centre-periphery systems (Frank1970, Amin 1976 & 1979, Cardoso 1972, Cardoso and Faletto 1979). The nations in the centre, the developed countries, profited from commerce while the peripherical nations, the developing countries, suffered from the unequal exchange process. For the dependency theorists development was first and foremost development away from dependency of the world market. In Latin American media research the structuralists uncovered and criticized all the ways in which the media promoted cultural imperialism and strengthened the unjust and dependency-creating development process which the theory of modernization represented. It was also from within this line of thought that Latin American scholars became leading articulators of the debate regarding a New World Information and Communication Order (NWICO) – a debate I return to below.

Finally Latin American Cultural Studies emerged in the 1980s, linked with the *theory of popular participation*, based on key issues such as empowerment of the people and community participation. This line of thought within participatory development theory was present in UN policy as early as the mid 1970s and it gradually spread, becoming the basis of most development theory from the early 1980s and onwards (Midgley et al, 1986: 21ff). The processes of political transition in Latin America in the 1980s included the development of large social movements which focused on popular participation, a perspective that began to be reflected in the epistemology and empirical focus of media and cultural studies. It was closely tied to the recognition of popular culture, not as a celebration of authenticity, but as the recognition of the culture and everyday life of the popular sectors of society. Cultural studies took an opposite stand from the ideological and counter-hegemonic discourse of the critical tradition, where the popular sectors were conceived in Marxist terms as broadly uniform mass social forces, by recognizing the multiplicity and complexity of the popular sectors; it began reflecting upon and empirically studying the needs, histories, trajectories and distinct socio-cultural profiles of these sectors.[1]

However, before elaborating further on the characteristics of cultural studies, let me briefly introduce the socio-political context in which critical media research developed in Latin America, and pinpoint some of this research tradition's main characteristics. As mentioned above, some of these characteristics and epistemological concerns have been carried over and re-addressed in contemporary Latin American cultural studies.

Media, science and politics hand in hand

Latin America in the 1960s and 1970s was in a process of profound structural transformation leading to substantial social and political turbulence. The Cuban revolution in 1959 had strengthened political beliefs among revolutionary and

---

1   Two recent books that summarize the main developments and debates on the Latin American field of communication are:1) Marques de Melo, Jose. 1998. *Teoria da Comunicacao. Paradigmas Latino-Americanos*. Petropolis: Editora Vozes and 2) Orozco Gomez,Guillermo. 1997. La Investigación de la Comunicación Dentro y Fuera da América Latina. Tendencias, Perspectivas y Desafíos del Estudio delos Medios. Buenos Aires: Ediciones de Periodismo y Comunicación. Universidad Nacional de la Plata.

progressive movements throughout the continent, contributing to the already heightened social tension. Simultaneously the process of industrialization and economic growth was going ahead at high speed leading to heavy internal migration and rapidly growing cities. Consumer societies began to take shape in urban centres such as Mexico City, São Paulo, Rio de Janeiro, Lima, Buenos Aires and Santiago, which however also consolidated and even increased social inequality. On the privileged side were the old rural oligarchy and the growing industrial bourgoisie in the cities, and on the other were the industrial workers, the shanty-town dwellers, the small peasants and the landless.

Part of the development process was the massive growth of television in the 1960s. North American television serials were sold in large numbers to Latin American countries. Film and television serials transmitted an idealized picture of the lifestyle which the modernisation theorists – and with them many Latin American government leaders – held as their ideal: "the American way of life". The Brazilian television educator Paulo Grisolli, with a life-long experience from Rede Globo, characterizes the role of television and especially telenovelas in the Brazilian development process of the 1960s and 1970s: "I usually say that in the evening the military created a country that did not exist, but when people read about it in the newspapers or heard about it in the television news, then they believed in it and became very proud. This phantom existed until democracy came and eliminated censorship, thereby revealing the desperate country the dictatorship had left behind" (Grisolli, 1994: 5)

The relations of economic dependency between the developed countries and Latin America grew, and a substantial part of the modernization process was financed by loans from the World Bank and the IMF. Many protests began to arise against the unsustainable and socially unjust process of development promoted by the authoritarian regimes ruling the region in the 1960s and 1970s. There was a continuous growth of social movements, especially in the 1970s and into the 1980s, and parts of the Catholic church became a progressive force in this movement of civic protest against the process of development and the repressive political regimes. The progressive movement within the Catholic Church began with the Second Vatican Council, held in Rome in 1962-1965. Responding to the global decrease in the number of believers, not least in Latin America, the World Catholic Church approved a doctrine supporting renewed social commitment. In Latin America this developed into a major political and social commitment among many priests and laymen. Out of this doctrinal renewal grew the *Theology of Liberation*, a socially committed theology preaching heaven on earth and using Marxism to explain the dynamics and structures of society. The *structural sin* of society had to be removed and the active participation of the people was needed. Local Christian communities grew up everywhere in Latin America, strongest in Brazil, Colombia and Nicaragua. They became important agents in the processes of re-democratisation (Tufte et al, 1986).

In the social context briefly described above, it was not only theologists and guerilla fighters who distanced themselves from the way in which modernization was taking place: the increase in social conflict, the widespread military coups, the establishment of profound economic dependency on international banks and agencies. A growing number of social researchers began criticizing the process of modernization for not leading to any social progress for the masses. Furthermore, some began to reflect critically upon the rapid development of mass communication and the way this communication was used politically.

10

The late Paul Freire, a Brazilian lawyer, adult educator and philosopher, contributed substantially to critical thought in Latin America in the 1960s and 1970s. Like Richard Hoggart, Raymond Williams and Stuart Hall from British Cultural Studies, he based his academic work on his practical experience in adult education. Paulo Freire is probably the most influential thinker to inspire the social and cultural movements in the past two or three decades, especially in Brazil, but also more widely in Latin America and in other parts of the world. His thought helped establish a framework of popular action and reflection which has been a main core in the democratization processes of numerous countries.

Freire did not relate explicitly to mass media, but focused primarily on the pedagogical process, the creation of human consciousness, originally working with literacy programmes among peasants in Northeastern Brazil in the late 1950s. Freire is best known for the method he developed for literacy work and awareness raising, where the individual can intervene actively in his or her own continuous process of becoming aware. The dialogue, the social commitment and the constant dialectic between action-reflection-action are some of the core elements in what has come to be known as the "Paulo Freire method" (Freire, 1975).

Latin American societies in the 1980s were characterized by two main factors. One was the *debt crisis* leading to economic crisis and bankruptcy in Mexico (1982), stagnation in Brazil (1985) and hyperinflation in many countries, the worst being Argentina. As a consequence of economic crisis, social and economic marginalization grew. A significant symbol of this was the return of cholera - a disease of bad sanitation and poverty - to the Latin American continent in 1991 after an absence of almost a century. The other factor was democratization and the fall of many of the military dictatorships (for example Argentina 1983, Brazil 1985, Uruguay 1986, Paraguay 1989, Chile 1989 and Venezuela 1988). The many Freire-inspired social movements played important roles in the move towards democratic elections in the region, the most significant movements being local Christian communities, community organizations, trade unions, womens groups, the Black movement (especially in Brazil) and human rights groups.

Finally, the 1990s have been characterized by difficulties in institutionalizing democracy. In many countries, neo-liberal presidents and/or political parties have been in power for several periods (Peru, Argentina, Brazil, Nicaragua, etc), and market forces have increasingly become a guiding principle in society, from the privatisation of the many and often very big public companies (telecommunications, transport, oil, mining, etc) to the running of universities and the agenda-setting in research.

Mass communication research in Latin America has, in the 1990s, experienced enormous growth in terms of student numbers and scientific production (Lopes and Melo 1997 eds). However, it is a contradictory process, where critical communication research has been fading as a research tradition, and where more market oriented functionalist research has experienced revival and growth. It is in this context that Latin American cultural studies has emerged and grown. It is taking place in a post-authoritarian period with liberal economies and politics dominating the region, and where postmodern thoughts have challenged and significantly influenced the social sciences. There has been epistemological change, and a questioning of the perspective of Critical Theory represented for example in the longstanding NWICO-debate, an on-going discussion in the 1970 and 1980s regarding media policies, media flow and media imperialism. Let me briefly introduce this NWICO-debate, an important predecessor of the current debate and research on media and communication in Latin America.

New World Information and Communication Order (NWICO)

UNESCO played an important role in initiating this media debate, both the global debate on a possible "New World Information and Communication Order" (NWICO), and especially the debate and research in Latin America (MacBride ed., 1980). The Latin Americans were active, outgoing and critical. Already in 1958 UNESCO, the government of Ecuador and Universidad Central in Quito, the capital of Ecuador, supported the establishment of the regional centre for advanced studies in journalism, CIESPAL, in Quito. In 1973 CIESPAL organized a Latin American media conference in Costa Rica. Here Latin American media researchers met in a common forum for the first time, thereby getting the opportunity to formulate a common attitude to mass communication research and to applied theories and methods.

The Costa Rica conference raised a fundamental critique of North American empirical media studies. The participants objected to the functionalist concept of objective, neutral research. They argued that social research could not, ultimately, avoid being political. Furthermore they opposed the idea that research should limit its scope to describing phenomena, as the functionalists did. Unlike the functionalists they interpreted mass media as a class phenomenon existing within the general framework of a society in which the majority of the media are privately owned. According to the Costa Rica critique, research had obviously ignored the power of these media and the use made of them as instruments for maintaining the status quo.

These criticisms resulted in a change in epistemological interest around media research (de Moragas Spà, 1985: 210). The consequence was an increased focus on critical content analyses, inspired by French structuralists and generally by the European semiotic tradition (Dorfman and Mattelart, 1972; Marques de Melo, 1971; 1974 and Pasquali,1963). Right up to the beginning of the 1980s UNESCO played a leading role: supporting conferences and establishing more media centres in Latin America, among them IPAL (Instituto para America Latina) in Lima. Many institutes of mass communication were established around Latin America in the 1970s and 1980s.

The NWICO debate has been a strong, long-lasting and highly political debate. It has been a global debate but largely led by protagonists such as Antonio Pasquali, Luiz Ramiro Beltran[2], Rafael Roncagliolo, Alejandro Alfonzo and many others from Latin America (Tufte 1996b, Marques de Melo 1998). The role of the mass media in the process of development has been a central issue, but ultimately the debate has been not only about a new communication order but also a debate on a new global order – a political discussion about power and a more just development of society.

---

2   Jose Marques de Melo and Jucara Brittes have in 1998 published the book *A Trajetoria Comunicacional de Luiz Ramiro Beltrán* (São Paulo: UMESP/UNESCO) which thoroughly documents Beltran's 40 years of activity in the field of communication.

The emergence of critical media research in Latin America was closely linked to these overall discussions about development. In the 1990s UNESCO continued to stimulate the Latin American debate on media policies, media training and the discussion of media and development, mostly with seed money for projects or conferences, but also in a more institutionalized way with the establishment of UNESCO Chairs of Communication (Marques de Melo (ed), 1996). Of 25 Chairs established at universities world-wide, four have been established in Latin America, in Uruguay, Brazil, Colombia and Mexico (Orbicom News 1998). These Chairs, co-financed by UNESCO, the hosting universities and private sponsorships in some cases, reflect the pragmatic, broad and interdisciplinary line of communications research present in Latin America today, representing all three lines of research outlined above. Most noteworthy for the Latin American chairs of communication, and for this field of research in general in Latin America, is that it is increasingly grounded in the socio-cultural and economic reality of the region, producing a more genuine knowledge than was the case in the earlier days of Latin American communications research.

The emphasis of critical communication and media research in the 1970s and 1980s has been along three overall lines: focus-areas that to some extent, although with a less dogmatic and ideological discourse, have a continued presence in contemporary communications research. Firstly, there is a basic concern about hegemony. There is a general belief that the dominant class use mass media for ideological control. Media research is thus concerned with uncovering media structures and structures of society in order to gain a better understanding of how the capitalist system tries to obtain ideological dominance via the culture industry. This implies concepts such as imperialism, economic dependency and cultural trans-nationalization. Only with a knowledge of these areas can a policy and a practice within communication be developed that can create a more democratic, participatory and liberating society.

Secondly, it draws attention to the inequalities of society. If constant attention is not paid to this, the risk is that the problems remain unsolved and the socio-economic situation in society is taken as natural, and not as something structurally determined. Thus information, documentation and conscientization all play an important part in stimulating critical thought. Thirdly, the critique is holistic, not oriented only towards communication and the culture industry but including a critique of the economic, social, political and cultural conditions of society. Communication is seen in a global context, thus placing media studies within the social sciences.

Positioning itself in this way, critical communications research in Latin America contributed to the development of an independent, non-colonialized academic space for Latin American media and cultural studies. The problems and difficulties in this venture do not lie in the fact that theories are developed and most often passed on to Latin America from European and North American "canons", but in the fact that Latin Americans have used them uncritically without translating the theories into a Latin American context and tradition. In this way foreign theory has often laid down the norms for what is scientific and for the role science has in society (Martín-Barbero 1987, Tufte 1997). This however, is changing, and it seems less evident in the growing strand of Latin American cultural studies which I will now address.

2. Cultural studies

> Once we take as the starting point of observation and analysis not the
> linear process of upward social progress but 'mestizaje' a mixing of
> cultures and lifestyles which creates continuities in discontinuity and
> reconciliations between rhythms of life that are mutually exclusive, then
> we can begin to understand the complex cultural forms and meanings
> that are coming into existence in Latin America: the mixture of the
> indigenous Indian in the rural peasant culture, the rural in the urban, the
> folk culture in the popular cultures and the popular in mass culture
>
> *Martín-Barbero, 1987: 188.*

In this statement, Martín-Barbero addresses what must be the central problematic
in any cultural study involving the Latin American reality. The complex cultural
reality, the mestizaje as Martín-Barbero labels it, is fundamental for analysing
cultural practices and cultural expressions, including telenovelas. Mestizaje must
be viewed as the cultural expression of a very conflicting, discontinuous and
complex process of modernization that has been going on in Latin America over
the past half century, in some countries much more quickly. The following pages
introduce Latin American cultural studies and place Media Studies within this
rather recent trend in Latin American academic research.

Culture and modernity

In addition to Jesús Martín-Barbero, Néstor García Canclini, an Argentinian
anthropologist living in Mexico since the late 1970s, is one of the most influential
cultural analysts in Latin America today. In several books and numerous articles
he has analysed cultural transformations in Latin America and the constitution of
modernity (Canclini, 1987a/b,1989/1995a English version, 1990a, 1990b, 1993,
1995b, 1997).

Canclini's overall perspective is to analyse the processes of modernization, that is
the complex development process consisting of social, economic and political
development, and analyse how this influences culture and vice-versa. Canclini has
also analysed the scientific development of anthropology and sociology in Latin
America and these disciplines' abilities to take account of the urban reality of the
1980s and 1990s. Earlier on, he analysed cultural policies (1985), which he
returned to with new perspectives regarding urban cultural policies (Canclini
1995b). In his most important work to date (Canclini, 1995a) performs a
groundbreaking analysis of culture and modernity in Latin America, introducing a
concept that indicates how he understands culture in Latin America today: he
speaks of hybrid cultures, being the cultural realities under which the new urban
masses live[3]. Speaking of hybridization Canclini attempts to grasp more of the
cultural complexity than the term mestizaje. Canclini explains:

---

3   Canclini's concept of *hybrid culture* has parallels to the reflections encountered among
    some British scholars of cultural study. For example Paul Gilroy's analysis of British
    youth cultures, where he distinguishes between Afro-centrism and Eurocentrism,
    analysing what he calls "the problem of hybridity" (Gilroy 1993: 2).

I found this term better suited for grasping diverse intercultural mixtures than *mestizaje*, which is limited to racial mixings, or "syncretism", which almost always refers to religious combinations or to traditional symbolic movements. I thought that we need a more versatile word to take into account those "classic" mixtures as well as the interlacing of the traditional and the modern, the educated, the popular, and the mass. A characteristic of our century, which complicates the search for a more inclusive term, is that all of these types of multicultural fusion intermingle and draw strength from one another.

Canclini, 1997: 22

The processes of cultural hybridization were readdressed by Canclini in a study where he links cultural hybridization with questions of globalization, multiculturality and cultural citizenship, although constantly maintaining the problems and challenges of Latin American modernity as a central focus (Canclini 1995b).

In his book *Hybrid Cultures – Strategies for Entering and Leaving Modernity* (1995a), Canclini carries out a thorough analysis of what today constitutes cultural studies in Latin America and the different ways in which anthropology and sociology have contributed to the development of this academic field. Historically speaking, anthropology has the longest tradition of studying cultures, and especially popular cultures. However, anthropology has traditionally studied small communities in rural areas, and not urban communities. These became central in Latin American cultural studies only in the 1980s and especially in the 1990s.

Meanwhile, many anthropologists have continued the same type of micro-analysis in urban areas as they have traditionally performed in rural settings. Only in recent years has a more holistic use of anthropology been developed, which is more closely linked to disciplines such as sociology and communications research, and provides a better analytical framework with which to understand the complexity of the cities. Many urban anthropologists have"done less an anthropology of the city than anthropology in the city (...) The city is thus more the place of investigation than the object" (Canclini, 1990b: 45). To Canclini, this raises a fundamental question as to whether a discipline that has a resigned attitude to modernity, and has only meagre theoretical and methodological instruments with which to understand modern society, is able to produce a pertinent discourse with which to intervene in the contemporary crisis in Latin America (ibid).

Canclini makes a similar critical analysis of the sociological tradition in Latin America. The early Latin American sociology of the 1950s and 1960s belonged to the functionalist school and served primarily as an instrument for understanding the macro-social changes that were occurring - focusing on migration, the changing labour force and the new work relations and content of work, where migrants adapted to urban work processes. There were many empirical studies, but no focus on local and traditional customs and the everyday life of the private sphere.

What did not seem to have developed in Latin American anthropology and sociology at the time began developing in the 1980s as cultural sociology. There is factual evidence for this emerging trend - as Canclini also points out - firstly in the growing number of empirical studies of cultural processes. These possess a growing clarity in defining their objects. Methodology is still a weakness, though

15

some methodologically sound research projects have been carried out, for example within the Programa Cultura at the University of Colima in Mexico. Secondly, there has been the determination of several distinguished Latin American scholars within sociology to study cultural processes, among them the Chilean Jose Joaquín Brunner, Sergio Miceli and Renato Ortiz from Brazil, the Argentinians Oscar Landi and Anibal Ford, and Gilberto Gimenez who is of Paraguayan/Mexican origin, among many others. Thirdly, cultural studies is becoming a key dimension in research within urban and political sociology, just as urban and political sociology, in addition to cultural and human geography, and not least communication studies, are among the disciplines that are entering the field of cultural studies. In other words, a growing interdisciplinarity is de facto emerging, a trend seen many places in the world.

Given the great challenge of trying to understand what the modernization process in Latin America has meant for everyday life, Canclini stated, as early as 1990 that "the sociology of culture exists and is one of the most dynamic areas of the social sciences in Latin America today"(Canclini, 1990b: 45).

Hybrid culture and popular culture

What exactly is this field of cultural research? In Latin America, the focus has been on the cultural phenomena of urban everyday life. The understanding of culture that has developed is very similar to that evolved in cultural studies at the Centre for Contemporary Cultural Studies (CCCS) in the UK, where culture is seen as "the area of production, circulation and consumption of significations" (Canclini, 1990b: 45), or to that referred to by Martín-Barbero when he says, in reference to communication: "In the redefinition of culture, the clue lies in the understanding of the communicative nature of culture, understanding culture as a process that is productive of meaning, and not just a "circulator" of information. Thus, the receiver is not just a decoder to whom the TV broadcaster transmits a message, but also a producer" (Martín-Barbero 1993).

As is rightly pointed out by other non-Latin American scholars (O'Connor 1991) as well as by the Latin American cultural studies researchers themselves (Canclini 1997), Latin American cultural studies is firstly not a uniform tradition, and secondly, not a genuine Latin American research tradition. Just like cultural studies in Britain, it has a highly mixed scientific background. British and Latin American cultural studies seem to have developed parallel to each other, with the occasional mediator and articulator of British cultural studies visiting Latin America. Only in the most recent years has a closer dialogue been established, providing a more massive and systematic inspiration the other way, from Latin America to Britain. This was seen with the conference "Cultural Boundaries:Identity and Communication in Latin America" organised at the University of Stirling in October 1996, with the participation of Renato Ortiz, Jesús Martín-Barbero, Néstor G. Canclini, Jorge Gonzalez and several others (*Media Development* 1997: No.1).

Latin American cultural studies have brought French semiology, Italian humanistic and social sciences (from Gramsci to Cirese), the German Frankfurt School and many other lines of thought together in their own constellation, or as Canclini states: "I find in most specialists in the humanities and social sciences, and in general in Latin American cultural production, a restructured appropriation of metropolitan canons and a critical use with respect to various national needs"

(Canclini 1997:26). This hybrid quality characterizes the academic traditions as well as the cultural production itself.

When we are speaking of popular culture in Latin America, we are dealing with a highly complex site of analysis, reflecting cultural matrices from Europe, Africa, the Middle East and elsewhere. The point to make is that culture is a dynamic process, and that when speaking of popular culture in Latin America we are not speaking of some authentic culture under threat from industrialization and modernization. William Rowe and Vivian Schelling have made one of the most comprehensive analyses in English of the complexity of Latin American popular culture, placing popular culture as a major force in the moulding of Latin American modernity: "Latin American modernity is not a replica of US or European mass culture, but has a distinctive character which varies from country to country. A major factor in its difference – probably the major factor – is the force of popular culture (Rowe and Schelling 1991:3)".

Culture and identity: navigating and negotiating

Brazilian and Mexican anthropologists and cultural sociologists have produced some of the most important cultural studies within this rising tradition of Latin American cultural studies. As early as 1981, the Brazilian anthropologist Roberto da Matta analysed traditional popular cultural phenomena as expressed in the urban cultures in Brazil (*Carnavais, malandros e hérois: Para uma sociologia do dilema brasileiro/* Carnavals, malandros and heroes: Towards a sociology of the Brazilian dilemma, Da Matta 1981). His interest lies in the analysis of the conflicting relationships between the social classes of Brazilian society, which is highly polarized: "I refer to a relational society, that is, to a system where the whole has a logic of which the parts can be totally unaware. For me it is basic to study the "&" that ties the mansion to the slum dwelling and the enormous, terrible, fearsome space that relates the dominant to the dominated" (Roberto da Matta, 1981).

A decade later Da Matta in his book *The House and the Street* (Da Matta 1991) developed what one might call a sociology of spheres, a thorough analysis of the concepts of time and space in Brazilian everyday life. He argues that in Brazilian society, parallel forms of time and space exist. He distinguishes between three discourses of time and space: the house, the street and what he calls "the other world". They are linked to three different spheres of signification, marked by different codes of conduct and each possessing a specific language. The three spheres are complementary and difficult to separate. One code of conduct may prevail, depending in particular on class status.

Da Matta's categorization of the social practices of mankind constitutes a special perspective, a sociology of spheres in which everyday life is lived, including watching television and producing meaning from it. I return to and use Da Matta later on in my case study, so will not enter into more detail here.

Another Brazilian anthropologist, Renato Ortiz, has been doing studies of national identity, analysing the historical matrices of the identity of Brazilians, characterizing national identity as an ideological construct created in the process of the modernization of Brazil. He analyses the racial aspect of cultural and national identities in Brazil (Ortiz,1985). In a later study, Ortiz analyses the relation between Brazilian culture and the culture industry, and thus the role of media in the reformulation of cultural traditions and identity (Ortiz, 1988). More recently he has, like Canclini (1995b), Martín-Barbero (1996 and 1997) and others focused increasingly on the problematic of globalisation and its challenges. In his book *Globalisation and Culture* (Original Title: *Mundializacao e Cultura*) Ortiz analyses the impact of what he calls "world modernity" upon collective identities (Ortiz 1994. See also Ortiz 1997).

Two of the most comprehensive empirical investigations of a whole country's culture, cultural transformation and the formation of its cultural identity have been and are being carried out in Chile (by the research institutions FLACSO or CENECA) and in Mexico (by Programa Cultura at University of Colima). At FLACSO researchers have sought to study a very broad variety of cultural production, including education, theatre, literature, art, popular culture, political culture, etc. FLACSO's book *Chile: transformaciones culturales y modernidad* (Chile: cultural transformations and modernity, by Brunner, Barrios and Catalán, 1989) operates with two main methods for determining the objects of analysis. The first distinguishes between two sorts of cultural production: (a) the institutionalized production of symbolic goods (education, science, technology, culture industry, art, religion, etc), and (b) everyday culture, covering the social interaction between groups and individuals. The second method is to characterize Chilean culture as part of the formation of modernity.

According to Canclini, FLACSO's analysis remains on a macro-sociological level, giving priority to analysing the modern forms of production, communication and consumption, studied in a quantitative way and without looking thoroughly into the interaction between these modern symbolic cultural artifacts and everyday life. FLACSO's work has undoubtedly delivered substantial methodological contributions to the development of cultural analysis, though missing central theoretical and methodological reflections on how to identify, limit and actually study everyday life.

In this perspective, the Culture Programme, directed by Jorge Gonzalez at University of Colima, in Mexico, is noteworthy, currently constituting one of the most interesting research centres of the region. The work carried out here is theoretically and methodologically very dynamic and innovative, and is always accompanied by empirically grounded research. Inspired by Bourdieu's reflexive sociology and Alberto Cirese's Gramscian-inspired work on developing a theory of folk culture, Jorge Gonzalez has developed his own concept of "cultural fronts", understood as a methodological and theoretical tool which can help understand "the historical, structural and everyday ways in which a web of relationships of hegemony in a given society is constructed" (Gonzalez 1997: 32). The polysemy of "fronts" lies in the double meaning of the concept, on one hand referring to boundary zones (porous and mobile borders), between the cultures of different classes and social groups; and on the other hand to battle fronts; "arenas of cultural struggles between contestants with unequal resources and conditions (...). The fronts describe general social relationships which, from the point of view of the daily construction of the meaning of life and of the world, elaborate the evident and the necessary, values and multiple identities. Precisely that which could unite us all" (Gonzalez 1997: 32). In this perspective, the articulation of cultural identities appear as socially constructed positionings, characterized by navigation between different cultural fronts and a constant negotiating of powers.

Empirically, among the many cultural phenomena that have been studied in the Culture Programme at the University of Colima are religious festivals, popular theatre, music traditions and telenovelas (Gonzalez 1992, 1994, Gonzalez and Galindo Caceres (eds) 1994, Covarrubias et al 1994, Gonzalez 1997 and Gonzalez 1998 (ed)).

3. Culture and communication: from media to mediations

Jesús Martín-Barbero's book, *Communication, Culture and Hegemony – From the Media to Mediations* (1987, English version 1993) is the first major contribution to the discussion of the role of mass communication in modern Latin American societies. A large part of Martín-Barbero's book is dedicated to the analysis of the historical matrices of popular culture, both analysing how scholars have understood popular culture throughout history, as well as analysing the historical matrices of popular culture itself, in particular tracing the cultural matrices of telenovelas back to the fairs of the late Middle Ages (Martín-Barbero1993a: 64pp).

Martín-Barbero's notion of communication and communicative action goes well beyond a concern with the media alone, placing these processes in a broader socio-cultural context, where mediation becomes a central concept. By 'mediations' he means "the articulations between communication practices and social movements and the articulation of different tempos of development with the plurality of cultural matrices"(Martín-Barbero 1993a).

Martín-Barbero analyses how culture is negotiated and becomes an object of transactions in a variety of contexts. Popular cultural expressions are seen in numerous ways within radio, television, cinema, film, theatre, circus, the press. These media and their content are then again in constant interaction with the socio-cultural contexts within which they exist and thereby develop as active components in everyday life. In this way the processes of mediation become infinite processes in which meaning is produced in the constant interaction between the media product and the viewers or listeners as well as in the social interaction between people. Ideological dominance seemingly becomes difficult to obtain, since any type of culture product is always interpreted and reinterpreted on a personal level, in ways dependent on a series of socio-cultural, psychological, economical, political and historical factors. Popular culture is obviously the hegemonic battlefield, but total hegemony is impossible to obtain.

Methodologically Martín-Barbero applies a highly interdisciplinary approach to cultural analysis and roots (mass) communication firmly in the socio-cultural and historical reality within which it occurs. He outlines a "nocturnal map" (Martín-Barbero 1993:211-225) indicating which particular types of mediations to study, among them daily life, social temporality and the cultural competence of the people in focus. By studying these mediations one should be able to capture the "sphere" in which the production of meaning takes place. Following this approach, communication – including mass communication – must be seen as a social process integrated in the cultural practices of everyday life. In a position that runs parallel to Herman Bausinger's (Bausinger 1984), Martín-Barbero argues that media and communication do not just influence everyday life – they are everyday life.

Popular culture and genre analysis

Martín-Barbero's book (1993a) largely contributed to the academic recognition of popular culture as a fundamental field of research in contemporary Latin American studies, announcing a break with the highly ideological and dualist dependency thinking represented by critical communications research. The focus on everyday life and popular culture, acknowledging the complexities in identity formation and production of meaning, represented some of the mayor innovations and advances in this rising tradition of cultural studies.

However, research into telenovelas and other popular genres in the culture industry only gradually became recognized as a serious academic field. Throughout the 1980s it was a contested and low-status area of research. An academic who spearheaded it from the very beginning was the Brazilian media researcher Ana Maria Fadul. Inspired by Martín-Barbero's work, Fadul raised a critique of critical media research in Latin America (Fadul, 1989). She said that researchers of this school were not interested in popular culture, and focused too narrowly on condemnation of the culture industry and its attempt to obtain ideological dominance. Instead of going into more thorough studies of why the products of the culture industry had become popular, their efforts had been directed to seeking alternatives and more participatory and politically mobilizing forms of communications than the mass communication of the culture industry. Fadul argued that researchers, instead of seeking alternative modes of communication, should recognize the popularity of the mass media and instead of rejecting them should relate actively and critically to mainstream television programmes, and in particular to the extremely popular telenovelas.

Fadul notes that in the 1980s nationally produced telenovelas gained a very large part of the market all over Latin America, having taken over and dominated prime time in many Latin American countries. *Dynasty*, *Beverley Hills* and other North American soap operas, serials and films were given screen time late at night or in afternoon time-slots. Serials such as *Twin Peaks* reached Brazil years after having been screened in North America and Europe.

Not only have Latin American telenovelas dominated their national and regional markets for decades, but they have also been exported to other parts of the world. For example Brazil's Rede Globo had already by 1988 exported television fiction, telenovelas in particular, to 130 countries throughout the world (Marques de Melo 1988). Fadul was thus in a strong position to argue for more Latin American research on this particular cultural product, and the reasons for its success. But the study which she demanded came about only gradually, a circumstance which I elaborate on in the final part of this chapter.

To understand popular television programmes' relation to popular culture, it is necessary to understand the different generic expressions by which they relate to popular culture. Fadul, and especially Martín-Barbero, argue for a very broad definition of what genre studies should include, in order to grasp the cultural matrices of popular television genres. Martín-Barbero specifies: "a genre is first and foremost a strategy of communication, and it is as traces of the communication that a genre becomes visible and possible to analyse in the text (Martín-Barbero 1989)". As a phenomenon situated between the production logic of the culture industry and the logic with which the viewers produce meaning in their TV-watching, the genre should be analysed from several perspectives:

> Each genre is defined both through its own architecture and its placement in the programme schedule...(This leads to) the necessity of constructing a specific genre system in each country. Because, in each

country the genre system relates to a specific cultural configuration, to the juridical status of TV-broadcasting and to a specific orientation as regards the transnational.

Martín-Barbero, 1989: 81

Obviously, the work of decoding is fundamentally different in for example Denmark and Brazil. Danes laugh at the boastful expressions of Brazilian men in a telenovela, about honour for example, while in Brazil these expressions are decoded seriously and naturally. Television reception is culture-relative, depending on the context in which it occurs. According to Martín-Barbero and Fadul a genre analysis must thus be more comprehensive than is traditionally the case, because it must encompass more of the process of communication: both the production and the reception (Fadul,1989: 82). Martín-Barbero's concept of 'mediations' encompasses this complexity, in that the mediations produce and reproduce the social significations, thereby creating a "sphere" which makes the understanding of the interaction between production and reception possible. According to Martín-Barbero: "the genres, articulating the narration of the serials, constitute a fundamental mediation between the logic of the system of production and that of consumption, between the logic of the format and how that format is read and used" (Martín-Barbero 1993a: 221).

These guidelines to genre analysis express a more holistic attitude to communication, and the close relation communication has with the social, cultural and historical contexts in which it is performed. This understanding has gained significant credence among researchers in Latin America in the course of the 1990s. In order to analyse the appropriation of products of the culture industry, interdisciplinary approaches are increasingly being adopted which take cognizance of the contexts within which the communication takes place, and thus of the complexities of the relation and interaction between producer and viewer/listener. Focus is increasingly on everyday life where culture, politics and communication are woven together in a totality.

Telenovelas

Taking a closer look at the research that has been conducted on telenovelas in Latin America, a rich and growing field of study can be identified. Apart from a few exceptions (Marques de Melo1973, Miceli 1972) the first studies are from the early 1980. Two bodies of research in particular mark the transition from critical ideological studies to more exploratory work along the lines of cultural studies: the Brazilian media researcher Carlos Eduardo Lins da Silva's study *Muito Alem do Jardim Botanico* (carried out in 1982, published in 1985) and the Brazilian anthropologist Ondina Fachel Leal's *A Leitura Social da Novela das Oito* (carried out from 1980-1982, published in 1986). Da Silva's reception analysis on television news led him to the conclusion that telenovelas, "despite their stereotyped and distorted expressions – represent true problems (...) types of problems that are totally absent in telejournalism. Thereby the absurd situation is achieved in which there is more realism in fiction than in journalism, which then becomes the world of fantasy ..." (Da Silva 1985: 114). Ondina Leal carried out an anthropological study of 20 families' social uses of telenovelas, a study that preceded media ethnography and at the same time instantly became a classic within media ethnography.

From Lins da Silva and Leal's ground-breaking studies, the field has grown in many directions, including quite a lot of reception studies, a very limited number of media ethnographical studies, a few studies of the production of telenovelas, some flow-analyses, a great deal of genre analyses and some studies trying to combine several of these different aspects of telenovela research. The best general overviews of the total field of research are found in McAnany and La Pastina (1994), which focus on audience reception of telenovelas, and in Fadul 1993, which takes in all fields of telenovela research. The Research Centre of Telenovelas at ECA at the Universidade de São Paulo is the best bibliographical centre in the region.

International interest in telenovelas in Latin America is another dimension of the field, exposing the phenomenon to larger international research communities. The international interest has been limited although it now is increasing. The principal studies by foreign scholars include those by the American media researcher Joseph Straubhaar (1982 and 1998) – focusing on the decline of American cultural influence on Brazilian television programming, due significantly to the national success of the telenovela, and those of the Belgian Armand Mattelart and his French wife Michèle Mattelart, who have 35 years of experience in Latin American studies. Their case study on Brazilian telenovelas (Mattelart and Mattelart 1989) provides a very insightful introduction to the generic development, the economy and the institutional setting of telenovelas, although I would argue that the Ph.D thesis of the Dutch scholar Nico Vink, published as a book: *The Telenovela and Emancipation, a Study on TV and Social Change in Brazil* (Vink 1988) reaches significantly deeper in some of the same topics as the Mattelarts, demonstrating very in-depth knowledge of the genre, genre history, and the social reality of the low income viewers. Vink's aim is to detect the perspectives of social change linked to the genre and to the consumption of telenovelas. Unfortunately, Vink does not then proceed to carry out his own empirical study of any particular audience's reception and social use of telenovelas.

The American anthropologist Conrad Kottak has carried out what is probably the most empirically grounded work done by a foreign researcher on television in a Latin American country, and published in English. His book *Prime-Time Society – An Anthropological Analysis of Television and Culture* was published in 1990. From 1983-1987 he investigated "television's role in moulding knowledge, attitudes, perceptions, emotions, and images of the world, and in stimulating economic development" (Kottak1990: 12). On telenovelas, Kottak gave particular emphasis on their role in the formation of national identity in six rural communities in different places in Brazil.

Regarding my own research on telenovelas in Brazil, this project – as will be described in chapter 2 – combines institutional and production analysis, genre analysis and audience analysis relating to the social uses and production of meaning in telenovelas. This holistic analysis is placed in the context of the development of modernity in Brazil. Aspects of this research have been presented at Latin American and other international communication conferences in the course of the 1990s, and published in journals and anthologies together with reflections on the overall project (Tufte 1993, 1995, 1996 b/c, 1997, 1998 and 1999a/b).

As mentioned above, telenovela research is growing in Latin America – language and cost being the principal obstacles to the lack of international (English-speaking) exposure. Among the principal researchers and research centres that carry out ongoing research into telenovelas in their domestic (national and regional) settings are the following: The Culture Programme at University of Colima, Mexico (Gonzalez 1988 and 1992, Gonzalez (ed) 1998, Covarrubias et al 1994,Covarrubias and Uribe 1998, Chavez Mendez 1992); the Colombians Martín-Barbero and Sonia Munoz (Martín-Barbero and Munoz, eds, 1992); the ECA/University of São Paulo, Brazil – Maria Immacolata V. de Lopes, which has been coordinating, since 1996, a large interdisciplinary research project: the Brazilians Ana Maria Fadul (UMESP) and Anonio La Pastina (University of Texas), the North American Emile McAnany (University of San Diego, USA) and Peruvian Ofelia Torres Morales (USP, Brazil) who has been researching since 1996 on telenovelas and demographic changes in Brazil (Fadul et al 1996, McAnany 1998): the Chilean Valerio Fuenzalida, (and in the 1980s also Maria Elena Hermosilla) researching on telenovela reception. Fuenzalida has since the early 1990s mainly explored the educational potential of telenovelas from the production side, experimenting with formats for public service broadcasting in Chile's TV Nacional where he is research director (Fuenzalida 1997); the Argentinian Nora Maziotti (Universidade de Buenos Aires) researching on the internationalization of formats and genres, with emphasis on genre and flow analysis in Argentina (Maziotti 1993, 1996 and 1998); Antonio La Pastina (participating in the above mentioned demography-project) who did ethnographic research on the role of telenovelas in a rural community in North-Eastern Brazil (since 1996). Many other individuals throughout the region are writing Masters and Ph.D theses on telenovelas, bearing witness to the huge growth that has taken place in telenovela research in the 1990s.

Finally, it is worth mentioning the specialist research being carried out on the international flow of telenovelas, outside of the Latin American region, linked to the commercial success of the genre on the international television market. Flow analyses of the penetration of other markets (Varis1985, Marques de Melo 1988, Biltereyst and Meers 1997 and 1998), reception studies on telenovelas in Europe (Intercom 15, 1992; Bouquillion 1992), and discussion of the telenovelas' export success in the light of the cultural imperialism thesis (Oliveira 1990, Reeves 1993, Sinclair 1993, Fox 1994).

Biltereyst and Meers' recent works lead to the conclusion that the expansion of telenovelas into international markets as, for instance, in Europe has been made possible by the rapid increase in broadcasting time due to the much larger number of television channels, and the fact that telenovelas have been relatively cheap to buy. However since competition in the 1990s has grown stronger, European programmers have tended to avoid "exotic" material, falling back on well-known and proven fiction programming, producing it themselves when possible or keeping to US programming (Bilerreyst and Meers 1998: 18). This has been negatively labelled as a bipolarization trend into domestic and US programming. Following John Sinclair (1993) Bilterreyst and Meers reject the thesis of reverse cultural imperialism, arguing that in fact there is an increased localization of media production developing parallel to greater globalization and formation of conglomerates, so that Brazil's Rede Globo and Mexico's Televisa are increasingly in competition with their North American counterparts on the global capitalist market (Bilterreyst and Meers 1998:18-19).

Summing up, the growing field of telenovela research is largely integrated into the broad stream of Latin American Cultural Studies, linking genre history and development, qualitative audience studies and production analyses to questions of popular culture, cultural change, formation of cultural identity, social development and modernity. Some of the flow analyses and institutional analyses however, fall rather into the tradition of critical communications research and more classical macro-sociological analysis. Telenovela research has today become a very broad interdisciplinary field, explained largely by the increased recognition and cultural and scientific significance accorded to culture, popular culture and everyday life, including the mass media forms of cultural expression like the telenovela.

4. A research field on the move

Cultural studies in Latin America is a scientific trend that is gradually getting a clearer theoretical and methodological scope, accompanied by – and based on – an increased number of empirical studies. Both anthropology and sociology have become more oriented towards analysing the mediations occurring in the mestizajes and the hybrid cultures that characterize the contemporary everyday life of most Latin Americans. Cultural studies developed in the 1980s, and became the overall context in which media studies was placed. This broad academic field experienced a gradual development in epistemological and political scope, being less dogmatic than the ideological discourse of the critical tradition, however maintaining a clear political and especially a social perspective in the studies carried out.

The development of Latin American cultural studies was related to the emergence of participatory development theory. It is based on a well developed cultural sensitivity, respecting the individual's thoughts and competences, taking popular culture seriously and seeing active participation and communication as key concepts in the process of development. Despite this general characteristic, Latin American cultural studies remains a diverse and very mixed academic field in Latin America. Nevertheless, there is a clear trend towards further studies of popular culture, including TV fiction genres, game shows etc.

A major challenge for Latin American cultural studies is to analyse cultural expressions, including mass communications such as telenovelas, in the context of the problematic of modernity. The new cultural realities in the huge urban centres of the region are characterized by very conflicting, discontinuous and complex processes of development which are difficult to understand without revising or adapting classical sociological concepts to the given reality. In other words, studies of this increasingly complex Latin American reality are challenging the classical canons of social research and of the humanities. As this chapter has briefly shown, Latin American cultural studies researchers are indeed generating intriguing knowledge and interesting theoretical reflections upon the cultural forms and social realities of modern Latin American societies.

2. Clarity of truth is but a saga: Making media ethnography operational

The constant availability of mass communications, particularly of a visual kind, in the modern world – in the home, the street, the workplace, and in transit – has meant the saturation of much of social time and space with cultural products. This has resulted in a qualitatively novel media environment, where the discourses of media and everyday life may become increasingly indistinguishable. If one traditional purpose of cultural practices has been the creation of a time-out from everyday life, the modern merging of mass communication with the rest of the social context may be creating an almost ceaseless time-in.

Klaus Bruhn Jensen, 1991: 40

It would seem to me that ethnography is less a prescribed set of methods than an ethos. It is a way of exploring aspects of human, social processes where living in and studying the local world become so intimately linked that fieldwork becomes a "way of life" in itself. But it is also a cultural practice, essential to anthropology and, as such, an academic discipline which relies on the goodwill of people to reveal themselves and to be revealed. In this sense it becomes too crude to talk about methods or ethnographic authority, and more fruitful to talk of ethnographic responsibility.

Marie Gillespie, 1995: 75

Introduction

In the above quotations Jensen and Gillespie lay down the two premises upon which this chapter develops: Jensen draws our attention to the increased mediatization of everyday life, creating cultural practices where the mass media and their discourses are indistinguishably part of everyday life. Gillespie shows ethnography to be an ethos with which the "indistinguishable relations" between media and everyday life can become distinguishable and understandable. Media ethnography, as I define it, recognizes the merging of mass communication with the rest of the social context and uses ethnography to identify the role of the media – whether as genre, flow or cultural form and expression – in everyday life.

This chapter explains how this research project on telenovelas fits into the growing, although often contested, research tradition of media ethnography. Firstly, I give an account of the key discussions evolving around media ethnography as a particular orientation within qualitative empirical media studies, and outline an analytic framework that makes several entry points to media ethnography possible. Secondly, I explain how this project developed out of an interrelated set of professional, personal and academic interests. Thirdly, I explain how I deal with each point of the analytical framework both in theoretical and empirical terms.

The analytical framework I propose has three main fields: first, genre analysis, which includes analysis of the cultural trajectories and communication strategies of the genre in focus, ieanalysing its historical matrices, intertextual relations and process of production; second, description of the everyday lives of the people in focus – covered in as much detail possible – and third, joint analysis of media and everyday life, covering firstly the social uses of the media, in this case of television, and secondly its reception.

Watching telenovelas is not a simple practice: it both influences and is influenced by the ways time, space and social relations are organized in everyday life. The rhythms and routines of everyday life are intrinsically linked to the presence of telenovelas in it. The challenge is to clarify the relations between the telenovelas – with their historic matrices and generic particularities, the rhythms and routines they articulate in everyday life, and the production of meaning that results from watching and talking about telenovelas. To address these complexities ethnography becomes relevant.

When focusing on cultural practices and using ethnography, there are in principle no limits regarding what to include in the analysis. The limits are defined and set by the researcher himself, in the strategic choices and selections he makes. I obviously have had to do the same. My choices are explained later in this chapter.

First, let me introduce this somewhat contested academic field of media ethnography.

1. Ethnography in media research

The American media researcher James Lull, who as early as 1980 called for the use of ethnography in qualitative empirical audience research (Lull 1980:199) remarked only eight years later that ethnography had become"an abused buzz word in our field" (Lull 1988: 242). Now, another decade later, it has become more or less established as a line of research within qualitative empirical audience research, although it still lacks some theoretical and methodological clarity. Media ethnography however still remains largely an academic "desk discourse" rather than a practical discipline nourished by empirical studies. My intention here is not to repeat the academic debate, but rather – based on a brief retrospective of the field – to suggest an analytical framework which I then seek to put into operation in the rest of this book, initially, in this chapter, by elaborating on the concrete trajectory, research design and methodology of my case study.

The emergence of media ethnography is a part of the epistemological shift represented by the development of cultural studies. Media studies went through a qualitative change, starting around 1980, an important component of which took place within qualitative audience research, namely the development of reception analysis. When exploring the contextual complexities of media reception many media researchers began increasingly to lean towards the qualitative methodologies associated with ethnography or media ethnography, very often when interpreting what could – according to anthropological or ethnographical norms – be characterized as ethnography. It was, and still is, first and foremost within media research that scholars have oriented themselves, theoretically, empirically and methodologically towards media ethnography. Ethnographers and anthropologists have only to a very limited degree entered into the field of media ethnography although Latin America is a region where a growing number of anthropologists are focusing on the media.[1]

Within media studies in general, and in the Anglo-Saxon ethnographic strand in particular, the term became too comprehensive, as Lull recognized in 1988, and attempts have since been made to clarify epistemological, theoretical and methodological differences and similarities, especially between reception analysis and media ethnography (see for example Drotner 1993 and 1996, Schrøder 1994 and Tufte 1993 and 1999b, Gillespie 1995). Broadly speaking reception studies are – naturally, one could argue – media-centric in their analysis of the text/receiver relationship while studies in media ethnography are more interested in the social interaction of particular groups of people.

The basic concern in reception analysis has been to determine the role of the receiver in the communication process. Since the recognition of polysemic texts (Hall, 1973) there has been increased discussion concerning the heterogeneity of the audience, especially from 1980 and onwards, with more attention being given to investigating how audiences use television actively as part of their own culture.

The text

Researchers working in reception analysis been been continually engaged in theoretical polemics concerning the status of the text, the context and the reading process in the production of meaning in communication. Some researchers carry out content analysis, arguing it is possible to say something about the dominant trends in society and the assumed decodings by the receivers simply by doing textual analysis combined with institutional and programme analysis. Others have argued that this focus is insufficient (Schrøder, 1984). Others again have argued for the continued use of content analysis combined with an increased attention to the role of the reader and the reading process (Jensen 1988). The Danish media researcher Ib Bondebjerg is one of the latter, arguing against those researchers who eliminate the explanatory potential of text analysis and only focus on the reception itself, the reading process. Bondebjerg says: "Polemically one could maintain that after one has eliminated textual analysis and intellectual critical evaluation, they suddenly reappear in a new form: the reception researcher is textual analyst when he interprets the interview, and it is also the researcher who both decides the experience-oriented quality criteria and ascertains whether they are present" (Bondebjerg, 1989). Bondebjerg's critique – shared today by many – touches a

---

1   See for example Borelli 1989 and 1993, Canclini 1995a/b, Gonzalez 1992 and 1997, Leal 1986, Ortiz 1988 and 1989.

weak point in many of the reception studies carried out so far. The fact is that many reception analyses are based mainly on the interview with the recipient, which, as Bondebjerg says, can be regarded as just another text analysis.

Methodologically, the field of empirical audience research is developing, including also a more nuanced conceptualization of text, emphasizing the various dimensions of intertextuality and distinguishing different layers, including historical and cultural matrices in media texts. John Fiske was one of the first to elaborate on the literary concept of intertextuality in relation to mass communication, distinguishing between the vertical and the horizontal dimension in intertextuality (Fiske, 1987a: p108).

The vertical dimension indicates the relation between what Fiske defines as three layers of text: The primary, secondary and tertiary texts (Fiske 1987: 108ff). The primary text is the actual media product, whether shown on TV, transmitted on the radio or published in print. The secondary texts are all the texts derived from the primary text, thus including advertizing, magazines, radio spots, etc. The tertiary texts are the texts the viewers produce themselves, their gossip, their letters to the broadcasters, their conversation. These three layers together constitute the vertical dimension of a text's intertextuality.

However, following Fiske, the horizontal dimension indicates the relation between primary texts. The most prominent form of horizontal intertextuality is that of genre. The genre-specific intertextuality may also reach back in history to take in genre comparability. Genres most often relate to several other genres, as for example the well-known intertextual relation between the French *feuilleton* and soap operas. Furthermore, horizontal intertextuality can also be understood as the relation between the evening's programmes, also expressed in Raymond Williams' concept of flow (Williams, 1975) or to the relation between yesterday's, today's and tomorrow's chapter of an ongoing narrative, for example telenovelas. The media flow into everyday life is thus an intertextual flow, with both horizontal and vertical dimensions.

Where the media text is the primary text in a reception analysis, Klaus Bruhn Jensen has argued for putting the priority in ethnographic analysis the opposite way round, with the conversations as primary and the media text as tertiary (Jensen 1992). This distinction is thought-provoking, and many media researchers with a background in language or literature keep questioning media ethnographers about "where the text is in the analysis". Obviously, the understanding of text and the different analytical approaches to the media text underlines the fundamental difference between reception analysts with their focus on the text-receiver relationship, be it contextualized or not, and media ethnographers with their focus on social interaction. A useful concept with which to grasp the conversations about the media texts could be Mary Ellen Brown's concept of the spoken text, by which she understands the text that people create when they talk about television (Brown, 1994: 67).

The audience

This also leads to different notions of audiencehood, depending on the overall aim of the empirical study. According to the Dutch media researcher Ien Ang the audience is a discursive construct which for a long time has not been defined broadly enough. Ang argues in her book *Desperately Seeking the Audience*

(Ang, 1991) that audience has for too long been a limited discursive construct mainly serving media broadcasting institutions in their aim to keep as big an audience for their broadcasting station as possible. They have not been interested in knowing why the audience reacts as it does, as long as they react actively.

Ang argues for a more nuanced understanding of the audience than the one the broadcasting institutions have been interested in so far. An ethnographic discourse, – knowledge and understanding of the TV audience can – "provide us with much more profound "feedback" because it can uncover the plural and potentially contradictory meanings hidden behind the catch-all measurement of "what the audience wants" (Ang, 1991: 169). Ethnographic knowledge "promises to offer us vocabularies that can rob TV-audiencehood of its static muteness, as it were" (Ang, 1991: 170). Ang operates in her analysis with a theoretical distinction between TV-audiences as a discursive construct, and the social world of actual audiences.

The first category refers to the discursive construct that media institutions (but also researchers I would argue) set up, in the first case in order to produce television, and in the second case to carry out research about the audience. The second category is Ang's attempt to develop a more nuanced understanding of who "the audience" is. She pleads for a stronger emphasis on the everyday life of the viewers in order to understand the multifarious nature of the audience.

Ang further draws attention to the problem of over-interpreting the multiplicity of polysemia. One might run the risk of positing an audience that is everywhere and nowhere:

> ... whenever I refer to the social world of actual audiences (...), I use the phrase nominalistically, as a provisional shorthand for the infinite, contradictory, dispersed and dynamic practices and experiences of television audiencehood enacted by people in their everyday lives (13)... But the social world of actual audiences consists of such a multifarious and intractable, ever expanding myriad of elements that their conversion into moments of a coherent discursive entity can never be complete.
>
> *Ang, 1991: 14*

Ang argues that further analysis of the social world of the actual audiences is necessary, however infinite this context may be. However, Kim Christian Schrøder put forward a polemical point of view by arguing that the increasing contextualisation of the reading process was leading to the problem of losing the audience and the media in the infinite globality of context (Schrøder, 1993: 73). This, I would argue, is only the case when the research design is lacking precision and a clear focus. As Ang also argues, the extent of the context must not prevent us from: "making the unfamiliar familiar, or more precisely, to make something that is so familiar in our everyday lives but has retained an "exotic" quality nevertheless, also familiar at the level of understanding, knowledge, discourse" (Ang, 1991: 14).

Ang touches upon one of the fundamental questions in reception analysis and media ethnography: Once one has acknowledged the multiplicity of polysemic readings how should one categorize the audience? If everybody has their individual interpretation, what should structure our empirical audience analysis?

Ang is very insistent about taking the social world of the actual audiences seriously and pleading for increased ethnographic understanding of the actual audiences. So frequently has she made this case that the Danish media researcher Kirsten Drotner labels her point of view 'ethnographic fundamentalism', "a morally founded belief that ethnography is better than other research approaches and should therefore be expanded" (Drotner, 1993b: 11).

What has been lacking has been a clearer understanding of how to conceptualize the people who are the object of study, both in reception analyses and media ethnographies. The Finnish media researcher Seija Ridell raises the fundamental question when she asks: "with what kind of voice are people in actual practice speaking in current culturally oriented audience research? Or, put differently, from what position are they led to express their 'inside views' by cultural studies scholars?" (Ridell 1998: 1). She rightly problematizes the lack of definition of the category of audience itself, emphasizing "the importance of reflecting the ethical and political implications inherent in researchers' methodological choices as well as (...) the ways they treat the informants in actual research situations and report their speech in academic discourse" (Ridell 1998: 2). Thus, when asking ourselves reception-oriented or ethnographic questions – and researching audience activity, pleasure or popular resistance – the insights should be related to the structural conditions of audiencehood. In other words, media use and media consumption should be critically assessed: "Attention needs also to be directed at people's opportunities of recognizing, problematizing and potentially challenging the conditions and constraints of the consumer-audience position they are offered as well as the ready-made choices inherent in it – in other words, the nature of people's gratifications as 'forced choice preferences'" (Ridell 1998: 9). The question of citizenship becomes a pertinent issue to address, without posing an either/or situation whereby either questions of media consumption or of citizenship are addressed.

To grasp this critical-dialectical approach, which seeks to link questions of media consumption with questions of citizenship, without excluding one or the other, Ridell suggests the use of the concept of the public, understood from an interactionist point of view. Instead of referring to a group of people, which would be the same as an essentialized conception of audience, 'public' should be conceived of as a collective conversation: "public would be seen 'spatially' as a site for (mediated) public activity – a communication space where explicit articulation of the differing values and interests of participants would be allowed, indeed fostered" (Ridell 1998: 10). Such a spatial approach, focusing on sites of struggle, is particularly relevant in the case of media ethnography, where – as emphasized above – the focus is on social interaction. It is also a logical continuation of Jensen's argument about media ethnography, according to which conversations between people are to be considered the primary text, or as Brown says, the spoken text.

Perceiving the audience as public is also the proposal put forward by Sonia Livingstone in an article where she reflects upon the development of audience research. One of her main points is to recognize the criticism which has been directed at many audience studies in recent years, of focusing too narrowly on the micro-sociological level of analysis. In outlining five approaches to the link between micro and macro levels of analysis within audience studies, Livingstone argues for the level where audience is conceived of as public; here is a version of social constructivism where agency plays a moderate role, a pragmatic middle-of-the road position compared with conceptions of the audience as either market or duped mass (Livingstone 1998: 208-210).

Livingstone seeks to capture the force of the micro-macro relation as conceived within democratic theory, understanding the subject as a citizen-viewer (Corner 1991) who acts within a "political system (...) built on the informed consent of the thinking citizen" (Livingstone1998: 210). Her preoccupation is similar with Ridell's – and my own – where the relation between media and everyday life is set into a larger framework dealing with questions of agency, social and political transformation, and focusing on strategic sites of struggle and interaction. Livingstone emphasizes the public sphere as the overall focus area, underlining her post-Habermasian conception of public sphere, which is discussed in depth in for example the work of John B. Thompson (1995) and also Livingstone and Lunt (1994).[2] The main point to make here is that media ethnography is a useful theoretical-methodological approach to these questions, transcending the text-receiver relationships to explore social and cultural transformation.

Ethnography becomes – as suggested by Gillespie – an ethos and a cultural practice for the social researcher, by which to explore human and social processes. While reception analysis evolves around questions dealing with the text-receiver relationship, media ethnography tries to understand how the mediatization of modern life has merged with the rest of the social and cultural context, with the reconfiguration of public and private spheres as a particular focus area. One could perhaps say that media ethnography becomes an ethos and cultural practice among media researchers particularly interested in culture and everyday life or among ethnographers and anthropologists particularly interested in media and ommunication. It is an area of research located in this interdisciplinary field between anthropology, sociology and media research, not forgetting the increased role of cultural geography (Morley and Robins 1995; Gripsrud 1997; Gonzalez 1997).

Ideally, an exercise in media ethnography becomes a comprehensive analysis of as many dimensions as possible of particular media environments or media situations in everyday life (intertextual relations, synchronic and diachronic dimensions of everyday life, trajectories of disposition among the people in focus, including for example life histories, etc). To deal with the multidimensionality of the study, it would usually encompass a series of both quantitative and qualitative methods brought together from, in particular, anthropology and sociology.

In this context, the epistemological aim of media ethnography is to clarify the role of the media and communication in the cultural practices of everyday life, thereby seeking to understand processes of social and cultural (including spatio-temporal) transformation, and to make clear the socio-cultural history, development and current characteristics of modern societies.

---

2   Both Ridell's and Livingstone's approaches to audience coincide fine with Jorge Gonzalez' focus on cultural fronts described in chapter 1, where his empirical focus is exactly on publics and their navigating and negotiating within particular sites of struggle. Suggesting this spatial emphasis in empirically oriented cultural studies furthermore writes itself straight into the core of contemporary debates regarding the reconfiguration of public and private spheres and the role of media and technology in these processes (see Meyrowitz 1985, Silverstone 1994 and Thompson 1995).

Making media ethnography operational

How do the above epistemological and theoretical-methodological definitions translate into empirical studies? How do we make the above principles operational? I shall now give a general framework which outlines three focus areas which in principle should be included in any media ethnography. The inspiration for the elaboration of this framework comes in particular from four scholars who, each from their own perspective address similar concerns; Firstly, Jesús Martín-Barbero's "nocturnal map" emphasizing the interactions where the social materialization and the cultural expression of television are delimited and configured. He identifies three places of interaction with the media that are central to explore: (a) the daily life of the family; (b) social temporality and (c) cultural competence (Martín-Barbero 1993: 211-228); Secondly, Roger Silverstone's book *Television and Everyday Life*, which is a sort of theoretical synthesis of the "qualitative change" seen in Anglo-Saxon audience research over the past 15-20 years. He outlines principal areas for attention in the complex relation between television and everyday life (Silverstone 1994). Thirdly, Jorge Gonzalez explicitly focuses on a particular fiction genre, the telenovela. He outlines what he calls a "cartography and mapping" of telenovelas as an analytical object, distinguishing between four areas of research: (a) Telenovelas on the air: (b) Telenovela production; (c) Description and analysis of the textual composition of telenovelas, and finally (d) Analysis of the readings and appropriations of telenovelas (Gonzalez 1992: 62-65). Finally, Mary Gillespie's book *Television, Ethnicity and Cultural Change* is a significant point of reference for empirical media ethnographical studies. It is a very comprehensive empirical analysis of the role of television in the formation and transformation of identity among young Punjabi Londoners (Gillespie 1995).

Obviously, the analytical and theoretical-methodological framework each of us designs must necessarily depend on the epistemological aim of our research: which questions do we wish to address? What is the purpose of the study? I outlined my position above, which leads me to the following three focus areas.

Genre analysis

This point refers on one hand to the historical trajectories of genres: from where do they spring? which intertextual relations can be traced? how are they linked with the history of popular culture and cultural formation within the public and the location in focus? Together, these questions form a substantial part of what Gonzalez calls trajectories of disposition, providing background knowledge about the genre's cultural and historical precedents and its historical relationship with the public.

On the other hand this point refers to the strategies applied in order to communicate to a public: How and why are the stories told? Who produces the particular genre? What interests – commercial/ideological/artistic – are considered? How is the public conceived of within the broadcasting institution – how are cultural characteristics and the organisation of everyday life among the public taken into consideration in programming, content and production? The political economy and institutional development of the broadcasting institutions should be included to the extent that they shed light on the communication strategies applied. When the focus of the study is not on a particular genre, but perhaps on a particular medium or on a particular media environment experienced by the public, focus should be on the institutional trajectories and strategies that have led to the particular media environments.

This point represents the macro-level of the analysis, together with the socio-demographic data collected as described below.

Everyday life

What constitutes the social order and cultural characteristic of a particular social group living their particular everyday life? Answering this requires information on socio-demographic characteristics, socio-economic data on (members of) households, knowledge about cultural factors such as race, ethnicity, religion, etc. The fieldwork on everyday life which is the basis for this description, aims at providing sufficient insight to produce detailed descriptions of the everyday life of a particular group, giving information on their organization of time, space and social relations and providing knowledge about their individual and collective dispositions and trajectories of disposition in terms of the formation of identity and production of meaning. Both the synchronic and diachronic dimensions of everyday life should be included, in order to provide a sufficiently deep knowledge. The diachronic dimension – which is often based on interviews about people's history or that of their family – can with advantage be related to the analysis of the historical matrices of the genre, providing a historical narrative on the role of particular genres in the lives of the people in focus.

The detailed description of everyday life serves to substantiate the analysis which is to follow giving particular attention to the role of the media in everyday life. This description of everyday life, provides the basis for a more factually grounded and in-depth analysis, both of the social uses of the media and especially of the way they are received.

Media flow

My identification and subsequent analysis of the role of the media in everyday life is structured along two principal foci: firstly, the social uses of television and secondly a reception analysis. These focus areas are kept apart here, in terms of analysis, from the dense description of everyday life, beginning by mapping out how and where the media texts and the secondary texts appear in everyday life and thereby making possible the identification and configuration of the media environment of everyday life. Who sees/uses/reads/listens to what programs/media? When, where, with whom and in which situation? How are the media used to structure time, space and social relations? The strategic sites of interaction, the sites of struggle become objects of particular attention. Secondly, a reception analysis is carried out.

When studying the role of media in everyday life from an ethnographic point of view, is it at all possible to focus on one specific programme or genre? When focusing on a specific programme, it can be difficult to carry out media ethnography, because people's everyday routines are literally linked to repeated practices that occur on a daily basis. Thus, if the priority is not on the media flow in general, but on a specific genre or perhaps even on a specific programme, the precondition must be that this media text has a massive presence in everyday life. Telenovelas in Latin America are good examples of this. They are screened daily, six days a week, and thus constitute a substantial media flow in themselves. However, their intertext relations ought to be included in any analysis, whether of cultural, historical, narrative or other aspects of generic intertextuality. The point should be that the media flow that is studied is a daily occurrence.

2. Project outline

I have often been asked how a middle-class Danish man can conduct ethnographic studies among low-income Brazilian women with all the possible biases of class, gender, nationality, religion, race and age that this may imply. To this, I hope the project trajectory below provides sufficient clarifications and answers. However, let me first present the actual data and field trip upon which this project is based.

Project data and fieldwork length

My main data for this research project were collected during two months' fieldwork in Brazil in January and February 1991, supplemented by a follow-up field trip of one month in August 1993. To this can be added visits to Brazil once or twice a year throughout 1994-1998. The data collected can be categorized under seven groups, the first four referring to genre trajectories and strategies: (1) Interviews with seven different representatives and agents from the producer side of telenovelas; (2) visits to the Rede Globo studios and interviews with representatives from different stages of the production process (editing, direction, production, etc); (3) identification and collection of secondary media texts – magazines, newspapers, records, etc; (4) obtaining 12 recorded chapters of the telenovela *Rubbish Queen*.

Regarding everyday life and media use, 13 women were selected as main respondents. To gather information and insights about them, three principal techniques were used: (5) participant observation in three low-income urban areas in Brazil: Santa Operaria in Canoas in Southern Brazil, Vila Nitro Operaria in São Paulo and Calabar in Salvador in North-Eastern Brazil. I spent between seven and twelve days in each of the three survey areas. (6) a quantitative data survey with 105 respondents from two of the case study areas. (7) thirteen qualitative interviews with women of all ages from 13-63 years, one with each woman.

One critical question was – and always is – how long the researcher should remain in the field. Lengthy stays in the field are a classical element of ethnographers' and anthropologists' work – with 18 months being the standard length of fieldwork required to obtain the "emic" or "native" point of view (Pike 1966 in Gillespie 1995: 55). Kirsten Drotner however, formulates what I consider a very precise, if difficult, principle to follow when designing your fieldwork: Drotner argues that one should "remain with the informants until one begins to question the obviousness of one's own culture" (Drotner, 1993b: 11). Despite the difficulty of this, it seems to be the most precise method to follow. How long one would consider it sufficient to remain among "the others" differs substantially from case to case. One may have previous knowledge or experience with the field or one might have almost no knowledge about it. However, the point to make clear is that time is an influential factor when seeking a deeper understanding of a society, a culture and a people.

Project trajectory

This project is the culmination of many years of personal interest, studies and work in Brazil and Latin America. It started 17 years ago, with my living for a year as an exchange student with a Brazilian family in southern Brazil in 1983, experiencing everyday life as an upper middle class student in a small town, experiencing family life with a "mother" who was crazy about telenovelas, and with at least one of the home's three television sets always turned on, from the moment I woke up and until the last light was turned off at night. It was also my first encounter with low-income urban areas in Brazil, where I participated as a volunteeer in the vaccination against polio of children in shanty towns – favelas – in the outskirts of Pelotas where I lived.

1983 was during the period of military rule (1964-1985), a period where politics and social criticism were touchy issues. The rich and very diverse Brazilian music culture was a powerful experience. Students of the early 1980s were singing songs by the old generation of composers and singers – songs by Caetano Veloso, Chico Buarque, Milton Nascimento, Geraldo Vandre, songs from the MPB-festivals of the 1960s and the Tropicalia movement. These songs had strong symbolic value, as a manifestation against the undemocratic and repressive political regime, songs that students of the early 1980s still incorporated as their own – not least Geraldo Vandre's Para Nao Dizer que Eu Nao Falei Das Flores ("So that it can't be said that I didn't speak of the flowers"). Simultaneously, Brazilian rock music was growing as a genre. Urban rock, which appeared especially in São Paulo, contained harsh social and political criticism, and was an important element in the growing social and political mobilization which culminated with free elections in December 1984. In January 1984 I experienced in Curitiba one of the first political rallies of the massive pro-democracy movement Diretas Ja which culminated in the free elections later that same year.

After this initial socio-cultural and political experience in and about Brazil, learning the language fluently and getting an insight into everyday life, popular culture, music and politics, came my university studies in cultural sociology in Denmark (1984-1989) which focused on Brazil and Latin America, leading to a more nuanced knowledge of Brazilian culture and society. My bachelor's degree (Tufte et al, 1986) was obtained on the basis of a study of the local Christian communities in Brazil that combined Paulo Freire's liberating pedagogy with their readings of Theology of Liberation. The local Christian communities exercised a social praxis where religion and politics where mixed in ways that stimulated my interest as a young secular Danish student.

Doing fieldwork for five months in 1987, mostly in the huge low-income urban suburbs of São Paulo, living in a seminary with progressive theology students, focusing on the study of everyday life in one particular favela, all this provided me with a deeper understanding of the work of the large, growing social movements in Brazil. The focus of my study was to explore the relations between everyday life in low-income areas and social mobilization and organization in the local Christian communities and in other social movements. The neighbourhood where I lived was situated only a couple of streets away the neighbourhood that a few years later became one of the three fieldwork sites for this current telenovela study.

However, the social movements of 1987 were building the foundations of a new democracy and in particular of the civil society that was struggling to establish itself after more than 20 years of military rule. The movements reflected the huge social and cultural diversity and complexity of Brazilian society. The biggest group involved was the enormous workers' movement, organized through a multitude of trade unions and with the workers party (PT) as their strongest political weapon. Other elements were the women's groups, the youth groups, parts of the Catholic Church, the landless movement, the Black movement, the Native Indian movement, the nascent ecological movement, the rock music and other musical trends inspiring the new era of development in Brazil. Living in São Paulo in 1987 provided a unique opportunity to follow the articulation of many of these social movements, their intersections, their methods of work, their quarrels and intrigues, their gains and their victories.

Following and observing their work provided me with the opportunity to observe some of the first urban land occupations by the landless movement which by the late 1990s had grown very large and well articulated. I participated in religious and political rallies, interviewed politicians on all levels, a large number of leaders and activists in these social movements, the local bishop and the archbishop of São Paulo. I also conducted numerous interviews and three months of fieldwork among the inhabitants of one particular favela-street. It became my most important cultural and methodological experience before the telenovela-study, bringing me into all the classic and often difficult fieldwork situations that require flexibility, careful conduct and reflexivity regarding the role of the researcher in the field.

Later, my studies and professional activities have included consultancy work for the Danish trade movement and working in the information department of a Danish development NGO, Danchurch aid, for three years. Both jobs took me to many parts of Brazil. Finally, working for two years with the United Nations Development Programme in Brazil's neighbouring country, Paraguay, increased my knowledge and understanding of some of the historical conflicts in Latin America: class conflicts, mistrust *vis-à-vis* state beaurocracies, institutionalized corruption, maintenance of the social and political status quo, misrepresentation in the media, among other issues.

Altogether, the above trajectory of personal, professional and academic activities serve to show how closely these three fields are linked, at least in my case: Firstly, my personal interest in Brazilian culture and society. Secondly, a cultural sociological approach and interest leading to a B.A, a Masters and a Ph.D all on Brazilian topics, and finally professional experience in non-governmental and international organisations relating to questions of social development in various dimensions, again with particular emphasis on Brazil and Latin America.

On one hand this trajectory has provided me with knowledge and insight regarding Brazilian society, popular culture and everyday life. The fieldwork experiences in Brazil have given me important methodological experiences regarding the practical use of ethnography, whether in interviews among low-income urban citizens, surveys in the field, or participant observation. Having spent more than two years in Brazil and more than four years in the region as a whole, living and working in a variety of contexts and with people of many distinct origins and natures, has given me a feeling for and insight into the characteristics and complexities of Latin American people, their cultural identity, their tastes and beliefs, their recent national history, and their dreams for the future. In other words, the above outlined project trajectory constitutes, for this research project on telenovelas, a significant part of what Mary Gillespie describes as ethnographic groundwork, consisting in achieving an adequate understanding of the local cultures (Gillespie 1995: 61-62).

Finally, and more pragmatically, the concrete research design of this telenovela-project builds not only on the experience and knowledge gained from the above trajectory, but also on the contacts established and maintained in the field in the course of previous fieldwork, as described later in this chapter. Meanwhile, let me initially turn to the first aspect outlined in my analytical framework for media ethnography: genre analysis.

3. Genre analysis: Trajectories and strategies

My genre analysis has three aspects. First, an analysis of the historical, cultural trajectory of the telenovela (chapter 3). Second, a genre analysis in a more classical sense, focusing on the dramaturgical and narrative structure and analysing how the genre has developed in content and language through three to four decades (chapter 4) and thirdly, an analysis of the production of telenovelas (chapter 5).

Telenovela (1): Roots in oral culture

The Brazilian public today has a lifelong experience of and a high competence in watching telenovelas. Their knowledge of the narrative conventions is however even older, springing from cultural forms going back into history. As I describe in detail in chapter 3, telenovelas – being today's principal form of storytelling in Brazil – contain intertextual references to a variety of genres and other forms of cultural expression: cinema, film, feuilletons, circus, cordel literature. The Brazilian media researcher João Luiz Van Tilburg's theoretical and methodological reflections on the reading of televised texts can be used to elaborate on the historical and cultural context that influences the viewer's knowledge of the narrative convention (Van Tilburg, 1993). Van Tilburg argues that there are some specificities related to the viewer's ability to understand television flow in general and telenovelas in particular. The specificities Van Tilburg emphasizes have to do with the text being audio-visual and of a high technological quality. A large number of Brazilian television viewers are illiterates or functional illiterates. This results in a reception process that is different from the reception process experienced by literate television viewers. Many Brazilian viewers have passed directly from an oral-based society (the rural background of many migrants) to a society of information technology with a high technological level in for example television broadcasting. This influences the cultural competence of the viewer, including the verbal competence.

The hypothesis Van Tilburg has explored in his analysis of 3,000 letters – written by viewers to actors and authors of Brazilian telenovelas – is the relation between the degree of writing ability and level of abstraction in the verbal discourse. This interrelation, he claims, influences the information provided by the audience and thus the character of output obtained, when researchers go out into the field and do in-depth interviews with TV viewers. Van Tilburg brings to researchers' attention the quality and level of abstraction in the verbal discourse of the TV viewers and its relation to literacy. This aspect is highly relevant in empirical reception analysis in developing countries, but should also be taken into account in the developed countries where indices of functional illiteracy are often surprisingly high.

Van Tilburg's analysis thus relates to the viewers' knowledge of the narrative conventions of the moving image. Every viewer has "the capacity of knowing the norms that rule the structure of melodrama" (Van Tilburg, 1993: 14) and thus obtains a competent knowledge of the structure of the specific genres. This is very pronounced in relation to the popular prime time genre of the telenovela. His findings are similar to the findings of for example Charlotte Brunsdon regarding the competence of women watching soap operas. Brunsdon argued they had a high cultural competence in decoding them due to their familiarity with the genre (Brunsdon 1981). Van Tilburg argues that there exists a televisual space (espaco televisivo) within which the communication – based on competences, expectations and conventions – takes place. One of the conclusions which Van Tilburg draws from his comprehensive analysis is that the televisual space is rooted in an oral culture.

Telenovela (2): The emotional relation between genre and public

Valerio Fuenzalida stresses another element of the relation between media, culture and everyday life: the emotional relationship which the viewer has to television. He argues that television, and especially TV fiction can create substantial emotional involvement in the viewers when they tell stories of everyday life. Recognition is fundamental in creating this identification and subsequently emotional involvement (Fuenzalida, 1992b). Fuenzalida talks about a kind of television that provides a testimony to ordinary people's lives: "The testimonial form presents ordinary people as actors and protagonists, and thereby validates audiences' daily life. In this televisual form many people may recognize themselves as actors in their daily story, with actions and circumstances like theirs; it is the true story of most people" (Fuenzalida, 1992b).

Fuenzalida, who after many years of working in the non-governmental research institution CENECA in Chile, conducting reception studies and elaborating plans of how to promote media education, has since the formal re-establishment of democracy in Chile (1990) worked as a director at the national TV station TVN. Here, he is very concerned about how to promote education and conscientization (awareness raising) through mass communication. He thus seeks to use his understanding of the emotional relation between programme and viewer in concrete production. His basic theoretical position is that the reception process is a very active process, where "the educational efficiency of the televised messages depends much more on the viewers' perception than on the (good) intentions of the broadcasting station" (Fuenzalida, 1994). He thus finds himself in a difficult situation, now being "a broadcaster" himself.

His argument for taking emotion seriously includes the proposal that telenovelas, due to their widespread popularity in Latin American countries, constitute a much more important and relevant educational instrument than for example news programmes. From a rational perspective it might sound strange, but as Fuenzalida states: "The redundancy of the serials makes its attraction rationally inexplicable; but the interest is, precisely, emotional" (Fuenzalida, 1987b: 25).

Fuenzalida argues however that not only TV fiction but the language of television as a whole is fundamentally emotional. This brings us back to the viewpoint established by Van Tilburg, of the oral characteristics versus the written characteristics. They coincide with Fuenzalida's distinction between the analytical-rational forms of learning versus the narrative-experiential (Fuenzalida, 1994). As Fuenzalida concludes in a paper presented at a UNICEF seminar on the developmental aspects and potential of telenovelas in 1991: "the language of television is more fit for narrative fiction and emotional identification than for abstraction and analysis: TV's associative language, polysemic and glamorous, has a stronger effect on imagination and desire" (Fuenzalida, 1992a: 39).

Thus, to deepen one's understanding of the "reading"process one must explore the emotional relationship which viewers have to television. This does not necessarily imply comprehensive psychological analyses, but can be viewed in the perspective of factually-grounded interdisciplinary analyses of the strategic sites within which the consumption and appropriation of telenovelas takes place. This constitutes a core aspect of my analysis in chapters 8-11. Fuenzalida argues further that a more profound understanding of the reception process should be sought, by understanding what relevance the programme has for the viewers, in conjunction with the viewers' concrete needs, as defined by them – a perspective I also include (Fuenzalida, 1992b: 15).

Telenovelas (3): Production

In order to get an understanding of how telenovelas are produced I interviewed a series of people participating in the production of telenovelas, both in Rede Globo and Manchete.[3]

The interviews represented a combination of what I sought and what was possible. Generally, it was extremely difficult getting access to the most central persons of the telenovelas. I tried in all ways possible to get an interview with both the author Silvio de Abreu (who wrote *Rubbish Queen*), with Regina Duarte (the main actress of *Rubbish Queen*) and with Jaime Monjardim (the main instructor of *Pantanal*). However, being a researcher from Denmark, with no substantial references within the TV networks, made it difficult to obtain the interviews I wanted. Furthermore, getting access to the studios of Rede Globo was difficult, and I was only able to visit them once, and this was outside production time. Ideally, I had planned to observe the production of a telenovela.

------

3   In Rede Globo I made interviews with Alexandre Avancini who at the time was deputy instructor on the telenovela *God will assist us (Deus nos Acuda)*. He provided me with detailed information about the working conditions in the Globo enterprise and about the role of author, director, actor and others in the production process. Paulo Grisolli I met three times, in Rio in Brazil, in Copenhagen, Denmark and in the Algarve, Portugal. He is a former instructor of tv-fiction (miniseries and one telenovela) having spent 20 years in Rede Globo. Through many conversations Grisolli has provided me with valuable information about the role of the director in the production of telenovelas. Margarida Ramos, who was a producer in the cultural department of the Roberto Marinho Foundation, provided me with information about the Marinho Foundation and their main activities. Jose Renato Monteiro, who was the director of Rede Globo's video school project, provided me with information about the educational concerns of Rede Globo.
In Rede Manchete I interviewed Attilio Riccó, the director of the department of teledramaturgy (Ricco 1991). He informed me in detail about the production process of *Pantanal*, about the competition between Manchete and Rede Globo and about the production process in general. He had worked for many years as a director in Rede Globo before coming to Manchete: Marcelo de Barreto, who was one of the four instructors of the telenovela *Pantanal* which instantly became a classic in the history of Brazilian telenovelas. He was very open about the role of the director, about the commercial interests influencing the production process and about the difficult process it is creating a product that can express and mobilize emotion. Barreto also provided me with his interpretation of the historical role of telenovelas during the military regime in Brazil. Finally I interviewed Ana Giannasi, who was responsible for production at the workers television station, TVT (Tv dos Trabalhadores).

In addition to acquiring knowledge about the production process I collected 12 chapters of the telenovelas I wanted to deal with, as well as a series of secondary media texts relating to telenovelas. I bought editions of the weekly magazines *Contigo* and *Amiga* which are the most important magazines when it comes to gossip about telenovelas. They publish detailed resumés of the coming week's chapters, talk about the private lives of the actors and often have interviews with actors, directors, authors or producers. Finally, they publish readers' comments on the telenovelas.

I read the daily newspapers and the special editions with TV supplements, for example in the *Folha de São Paulo* every Sunday. *Folha de São Paulo* also has daily "culture pages" relating to telenovelas and other TV programmes. Finally, I listened to some of the LPs and CDs with the music from the telenovelas. They are played a lot on the radio during the period when a telenovela is being broadcast. I also watched several hours of television daily on my travels round the different regions of Brazil, watching and comparing channels.

Altogether, the above three points, telenovela 1, 2 and 3, outline central trajectories regarding the role of telenovelas in the lives of the chosen Brazilian public. Together these trajectories constitute important keys to understanding the relation between telenovelas and their public. The matrices of these trajectories are found in pre-modern oral culture, in the historical emotional relation between melodramatic narratives and their public, and finally in the history and industrial dynamics and interests of familiar mass-cultural formats. By studying these historical, cultural, narrative and culture-industrial matrices, many explanations will be found of the contemporary role of telenovelas in the Brazilian and Latin American society.

The explanatory potential of the above analyses is however significantly increased when linked with studies of the social and cultural practices of the public. The next section deals with my methodology in approaching the study of everyday life.

4. Everyday life: Doing fieldwork

The dilemma is not if we will disturb, but how we will disturb.

Bovin, 1988: 35

We have gone through a passage in social science, from a basic lack of sensitivity to a paralyzing preoccupation with reflexivity (...) Reflexivity must be in the text, but it shouldn't be the dominant theme. It can be in the way you prepare the text for the reader, for instance.

Lull, 1998

These two quotations reflect on one hand the typical preoccupation of anthropologists with reflexivity (Bovin) and on the other hand the process experienced by media researchers who have drawn closer to ethnography over the past 15-20 years. Lull's mention of a "paralyzing preoccupation with reflexivity" in social science has indirect references to the discussion and problematization of the author's authority in ethnographic texts, an issue raised in the essays in Clifford and Marcus' *Writing Culture* from 1986. This book stirred up a major discussion, especially in American anthropological forums regarding the authority of the ethnographer to represent the "other" through the text. In brief, my main preoccupation – which I share with Lull and Gillespie – is to ensure that when doing fieldwork, one reflects the whole process, and the subsequent (re)construction of the reality experienced in the field. It should not result in autobiographies, but ought to show the limits of the study.

Methodological transparency lays open the premises upon which your analysis is based and your conclusions are drawn. I therefore go into considerable detail when presenting the main phases of my fieldwork experience. After reflecting critically on the use of participant observation, I describe the remaining phases of the fieldwork process; the selection of survey areas, the use of gatekeepers to approach the field, conducting a data survey and finally carrying out qualitative interviews.

Participant observation and the question of reflexivity

A very central part of ethnographic knowledge is generated through participant observation. My participant observation consists of two main activities: (1) general observation in the area, and (2) specific observation of the everyday lives of the women in the survey.

Firstly, while moving around in all three areas, I have sought out both the traditional male and female spaces of interaction. Despite the fact that social spaces are very gender specific, I have participated, to the extent that was possible, in both universes. The female universe was largely the household, doing the cleaning, washing, cooking etc. And often the women meet and chat among neighbours or visit each other. However their sphere also includes doing the shopping, participating in community work, church related activities, etc. I participated in all of this sort of activities. The men often frequented the bars or hung out on street corners playing dominoes or talking. In the mornings they went off to work together, taking the buses for hours and hours (as do many women). I followed the men to work in the São Paulo industries and back again, participated in their billiard games and drank beer and cachaça with them in the bars. In this way I have tried to get a overall idea of the social and physical spaces men and women move around in and their interrelations. It took me into a lot of shops and bars, supermarkets and football fields, church services and community meetings, women's club meetings and demonstrations, schools, streets and not least into many households.

Secondly, I focused on the everyday lives of the 13 women who were my main study. I went into all of their homes at least twice, and spent a lot of time in some of them, had many meals, played with the children and drunk many cafézinhos. I met most of the family members as well as other (visiting) relatives, friends and neighbours. My observations in their homes, including during telenovela screenings, provided insight into the socio-economic conditions the women live under, their organisation of time, space and social relations and their social uses of the television. However, the diachronic dimension of this data collection – their life-stories and family histories – were only briefly touched upon for lack of time, and would have required more time in the field. To give a more detailed account of their everyday lives would also have needed more time (chapter 8).

Using participant observation as an ethnographical technique is on one hand fundamental for media ethnography but simultaneously it contains the inherent danger of objectifying the field of interest. The dilemma is expressed in the

41

concept itself, containing the wish both to observe and simultaneously participate in a social practice. The method implies the intention of not disturbing the cultural practices. Paul Willis argues that implicitly participant observation is a "secret pact with positivism": The stubborn insistence on the passivity of the participant observer is thus a stubborn belief that the research object truly is an object. The aim is to minimize the distortion of the field, because one fears that the object might be contaminated by the subjectivity of the researcher (...) The first principle of the participant observer, to defer theory, contains the danger of hidden positivism (Willis, 1986:91).

Willis's point is that it is not possible to "have a clean slate". It is of course possible on the concrete level to postpone theory and adopt an open position *vis-à-vis* the reality in which one is situated, however whatever the researcher observes will be understood from his perspective. This recognition is an indispensable adjunct to any research, especially when carried out in a different culture from one's own.

To achieve a clear distinction between subject and object is however difficult. The most important point is to clarify one's theoretical position, including recognizing the difficulty of distinguishing between subject and object. Furthermore, one must consider the consequences of one's theoretical position and methodological choice. What will happen to so-called scientific validity?

When the Danish anthropologist Kirsten Hastrup talks about scientific validity and the mixing of subject and object, she does not imply that the former disappears, but that the definition of scientific must be changed. Hastrup operates with the concept of a third culture (Hastrup 1986). The moment an anthropologist appears and temporarily resides in another culture, a new situation arises. The anthropologist adopts parts of the other culture and also arrives with her own culture. The anthropologist does not become one of them, but is on the other hand no longer the same. Likewise, the other culture also changes in this encounter of cultures. The meeting should not be understood just as a putting together of cultural expressions, but becomes a mixture of its own. Everything is changed.

However, the establishing of a third culture remains an ideal condition which in practice is difficult to obtain. The cultural encounter is always full of confrontations and inner conflicts which have to be got over before a symbiotic third culture can emerge.

In the encounter between two cultures ruptures occur that reveal the self-evident structure which ties the everyday together. In this rupture a possibility is created where the cultures can both seek mutual sympathy and understanding. In other words, it is not until the occurrence of this encounter that a distance to one's own culture becomes possible, producing a consciousness of the underlying structures of one's own culture However, first and foremost this cultural encounter provides one with the possibility of uncovering and possibly understanding what is self-evident to the "others' in everyday life. The concept of "third culture" is in other words the establishment of a new culture.

Some anthropologists have worked out radical methods for creating mutual cultural understanding. Paulo Freire talks of cultural invasion as a methodology with which to initiate one's relation to "the other" (Freire, 1972). The Danish anthropologist Mette Bovin has elaborated what she calls provocation anthropology (Bovin, 1988: 21ff), explicitly gambling on and subsequently analysing the consequences of an active cultural invasion. Since it is impossible to avoid interference, she prefers rather to make the problematic explicit and thus place the question of reflexivity, cultural encounter and the relation between the researcher and "the field" centrally in the research design.

The point is not that one approach is better than another. In order to carry out media ethnography, the role of the researcher must, as mentioned earlier, be thoroughly reflected upon. Instead of seeking to hide away and become an observing fly on the wall, integration into everyday life is more productive. In the course of this process, researchers must be aware of their personal reactions to, as well as carrying out analyses of how, when and why "the others" react to them as cultural "intruders". Through a conscious and deliberate integration – however not necessarily as provocative an invasion as Bovin argues for – I believe that the researcher reaches further into the dense layers of the everyday.

Selection of survey areas

The three survey areas were selected on the basis of two main criteria: (1) I needed low-income urban areas and (2) I wanted to have regional variations in my data. Urban areas were chosen because 75 per cent of the population in Brazil live in urban areas (IBGE in *Veja*, January 1991). Of these, more than half live in the urban peripheries as first or second generation migrants from the rural areas. It was among some of these people that I was interested in conducting my case study.

By choosing three very different regions of Brazil I wished to reflect some of the cultural multiplicity of Brazil, exploring to what degree this would be observable in their social customs and especially in their reception of telenovelas. My search for regional differences was to be matched with the more pragmatic constraint of accessability. Given this condition, the choice fell on the following neighbourhoods: Vila Nitro Operaria in São Paulo in the centre of Brazil, Santa Operaria in Canoas in the southernmost region of Brazil and Calabar in Salvador in the Northeastern region of the country.

Salvador, the capital of the state of Bahia in northeastern Brazil, is interesting because it has the country's largest concentration of black inhabitants, thereby – together with the racial characteristics of Southern Brazil – providing an important variable for the reception analysis. Salvador is the former capital of Brazil, a city to which the slaves were brought from Africa in the 16-19th centuries. Calabar is a 40-year-old shanty town area (a favela) in the centre of town, having predominantly black inhabitants.

Unlike Salvador, Canoas – 2500 km further south in Brazil – has many inhabitants who are descended from German immigrants who arrived at the end of the 19th and the beginning of the 20th century, and have thus brought very different cultural traditions along with them in history. In addition to different cultural characteristics, the religious practices of the chosen regions differ substantially, containing many variations and nuances within Afro-spiritual and Catholic beliefs.

São Paulo is the country's largest economic, political and cultural centre. Migration has been largest in São Paulo and at the same time São Paulo was the city which mobilized the largest opposition to the military regime in Brazil. It is a city with many political and cultural conflicts and divisions. Furthermore, São Paulo's eastern zone contains the urban peripheries in Brazil that I know best, having carried out several other studies here prior to this case study (see project trajectory). Finally, São Paulo is the city where the broadcasting company Rede

Manchete has the biggest ratings and thus – at the time of my fieldwork – constituted the largest threat to Rede Globo's national dominance. The workers' quarter Vila Nitro Operaria was chosen because I had been in the area before and knew some of the people there. It is a workers' suburb dating from the 1930s, situated approximately one and a half hours by public transport from the centre of São Paulo.

Gatekeepers

The contact to the survey areas was established through a series of gatekeepers. In all three cases the contacts were made through local community organizations or non-governmental organizations. In Calabar in Salvador my contact was established through the Brazilian NGO, CESE, that provides technical support to the local organization for community schools. A board member of this local organisation, Maria, was also the chairperson of the community organization of Calabar. I was introduced to her and she then became my gatekeeper in Calabar.

Maria's position as local community leader had several implications for my encounter with the inhabitants of the community. First of all it meant that Maria was very well known locally. On our first walk around in the community she greeted very many people, and being seen with her later facilitated my contact to some of the people. On the other hand some people most probably disliked her for her work, which may have prevented them from speaking openly to me. This never became explicit to me, but is a bias to be aware of. Furthermore, Maria was associated with donors, the CESE organization, which might lead some to devote special attention to pleasing "outside" visitors she brought along. However, I made it clear to everybody I met that I was not a potential donor, but a researcher interested in telenovelas.

In Vila Nitro Operaria in São Paulo my contact was established through the Brazilian non-governmental organisation FASE. This gatekeeper process had started back in 1987 when I carried out 3 months of field work a mere 15 minute walk from Vila Nitro Operaria. I maintained contact with the priest who had been my host at the time, and who in 1989 had put me in touch with an industrial worker, Servilho, who became my gatekeeper for my study of the trade union movement in São Paulo. Servilho lives in Vila Nitro Operaria and, in 1991, when I was setting up this study, he became my gatekeeper again.

Like Maria in Calabar, Servilho is a well-known person in the local community. People know him because of his political and trade union activities. This political bias was obviously present when he introduced me to some women in the area, influencing his selection of people and most probably influencing what they said – I noticed this clearly with the first woman he introduced me to. To counteract this bias I chose three of the five women at this site by other means than by Servilho's introduction, mainly through contacts I established in the course of my fieldwork. It was thus a pragmatic solution, which kept up good relations with Servilho while avoiding too significant a bias through his choices.

In Santa Operaria in Canoas the local Catholic church movement was my entry point. The contact person was the priest Antonio and on the more local level it was a young monk João Carlos. João Carlos helped the local Christian community organization in their social work. João Carlos lives in the area and Antonio was one of the leaders in the occupation of the area in the early 1980s. He is thus well known. Antonio provided me with a place to stay, in the house of some nuns, which also was the meeting place for the Christian community. João Carlos provided the contact to the women of the community. Due to time constraints, I did not carry out a quantitative survey in Santa Operaria.

My access to the 13 selected women necessarily had to go through gatekeepers, people who had my confidence as well as confidence among the inhabitants of the selected communities. No matter who I chose they all had either religious, political or community organizational biases. They were however fundamental for my entry into the field, proving very useful in introducing the neighbourhood to me and vice-versa.

The data survey

The survey included 105 women, 49 in Vila Nitro Operaria in São Paulo and 56 in Calabar in Salvador. The women were randomly selected. The survey was carried out at the weekend in both places, as it would be more likely that people would be home. In both places I had assistants helping me visit the many homes and ask the questions. The questionnaire was to cover three main areas of interest for my study: socio-economic data, data on media habits and data relating to the social uses of television (Appendix 1). Part 1 dealt with conditions: family status, work and income of everybody in the household. It included questions on how many children there were in the household, the marital status of the woman, type of job and who earned how much. These answers, combined with participant observations in the area provided me with a general overview of the socio-economic situation that the survey groups live under (see chapter 8 for further elaboration).

Part 2 concerned the TV habits of the women. I mapped out whether they saw television, what, how much, how often, when and with whom. The questionnaire included a small diagram where the person asking the questions filled in what the women watched in the morning, in the afternoon and at night. I also wanted to know whether they had watched specific telenovelas, including *Rubbish Queen* and others. By mapping out their novela habits I sought to obtain an overview of their use of telenovelas as well as which TV station they preferred and how much of their TV-viewing was a collective or an individual activity.

Part 3 of the survey concerned the women's other media habits, such as radio and the written media. From this I could obtain a picture of the overall media patterns and from there look closer into the intertextuality of the media. To interpret the data of this survey I constructed 18 different tables from each of the two areas (Appendices 3 and 4) and calculated a series of percentages that are used in my analyses.

Research assistants

Three women from Salvador assisted me in carrying out the data survey. They were all friends of mine. One was a law student, one an educationalist and one a teacher. They were middle class Brazilians and happened to be sisters. I instructed them carefully, explaining how they were to go from house to house and explain that they would like to ask the woman of the house some questions. In practical terms they did not succeed in doing very many presentations themselves because Maria Jesús, the chairperson of the community organization herself took the time to walk with them and present them to every household with just one phrase, something like this: "Hello Dona Paula, I brought with me a young student who would like to ask you some questions about television and telenovelas. Can she come in for a short while?" With this introduction the women let me and my assistants come into their homes. In São Paulo a friend of mine assisted me with the questionnaire. She is a student, a middle class Brazilian with former experience from similar surveys.

Neither in São Paulo nor in Calabar did I or my assistants once get 'no' for an answer. However, we did at times sense a reluctance or a feeling of uncertainty as to what we were wanting to know. However, with the subject being so everyday and familiar as telenovelas, the women generally relaxed and responded to all the questions. The respondents did not fill out the questionnaire themselves but were asked the questions by myself or the research assistant. Households without television were also asked, because not having a television set did not automatically imply not watching television. The women in these households often went and saw television with other people.

Having assistants to help carry out the survey gave me more time and energy to concentrate on the time-consuming process of participant observation and in-depth interviewing.

Obviously, I do not intend to argue that these 105 women are statistically representative for any neighbourhood(s) or even less a particular social class. However, I do wish to argue that they were to a degree analytically representative (Kvale 1996: 227), and that this survey can thus plausibly be held to provide useful information about the general patterns of consumption of telenovelas and other media among low-income Brazilians in urban peripheries. Obviously one can discuss how true this is, and whether it is the researcher or the reader who should be the judge. I have simply presented the premises and overall line of content of the survey, leaving it to the reader to decide.

The qualitative interview

The 13 women constituting the qualitative basis of this case study were chosen at random. I had met a lot of them in other contexts than their homes, eg. at various types of community meeting, in their jobs or in the street. All of them had a positive attitude to my approach and some found it rather amusing that I wanted to discuss telenovelas with them. My impression was that this positive attitude and the familiarity of the topic facilitated communication between us. I carried out all the qualitative interviews myself, as open, semi-structured conversations ranging from 45-90 minutes in duration. They took place after previous visits in the households and towards the end of my stay in the local community. All interviews were tape-recorded and transcribed.

Choice of telenovela

Rubbish Queen was chosen as my sample telenovela because it had recently been screened, but was now off air. I wished to explore to what degree telenovelas that were no longer being screened remained present in the women's memories. What made the women remember the telenovela? Which elements did they highlight now, several months later? While the choice of this novela was important for exploring narrative memory, it only constituted a point of departure in my study. My fieldwork took in a series of other telenovelas currently on air, a total of 11, spread over three different television channels. The basic point with the *Rubbish Queen* was to focus on one particular textual representation of a popular cultural phenomenon which is massively present in everyday life.

I obtained access to all the recordings of the *Rubbish Queen*, choosing to record three blocks of four chapters each, a total of 12 chapters of the telenovela. The questions I asked in the interviews were related to the telenovela as a whole, to the characters as a whole, and not to one specific chapter. It was the everyday flow of telenovelas I sought to uncover, and the traces that a telenovela which was now over had left in people's minds.

The qualitative interviews all followed an interview guide which I had devised. The dual aim was to capture the reactions relating to a specific telenovela (which was my original idea), and to grasp the production of meaning articulated by daily exposure to telenovelas. My interviews always began by me asking the women to retell the basic story of the telenovela. On the basis of their résumé issues arose, such as love, social conflict, gender, labour, family, lifestyles, race, etc. I asked them to tell me who they liked and disliked the most in the telenovela. From there many of them entered into comparisons of different actors and telenovelas, which led the way into general discussions of telenovela content, characteristics, highlights, etc.

Another fundamental part of the interview was to obtain information and comments regarding their daily routine from they got up until they went to bed, focusing on their media use. This provided an important basis for analysing their social uses of the media. In conclusion, I often got them to tell me which story they would like to tell, if they were able to have a story produced as a telenovela.

In all but two I cases interviewed the women in their natural social contexts, their homes. The two youngest, 13-year old Estella and Christiane, were interviewed outside of their homes, in a room on the premises of the Catholic church to which they belonged. Most often the interviews were carried out in the living rooms, which in many cases were simultaneously bedrooms and kitchens. However, I followed most of them in non-domestic settings as well, in the course of my participant observations.

The TV was often turned on while I interviewed, just like it usually was in their everyday lives. In the interview situation I aimed at being alone with the interviewee because I personally would find other people's presence disturbing. However, this turned out to be far from the case in many of the interviews. There were often no other places where the other family members could go other than out of the house and/or into the street. Furthermore, many of the family members were far too curious to move away when I was visiting the house. To my surprise their presence turned out to be an advantage. When analysing what actually happened in the situation, and while studying the transcripts of the interviews I have become convinced that the presence of others was very useful and obviously more natural a setting than the one I had intended to establish. Instead of being a hindrance it was a help in my conversations with the women. The others' presence was part of their natural setting and also gave them a greater degree of confidence. The moral codes of conduct would tend to make women uneasy about sitting alone and talking to me, and with some of them this probably was the case. Because they live in very close social contact with members of the household as well as with friends and other relatives, and because there was very limited space in many of the homes, it was natural for everyone to participate in any social activities that were taking place. It occurred to me that almost none of my repeated visits in these households took place without at least one or two additional persons present in the house, and most often in the living room where I was conducting an interview with one of my respondents. My visits were social events. In the interview situations, other people were present in the house and most often in the same room, in 12 out of the 13 interviews.

The main bias in the interview situation was undoubtedly the gender bias. In the initial comments from the women, prior to the interview, most of them found it amusing and funny that I wanted to talk to them about telenovelas. I think it added to the amusing aspect of the exercise for them that it was a man who wanted to talk to them about telenovelas. This fact may very well have prevented me from obtaining the same degree of intimacy as could have been obtained if a woman, and especially a Brazilian woman, had conducted a similar exercise. Despite this bias, my retrospective autoanalysis and analysis of the situation makes me believe that the atmosphere was generally very relaxed and natural.

Another element of gender bias lay in the reactions of the husbands. They could not really understand my interest in telenovelas, which stimulated their curiosity, and made some of them hang around, especially outside the house. This may have limited the confidence shown to me by some of the women.

As will be seen from the above, the whole process of fieldwork is characterized by many pragmatic solutions taken in the situation. It requires tolerance, flexibility and time to spare, along with good preparation, cultural-linguistic competence and general knowledge about the field. There is no single solution, and each empirical study is thus unique. The aim is to say something valid about the people and culture in focus, and seek to make some analytical generalizations, as I will do in the course of my case analysis. I consider that the validity of this study lies largely in my having presented and argued for the fieldwork process, and made clear my choices and priorities, as well as the limits and limitations.

5. Television in everyday life

In media ethnography the social interactionist approach is crucial to getting answers to overall questions on the role of television in everyday life. Analysing the social uses of the media, in this case television, is a fundamental first part of this social interactionist approach. As I argued earlier in this chapter, focus should likewise be on the collective conversations which publics take part in, in other words, a reception analysis. This conversation, in particular the talk about TV, must be interpreted, which constitutes the second part of this analysis.

The social uses of the media

In order to systematically analyse the role of TV in everyday life, we must distinguish between television's role in the constitution of time, of space and of social relations. The social use of television is further structured according to two overall parameters which help systematize the total analysis: the structural and relational use of television. The use of these concepts in media analysis originates from James Lull, who used them in his analysis published in the article "The social uses of television" (Lull, 1980). Here I seek to link these two characteristics of the social use of television with the organization of time, space and social relations in everyday life, creating an altogether more complex panorama.

The structural use of television is predominantly linked to the organization of time and space and less to the organization of social relations. Contrary to this, the relational use of television is chiefly linked to the organization of social relations and the organization of space, as will be seen below.

Figure 1: Constitutive elements in the analysis of media in everyday life

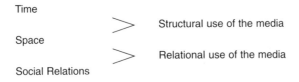

Time

The concept of time is a symbolic construct which is very much related to cultural specificities. In traditional societies, time is linked to specific social activities. Time is reflected in what you do. This stands in opposition to the rational understanding of time as something individualized and concrete in itself, something you can lose or save, buy or sell, independent of how you use it (Martín-Barbero 1993: 218). Here time is a value, linked to the rational, capitalist mode of production. In traditional societies time is often a cyclic concept, linked to the repetitive nature of the days and seasons. On the opposite side, you find the linear time perception, related to the more rational and product-oriented culture, independent of the cycles of nature. The perception of time in contemporary urban societies is not the same as in traditional societies, nor is it a rational linear time perception. It is something in between, linked tightly to the organization of space and social relations.

Television, as a flow and as a composite of different genres influences the symbolic construction of time. As industrial products, television programmes are the output of a rationalized process of production, but they also integrate creative processes which can be difficult to rationalize completely. Thus, the degree to which and the manner in which TV programmes influence the symbolic construction of time are highly dependant upon a large number of other factors which must be dealt with ad hoc, according to the specific situation to be analysed.

On the material level, as one of the "objects of everyday life", television contributes to the creation of obviousness and entirety (Bech Jørgensen 1994), a set of concepts very closely related to Giddens' understanding of ontological security. As I found out in my case study, television for many people has a time-structuring function, and different programmes orient the viewer in his or her everyday life. Jennifer Bryce distinguishes very usefully between monochronic and polychronic conceptions of time in the way her respondents relate to television viewing in relation to other social activities (Bryce 1987). Bearing this distinction in mind, we can say that the achievement of ontological security through media consumption occurs in many different ways.

Space

Space should be understood as both a symbolic construct and a materially existing site, although distinct from a "place". De Certeau makes this distinction, indicating space to be a place created by practice (De Certeau 1984). A space does not exist all the time, but is constituted in the interaction of social agents with time and social relations. A living room becomes a 'practised place': where family members, friends and relatives sit and talk, relax, watch television and have a drink, where children play, etc. However, as a place it is just a room, like the bedroom or the kitchen. It becomes a space, a living room due to the practices of everyday life occurring in the specific organization of time, place and social relations.

On the symbolic level television can contribute to the constitution of spaces. As the Brazilian anthropologist Ondina Leal showed in her study on the role of telenovelas in everyday life among Brazilian families, television becomes a significant element in the constitution of"spaces of modernity", both through the bricolage surrounding the TV set, but also through the role attributed to the content and reception of the TV flow (Leal 1986). Thus, television, both as a material possession, as a centre in a field of ornaments and decorations and finally through the interaction of content and flow with the viewer, can contribute in multiple ways to the constitution of spaces in everyday life. The organization of space thus relates to both the structural and relational use of television.

This "practised place" or "space of modernity" is exactly the site of struggle Ridell refers to, or the strategic site of interaction Murdock refers to. It also has direct relation to Van Tilburg's "televisual space". These concepts emphasize different aspects of what occurs in this or these space(s). The concepts complement each other and I use them to point the way to different perspectives in my interpretation of the social uses of television and telenovelas in particular.

Social relations

The ritual viewing of the daily TV programmes influences the social creation of a feeling of wholeness in everyday life. In the viewing process, it might not be so much the concrete programme content which is important as the feeling of gathering around the daily entertainment or news programmes and thereby becoming part of a social unity, be it a family, a nation or other social unities. The character of the social relationship obviously differs from case to case.

Because of the para-social interaction between the viewers and characters on the TV screen, some degree of social relations can develop with talk show hosts, actors, or news readers, as empirical studies have shown (Horton and Wohl 1986). The recognition of the screen characters mobilizes positive or negative emotions, and becomes an element in the constitution of social relations in everyday life. The organization of social relations is thus relates linked to the relational use of television.

Finally, TV can also provide the possibility of insight into the non-obvious, the possibility of something different, thereby helping to create shifts and ruptures in everyday life. Utopias, dreams and wishes may be stimulated or formulated by TV viewing. For example involvement with and projection towards a television character may promote the desire for another life and perhaps stimulate action for change among the viewer(s).

TV talk

> Reception analysis (...) combines a qualitative approach to media as texts, producing and circulating meaning in society, with an empirical interest in the recipients as co-producers of meaning. It is, in other words, audience-cum-content analysis.
>
> *Jensen, 1988: 3*

While the analysis of the social uses of television outlined above focuses on interpreting social interaction and the factual organisation of time, space and social relations, articulated and structured by the use and consumption of television, reception analysis – analysing the talk about TV – focuses on discursive practices. It is an analysis of the talk about the telenovela as it is manifested both in the conversation between viewers as well as in the interviews between researcher and respondent. How does the audience compare and contrast the telenovela world with their own social world? What attracts attention, who do the viewers identify with, what, in the narrative, is criticized or rejected? These and other questions are set in relation to the actual media text, becoming, as Jensens says:audience-cum-content analysis.

The aim is to explore how talk in a telenovela, and talk about the telenovela become linked in everyday communication, exploring the social and cultural consequences of this in terms of the articulation of identity, social relations, social action, opinions, etc. As Fiske says, the way TV is talked about provides us with two sorts of clues about these questions: "...clues about how TV is being assimilated into the social formation and how that social formation is read back into the text, and clues about which meanings offered by the text are being mobilised in this process. This form of intertextual relations is a bridge between the textual and the social" (Fiske 1989: 66).

The ideal but also the most difficult procedure is to observe the viewers' natural discussions about the telenovelas. In practice I achieved this on a few occasions. I also experienced interview situations where the respondent began discussing a telenovela with a friend or relative who was present during the interview. The main substance in my analysis was achieved in the interviews and only to a limited degree through participant observation.

6. The clarity of truth is but a saga

Niels Bohr once asked an audience what was the opposite of truth. It was neither lies nor falsity, he claimed, but clarity. If clarity is the opposite of veracity, we need not despair even if we cannot entrap the truth with a few words (Hastrup, 1986: 9).

Following Bohr's argument, objective truth is non-existent and therefore cannot be pinned down, no matter which method one uses. The way to design a media ethnographic research project is thus to make clear the subjective choices taken in order to shed light on a specific problem in the most relevant way. Many conditions and situations will be difficult to understand due to the cultural differences. The dynamics of the cultural encounter will give moments of clarity, "aha" experiences, but can also lead to conflicts and contradictions between the researcher and the "otherness" of the situation. All that, however, is part of the analysis.

Coming from another culture will however provide the researcher with the possibility of discovering aspects of culture and social action that the people studied do not perceive for themselves. The point of these methodological considerations is obviously to try to prepare oneself for any conflicts and problems that might arise. However, by linking methodology with theoretical reflection and making explicit the epistemology of the project, the outcomes and findings may become less vague. In principle, as I have stated already, there are no limits to what should be included in the analysis. The limits are defined and set by the researcher himself in his strategic choices and selections. I have now outlined my strategy, and will seek to put it into operation in the rest of this book.

3. Rediscovering Brazil: Samba, saints and social movements

A story only becomes a success when the storyteller tells about something that is recognizable, or at least understandable. The story and its audience must have some common cultural denominators, where the issues or situations of the story are understood and strike some chords in the cultural repertoire of the audience. It is difficult to understand a joke if you do not have the same understanding of what is funny and what is not, or you might misinterpret a statement – for example an ironic remark – if you are not used to irony or have another concept of right and wrong. The story being told might be rooted in some norms and values that simply are too different from yours to make it an interesting or understandable story for you.

To understand telenovelas and their success we must understand the cultural context in which the story – in this case the telenovela – is being told. First of all it is worth noting that telenovelas are stories told to a national audience. The concepts of nation and national identity are both ideological constructions, so to get an understanding of the national context in which telenovelas operate, it is necessary to analyse what constitutes these ideological constructions. The focal point of analysis – part 1 of this chapter – will be the dominant ideological and cultural discourse and its special emphasis on the national.

Telenovelas are also often closely linked to the collective memories of the viewers. Analysing these collective memories is not the same as analysing "the national". The rituals and social actions of everyday life are constituted around past experience. The collective memories are deeply rooted in the past, and tracing them means studying historical events that are imprinted on the minds of people. It may be recent events or events from a previous era that have been passed down from one generation to another establishing the trajectories of disposition upon which cultural identity is articulated. An example of this is when Afro-Brazilian groups in my survey area of Calabar cultivate their African past and their past as slaves in Brazil in their ritual celebrations. An example of a recent event was when the neighbourhood of Santa Operaria in Canoas commemorated the 10th anniversary of their invasion and occupation of the area where they now live, thus reviving a recent experience of tension and confrontation closely related to their establishment of new homes and lives. Collective memories – or cultural markers of the past – are configured around varying communities defined along such lines as the national, race, gender and class.

In part 2 of this chapter I will focus on two major discourses based on memory which, according to my experience in Brazil, are significant for the constitution of identity. One links the history of migration, the urbanization process and the rural past with the constitution of urban neighbourhood cultures and, in a larger scale, with modernity. The other is belief. Here, I will examine the signification of Catholic and Afro-Brazilian religions and relate them to race and class.

Dominant cultural discourses, memory and the constitution of modernity are key words in this chapter. My analysis will use all three to gain insight into the chronology of the symbolic construct 'Brazil', as a nation and as a cultural discourse, on one hand reflecting common ground to which all Brazilians relate and on the other hand reflecting the complexity and the "otherness" of Brazilian modernity compared with, for example, Anglo-Saxon understandings of the concept. The point of this chapter is to establish a basic appreciation of the significant cultural discourses that both precede, anchor and in multiple ways condition the role of telenovelas in the everyday life of low-income urban women in Brazil.

1. Modernity and the nation

Characteristic for Brazil, as for many other third world countries, has been the arrival of new ideas far before the socio-economic and cultural conditions were ready for them. The Brazilian sociologist Florestan Fernandes analyses in his book *The Bourgeois Revolution in Brazil* (Fernandes, 1975) that in dependent societies of colonial origin, capitalism was introduced prior to the constitution of a competitive social order. In Brazil, this led to a social and economic situation in the 1960s and onwards generally known as wild capitalism. Fernandes portrays the national bourgoisie in Brazil as bearers of a moderate modern spirit, implementing a restricted democracy, and thus preventing civil rights from being obtained by the whole population. The bourgoisie in third world countries such as Brazil acted for the benefit of their own economic advantage and thus did not have the "civilizing" role the bourgeoisie had in Europe. In Europe, cultural and material development occurred simultaneously, and modernism flourished within literature while profound changes took place in society, so that the effects on everyday life were social, economic and cultural. What happened was a gradual learning and adaptation to mass society.

Brazil was and is still characterized by the importation of ideas, within art, politics and science. Referring to the late 19th century, Rowe and Schelling remark, "Brazilian elites became receptive to European cosmopolitanism and the current belief in progress and enterprise"(1991: 38). The development of Rio at the turn of the century is an example. In this period, inspiration from the Belle Epoque and Art Nouveau in Europe reached Rio, but remained confined to an uban elite. Inspired by these literary and cultural influences, they remodelled the city, constructed avenues and squares with electric lighting. Animated by the new ideas and possibilities, they left their colonial verandas and salons to come out and experience the new times (Ortiz, 1988: 31pp). The optimism expressed in these ideas was however contradicted by the slum areas, which bore witness to the marginality and poverty in which many Brazilians lived. La Belle Epoque and Art Nouveau were based on ideas of progress and civilization. In Brazil, however, they expressed its underdevelopment.

São Paulo - modernity

Another example emphasizing the huge contradictions of Brazil was seen with the cinema industry, where an incredible optimism was seen in *Cine-Arte* magazine and the cinema industry of the 1920s. On one hand there were the great ideas and ambitions of the developing Brazilian film industry which saw development in terms of the number of cinemas in the country, and on the other hand there were the material conditions which made such schemes impractical. The cultural and economic elite basically used the social and economic contrasts to create a distance between themselves and the great majority of society.

These examples show how the ideas within the cultural, political and economic elite in Brazil constituted an artificial superstructure which was contradicted by the social and economic reality of the time. For this elite, the modernization of Brazil, including avant-gardist cultural trends, modernism, integration into consumer society and the industrialization of the nation, was a sweet dream they sought to realize without any critical dimension and which did not reflect the reality of the country. Their ideas simply belonged to another world than that of Brazil.

The rediscovery of Brazil

In the 1930s something happened. Renato Ortiz calls it "the rediscovery of Brazil" (Ortiz, 1986: 130). In these years mass society began to be established. The country experienced fundamental changes, especially a significant growth of industry in the urban centres of Rio and São Paulo.

The world crisis favoured Brazil and gave the economy a lift. Rapid industrial growth led to heavy internal migration, which brought about substantial changes in the composition of society. With the arrival of country people in the cities, a "hybridization" of cultures occurred. These changes soon transformed urban society, new ways of life were established and gradually the whole physiognomy of the cities changed. In the outskirts of the cities, new suburbs developed in an unplanned way and the occupation of new areas gradually transformed the outskirts of the cities into favelas and popular housing zones. "The city began to lose its centre"(Martín-Barbero, 1993a: 158).

> The people from the country had to learn to cope with a host of strange ways. It was necessary to learn how to catch a bus, how to find one's way through the streets, how to apply for identity papers. The old society responded to the immigrants with a disdain that covered not just repugnance but fear. More than an assault, the appearance of the masses meant that it was now impossible to continue maintaining the rigid hierarchy of differences that constituted society. For this reason the onslaught of the masses, though non-violent seemed equally dangerous; it was not the uprising of a social class but the freeing of an uncontrollable energy.
>
> *Martín-Barbero, 1993a: 158*

Populism became the political answer to this development. It became the way the state sought to legitimize itself and to mediate in the growing tensions between more and more diversified social groups. President Vargas (1930-1945 and 1950-1954) led this political and economic process.

The rediscovery of Brazil lay in the redefinition of the national, the wish to transform Brazil into a modern nation. Vargas had a very nationalistic policy, promoting a new vision of development, differentiating himself from the traditional oligarchy that had led the country. He introduced a modern concept of the "state", and a plan of action, *O Estado Novo* (The New State). In his second period in power (1950-54) Vargas emphasized national capitalist development, attempting to forge a strong alliance between the industrial bourgoisie and the working classes. Meanwhile, considerable sectors of the industrial bourgoisie were against this isolationist policy, preferring an alliance with international capital, thus pursuing another strategy in the development of the nation. With the suicide of Vargas in 1954, the path lay open for internationalism, "the open door policy" of President Kubitchek in the late 1950s.

National identity, a Mestizo *identity*

Within the cultural reflexions taking place in literature, art and social sciences at the time, the understanding of culture and Brazilian cultural identity gradually changed. The reinterpretation was rooted in Brazilian modernism. From the 1930s on, "the idea of modernism as a project can be seen as a paradigm for interpreting the relation between culture and modernization in Brazilian society"(Ortiz, 1988: 35).

There was a redefiniton of the "modern" and the "national", bringing these concepts closer to each other. In this process the Brazilian author and social scientist Gilberto Freyre produced one of the first interpretations of Brazilian national identity within the new paradigm. In searching for a clearer interpretation of identity and how Brazilian cultural identity could be defined, Freyre's work went beyond the growing polarization between urban and rural thought.

Freyre was very critical to the process of modernization. He praised tradition and the values of rural Brazil. However, compared to earlier writers he was innovative in his analyses of rural Brazil. He considered national identity to be based not only on the culture of the whites, but to include both indigenous and black culture. In his classic analysis of Brazilian culture, *Casa Grande e Senzala*, from 1933 Gilberto Freyre offered a "national identity card" to the Brazilians (Ortiz, 1986: 42). While the 18th-century intellectuals searching for the identity of the national "being" produced ambiguous interpretations, ignoring the presence of blacks in society, Freyre offered a clear identity in the *mestizo* of the Brazilian. He is one of the first social scientists to acknowledge the presence of blacks in Brazilian society. Freyre recognized the multiple racial origin of Brazilians, characterizing the national identity as a mixture of the cultures of the indigenous, the black and the white races in Brazil: the *mestizo* identity.

Brazilian cultural identity was now no longer, in official discourse, related to skin colour. This was later, in the 1980s and 1990s, to give the Black movement of Brazil a problem, because once blacks identified themselves as Brazilians it made cultural redefinition as 'black' more difficult. Thus, Freyre's positive interpretation of the cultural mixtures, which became the discourse of the dominant ideology, on one hand covered up the racial conflicts while on the other hand made it possible for all Brazilians to recognize themselves in a national identity.

Developmentalism and directed humanism

Where nation was a key word in the process of modernization of the 1930s, the focus had by the 1960s altered to development. Progress lay in economic development, and democracy was initially expected to be a spin-off of modernization. The trans-nationalization of the Brazilian economy was expected to speed up the process of development and lead to a mature and modern mass society where increased consumption and a redistribution of goods would ultimately increase democracy. However, this optimistic ideal of development was contradicted by reality, which showed increased inequality and growing class tensions. Thus, instead of democracy almost insoluble contradictions arose: "For the left, these contradictions simply made visible the incompatibility between capitalist accumulation and social change. For the right, the contradictions demonstrated the incompatibility of economic development with democracy" (Martín-Barbero, 1993a: 179).

In Brazil the contradictions led to political and economic instability, which resulted in the military coup of 1964. The aim of the regime was to stabilize the economy and thereby develop the nation. Economic growth was achieved, with Brazil obtaining world records in economic growth in the late 1960s and beginning of the 1970s. The instruments used to reach these figures were severe political repression, heavy borrowing to finance huge state projects in all branches of the infrastructure, and finally massive international investment. The regime had acknowledged that economic growth needed strong political control, which it also sought to establish through a very conscious and directed communication policy – a policy that included the support and development of Rede Globo's infrastructure. However, the drive for political control resulted in authoritarianism and not democracy.

The philosophy of the 1964-regime was an uncritical attitude towards the process of modernization. Modernization obtained a value in itself, linked to a neutral and very ideologically biased understanding of culture. The regime developed a hybrid concept of culture; the humanization of technology. This was introduced in the policy of the regime's Federal Commission of Culture (CFC) established in 1966. This "directed humanism" secured "the democratic neutrality of cultural action while bringing a discourse of human values to economic development" (Ortiz, 1986; 105). What the regime ended up doing was basically to reutilize the arguments Freyre used about the Nordeste of Brazil, conceiving of Brazilian culture as a *mestixo* culture. While Freyre based his concept of national identity on the diversity of races, the regime understood the nation as a unity of diverse regions each with their own culture. The regional replaced the racial.

This pluralistic understanding of national identity and unity was not only humanistic. It was based on an ideology of harmony, eliminating the questions of power and conflict. Any conflict was to be resolved within the concept of diversity, not disturbing the harmony of national unity: "The master does not oppose himself to the slave but differs from him. The slave-house does not represent an antagonism to the mansion, but simply imposes a differentiation which often is complementary to the global situation in society" (Ortiz, 1986: 96). This was an ideology of syncretism, ignoring conflicts, considering culture disconnected from society. There are parallels to cultural anthropology, in the regime's refusal to admit the existence of power relations (Ortiz, 1986: 95). For example the world football championship of 1970 contributed to a unification of Brazil, especially when the Brazilian football team with Pelé won the world championship. The country burst into pure harmony for a moment, forgetting social conflict and political repression.

Popular participation

The power relations in society were challenged when social movements began gaining support and strength in the 1970s. As early as 1974 the regime suffered a major moral defeat when it lost an election to the only opposition party allowed under the military regime. This became the turning point in the history of the military regime. During the decade local Christian communities emerged in more and more places, inspired by the Theology of Liberation, beginning a long process of political conscientization. In the late 1970s huge strikes swept through the country, initially for higher wages, but soon becoming a national political movement against the military regime. In 1979 President Figueiredo was forced to award an amnesty to exiled Brazilians and also had to launch A Abertura, the democratic opening of the political system. One of the trade union leaders heading the workers movements was Luiz Ignacio Lula da Silva, called Lula, who in 1980 became president of the new established Workers' Party (Partido dos Trabalhadores) and who in 1989, in the first direct election for president since 1960, obtained 47 per cent of the votes, losing to Fernando Collor de Melo.

The military regime in the late 1970s gradually changed their attitude to culture. So far they had operated with a uniform concept of culture, based on the ideology of directed humanism, promoting the development of a national culture and thus a national identity. However, the late 1970s were characterized by two things: a growing economic crisis and a growing political movement against the military regime. This led to a change in the regime's concept of culture, reviving the old dichotomy of high culture and low culture. The regime's Portela-plan which began in 1979, distinguished between three sorts of culture : (1) Culture linked to national identity, encompassing the cultural values applicable to any Brazilian; (2) Culture understood as "subsistency culture" being the culture of the poor; (3) Alienating culture or intellectualized culture, being the high culture of the elite (Ortiz, 1986: 138).

This new understanding of culture and cultural diversification helped legitimize the strategies of the regime. Many years of developmentalist action had industrialized the country but had not changed the living conditions of the majority. The contrast between the elite and the large majority of low-income people had remained unchanged. Under increased political pressure from the social movements, the rhetoric of the military regime changed, no longer trying to impose uniform cultural values on everyone – the mestizo culture – but instead acknowledging a difference and especially giving value to what they called the subsistency culture. "Subsistency culture means the art of surviving within a reality of poverty" (Ortiz, 1988).

This understanding of one uniform culture among poor people followed the lines of thought of the Mexican anthropologist Oscar Lewis who in the 1950s developed the concept of a culture of poverty based on fieldwork in low-income urban areas in Mexico (Lewis, 1958). In this concept lay a recognition of the survival strategies of the poor; the social networks and the creativity that made it possible to survive. This discourse, in Brazil, apparently rehabilitated the cultural values of low-income groups, acknowledging the poverty and the struggle of everyday life. However it remained rhetorical. The recognition was not aimed at trying to solve the problems but to maintain the status quo. The Brazilian regime went as far as directing its policy towards the low-income areas. In 1980, the Secretary for Cultural Issues described its community action plan as follows: "It is based on thorough work on the ground (grassroots work) together with the communities, aiming at making them conscious of the value of the cultural and natural patrimony of the region, decentralizing the spontaneous cultural activities and making them less elitist, involving associations and local leaders in the search for alternative resources" (Ortiz, 1986). Meanwhile, even though this action plan may have led to some extra musical and cultural events within the communities, it did not question the social and economic structures of society. It was a new strategy for participation, aimed at pacifing the popular movements.

The modern Brazilian identity

Ever since the Declaration of Independence in 1889 and since the avantgarde trends flourished among Rio's bourgeoisie in the late nineteenth century, the construction of modernity in Brazil has been developing. Modernity in Brazil became much more than just the process of industrialization. It became a state of mind, a set of norms, a code of conduct developed and spread by the urban bourgoisie. In rather simplistic terms, modernity became a rejection of the rural Brazil, and a promotion of urban values, first of all expressed in materialism, continuous economic growth and as a directed humanism practised towards the low-income strata.

Industrialization gradually enabled the numerous remote and in many ways independent regions of Brazil to become united, both in terms of infrastructure as well as in the minds of the Brazilians. Here television came to play a central role, as we shall see in chapter 4. The idea of a national identity was promoted by the dominant classes, with a generalized discourse to the effect that class-, social- and racial inequality and difference was nothing more than mere regional differences in Brazil. However, this directed humanism and the uncritical belief in economic growth as the key to developing a modern Brazil was – and is still – severely contradicted by the socio-economic reality of the vast majority of Brazilians.

Brazil is in many ways a modern country, in some areas as highly industrialized as the USA, Germany or the Nordic countries. Seen in terms of its technological and economic capacity, the number of its urban inhabitants , and the potential of its literature, music and fine arts, Brazil looks like a highly developed and industrialized society. However, the indices of illiteracy, level of education, birth mortality and the living standards for the majority of the population point in the completely opposite direction.

Brazil has a colonial past, with a long history of social conflict, of poverty and of sporadic economic and political repression. Out of these socio-economic and historical conditions has grown a cultural identity full of tensions, contradictions and multiple influences: rural and urban realities; rich and poor people; red, white, black and yellow races; "high tech" and medieval industries side by side; all these tensions and contradictions co-exist, often mixed up, creating various hybrid cultural forms and expressions. All of this exists today and together forms the history, culture and society of modern Brazil.

An issue which today, retrospectively, is seen as characteristically Brazilian is that "social change was achieved less through a radical break with the past than through a conciliatory accommodation of divergent interests and moderate social reforms introduced by the state. Capitalist development and modernization in Brazil went hand in hand with the creation of a heterogenous mass society" (Rowe and Schelling 1991: 44). This heterogeneity is significantly present today in the urban neighbourhoods, where a multiplicity of trajectories and experiences intermingle creating unique mosaics of social and cultural practices, mosaics that at a distance seem uniform and more or less homogenous, but looked at more closely reveal a multitude of constituent components.

Telenovelas are simultaneously a result of and representative of these manifold trajectories and experiences. Television and telenovelas are mediators in the processes of social change and formation of identity, and thus in the making of the heterogenous cultural mosaic that is Brazil, where capitalist development, social change and identity formation are elements of the same reality.

2. Memory and cultural identity

> Social memory is not just continuity and unchanging identity, it is also memory of destruction and discontinuity – there are a variety of differentiated memories.
>
> *Rowe and Schelling, 1991: 228*

In part 1 of this chapter I sought to analyse the constitutive elements of the dominant ideological discourse which sets the agenda of national identity. Part 2 enters into an analysis of the collective memories that influence the constitution of personal cultural identities.

Cultural identity is related more to the everyday life of the people. Whereas national identity transcends everyday life, people's cultural identity is a part of everyday life. However, both cultural identities and national identity are rooted in one specific issue: memory. Memory is a resource of references, a cultural capital that is used in the formation of everyday life and in planning the future. As Halbwachs observes, memory is always relived in the present (Halbwachs,1968) and as Rowe and Schelling state above, "there are a variety of differentiated memories".

Memory can be individual as well as collective, but is in both ways fundamental for the constitution of cultural identity. Cultural identity, according to the Brazilian media researcher Nilda Jacks, is an important mediator between the subject and the reality around it:

> ... cultural identity fulfils a fundamental role between the subject, individual or social, and the reality surrounding it, mediating the processes of production and the appropriation of cultural goods. It is this mediation that guarantees the significance of cultural production and the meaning of the consumption of symbolic goods, without which it turns into an empty process, with the danger of turning into an alienated and alienating act.
>
> *Jacks 1999*

Collective memories, being central to the constitution of the subject's cultural identity, thereby become central for the analysis of television reception. The methodological challenge lies in identifying the common denominators – as well as the differences – in the interpretive communities to which the viewers belong. The interpretive communities which I shall return to later in my reception analysis (see chapter 9) will be defined on criteria such as gender, socio-economic status, job, race, family status, religion and regional and even national affiliation. Based on the general socio-economic development trends in Brazil I have selected two discourses within memory that are significant in the constitution of identity, thus providing information that will be useful when analysing television reception. The first one relates to the history of migration, the urbanization process and the rural past in the constitution of urban neighbourhood cultures.

Suburbs: the centre of everyday life

One of the characteristics of the urbanization process in the modernization of Brazil has been the way migrants, moving from rural to urban areas, have organized themselves socially and materially. Many have been pushed to marginal areas that either for economic or strategic reasons have been of little interest to the state or to private enterprises. Most migrants went to places where they already had relatives or friends. Thus, they often moved directly to areas in the outskirts of town, where many earlier migrants live due to the restricted areas in the centre. Via their contact with relatives or friends the new migrants obtained information on housing, jobs, etc. The network of family and friends also functioned as protection against the unknown social reality surrounding them.

Suburbs naturally differ in their degree of development. If it is a very poor area, a favela, the state often ignores it, and avoids providing assistance with housing, sanitation or other facilities. This inaction on the part of the body politic is legitimized by pointing out the illegality of the areas – often they have been squatted – and the assumed peripheral position they possess in relation to the economic life of the city. All three survey areas in this book's case study have had these experiences of state passivity in meeting the rights of these marginalized citizens.

Clearances of illegally occupied areas frequently occur, but have no long term effect because the squatters go looking for a new place or return to the same place later, having nowhere else to go. On some occasions resettlement in social housing occurs, although this is often considered too expensive a solution for the state:

> Unable to provide cheap housing yet willing to acknowledge the migrant's desire to build his own house, governments have recourse to two solutions. In "site and service" schemes, the public authority lays out the area with roads and services, the site owner then constructing his house with materials provided centrally. (...) Alternatively, the existing squatter settlement can be recognized and services provided; it is "upgraded".
>
> *Lloyd, 1979: 26*

Upgrading leads to acknowledgement – even though often under pressure – of the self-help potential of the squatters. However, upgrading is expensive, so more often when something happens it is site-and-service projects, where the present situation of the area is bettered, roads are paved, building materials provided for the inhabitants to better their own houses, etc. However, the unsatisfactory nature of the housing, often illegal, overcrowded and without basic infrastructure, frequently leads the migrants to conceive a burning desire, an overwhelming wish, to have a proper house of their own, on their own little piece of land, as they might have had in the past when they lived as small peasants in Nordeste.[1]

Cultural marginality

What characterizes the urban peripheries (outskirts) is marginality, culturally, economically and politically. Cultural marginality derives from the "centre's" estimation of the inhabitants of the periphery as belonging to a subordinated subculture, either cast out from or integrated into society on the conditions of the dominant groups.

> In the sense of integration the term marginality is descriptive and ethnocentric. It locates certain groups – here the shanty-town dwellers – with reference to the dominant groups in the society. They do not quite belong to the society perceived by the latter. The problem posed is: "will they become integrated in time, will they persist on the margins, or will they develop a sub-society of their own, in antithesis and opposition to that of the dominant groups?
>
> *Lloyd, 1979: 62*

---

1 This was a general conclusion of a fieldwork analysis I participated in a shanty-town dwelling in the outskirts of São Paulo in 1986-1987. See Tufte et al, 1990.

It is the fear of a counter-culture challenging the dominant ideology that makes the surrounding society regard the counter-culture as diverging from the dominant norm. This sort of stigmatization is interpreted by the social psychologist Erving Goffman as an attempt to separate the "different" people from oneself, because by being different they threaten the system of attitudes and behaviour that constitutes the identity of the "normal": "By setting up a stigma theory, an ideology, we explain his inferiority and convince ourselves of the danger he constitutes" (Goffman, 1975:17). If a person is continuously confronted with the stigma, it may end up becoming internalized in the person. On the other hand, the confrontations can also provide the stigmatized person with a better understanding of his or her own position in relation to the national culture. It can open up a strong wish for change, a dream of a better life. Telenovelas, as we shall see in my analysis, may very well open up such reflections and dreams. Occasionally, the experience of "difference", most often seen as social inequality, can result in a change in the practice and forms of resistance in everyday life. Continuous confrontation with the fact of being marginalized, the experience of not having your own land, being pushed from suburb to suburb – and simultaneously retaining the perhaps romanticized memory of your rural past in Nordeste – all this together may lead to just such a change in everyday survival strategy and resistance: for instance setting up an occupation of land.

Neighbourhood culture

The above described socio-economic and cultural characteristics apply to the vast majority of the low-income urban dwellers in Latin America. The social reality of the urban peripheries has existed in some places for more than half a century. What has developed in these places is a new neighbourhood identity: "A new culture emerges specific to the popular neighbourhoods, different from those of the heroic workers at the turn of the century and different from the centre (of the city) which often provides a reference point for its definition" (Romero, 1984 in Martín-Barbero, 1993a: 197).

Seen in the perspective of modernity, the notion of the suburb and its role in the process of modernization requires a different approach from that of classic theories of modernity. Roger Silverstone performs a very thorough analysis of the role of (Western) suburbs in the process of (European) modernization and the role of television in the development of what he characterizes as a "suburban identity" (Silverstone 1994). Parallels to Martín-Barbero's "neighbourhood identity" are tempting, however not so simple, the main point being that the social realities of European and North American suburbs are different from suburbs in a Latin American context. This serves to illustrate the difficulties in universalizing theoretical concepts developed on the basis of one specific social reality (see also Tufte 1998).

The particularities of Latin American suburbs (*periferias*) appear in Martín-Barbero's reflections upon them. Neighbourhood culture in Latin America is, according to Martín-Barbero, formed of three different environmental influences:

> ...those coming from the agencies external to the neighbourhood such as
> the school; those formed by agents from outside the neighbourhood but
> nevertheless rooted within the community such as the cafés; and those

institutions that are created quite independently by the popular classes on their own such as the libraries and clubs.

Martín-Barbero, 1993a: 197

This distinction is useful, although neighbourhoods obviously vary. A central agent, contributing substantially to the culture of many neighbourhoods is the Catholic church, especially the part of the church inspired by Theology of Liberation. The communidades eclesiais de base (local Christian communities) have been influential in grassroots work throughout Latin America since the 1970s. Back in the early 1960s, after the Second Vatican Council in Rome, the Catholic Church decided to resituate their work, bringing their gospel out into the neighbourhoods where people lived. Many priests literally moved out, thus creating the base for the emergence of Theology of Liberation and the local Christian communities.

Skyscrapers in downtown São Paulo

Within the church structures there are also a range of activities for young people, women and the neighbourhood in general. In addition, many of the social movements that emerged in Brazil throughout the past two decades have often used the infrastructure of the church for their meetings and preparing their activities. The church has largely been – and continues to be – an institution that provides the space where migrants, very often women, can establish and develop social networks of the utmost importance for their gradual integration and adaptation to urban life. As I describe later on, telenovelas become a frequent topic for conversation within the networks established around church activities, thus contributing to meaningful, albeit complex, processes of social interaction and integration.

A central aspect in the neighbourhood is the gender division of activities. The cafés, bars, sports clubs and football fields are among the preferred social spaces where men gather after work and at the weekends; the numerous unemployed men also gather here on weekdays.

The women have their own networks and social spaces, of which those described above that are based on the church are often the most central. The leading role played by women in the organization of time and space, and in the ongoing struggle to improve living conditions in the neighbourhood is a characteristic aspect of these people's lives. Women look after the children, do the shopping, cleaning, cooking and often also some minor jobs to earn some money. This can be washing the clothes of the local football team, selling cakes, sweets or other things, sewing clothes, etc. Furthermore, women are the most active in the grassroot activities, like the Black movement, the community organization, the Christian community or the women's clubs. They also borrow food from each other and look after each others' children. The social networks of women become the fabric that keep the neighbourhoods together (Tufte et al, 1990).

Neighbourhood culture in Vila Nitro, Operaria

Martín-Barbero interprets the leading role of women as being configured on the basis of maternity: "It is a social maternity that instead of closing in around the family connects the whole neighbourhood as its place of development and operation" (Martin-Barbero, 1993a: 199). However, this social maternity is not so strong a feeling that it prevents them from wishing for another way of life, as one woman I interviewed in 1987 stated in a favela in Brazil. This woman – Dona Jurema – was 54 years old and already a great-grandmother: "If I could live my life again I would work in a firm, live my life alone, earn my money, pay my INPS (a pension fund) and have a whole house to myself, without a man, children all married...to be able to be free, more relaxed and not have worries" (Tufte et al, 1990: 76).

The neighbourhood culture is complex. It is a social, cultural, economic and political organization of time and space that transcends classical models of comprehension and analysis in all aspects of life. It is often irrational and incomprehensible for people who are not a part of it. The family and other close social networks form the fabric that keeps the neighbourhood together. Politics is reconceptualized and reformulated, including the everyday strategies of survival and resistance taking place in the neighbourhood.

The neighbourhood becomes a space of social interaction founded to an intense degree on oral cultures and rural ways of life that have been remoulded in an urban setting, and in which the telenovelas come to play a fundamental role in the processes of socialization, social integration and identity formation. Thus, as we shall in the case analysis, the specific organization of time, space and social relations characteristic of low-income urban neighbourhoods is closely linked, in a dynamic and articulate manner, to the use and consumption of telenovelas.

Catholicism and spiritualism – cultural dynamics

The role of religion among Brazilians is a very complex one, due to the great number of religious manifestations, within the broad parameters of Christianity and Afro-Brazilian spiritualism. Religious syncretism, mixing Catholicism with Afro-Brazilian spiritualism, is also widespread, thus establishing even more complex situations. A good starting point for analysing the role of religion is the hypothesis advanced by the French anthropologist/structuralist Claude Levi-Strauss. Levi-Strauss' hypothesis is that myths and the ritual symbolic world are attempts to interpret contradictions experienced in everyday life. The myth dissolves the limits of the possible, thus liberating the mind. Levi-Strauss' interest is in the content of the ritual, whereas the French philosopher Durkheim and the British ethnographer Radcliffe-Brown emphasize the function of the ritual.

Clifford Geertz, like Levi-Strauss, sees religion as a potential force of resistance and change. Geertz regards religion as a cultural system, representing models of a non-symbolic reality and models for a non-symbolic structure of reality. It is both an image of what society is and how it will be, and thus a self confirming system (Geertz,1965: 215). This system attempts to make the explanation of the world plausible by engaging feelings, while the system of comprehension of the world must make the feelings rational. Nevertheless religion can contain thoughts about how society might be able to develop. When these thoughts and everyday life do not correspond, the thoughts can appear as possible alternatives to the existing reality.

When Levi-Strauss talks about myth as an area where thought is free, or when Geertz describes religion both as a model of and a model for the social order, it means that the images created in the myths of Paradise often transcend the limits of experience and comprehension. The images can be a protest stemming from the experience of an unbearable life situation but at the same time an indicator of a new and better way.

Aspects of this potential of resistance can be seen in the religious rituals in the neighbourhoods on the outskirts of the big cities, both in the Catholic and Afro-spiritual celebrations. The action of the Christian communities can be interpreted as an attempt to transform their myth of Paradise into reality. Many Christian communities have obtained substantial improvements for their neighbourhoods. Combining the stigmatized contradictions experienced in everyday life with collective memories and religious and mythical dreams and aspirations for the future, the Christian communities have managed to create dynamic social, cultural and political movements in many neighbourhoods. They shaped the base of an extensive and profound process of political, social and cultural conscientization that took place amongst low income groups in Brazil in the 1980s. This process has emerged and has been kept alive from within the dialectics between social reality and faith.

The role of telenovelas in the lives of low-income Brazilians relates to the religious beliefs of the viewers and can also itself be seen to possess some of the characteristics of religion put forward by Levi-Strauss and Geertz: The liberating of the mind created by the myth of religion interacts with the images and content of the telenovelas as interpreted by the viewer, creating some significant emotional dynamics in the process of reception. The images of telenovelas can be seen as visual interpretations of the myths, the realisation of material, emotional and spiritual ideals. A central core in the analysis of telenovelas must thus be to work out which myth is constituted by the telenovela and which images are created in it. Is it a myth of paradise which is transformed into reality? Do televisual myths contain potential forces of resistance and change like religious myths?

Afro-Brazilian spiritualism

The Afro-Brazilian religions have not had the same transcending effects on popular participation in social movements, but nevertheless constitute an important cultural base for a large, and growing number of blacks, mulattos and also whites in the low-income urban areas. These religions have cultural roots originating in the time of slavery and further back in Africa. They reached Brazil with the West African slaves who worked in the mines and plantations under the Portuguese colonialists. They were forbidden during the period of slavery but were later taken up and reshaped in their contemporary forms.

In order to understand what Afro-Brazilian spiritualism is, Halbwachs' concept of collective memory is useful (Halbwachs, 1968). The religious praxis can be interpreted as a process of reliving and remaking the past. This is manifested in the religious celebrations. The cult of *Candomblé* can be seen as an example: "*Candomblé*, by defining a sacred social space, the terreiro, makes the incarnation of the collective African memory possible in specific enclaves of Brazilian society" (Ortiz, 1986: 131). The conception of the world in cults like *Candomblé* is based on the fundamental assumption that the development of life is based on the will of the Gods. The solution to problems therefore lies in calling on the Gods. This occurs through rituals, where the Gods may appear (*baixar o santo*). The numerous rituals reproduce and reactivate gestures and beliefs held by the people's negro ancestors in Africa, in some cases maintaining a great similarity to some rituals still occurring in African countries.

This process of remembering and reliving is not something static. Though the tradition looks back to the ancestral past, it is not preserved as it was. What often happens in the Afro-Brazilian cults is a religious syncretism, or as Renato Ortiz calls it: cultural mutations (Ortiz, 1986: 132). The classical example of religious syncretism is found in the merging of African gods with Catholic saints. Iansá is related to Saint Barbara, Iemanjá with Nossa Senhora (the Virgin Mary) and Oxalá with Jesus. In the history of the saints, the collective African memory retains some elements that have some analogy to the orixá or God.

However, syncretic or not, the ritual and individual models of resolution offered by these cults do not confront the major mechanisms of repression experienced in everyday life, such as social and economic inequality and political and racial repression. The individual solving of problems manifested in the celebrations prevents the development of collective strategies of resistance: the explanations given by Afro-Brazilian religions of everyday affairs are all attributed to the interference of the gods in everyday life. This prevents an acknowledgement of the power relations behind everyday problems (Sjørslev, 1983: 103). The growing participation of the Brazilian (often white) middle class in some types of cult backs up this conclusions. Cults provide individual solutions that do not threaten the dominant ideology. So they tend to become integrated into society rather than challenging and transcending it, precisely because of their hidden, passive and non-threatening aspects (Sjørslev, 1983: 95).

However, the cults also constitute an important basis of identity and survival for many blacks and mulattos. The transcending potential in the cults thus lies in their connection to everyday life, in the felt contradictions of that life, and in the visions of something else, something better.

The Black movement – music, body and politics

When it comes to the political aspects of the life as a black Brazilian, *o Movimento Negro* (the Black movement) has grown substantially in recent years, articulating a black cultural identity, working explicitly on recovering of Afro-Brazilian history, promoting Afro-Brazilian musical rhythms and in a multitude of ways making black Brazilians conscious of their collective past, in terms of their race and historical origin. Some of the strongest groups within this movement are Grupo Axé and Grupo Cultural Olodum. They are both from Salvador in Bahia, where 70 per cent cent of the population are of black origin, 30 per cent being pure black (Olodum, 1991).

However, one of the challenges in their work lies in the recreation of a black identity, after many years of "directed humanism" under the military regime and further back a promotion of a national cultural identity minimizing the racial aspect. The Black movement considers the recovery of a racial identity important, arguing that the economic racism will have to pass through a revival of ethnic and racial awareness. Brazil cannot hide racial problems away by solely interpreting the differences as regional differences, cultural differences. It remains a problem of race. This is most manifestly expressed in the petty racism that blacks experience in everyday life, while waiting for a bus, when going shopping or when applying for a job. It can range from pejorative remarks and jokes about blacks, to racial preferences in jobs. Recent research conducted by the Brazilian Institute of Geography and Statistics (IBGE) shows that black Brazilians in general are significantly lower paid than white Brazilians. In Salvador, Bahia, the average wage for white men was more than three times the wage for black men, and for women the difference was somewhat larger (IBGE in Veja, 16.03.94). In many leisure clubs for the middle class, blacks are not accepted – it is not stated anywhere, but it is the everyday practice of many clubs. Racism exists in the everyday life of many black Brazilians.

Thus, the political movement of the blacks works explicitly with the questions of cultural identity and racism, stimulating and strengthening the collective memories of the black Brazilians and thereby creating the foundations for social change and the abolition of racism.

A fundamental element in their work is the use of music, song and the body as repositories of a black Afro-Brazilian identity. This form took off the 1980s and 1990s, articulating a particular cultural identity through music and rhythm, and using memory as a vital element. It has its parallels to the urban popular music of the beginning of the 20th century, a popular cultural form of expression which led

Afro-Brazilian dance in Crioula's school where she teaches

to the samba and the Carnival. This music, explicitly black, sang – and still sings – about life on the margins of society, in the suburbs of the growing cities, about work which is "the opposite to a life of pleasure, idleness and subterfuge" (Rowe and Schelling 1991: 128). The hero, in what came to be known as samba, is the *malandro*, an anti-hero praising these values of pleasure, idleness and subterfuge, an anti-hero who in the late 1960s and 1970s became a protagonist in telenovelas, as I show in chapter 5.

Thus, black music, life at the margins of civil society, a strong, often syncretic, religious belief, and a history of recent migration, intermingled to become characteristic aspects of everyday life among Brazil's the numerous low-income urban dwellers who are black.

Popular culture in everyday life

The investigation of popular culture poses the rethinking of the whole cultural field, from the practices of everyday life to artistic production. Its proper documentation shakes up influential paradigms of cultural history (both folklore and media studies for example), challenges discourses of identity (populist ones, for example), and undermines literary and art-historical theories (magical-realist ones, for example). Inevitably a multidisciplinary action, it requires taking the cultural sphere as neither merely derivative from the socio-economic, as a merely ideological phenomenon, nor as in some metaphysical sense preceding it. Rather, it is the decisive area where social conflicts are experienced and evaluated.

Rowe and Schelling, 1991: 12

69

Such spheres of culture, popular culture, are precisely found in the neighbourhoods described above. The widely-scattered sites where the popular cultural genre of telenovelas meets its audience is where social conflicts are experienced and evaluated. The "hegemonic battle" between differing ideologies and ideas is also fought here producing ambivalent interpretations between, on the one hand, the internalized stigma of the dominant ideology. and on the other, the potential of anger and resistance.

Neighbourhood culture is a unifying concept signifying the socio-economic, temporal, relational and physical limits within which the everyday life of low-income citizens is carried on. Neighbourhood culture is impossible to understand using a traditional model of class analysis. Inside the neighbourhood there exist a multitude of different social, ethnic and cultural subgroups, intersecting and interacting. The neighbourhood cultures are rooted both in the religious beliefs of the inhabitants as well as in the collective memories that occasionally become conscious and are relived in the present in everyday life. In the interaction of the past with the present, cultural identities emerge and develop into manifold popular cultures. "The popular does not define itself in its origin or in its traditions, but in the position it constructs *vis-à-vis* the hegemonic" (Canclini, 1995a). The "popular" is thus expressed in the hybrid cultures of everyday life in the neighbourhoods, and more specifically in the survival strategies and in the symbolic negotiations and positions that people develop in these contexts.

4. *Globo*lizing the television industry

"I feel happy every evening when I turn on the television to see the news. While there is news from different parts of the world about strikes, assassinations and conflicts, then Brazil marches in peace, on its way towards development. It is like taking a tranquilizer after a hard days work"

President General Medici, 1973

"...ce qui compte, c'est que, à 20 heures, chaque soir, 82 per cent des téléspectateurs soient devant leurs postes, bien plus qu'aux Etats-Unis, ou en Europe. Ce chiffre prouve que nous avons fait de la télévision une véritable culture populaire, un instrument d'intégration nationale unique en son genre. Une télévision brésilienne programmée pour les Brésiliens et non un de ces mélanges internationaux sans identité que sont devenues la plupart des télévisions du monde"

Roberto Marinho, Owner of Rede Globo, 1984

The history of Brazilian television is closely tied to the struggle of the military regime to unite the huge country, create a national identity and impose political and economic control. The state had two major preoccupations: one was to transform Brazil into a modern industrial nation and the other was to create a national integration, to unify the culturally multiple and geographically dispersed regions of Brazil.

The TV industry in Brazil started as a risky initiative by a businessman looking for new profits, but gradually television came to play a leading role in the political process of integrating the people into the nation. Simultaneously the technological innovations and the development of the infrastructure of communication gave access to enormous markets that had not been accessible before. Thus, television came to be both a political and an economic motor in the process of modernization of Brazil.

71

1950-1963. A private initiative showing high-culture TV

Brazil was the first country in Latin America to get television – shortly ahead of Mexico and Cuba. The first public broadcast by Brazilian TV Tupi was on 18 September, 1950. The owner of TV Tupi, Assis Chateaubriand, was a wealthy businessman, owner of the largest media empire in Latin America, a conglomerate covering press, radio, records and shares in the rapidly growing cinema industry. Chateaubriand decided to launch television hoping that the prestige linked to the project would favour his media empire Diarios Associados. Thus, the launching of television in Brazil was a commercially-motivated private initiative. The very first transmission was sponsored by four companies. Commercial interests were fundamental in Brazilian TV at this moment and has been ever since. The state's interest in television did not become explicit until years later.

When television was launched, there were only 200 TV sets in the country, of which the large majority were imported by Chateaubriand himself. Two years later there were 11,000 TV sets. Chateaubriand acquired the knowhow and the technology for TV production from the Brazilian radio industry and importation from the USA. McCann-Erikson and J. W. Thompson (subsidiaries of American companies) were the biggest importers of technology from the USA. They also participated in the production of TV programmes in the 1950s, due to the lack of expertise within TV Tupi and other emerging TV stations (Simões, 1986: 24).

TV programming in the 1950s was characterized by élitism and and a bias towards programmes for cultured viewers. The programme schedule consisted basically of live music shows and live theatre. In addition to the entertainment programmes, in 1952 Chateaubriand launched what came to be one of the most famous news programmes in the history of Brazilian television: Reporter Esso, named after its sponsor. It was a television adaptation of a news programme that had been a great success on Radio Nacional. The success it obtained was attributed to the international news. The fact was that the programme was entirely produced by United Press International (UPI) under the auspices of an agent who delivered the programmes packaged and ready to broadcast to TV Tupi (Nogueira, 1988: 86).

Meanwhile, televised theatre occupied the prime slots. Gradually, more and more tele-theatre was produced, made specifically for TV audiences. Instead of going to the theatre, the bourgoisie watched television at home. It was accorded the same high cultural esteem as real theatre. The actors could even received telephone calls from enthusiastic spectators in the same way that they received visits in their theatre dressing rooms.

The larger sections of the population in those years favoured the cinema and especially radio. Both were national phenomena. Going to the cinema was predominantly an urban pursuit, even though travelling cinemas also were common. In the second biggest city of the country, São Paulo, advertisements in 1950 claimed they sold more tickets to the cinema than in all of Sweden (Simões, 1986: 24). Radio was even more widespread, including the rural areas, but according to Milanesi it represented an extension of urban norms and values to a rural setting (Milanesi, 1978: 111). The Brazilian sociologist Florestan Fernandes goes further, saying that the gradual but slow expansion of television to rural areas is also an extension of the urban to the rural: "The city imposes itself on the rural areas, pulling away capital and workers, propagating consumer necessities essential for existence in the city, but still not within the reach of the average inhabitant of rural Brazil if no compensation is given that can guarantee the rhythm of development and the differentiation of the rural products" (Fernandes in Milanesi, 1978: 111).

From its beginning Brazilian television had a series of technological and economic characteristics promoting a way of life, specific norms and values oriented towards a modern, urban consumer society. All broadcasting stations were placed in cities, programmes were and are directed mainly towards urban populations and commercial interests were continuously stimulating consumption (except on the state-owned tv-stations). These characteristics remain present today.

The first telenovela

Despite the dominance of high culture on the Brazilian TV screen of the 1950s, the telenovela was present almost from the beginning. The first telenovela went on air on 21 December 1951. *Your Life Belongs to Me* (*Sua Vida Me Pertence*) was transmitted in 15-minute episodes twice a week for three months. While teletheatre was a copy of the theatre genre, the first telenovelas were visualized radionovelas.

Radionovelas, like the old radio plays on many European and American radio stations, were very widespread and popular at that time. Radio São Paulo alone transmitted 22 radionovelas a day! (Vink, 1988: 23). TV Tupi adapted the radionovela to television, but without elaborating much on the visual language. The first telenovelas were considered by many people within the media industry as a poor substitute for theatre – melodramatic and cheap.

During the period of 1951-1963, 1890 teletheatre productions were broadcast (including live theatre transmissions), while only 164 telenovelas were broadcast. An average telenovela lasted 20 minutes per chapter, with two chapters a week being broadcast over a period of one to three months. A teletheatre play lasted one and a half to two hours, corresponding to four to six telenovela chapters (Ortiz et al, 1989). The priority given by the TV stations to teletheatre productions was obvious, as it corresponded to the wishes of the predominantly well-off TV viewers. Telenovelas never really became popular during these early years.

American TV series quickly got a solid grip on the Brazilian market. Hollywood TV series began spreading on the American market in the mid 1950s. By the late 1950s they began gaining a share of the international market, including Brazil. Until the late 1960s American TV series and films continued to be quite popular on Brazilian television. After that date, Brazilian domestic production won back the market share, especially in prime time.

The telenovela with its typical 1950s form and content was a low-priority programme both among producers and viewers. However, as the TV audience grew and spread to new social strata, programmes with a more popular content were needed. At the same time, the state began to take an interest in the potential of mass communication through television.

1963-1969. TV to the masses: A national culture industry emerges

In 1963 videotape was introduced in Brazilian television. This had a tremendous impact on television, providing not only the possibility for broadcasting telenovelas daily, but also of elaborating a strategy for horizontal programming.

In the 1960s television developed into a regular industry. It was the launching of TV Globo in 1965 that marked the beginning of this new era in Brazilian television. Politically and economically Brazil was at a vigorous stage. The military coup in 1964 led to a strengthening of the development strategy of modernization and to an elaborate plan for the strategic use of mass communication in the development process.

Industry developed, attracting many people and thus stimulating internal migration. In spite of military repression and the tensions created by the fundamental changes in people's lives, the contours of a modern consumer society began to take shape around the big cities. TV became a symbol of modernity and also a status symbol which an increasing number of people in the growing middle class acquired. From 1960 to 1964 the number of TV sets in Brazil almost tripled, from 598,000 to 1,663,000 (Abinee in Mattos 1990: 10).

The increase in TV sets indicated a growing market and thus led to an increased interest among companies in reaching these new markets by advertising on television. In 1958 only 8 per cent of the total costs spent on advertising in Brazil were spent on TV commercials, while 22 per cent were spent on radio and 44 per cent on advertisements in the press. In 1967 the amount spent on TV commercials had risen to 42 per cent of total advertising expenditure, while radio had decreased to 16 per cent and the press to 15 per cent (Ortiz et al, 1989: 56). TV was quickly becoming the most important medium for reaching consumers.

The genre that was increasingly able to attract large numbers of TV viewers and thus advertising money was the telenovela. The first daily telenovela came in 1963 on the relatively new TV Excelsior.[1] TV Excelsior was the first television station to be run professionally, on commercial terms, with a clear programme policy and with precise broadcasting schedules, even running promotional slots for its own programmes. TV Rio, following Exelsior's lead, began transmitting daily telenovelas, and managed in 1964 to reach ratings as high as 73 with the telenovela *The Right to be Born (O Direito de Nascer)*. From this time onwards telenovelas were always transmitted daily, except on Sundays. The number of chapters, the length of each chapter and not least the content continued to be subject to a lot of experimentation throughout the 1960s. In spite of this, the telenovela consolidated its position through the 1960s as the most popular programme to be broadcast in prime time.

The number of telenovelas produced from 1963-1969 was larger than the number produced between 1951-1963. Telenovelas increasingly became the product used by TV stations to conquer new audiences and gain a larger share of the market – all TV stations were involved in producing them. Meanwhile, not all stations came out winning. Towards the end of the 1960s the tendency was clear: the market shares of TV Excelsior and TV Tupi were dropping, and Globo was gradually winning the dominant position, increasing its production of telenovelas as the market expanded.

---

1 TV Excelsior was bought by Mario Simonsen in 1959. He was the biggest coffee exporter in Brazil. Due to an international boycott against his powerful position of the global coffee market he turned his back to the multinational enterprises and their allies in Brazil; the internationally oriented national bourgeoisie and the liberal politicians. Instead Simonsen supported the populist and very nationalistic President Goulart who won the presidential election in 1959 and took office in 1960. When Simonsen bought TV Excelsior it was see nas an attempt for him to get a political instrument and support Goulart. Therefore, there were clear underlying political motives behind the regime's withdrawal of the licence to transmit from the Simonsen family in 1969.

Although telenovelas were domestically produced, major foreign influence existed, especially in the early years of the daily telenovela transmissions. Of 24 domestically produced telenovelas in 1969, 16 of them were sponsored by three large foreign soap and toothpaste companies: Gessy-Lever, Colgate-Palmolive and Kolynos-Van Ess (Kehl, 1986). Their influence on the programme content was considerable, judging by a statement of Pola Vartuck, interviewed in 1986. She was one of the first managers of Colgate-Palmolive in São Paulo: "The bureau owned the programme. It was the bureau that decided how the telenovela should be, and that negotiated with the managers of the TV station about who should direct the programme, the actors, everything" (Ortiz et al, 1989: 60).

The military regime and Rede Globo

In April 1964 the government in Brazil was overthrown. President Goulart had been forced to resign in 1963 and had been succeeded by his vice president, Janio Quadros. He remained in office less than a year, when the military took power in a coup. The military takeover had serious consequences for cultural life in Brazil. Heavy censorship was imposed, making life very difficult for theatres and cinemas. The year after the military coup, on 26 April, 1965, TV Globo started transmitting.[2] The owner of Globo, Roberto Marinho, who is now over 90, began with a television station in Rio. After one year Globo had ratings of 40 in Rio. In 1966 Globo bought itself into São Paulo by taking over TV Paulista. Very quickly Globo became one of the leading television networks in Brazil.

The story of the Globo enterprise goes back to 1925, when Roberto Marinho started the newspaper *O Globo* together with his father Irineu Marinho. Today it is the second largest newspaper in Brazil, with a daily issue of almost 30,.000 (Almanaque Abril, 1991). In 1944 Globo set up a broadcasting system – Sistema Globo de Radio – which today includes 20 radio stations. In 1957 President Kubitschek gave Roberto Marinho a television broadcasting license for Channel 5, but it was not until 1965 that TV Globo went on air.

In 1962 Globo had begun negotiations with the publishing concern Time-Life, who had offered their services to one of the largest newspapers in Brazil and, to the TV network belonging to Assis Chateaubriand, TV Tupi. Meanwhile, as it was against the constitution to have foreign companies as co-owners and participants in the running of Brazilian companies with television licences, both TV Tupi and Globo declined the offer from Time-Life. Nevertheless, Globo was interested, and after the military coup in 1964 and following the direct intervention of President Marchal Castelo Branco, an official agreement was settled between Time-Life and Globo. From 1962-1969 Time-Life transferred over 6 million dollars to Globo.

The co-operation was not without problems, especially the first two years, where it took place secretly. It almost developed into a national scandal in 1964-65, had not President Branco intervened and declared that the co-operation between Globo and Time-Life was legal. Legalising the cooperation took time however; the process lasted from 1966 to 1968. Later, the initial co-operation was judged unconstitutional, but by now Globo had reached its position as the national leader of mass communication. As Daniel Herz states it: "Based on unconstitutional

---

2   This account about Globo is mainly based on the book by Daniel Herz: *A historia Secreta da Rede Globo* (The Secret Story about Rede Globo), Herz 1989.

transactions, Rede Globo managed to acquire the necessary capital and knowhow to launch a professionally run TV network which quickly developed into the leading network in Brazil and into one of the biggest in the world" (Herz, 1989).

In 1969 Rede Globo bought the 49 per cent of Globo shares owned by Time-Life. Through the cooperation with Time-Life Globo had obtained considerable knowhow about TV production, of a kind which had till then been unknown in Brazil.

> The Brazilian stations could profit greatly by making similar agreements to the one we made with Time-Life, because in that way they would contribute to improving the technical and operational level for Brazilian television. The technical assistance from Time-Life helped us a lot, especially their advice as to which equipment was best and on acquirinbg the most modern antenne so that we could have the best pictures of the all the TV stations in Rio.
>
> *Marinho 1966, in Herz 1989*

The active role of the military regime was not motivated simply by a wish to help Globo gain new markets and profits. Their support was politically motivated. The regime was concerned about the building of a modern nation, and thus concerned about creating the sense of nationhood amongst the Brazilians. At the same time, the regime was interested in using the mass media, especially television for ideological and political control of the country.

In 1969, five years after the military coup, the regime, now under President General Medici, launched a plan for national integration, PIN (*Plano de Integraçao Nacional*). The idea for PIN had been formulated as early as 1962 in the War Academy (*Escola Superior de Guerra*). PIN was part of the regime's gigantic development project for Brazil, where a basic infrastructure was to be built in the Amazon Region, linking this huge area more closely to the rest of the country. The idea was to make the Amazonas accessible for massive colonisation by people from other parts of Brazil, and to begin to use the huge amounts of natural resources in which Amazonas was rich. PIN was an economic as well as a political plan of integration, with a strong nationalistic flavour (Van Tilburg, 1991a).

As with all development projects under the military regime, the precondition for their realisation was to be found in "The Triple Alliance". This was the name given to the informal alliance between international capital, local capital and the state apparatus in Brazil. Behind the idea integration lay the hope of politically and economically "uniting" Brazil, developing a strong feeling of nationhood and simultaneously establishing the possibilities of political control of the whole country.

In this period of undeclared war, where a military regime was in power, the situation was handled like a state of war. The regime introduced censorship and sent their political adversaries either into exile or to prison. PIN was the plan of the regime, the Triple Alliance the economic basis, and mass communication via television was to be an important instrument with which to reach the whole nation with ideological and political messages. In 1967 Brazil's Ministry of Communication was established. Here lay – and still lies – the authority for granting communication licences, and the control over who has permission to transmit television and radio.

The land-based communication system for receiving satellite television was built by 1969. That same year Globo launched the first national television programme, the news programme Jornal Nacional. This was a landmark in Brazilian television. The national net of radio waves (micro waves) was achieved in 1972 (Van Tilburg, 1991a).

The close relationship between the commercial interests of Rede Globo and the political interest of the military regime created perfect conditions for the growth of Rede Globo. The knowhow obtained from Time-Life, political contacts, and the industrial attitude permeating the running of the Globo network: centralized production, professional leadership and planning, together moulded the base for the absolute dominance Rede Globo was to acquire in the Brazilian culture industry and especially the television market in the 1970s.

1969-1978. Unifying Brazil and consolidating Globo leadership

The number of TV sets continued growing steadily through the 1960s and the 1970s. In spite of substantial progress socio-economic development did not happen overnight, and national coverage in terms of TV sets was still a long way off. At the beginning of the 1970s more than half the households in Brazil did not have electricity and 75 per cent did not have television. Nevertheless, television was a very popular phenomenon. So, even though many households did not have television yet, people got access to television by gathering in public spaces or at the homes of friends or family. In 1970, technological conditions and the widespread popularity of TV as a daily social activity, laid the foundations for televsion to become the first mass medium with truly national coverage in Brazil.

The organisation and the provision of money needed to administer the continuous expansion on the TV market, to cope with technological development and to manage the increasing production of programmes, required quite an amount of professionalism. It was in these years that the competing TV stations fought their toughest battle for the audience. The demand was for more and better productions, stability in the programme schedule and transmitting periods, and quality in the fiction programmes, first and foremost in the telenovelas that rapidly became the flagship product of TV stations. In this context Rede Globo developed as the exemplary TV network.

The development of society at this moment was characterized by two trends, both contained within the process of modernization, as described in chapter 3. On one side there was the rapidly expanding economic activity, leading to ruptures with old norms and traditions, migration, new cultural interaction, new lifestyles – a challenge to traditional norms, values and popular cultures. On the other side – in the midst of this process of disintegration and change – the repressive and authoritarian regime tried to impose a sense of cultural uniformity reflected in the concept of nationhood, trying to prevent people from challenging the status quo, in spite of the major social, cultural and economic changes that were occurring. Somehow, Globo managed to grasp the many simultaneous tensions and contradictions of this process of modernization, fuelling the telenovela in that process and forming a narrative that gripped the attention of the entire nation evening after evening.

In spite of commercial success and expansion, this period was also characterized by strong state control. Although it supported the development of an infrastructure for national television, thus benefiting Rede Globo, the state also wished to control the TV stations. During the period 1968-1979 the media of mass communication were subjugated to the restrictions contained in the Institutional Act No. 5, from 1968. Under this Act the executive federal powers had the right to censor the TV stations, subjecting anything suspicious to state censorship control. They even published lists of thousands of words and themes that it was prohibited to touch upon (*Estado de São Paulo*, 11.11.92). This also prompted self censorship. One of the most outstanding cases was the total censorship of the telenovela *Roque Santeiro*, planned to go on air in 1975. It was not until after the fall of the military regime that *Roque Santeiro* in 1986 could be shown, then becoming the only telenovela in the history of Brazilian television to reach a rating of 100 (Fernandes, 1987).

The number of telenovelas produced from 1970-1980 decreased compared with the period 1963-1970. This was mainly because the telenovelas lasted longer. It was also caused by the decrease in competition. TV Excelsior transmitted its last telenovela in 1970 because its license was withdrawn, and TV Bandeirantes only produced one telenovela in 1970, not returning to production till 1979-80.

The competition between TV Globo and TV Tupi continued through the1970s, but the tendency was clear: Globo extended its amount of transmission hours, developed new types of programmes and consolidated and even fortified ratings while TV Tupi obviously became more unstable. There were frequent breaks, a lack of punctuality in broadcasting times and instability in programme content. In 1980 TV Tupi was declared bankrupt and had its licenses withdrawn. These licenses were divided between Rede Manchete and Rede SBT.

Rede Bandeirantes was the most recent network,which managed to grow throughout the 1970s, appealing specifically to what the director of programmes and production at Rede Bandeirantes at the time, Claudio Petraglia, called "the qualified audience". By this he meant viewers who were better-off and better-educated than those being targeted by the majority of the TV stations at the time. Rede Bandeirantes was the first TV network to transmit in colour, the first transmission (in 1972) being from The Festival of Grapes (a tradition of the Italian immigrants) in southern Brazil (Petraglia, 1988: 73). In the late 1970s Petraglia left Bandeirantes, and the network changed course, aiming at more popular segments of the viewers (C and D), with for example the widely-watched talk show Bolinha, which was very much designed for the popular audience. Later, in the mid-1990s, Bandeirantes also entered into telenovela-production.

After the closure of TV Exelsior and the decline of TV Tupi, Rede Globo obtained a de facto monopoly, pushing all the rest of the networks, which were unable to compete with it in the fight for ratings, into second rank.

Cultural imperialism – which way?

Domestic production, mainly by the networks themselves, has historically been the overall trend in Brazilian television. Compared to international statistics the ratio is very high: in the 1980s Globo was the largest producer of TV fiction in the world (Barreto, 1991). There is no doubt that there has been substantial international influence in terms of technology, content, formats, programme concepts and dramaturgy. The whole concept of commercial television is based fundamentally on the North American model for the organization of broadcasting. However, I will argue in chapter 5, that in spite of these basic commercial rules of the game, the Brazilian telenovela is a very national genre. It has natural links to international and historical genres, but was already by the early 1970s established as a genre on its own.

However, Brazil continued to import – and naturally still does import – foreign products, mainly from the US. Throughout the 1960s the imported, mainly North American, TV series obtained a considerable percentage of total viewing-time, compared with telenovelas. This was a trend that decreased throughout the 1970s, but did not stop. Telenovelas increased their share of viewing time from 12-13 per cent of the total in the mid 1960s to 20-22 per cent in the mid-1970s (Straubhaar 1983). During the 1970s national production increased in journalism, sport and TV fiction. While imported programmes in 1972 occupied approximately 60 per cent of the total programme share, it decreased to 30 per cent in 1983 (Antola and Rogers, 1985 and Varis, 1983 in Ortiz, 1988: 201-202).

Considering only the prime time programming, the ratio of imported programmes fell to 23 per cent. This placed the Brazilian ratio of national versus imported programming in prime time on a par with European countries such as France, Italy and UK/BBC which have, respectively, 17 per cent, 19 per cent and 21 per cent imported programmes in prime time, while other Latin American countries like Mexico and Venezuela have a considerably higher ratio: 44 per cent and 42 per cent (Varis, 1983: 19). Two excellent studies, both done by North American researchers, document and analyse the development of foreign influence in Brazil and Latin American, emphasizing the decline of North American influence, and raising the question of whether the growing export of Latin American fiction is to be interpreted as an inverse cultural imperialism or not (Straubhaar, 1982 and Antola and Rogers, 1985). Straubhaar develops the concept of "cultural proximity" to explain the success of national Brazilian programming in the competition with imported North American TV programmes. Cultural proximity signifies the desire and tendency to choose programmes that are culturally as close to one's own cultural universe as possible (Straubhaar 1982, 1998).

Summing up, the 1970s were the years where the process of industrialization and technological development was at its height in Brazil. There was a sense of optimism among a broad spectrum of the middle class. In those same years, the social movements began to grow in Brazil. The pressure on the regime thus grew, leading to President Figueiredo's initiative in 1979, launching a political process of democratization called the Abertura (opening).

Rede Globo had grown thanks to the political support from the military regime and the financial and technical support from Time-Life. In the 1970s this resulted in the definite consolidation of Rede Globo as the number one TV network in Brazil. The culmination was in 1978, where Rede Globo became the first television network in Brazil to obtain national coverage, with either its own or associated TV stations in all state capitals. This technological milestone was reached just a few weeks before the world championship in football was to be played in Argentina, in June 1978.

The years to come were to be marked by economic recession in Brazil and by fundamental political changes. Globo thus directed their attention to the international market, while they simultaneously adapted to the domestic political changes, securing their role as the leading national network. We will look further into this below.

1978-1990. Internationalization and democratic "opening"

The spread of TV sets in Brazil continued. In 1980 more homes had television than a refrigerator; in the cities 73.1 per cent of households had television and only 37.8 per cent had refrigerators (Da Silva, 1989). The rapid spread of television was not caused by a sudden increase of wealth among people in general, but reflected the high priority people gave to television. Increasing market competition, including the offer of payment by instalments, facilitated and stimulated the process of buying TV sets.

By 1990 there were 30 million TV sets in Brazil, equivalent to one for every five inhabitants. The popularity of television was not only seen in the widespread acquisition of TV sets, but also reflected in ratings. A study showed that at 8.30 pm every day 80 per cent of TV sets were switched on in Brazil. Globo had ratings of 70, the equivalent to 85 per cent of viewers, watching their eight o'clock telenovela (Salles,1988: 18-20)! Put in another way, these facts show us that on ordinary weekdays more than 70 million Brazilians were watching television in prime time, more than the total population of Argentina, Uruguay, Paraguay and Bolivia, or more than triple the population of all the Nordic countries put together (Denmark, Norway, Sweden, Finland, Greenland, Iceland and the Faroe Islands). And the large majority of these people watched the same television network: Rede Globo!

Today Sistema Globo de Communicações is an enterprise including more than 100 companies with more than 20.000 employees. The yearly turnover was in 1989 1.3 billion US dollars (*Folha de São Paulo*, 9.2.91). The conglomerate includes a bicycle company, furniture companies, microelectronics businesses, cattle farms in Amazonas, a record company, a publishing firm, newspapers, more than 20 radio stations and Rede Globo de Televisão. The Globo publishing firm controls 12 per cent of the magazine and book market in Brazil. The record company Som Livre is one of the four biggest of its kind in Brazil that together control 80 per cent of the music industry. Som Livre is the main promoter of the numerous novela music records.

Roberto Marinho is also the biggest individual shareholder in the petrol company Petrobras, producing all of Brazil's oil, in which the state has the majority of the shares. Marinho has also, via some of his many political contacts, become associated with the Japanese multinational company NEC specialized in electronic equipment (Vink,1988: 30). Furthermore he has recently become a member of the most exclusive cultural association in Brazil, the Brazilian Academy, together with the finest artists and authors of the country.

Roberto Marinho, who on his card presents himself as a journalist, is sometimes labelled the most powerful man in Brazil, a description he prefers to avoid: "I don't like the word power. Power is such a crushing word, and I don't want to destroy anyone. My purpose is not monopolistic" (Marinho 1985).

In the wake of Rede Globo's consolidation as absolute leader within the Brazilian culture industry, the company turned to the international market. Since the beginning of the 1970s Rede Globo had exported telenovelas and mini-series, but it was not until the late 1970s that Rede Globo got a major breakthrough on the international market. In 1978 they began presenting their telenovelas and mini-series at the annual TV festivals in Cannes. In 1977 Rede Globo sold 300.000 US dollars' worth of fiction. This figure had by 1987 reached an annual sale of 20 million US dollars (Ortiz, 1989: 119)! In 1985 Rede Globo bought Telemontecarlo in Monte Carlo. The strategy was obviously to get a foothold in the European market, challenging firstly the Italian market. Telemontecarlo covered 5 per cent of the Italian market, and was the country in Europe that had bought most telenovelas. From 1981-1988, 27 Brazilian telenovelas were shown on Italian television (Marques de Melo, 1988). But Rede Globo was up against an opponent who was too big and powerful. A few years later Rede Globo had sold Telemontecarlo. The king of Italian television, Berlusconi, obviously disliked the challenge of Rede Globo. Sources in Rede Globo, who prefer to remain anonymous, have told me that threats and sabotage in the Telemontecarlo studios forced Rede Globo to sell.

This was a setback to Rede Globo's international expansion but did not stop it. When Brazilian telenovelas entered the French market in 1985 it was the ninety-second country to which Globo had sold programmes (*Le Monde*, 22-23.07.84). The telenovelas *Dancin' Days* and *The Slave Girl Isaura* were the first Brazilian products on the French market. Since then Globo have conquered new markets. By 1988 Brazilian telenovelas and mini-series had been sold to 128 countries throughout the world (Marques de Melo, 1988).

Rede Globo's rise had now reached its climax: national domination of television, efficient production of fiction, international success with fiction programmes and a national consolidation of its influence and its media empire, spreading the risk to other areas, predominantly within the culture industry, but not only within that industry. The dominant role which Assis Chateaubriand and his media empire Diario Associados had possessed in Brazil in the 1950s and1960s,[3] was in the 1980s replaced by Roberto Marinho and his Sistema Globo de Communicaçoes.

Rede Globo felt secure and economically safe on the national market. Since the closure of TV Tupi in 1980 no network had been able to challenge the leadership of Rede Globo. Two networks were trying, TVS and Rede Manchete. They continuously attempted to win market shares, TVS aiming at conquering shares within the D and E segments of the audience, while Manchete went for A and B. A major battle with Manchete took place between April and June of 1990 which was fought out between two telenovelas, Manchete's *Pantanal* and Rede Globo's *Rubbish Queen*. TVS only began to challenge Globo's market share seriously in 1990 and 1991, introducing Mexican telenovelas and a telejournalistic programme called *Aqui e Agora*. I will return to this in the analysis of the developments in the 1990s.

Adapting to democracy

In the late 1970s and especially in 1983-1985 the political process of democratic transition accelerated, culminating with the election of Tancredo Neves in November 1984 as the first civilian president since the early 1960s. This brought about a relaxation of censorship, and gave a sense of renewed hope to the masses of people suffering the economic crisis into which Brazil had plunged after more than two decades of expensive economic expansion.

---

3   Assis Chateaubriand's media empire, *Diarios Associados*, that Tv Tupi belonged to, had at this time reached its peak: The prestige daily newspaper, *O Jornal do Rio de Janeiro*, another approximately 30 newspapers, 18 tv stations, 30 radio stations, its own news agency, advertising agency and public relations firms and several of Brazil's leading magazines – including *O Cruzeiro* which, until 1967 was Latin America's biggest selling magazine (Tunstall, 1977: 182).

Despite the severe economic crisis, the struggling regime continued to develop its telecommunications projects. In February 1985 the Brazilian state bought its first telecommunication satellite, Brasil Sat I, from the American company Hughes Aircraft – Space Aerospace. The year after, in March 1986, Brasil Sat II was bought. These investments marked the final purchase by the Brazilian state, the last technical step along the strategic line of thought initiated in 1962, aiming at national integration. The technical aims of the regime, described earlier, were fulfilled. So was national integration, in that a greater sense of nationhood had developed.

Meanwhile, it is more difficult to evaluate to what extent political and ideological control was obtained. The whole process of abertura and formal political transition obviously indicates a decreasing political control. The role of Rede Globo in this process is described with great precision by Elisabeth Fox in her book *Media and Politics in Latin America* (Fox, 1989). Rede Globo entered into the conflict of interests, mediating between the popular demands for direct elections and the unwillingness of the regime to grant them. Rede Globo gradually transformed the popular demand of *Diretas Já* (Free elections now) into *Tancredo Já* (Tancredo now), reflecting the policy of gradual transition to democracy accepted by the regime and – through the intermediary of Rede Globo – finally also accepted by the people in the streets.

This balancing act performed by Globo between the conflicting interests appears to be a continuation of the populist tradition developed by President Vargas in the 1930s, continued by President Goulart in the early 1960s and later attempted again by President Collor de Melo in 1990. Thus, even though the Triple Alliance lost formal political power in 1985 and real political power with the first direct presidential elections in 1989, the aim to modernize Brazil and to maintain economic control within the Triple Alliance was carried out successfully.

Though successful for a while, the strategy of the state then began to decline, but one entity that came out of it successfully was Rede Globo. Globo's ability to link high technical quality in its productions with a modernist discourse, became central for the commercial success of the network: it signified 'modernity'. As the critic Inácio Araujo explains:

> What is central in Globo's way of producing is the way it linked the notion of modernity with that of quality. Globo had quality because it propagated modern values, values of change, and projected itself towards the future. And it was modern because the futuristic belief inherent in this project promoted a desire to consume, to be integrated into the developed world, to belong to an ascending middle class. In synthesis, the link between modernity and quality was consumption. All the values spread by the network passed through this concept.
>
> *Araujo, 1991: 273*

1990s. Transition: Polarisation and/or democratization?

Brazilian television celebrated its 40th anniversary in 1990 and Rede Globo celebrated its 25th anniversary. The media situation in the 1990s grew more complex because of the latest developments in technology. Furthermore, serious attacks on Globo's leadership occurred and continued occurring. Brazilian TV in the 1990s has been marked by three major trends: (1) the increased pressure on the monopoly-like situation of Rede Globo; (2) the video cassettes, parabolic aerials and cable television currently sweeping the country; (3) a fall in the price of production equipment which has brought about a diversification of production and transmission.

However, these trends on the TV market must be seen in the perspective of the viewers' situation: the socio-economic polarization of Brazil is greater than ever, having deteriorated substantially in the 1980s – known generally as the lost decade – but also in the 1990s, despite – or perhaps as a consequence of – President Cardoso's strong economic policy (UNDP 1996-7).

At the turn of the millennium mass communication in Brazil is in a period of substantial technological transition, with experimentation, change and fierce competition occurring, not least within the production of TV fiction.

Increased competition

A challenge to Globo's dominant position in the 1970s and 1980s came from Manchete in 1989-1991 and is today coming especially from SBT, but also periodically from TV Record and Bandeirantes, all of which are telenovela-producers. In the 1990s the telenovela has been an important area of competition, along with news formats and more recently talk shows, for example with TV Record's *Ratinho* in 1998, which affected Globo's prime time ratings.

In the area of telenovelas Manchete began in the second half of the 1980s to invest money in telenovela production, expensive, high-quality production, with mixed results. The telenovelas *Kananga do Japao* (1989), *Pantanal* (1990) and *Ana Raio e Ze Trovao* (1990-1991) all obtained fine ratings. Toughest was the battle around the 25th anniversary of Rede Globo, in April 1990, where Rede Manchete, with *Pantanal*, managed for the first time in decades of Globo dominance, to beat Globo in the ratings. This shocked Globo, and they tried in various ways to recover the lost ground. The main reason for Manchete's success was the excellent quality of *Pantanal*, which broke new ground in terms of content and dramatic form and struck new cultural chords in the viewers. It immediately became a trendsetter in the history of the Brazilian telenovela. I will return to *Pantanal* in chapter 5.

Rede Manchete did not manage to repeat this success. *Ana Raio e Ze Trovao* had some of the same elements as *Pantanal*, but not the same appeal to the audience. Rede Manchete subsequently went into decline, shifted to another owner and back again, and finally had to close down. In ratings terms, it has fallen from being the second to the fourth network in Brazil. Nevertheless, the fact that it had obtained telenovela ratings superior to those of Rede Globo seemed to indicate that Globo had lost some of its rapport with the audience. Globo was not unassailable.

SBT attempted a double strategy in their challenge to Globo. One was to transmit imported telenovelas, mainly from Mexico (*Carrossel, Vovo e eu, Alcançar uma estrela, Marielena*, etc), but also Argentina (*A Estranha Dama*) and Venezuela (*Topazio*). The other was the launching of *Aqui e Agora*, a sensational exercise in telejournalism. Both aimed specifically at the least educated and worst off segments of the audience. And SBT is obtaining steady and increased success in both projects. The Mexican telenovela *Carrossel*, transmitted in 1991 at 8 pm, challenged both Globo's 8 – 8.30 news broadcast, *Jornal Nacional*, as well as the telenovela that followed it. *Jornal Nacional* fell from 54 in the ratings to 41 within the first 3 weeks of *Carrossel*, while *Carrossel* subsequently reached 21in the ratings, where SBT at this hour usually had 6-10. Since 1991, SBT continued screening Mexican and other Latin American telenovelas, though gradually giving priority to *Aqui e Agora*, which from June 1993 was extended from 1 hour 15 min to 1 hour 45 min, divided into two blocks, still within prime time.

By 1995, SBT had conquered 19 per cent of the audience (an average national percentage for all of 1995) compared to Globo's 64 per cent (*Isto E*, 3.4.96). SBT continues as the number two television network in Brazil, with TV Record and Bandeirantes as the runners-up. What is happening is that there is a continuous challenge to Globo's leadership. In the process experimentation with new genres is occurring. While SBT is investing a great deal in telejournalism and telenovelas, Globo are diversifying into, among other types of programme, the short serials known as mini-series (see chapter 5 for further elaboration on this genre). However, Globo continues giving telenovelas top priority, filling most of prime time with them and gaining ratings around 50. Manchete had a few telenovela successes around 1990, but thereafter went into decline and closed. Thus, SBT seems currently to be the prime challenger to Globo's dominance.

While this is the current situation among the regular TV channels, the situation is equally or perhaps even more competitive and fierce on the pay-TV market, where Globo also has a dominant position, although here in close partnership with a series of international media conglomerates, as will be elaborated upon below.

Pay-TV in Brazil: Conquering the largest market in the world

Current technological changes, which are happening all over in the world, are leading development in Brazil in two directions: on one hand there is a tendency towards localization of media infrastructure and media production, and on the other hand the tendency is towards globalization, with an increased concentration of power, money and programme production. Globo is gambling on both horses, creating strategic alliances with large multinational corporations, and simultaneously creating alliances with – and investing in – local concessionaries around Brazil.

In recent years, video cassettes have become widespread, mainly among the middle class but rapidly spreading due to a drop in price making them more accessible. On the production side new and cheaper technology has made better quality production affordable and increased the possibilities for independent producers to enter the production scene. Today Brazil has a enormous number of alternative video producers, mainly producing for the social and popular movements. As these producers gained in experience, working in enterprises like TV Viva in Recife, TV Cultura in São Paulo and TV Maxambomba in Rio, a process has got underway leading to better quality low(er)-cost TV, and to a gradual strengthening of regional and local TV initiatives. However, it cannot be compared with the impact and influence of mainstream television like Globo and the other national networks. CGP, Central Globo de Produção, is still a huge producer of TV fiction. Only very few independent producers, like DEZ (lead by former Globo director Daniel Filho) have obtained funds and expertise enough to produce for the national networks.

Parallel with this local/regional trend, and with the continuing strength of national production, satellite and cable TV is leading to a concentration of ownership and of production in a limited number of media corporations (Sinclair et al 1996, Wildermuth 1998). In Latin America Globo is the strongest media corporation to have established, in addition to a solid national base, a strategic partnership with other companies: Latin America DTH Consortia formed in 1995-96. This consortium is owned by Rupert Murdoch's News Corporation (30 per cent), Mexico's Televisa (30 per cent), Globo (30 per cent) and the American TCI (10 per cent) (Sinclair 1998). In Brazil, Sky DTH is offering 72 channels (Folha 4.4.96). Competing with DTH is the Galaxy Latina America (Direct TV) owned by the satellite division of General Motors Hughes Electronics Corporation (60 per cent), Mexican Multivisión (10 per cent), Globo's competitor in Brazil, TV Abril (10 per cent) and Grupo Cisneros from Venezuela (20 per cent) (Sinclair 1998). Direct TV began transmitting in Brazil in September 1996. In cable distribution and subscription TV, two companies control the Brazilian market: TVA (TV Abril) and Net Brasil (Globo 68 per cent) (Folha, 9.5.95).

Both direct satellite consumption and cable television are very strong trends, in particular within the Brazilian middle class; they are also accessible to the lower middle class. However, due to economic constraints, the large majority are prevented from obtaining these channels. This development process obviously points in the direction of a polarization, where cable and satellite TV are for the higher social levels, and the "traditional" open TV channels remain mass-oriented, aiming at a national coverage.

To sum up, several processes are occurring parallel to each other in Brazil, on one hand an ongoing democratization in the access to production and transmission, but on the other hand a centralisation in the ownership and financial control of the largest channels and the best-quality programmes, with the Globo Organisations and the Abril Group as the major players.

Still hand in hand

In spite of the fact that mass communication is commercial and privately owned in Brazil, the major players have always been, and continue to be closely related to the political circles and to the government. For many years the military regime operated strategically with the use of mass communication, supporting the development of nation-wide television coverage. This was used in the regime's strategy of national integration. There was very limited public service television, however. Censorship and self-censorship became the control mechanisms governing the media.[4]

An increasing number of Brazilian politicians became the owners of mass communication companies, both television stations or networks, and newspapers and radio-stations. This was and is still most widespread on a local and regional level. However, the owner of Globo's largest competitor SBT, Silvio Santos, ran for president at the first democratic election for president in 1989. He had almost

---

4   The public service channels, the *TV Educativas* that exist on a state level (a total of about 20 stations), are all so insignificant and with so low ratings, that I have chosen to exclude them from my analysis, thus limiting my focus to the commercial television in Brazil, which furthermore is where telenovelas are transmitted.

no programme and barely a political party, but managed very quickly to obtain substantial support, reaching more than 10 per cent in the polls in just a little over one week. However, he had not registered in time and was therefore disqualified. The winner of the 1989 election, Fernando Collor de Melo, had heavy support from Roberto Marinho's TV network, Rede Globo, a political support that later was officially admitted by Roberto Marinho. Even in the 1990s, these close relations were confirmed when President Collor, in 1990 and 1991, provided 101 concessions, free of charge, many to small businessmen, friends or relatives of congressmen (dos Santos 1997: 100). These examples thus confirm the close interrelation between media and politics in Brazil.

The concrete development of the mass media, and especially the development of Rede Globo, went hand in hand with technological development, although Rede Globo's high quality-level was misleadingly equated in their publicity with the modernization of Brazil. The slogan was that the better the technological capacity, the more modern Globo – and Brazil – was. Rede Globo has always been characterized by a high technological standard, competitive on an international level. However, this "GLOBAL" quality (Padrao Globo de Qualidade) stood, and still stands as a contrast to the indices of poverty, illiteracy and the generally low standards of social and educational development amongst the majority of the Brazilians. Nevertheless, commercially speaking, TV sets and Globo programmes became outspoken successes!

As we now have seen in chapter 3 and 4, the regime's discourse of modernization and national integration – transferred to the programmes of Rede Globo – supported the status quo in the social organization in Brazil. Nevertheless, Globo did not remain untouched by the political developments in the process of democratization. The ideological discourse in the programming became more nuanced with more elaborate critical discourses appearing in the 1980s. For example, the telenovela *Roque Santeiro* which was forbidden in 1974 was allowed to be shown in 1986, and was screened, although in a new version. The telenovelas in the 1990s, as will be described in chapter 5, provided interesting links between the continued development of a genre and the evolution of civil society in Brazil.

Thus, despite Globo's close relationship to the political and economic agenda of the military regime, and later of the elected president, the official discourse – the preferred meaning – as communicated to the public, was not always "read" as such, neither are the media discourses so univocal. Television has since its beginning been an integral element in the process of modernization in Brazil, and telenovelas have been the flagship of the process both as programmes and as commercial products, reflecting the many contrasts and ambivalences that constitute the actual process of modernization in Brazil. The narrative characteristics and the history of the genre will be elaborated on in the next chapter.

5. The Brazilian telenovela

Novelas are folk art adapted to modern communication, without losing its original glory

Alberto Moravia, 1985 in Mattelart 1989

Whoever you ask in Brazil, they can all recognize a telenovela when it is on television. However, when you ask them to define what a telenovela is, it becomes more difficult. Knowing what a telenovela is lies implicit in Brazilians' cultural and televisual competence, it is a self-evident aspect of everyday life. Telenovelas are easily recognizable because they – as I will explain in the first part of this chapter – grew out of the history of popular culture, having historical matrices in ancient oral and literary storytelling as well as in more recent narrative mass communication within theatre, circus, radio and cinema. With 30-40 years of telenovelas and with more than 50 years of radionovelas, most Brazilians have been born with novelas as part of their everyday life.

In the second part of this chapter, I analyse some of the overall characteristics of the narrative and emphasize the elements constituting telenovelas as a different genre from American soap opera. Brazilian telenovelas are, like the *cordel* literature, *open works*, in the understanding Umberto Eco gives to this term (Eco,1981b). The narrative is not concluded when the telenovela goes on air, but unfolds in a process dependent on audience response. Typically, when a telenovela starts, 24 chapters are filmed, the author has written 15-20 more and thereafter seeks to keep about 20 chapters ahead of the chapter on air. A telenovela normally develops into 150-200 chapters.[1]

Thirdly I analyse the development of the telenovela genre, from its very beginning in 1951, structuring its history in three major phases of development: Romantisicm from 1951-1963; Realism from 1968-1985/6 and Post-Realism from 1986 onwards. Finally, the fourth and final part of this chapter introduces the *Rubbish Queen*, its main plot, characters and settings, and places the narrative in the context of contemporary Brazilian reality which in many ways is reflected in the story,

---

1   The word chapter is chosen instead of episode to label the part of a telenovela shown every evening. Episode would be misguiding, because it would indicate a closed narrative, which is not the case in telenovela chapters. Furthermore, in Brazil they use the word *capitulo* and not *episodio*.

Recalling Fuenzalida's reflections in chapter 2 on the emotional relationship between a genre and its public, this chapter will explain how this relationship has evolved over time, simultaneously reflecting the process of modernization of Brazil. By drawing on well- known cultural matrices within the art of storytelling, and by exploring the needs and aspirations of the public, telenovelas serve as mediators of and socializers into the society of which they are at the same time a product,

1. Historical matrices

Three cultural phenomena: storytelling, *repente/cordel* and circus are all central historical matrices in today's mass communication narrative form: the telenovela. Usually, these popular forms of communication are not explicitly linked with the narrative and genre history of telenovelas. However, there are a series of traces from the oral culture of storytelling and *repente*, passing through the oral literature of the *cordel* and the fabulous and grotesque comedies of the circus which lead up to the telenovela. Alongside the *feuilleton* and the radionovela, these phenomena constitute central though often overlooked aspects of the history of the telenovela.

Storytelling

The world of the story is no other than the world of the people: a world without fatherland, over and beyond any fatherland, rooted in a collective language. A diversified world, apparently fragmented, but fertile in its heterogeneous forms. Resistant in its norms and values, intercommunicative in its imaginary, and versatile. The world of the storyteller is his History, etched into the stories he tells (Lima, 1985: 56).

Storytelling has always existed. The story genre covers a wide range of sub-genres, but they all have the characteristic of being an entertainment told by one, or sometimes various storytellers to an audience. It is an oral tradition transmitted from generation to generation, an element of everyday life, most widespread in rural areas but also existing in urban settings. Storytelling in its traditional form has in Brazil entered into decline and is today only performed by a limited number of elderly people. However, the structure of stories, the content and the time and space in which storytelling occurs contain some of the historical matrices of the modern mass media storytelling of the telenovelas. The incorporation of storytelling into the everyday life of the listeners has many similarities to what occurs with the mass media today.

Francisco Assis de Sousa Lima has made one of the most thorough analyses of the story and the narrative community in a Brazilian setting (Lima, 1985). In the local community of Cariri in the Northeastern state of Ceará, Lima interviewed 37 informants of which 21 identified themselves as storytellers and another 9 occasionally told stories. They were both men and women. Together they told 182 different stories, as well as explaining the how, where, when, why and for whom the stories were told. In addition, Lima made a thorough analysis of the socio-economic and political history of the region, to be able to place the stories in a context, and understand the historical context from which they sprang.

Stories in Cariri are called *Historias de Trancoso* (Trancosos stories). When asked what Trancoso stories are, one of the locals, Julio, answered: "What it is, I don't know, I really don't know what it is. I can tell you a story, but I really don't know what it is"(Lima, 1985: 57). The structural characteristics of the storytelling form are taken as self-evident and often stories are told spontaneously at given moments either during collective work or in a pause while in the fields or as a leisure time activity.

The Trancoso stories are fiction, classified by the community as stories originally told by a man named Trancoso. Who he was nobody knows. The stories are long, endless and are not really believed to be true. For example the animals in them talk. Sometimes they do include some events that probably occurred in real life. Many stories take place in times of emperors, kings and queens.

A person who often appears in the Trancoso stories is the *Turco*, a turk. This person is always big and evil, originating in stories coming from the Iberian Peninsula and the horror of the wars and conflicts between the Portuguese and the Ottoman empire. Other stories are rooted in events that took place in the recent history of the region, like the popular uprising against the oligarchy, the almost mythical stories of *Padre Cicero*, a priest who became mayor of the town and helped the poor. Lima divides the Trancoso stories up into several categories. No matter what the category, they have the same function in the community: as entertainment, like games, dances, etc. Stories are told for all ages. They are told both in rural areas and urban areas (Lima,1985: 67). In the rural areas, Trancoso stories are told by people living on small farms or by the employees at the farms. Storytelling constitutes a moment of relief, relaxation and inspiration. Important for storytelling is the presence of an audience of attentive listeners – only interested listeners gave the optimal resonance and the full impact of the story – "a polarized, vibrant and silent listening" (Lima, 1985: 68).

In the 1950s storytelling in Cariri went into decline. The locals give two main reasons for this. One is the emergence of mass media like radio, magazines and television taking over storytelling and increasing the entertainment on offer, with more appeal to the younger generation. The relationship to the old people, who usually told the stories, has changed, a change in social relations in general has occurred. In this context Alexandre Leite Moreira says that stories used to be told due to lack of options for leisure time: "Stories are things of the past, of leisure time. It is getting out of fashion, because there is lots of entertainment, lots of television, day and night" (Lima,1985: 71).

With the spreading of radio and TV in the region – radio as early as 1939, but massively from 1959 onwards, and TV from the beginning of the 1960s, storytelling in its original form declined. The routine of listening to endless stories was taken over by the mass media:

> I think the Trancoso story does not have a future, it's going to disappear with time. In general storytelling will be provided by the novela, in television, in radio, these will occupy the space, and with more advantages. The novela of television is happier, it is a kind of developed story. In the novela many things are not stated because it is shown, there are no lies and it is accepted by all of humanity.

> *Lima, 1985: 71-72*

The traditional stories also disappeared due to changes in methods of production in the rural areas. The collective ways of peeling and cleaning crops such as corn and beans disappeared around 1950. Before that time people used to get together in the house of the owner of the crops that had to be cleaned and stories were told. This type of gathering stopped with the introduction of quicker and more effective ways of cleaning the crops, not needing the same amount of labour.

The decline of storytelling cannot only be explained by the introduction of new media and new modes of production. Part of the explanation lies in the disappearance of old values due to the social and economic decline of rural Brazil, resulting in the breakdown of some of the social networks upon which storytelling in its older forms was based.

Despite the decline of oral storytelling as an element of everyday life, it has not disappeared as a "folk art". Storytelling developed, and was articulated in new ways, especially through radio and later television, with the novelas being the new genre. Mass media enter into the cyclic time of the everyday, the habitus, where the rhythm is relaxed and the flow of stories continuous – a relaxation but also an inspiration, an incorporation of mass communications into everyday life.

Literatura de Cordel and Repente

The *literatura de Cordel*, which Cariri calls "the market verses"constitutes one of the literary matrices of contemporary mass communication in Brazil. *Cordel* literature is a mixture of genres incorporating news with entertainment, taking up religious, political, social and cultural issues. It is a tradition of storytelling based on literature in verse, which is either read aloud or more often sung in public settings such as market places, squares and street corners. It is a phenomenon which finds its strongest expression in its traditional home among the poor and often landless peasants in the *sertão* (the outback) of *Nordeste*. However, it has spread all over the country with the migration from *Nordeste* southwards to the big cities as well as to the West to the huge Amazon region. The term *Cordel* literature originates from the Iberian Peninsula and originally signified the literature hung upon strings to be read on public squares. Meanwhile, in Brazil it is more often referred to as *folheto*, referring to the small booklets in which it is printed.

Cordel literature has an oral parallel in the tradition of *repente* – verses recited from memory, or very often improvised. The tradition of *repente* has a broad variety of local and regional characteristics and expressions, many belonging to the category of *defeiteiras*, which consists of two or more poets reciting in turn, challenging each other in the creativity of their improvisation. Within the *defeiteiras*, the *boi-bumbá* is special because this is a collective recitation, where everybody takes part. Another element of both *repente* and *literatura de cordel* is the accompanying music: guitar, accordion and other instruments. *Cordel* literature however is limited by definition to situations in which verse predominates, accompanied only by music and with no dancing (Salles, 1985).

Cordel literature has served as a popular way of spreading news about what is happening in the political and economic centres of the region, the state or the country. It is a means by which illiterate peasants and landless people gain information about current events, as for instance in this an example from an uprising in São Paulo in the 1920s:

O Exército brasileiro	The Brazilian army
Não mais querendo aceitar	Wanting no longer to accept
O govêrno da nação,	The gov'ment of the nation
Resolve se revoltar	Decides to revolt
Depor os governadores	Depose the governors
E instituir sem rigores	And to institute without harshness
Dictadura militar.	Military dictatorship.
O Exército quer a república	The army wants a republic
Democrática federativa;	Democratic and federative;
Onde a vontade do povo	Where the people's will
É soberana e altiva,	Is sovereign and haughty,
Quer que o chefe da nação	It wants the nation's leader
Respeite a constituição	To respect the constitution
E a lei que della deriva	And laws deriving from it
...	...
Quer que a igreja continue	It wants the church to continue
Separada do estado,	Separated from the state
E que cade cidadão	And that every citizen
Tenha o direito sagrado,	Has the sacred right
De ter fé ou ser atheu,	To have faith or not
Porém que o pensar seu	So that his views
Seja sempre respeitado.	Are always respected.
O voto será secreto	Voting must be secret
Para qualquer eleição,	For any election
Nem um eleitor humilde	No poor voter
Soffrerá mais coação	Will suffer coercion again
Ninguém poderá privar	No one will remove
Do direito de votar	The right to vote
A qualquer um cidadão.	Of any citizen.
O ensino obrigatório	Compulsory education
Primário e proficional	Primary and professional
Será logo instituido	Will soon be instituted
Para o Brasil em geral;	For the whole of Brazil;
Matar o analphabetismo	To kill off illiteracy
E acabar com o almofadismo;	And finish with laziness
Eis do exército o ideal	This is the ideal of the army.
Salles, 1985: 230	*Salles, 1985: 230*

One major issue raised in *cordel* literature is everyday life in the sertão, reflecting the sertanejo's desire to revenge social injustice. An almost mythical hero of the sertao is the bandit leader *Lampião* who in the 1930s swept the region robbing from the rich and helping the poor. He was a Brazilian parallel to Robin Hood. Lampião and his group of bandits, the *cangaceiros*[2] have often been the subject of

---

2   *Cangaceiros* is the name given to the bandit groups in general living on the sertão in the first half of this century, robbing the big farms, protesting against social injustice, and to some extent passing on the robbed goods to the local population among whom they often had support and originated from.

cordel literature, focussing on their machismo, their physical strength, their heroic fight against social injustice and describing the conflicts and fights they fought. The verses also reflect the *sertanejo*'s revolt against his own poverty and misery:

Pedir esmola hoje em dia	To beg money these days
Não é boa profissão	Is not a good profession
Segue a pé para o sertão	Walk to the outback
Sòmente para se vingar	Just to get revenge
Vai pedir para se alistar	Ask to be enlisted
No grupo de Lampião	In the group of Lampião
Braga,1989: 37	*Braga, 1989: 37*

The authors of *cordel* literature and *repentes* were always very popular and well-known in their region, like Master Noza in Ceará, Xico Santeiro in Rio Grande do Norte or Master Vitalino in Caruaru (Salles, 1985: 31). These poets or authors were always very proud of being poets and always seemed to maintain an optimism in their poetry, no matter what the subject (Braga, 1989: 38). Joaquim Jaqueira, a *repentista* (reciter of *repentes*), was also a guitar player and singer, and became famous in the *sertão*. He lived in Rio for years, working as a guard at construction plants. He often met Northeastern *repentistas*, among them Azulao, with whom he occasionally sang on the Programme *Almirante* on National Radio. Joaquim Jaqueira used to present himself with the following verse:

Eu sou Joaquim Jaqueira	I am Joaquim Jaqueira
Canto até escritura	I even sing writings
E no braço da viola	With a guitar in my arms
Eu faço verso em altura	I write poems
E todo mundo aprecia	And everybody appreciates
Uma Jaquinha madura...	A mature Jaquinha...
Salles, 1985: 215	*Salles, 1985: 215*

Both *repentes* and *cordel* literature originate from the sertão but, as I mentioned above, they spread to the big cities of Brazil with the process of migration from *Nordeste*. Thus, many of the singers and authors today live in cities and have brought the traditions with them. Unlike storytelling, these genres have to some extent survived migration and modernization, and are one of the continuing ways in which people interpret and reinterpret the society around them, becoming incorporated into the lives of the people in the outlying neighbourhoods of towns.

Repentes and *cordel* literature are both related to oral storytelling, the *cordel* being orally recited literature and *repentes* being stories told in verse with music and dance. Both of the verse-based genres are related to storytelling as described before. *Cordel*, *repente* and the oral telling of stories often have the same audience though the settings are different. The interrelation lies not only in the audience, but in the mutual inspiration between these genres. Usually it was the *cordel* literature that inspired the stories, but it also happened the other way around (Lima, 1985: 77).

You never know when *cordel* poetry and especially *repente* ends. They are continuous narratives, leaving room for inspiration and dialectics, with an openness in terms of time, and in the way they are produced, and their relationship to what is happening around the performance. *Cordel* literature reflects the social, political and cultural situation surrounding the author. The fact that there is an author differentiates this form from storytelling where the stories are passed on orally from one generation to the next.

Some of these aspects link the *cordel* and *repente* to the telenovelas: (1) all are the work of a specific author, recognized through having characteristics specific to that author; (2) they are open works reflecting contemporary concerns on local, regional and national levels; (3) they enter into a dialogue with their audience, (4) as a consumer product, *cordel* literature has to use some of the same mechanisms to reach its audience as those developed in the culture industry of which telenovelas are a part.

Circus

The third and last historical matrix of the telenovela as a mass medium lies in the circus. Like the traditions described above, the circus has its origin in popular oral culture, going back to the fairs of the medieval Europe and to the origins of the melodrama (Martín-Barbero, 1993a: 114ff). In Brazil the tradition was similar. The travelling troupes of acrobats, jugglers, clowns, magicians, musicians and animal trainers set up their circus tent in villages and towns, preferably aiming to arrive at the time of religious holidays, when the people from the nearby rural areas came to the village to pray or just to participate in the social gatherings and events linked to this day (Milanesi, 1978: 39).

The troupes of medieval Europe aimed at presenting "farces and comic interludes", mixed with acrobatics, puppetry and juggling. Often exaggerated symbolism was used, emphasizing gestures, emotions and action. Words were of less importance than technical and optical tricks, and music and sound played an important role in the emphasis of dramatic moments. Many of these elements developed and became rooted in the circus tradition, well known even in the circus of today.

The circus sought to tell stories, most often comedies and often with grotesque situations. The clowns had the leading role in most circuses. Gradually, from the 1930s onwards, the annexation of the theatre into the circus became more frequent in Brazil (Milanesi, 1978: 41). Instead of short jokes and grotesque action, longer comedies and dramas were developed. This mutation of the circus towards theatre was partly a response to the growth of the film industry in Brazil. However, it was also a natural development of the circus traditions. An Argentinian study of the relation between circus and radio showed how the world of minstrels and travelling circuses helped to build a bridge between gaucho novels, wandering comedians and the radio (Rivera, 1980). Thus it was in the circus that a tradition of popular theatre was formed, gathering collective memories and adapting them to modern melodramatic expression. This gradually developed into the radio theatre in Argentina and radionovelas in other Latin American countries (Martín-Barbero, 1993a: 169).

Today circus is predominantly a phenomenon existing of the outskirts of major cities. Here circus exists as a form of entertainment just like football. It is only here that it can find a market. The rural areas are too poor and too sparsely inhabited to make it economically viable for circuses to pass there. What has happened in Brazilian circus tradition since the gradual integration of theatre into circus has been a greater adaptation to the modern world where a massive culture industry influences the potential customers of the circus.

Thus the incorporation of the circus into everyday life continues, as it tries to keep up with the entertainment offered by the culture industry. Many of the dramatic, artistic and technical characteristics, the special way of telling stories that developed in the earlier days of the circus in Brazil, have been integrated into the culture industry, as I described in relation to radionovelas and radio theatre. This also accounts for telenovelas, as we shall see later in this chapter, not least in the case of the *Rubbish Queen*. The circus today has remnants of what it always was, but as with any other cultural expression n the arts, it tries to adapt to the trends in form, aesthetics, rhythm and content of the modern world. The circus is likely to survive in Brazil. In the region of São Paulo there are about 200 circuses around the neighbourhoods (Magnani, 1984 in Martín-Barbero, 1993a: 169pp). Today circus "is a mishmash of historical dramas, parodies of telenovelas, wrestling, magic and modern pop music".

The culture industry is today part of the modern world and thus the actors, musicians, presenters etc. of this industry figure in the world of circus performances. Conversely, circus has, ever since the film industry started, influenced the genres of film, radio and television, thus forming one of the central but often overlooked historical matrices of the mass media.

From oral culture to television culture

Storytelling, circus and *repente* and *cordel* literature together constitute the fundamental historical matrices of the telenovela. The ways in which these phenomena take part in the everyday life of the audience have many similarities to the roles of the telenovelas. Storytelling used to occur in Brazil both in collective work hours as well as in more joyful moments of leisure. The stories were a natural part of people's everyday lives. Storytelling was a collective activity following the rhythms of daily routine, inserting itself wherever there was a gap, as telenovelas do today . When oral storytelling went into decline in the 1950s it was rearticulated in new forms. Mass media took over the role of the storyteller.

Cordel literature and the *repente* brought in new aspects, such as the fact that the stories were produced by authors. The *cordel* was one of the early "open works", developing in relation to the taste, interest and feeling of the audience. This market orientation was essential, if the authors of *cordel* literature were to survive. A further similarity with the telenovela lay in the contextualization of the stories, relating to current political and social events on all levels of society.

Circus emphasized comedy and developed melodrama. It also evolved a way of telling stories, where the audio side – the music, the effects and noisy gestures and expressions – became central to mark important moments, dramatic climaxes, special emotions and other aspects of the story. This has since passed through radio to TV and is today considered one of the more "radiophonic" elements left in telenovelas. Comedy has remained a specific subgenre of telenovelas ever since the 1960s (see final part of this chapter).

Thus, the historical oral cultures and the modern television culture occupy similar roles in the everyday life of the people. Sociability, collective activity and entertainment are some of the common denominators in the role that oral cultures have played in Brazilian history and in the role that telenovelas play in contemporary Brazilian society. However, in what way are these modern stories told? What are the characteristics of this narrative?

2. Dramaturgical complexity

The Brazilian telenovela has a complicated dramaturgy, linking stories contained within a single episode to others spanning the series, in such a way as to keep the regular viewer watching every chapter, but also to enable the infrequent viewer to make sense of an odd chapter here and there, so that they will, the broadcasters hope, get 'hooked'. Finally the dramaturgy has to suit the commercial interests; there are breaks every 10-12 minutes to give room for two or three minutes of commercials. The dramaturgy unfolds on three related levels: the overall narrative, the chapter, the scene.

The Brazilian media researcher and critic Decio Pignatari structures the plot of the telenovela in three main phases: In the first phase, a prelude of 30-40 chapters, all possibilities are laid open, two or three themes are emphasized and the characters are rather vague. In the central phase, containing at least 100 chapters, the plot develops. The characters get clearer profiles and primary and secondary plots are hierarchised and made plain. The narrative proceeds slowly, and undergoes changes based on the response of the audience which is assessed partly through audience polls and partly through the direct response of the viewers in letters and phone calls to the TV-networks and especially to the actors.[3]

In the third and ultimate phase of the telenovela, consisting of approximately 30 chapters, the closure of the narrative is carried out. Some characters are suddenly changed, some disappear and new ones turn up in order to resolve the puzzle that has been set up by the profusion of plot-lines (Pignatari, 1984: 60-85).

Depending on the popularity of a telenovela it is either prolonged or cut short. If a character is popular her or his role can be given more priority, and more chapters can be written where the popular character gets a more prominent place in the plot. The fact that author is only 15-20 chapters ahead of the chapter on air makes it possible for him or her to react to audience response as well as to current social and political affairs.

Both in the main plot as well as in the plot of each chapter there are many parallels to the French *feuilleton*. In his book *The Role of the Reader* the Italian semiotician and philosopher Umberto Eco describes some of the semiotic characteristics of the French newspaper feuilletons in the middle and late 19th century, with Eugene Sue's feuilleton *Les Mysteres de Paris* from 1848 as an example (Eco,1981b: 130pp). Eco analyses which textual constructions are able to keep the attention of the reader over longer periods of time. According to Eco it is important that each chapter ends with a series of unresolved conflicts, cliff-hangers, thereby keeping the attention of the readers until the next chapter. To hold onto that attention it is also important that the reader's need for suspense is satisfied. The suspense technique activates the reader and makes her consider what will happen next and begin to imagine possible solutions. Eco calls this the reader's own search for new information (Eco, 1981b: 133).

These characteristics of the *feuilleton* are shared by the telenovela. New conflicts are set up in every chapter so that the viewer "needs" to see the next one to find

---

3   The actress Regina Duarte got more than 2000 letters as a feedback to her leading role in *Rubbish Queen* (Van Tilburg,1991a).

how they are resolved. New characters are placed in the story and new plots are established. The viewer continues to search in the next chapter, finds the answers, then new conflicts arise. In this way the need for new information goes on continuously.

To avoid losing the reader in between the conflict and its resolution, the plot must contain what Eco calls stretches of redundant material. Since identification is only possible in a situation of recognition, these moments must be sustained for a while, which creates a margin of redundancy. They occur after something surprising happens in the story, reestablishing stability. This continuous change between the building of and the release of suspense Eco describes in terms of a sine graph, equivalent to the regular and constant movement of a wave. In other words, it is an undulation, moving from excitement to stability, excitement to stability, all the time (Eco,1981b: 132).

To be able to keep the attention of the viewers in this constant undulation between excitement and stability, the dramas must necessarily be spread over more than just the main plot. Eco operates with the concept of what he calls a centrifugal novel. Sue's feuilleton *The Mysteries of Paris* is an example of such a novel (Eco, 1981b: 133). There is a main plot: Prince Rudolph's search for his lost daughter. This is the trunk of the novel. From this grows a lot of branches, secondary plots, performed by a large gallery of characters that all have some sort of relation to the main characters. To a large extent it is thus the secondary plots that create the movements. This centrifugal model thus combines the constant wave movement of each chapter with the narrative of the main plot.

The wave movement passes through all chapters of a telenovela, simultaneously being integrated into the drama curve of the main plot. The peaks of the drama are followed either by margins of redundancy or are cut off at a cliff-hanging point just before the climax by a commercial break or the end of the chapter..

The specific scene

In addition to the *feuilleton*-like dramaturgy of the main plot and the chapters of the telenovela, each specific scene contains dramaturgical characteristics which can be traced back to the oral culture of storytelling. Every chapter is shaped like a serial, with cross editing from one secondary plot to another. In other words they operate with several narrative sequences within the same chapter. Each of the scenes is a small episode with its own easy-to-grasp dramatic plot. Unlike the feuilleton structure of the main plot, developing throughout the telenovela, the minor plots or episodes of each scene give the infrequent viewer the possibility of catching on to novela-viewing. The many minor episodes serve to keep the attention of viewers who are not familiar with the story. They are related to, but without consequences for the overall narrative.

The Danish media researchers Tove Arendt Rasmussen and Peter Kofoed point out in their book *Dallas* (1986) that *Dallas* is the television serial that has developed one of the most precise steering instruments for the unfolding of conflict, by securing suspense and release in every episode (here equivalent to chapters in a telenovela). This is done by dividing every episode up into 4 modules (Rasmussen and Kofoed, 1986: 48ff). By having serial, *feuilleton*-like elements in module one, some of the unanswered questions from the previous episode are answered straight away while new unresolved conflicts are established. Modules two and three use episodic elements, and keep the attention of the viewer with dramatic scenes.[4] The telenovela contains the same basic structure. The first and last modules are usually very short and dramatic. In between there are often more than two modules. Each module consists of the scenes between two commercial breaks.

In terms of Eco's sine graph, the initial secondary plot in the graph contains the follow up to the minor plot which was interrupted by the commercials. Hereafter follows a series of minor plots of one scene each and finally a scene where the narrative is cut short, leaving a cliffhanger that keeps the viewer in suspense until the next module appears after the break or next day, if it was the last module in the chapter. The division into modules and minor plots is shown in the form of a sine graph in Diagram 1:

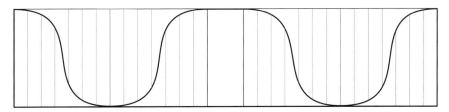

Diagram 1. The minor plots in the sine graph of a chapter

The long time-span of the main narrative, the repetition from one chapter to another, the dramas which occur, the suspense and emotion, the love story, the bipolarity between good and evil – all these elements melt together in a melodramatic form of expression that fits very well into the everyday life of Brazilians. The many chapters and the colloquial language creates a familiarity with the telenovela; you easily recognize it even though you might not be able to define it. The thematic and dramaturgical characteristics are recognizable elements of everyday life facilitating the adaptation of telenovelas to the natural rhythm of your life.

Telenovelas and soap operas – two different genres

The narrative structure of telenovelas and soap operas is basically the same. As the Brazilian media researcher Helio Belik argues in his master's thesis, the difference lies in the production of meaning and the impact on the audience (Belik, 1989). Telenovelas and soap operas do not reflect the same social and cultural needs and aspirations.

First of all, telenovelas are prime time products while soap operas are day time products. The American evening serials like *Dallas*, *Dynasty* and *Beverly Hills* are

---

4   David Jacobs, the director of *Dallas*, does not want *Dallas* characterized as a soap opera. He indicates two major differences between soap opera and *Dallas*. One is that *Dallas* ends. It has a determined number of episodes contrary to soap operas that continue almost infinitely. The other difference is, that in *Dallas* every episode is a closed narrative, whereas in soap operas they are parts of a continuous narrative.

still a minority among American programmes of this type. The target group for soap operas is 18-49 year old women (Cantor and Pingree, 1983), while telenovelas reach much broader audiences. As a result of their being shown in prime time, most of the family see them. Consequently, telenovelas have a major social and cultural impact.

Furthermore, soap operas are still financed in the USA by large companies manufacturing soap, cosmetics etc, who thus have an interest in directing the soap operas precisely to the specific target group buying these products. Telenovelas were produced and financed in similar ways until the late 1960s, but then the TV networks took over the production themselves and diversified their financial support and thus the market orientation. The commercial interest is still predominant and is a major part of the financial basis enabling telenovelas to be transmitted. However, the market orientation is the whole family.

Unlike soap operas, telenovelas come to a definite end. They usually last from five to eight months, where soap operas go on almost eternally. The soap opera *Guiding Light* has been on for more than 50 years, first as a radio soap and for the past 40 years on television.

The last difference to be emphasized is the aspect of class always contained in story of a telenovela, but only seldom in North American soap operas. In this sense telenovelas reflect the extreme polarization of Brazilian social reality.

It is this evocation of social and cultural needs and aspirations – the interaction between the telenovela and the surrounding society – that constitutes the major difference between telenovelas and soap operas. The following analysis of the historical development of the telenovela is thus structured according to the relations between the development of society and the development of the genre. The three phases also reflect the development of television's role in Brazil, as described in chapter 6. The telenovela genre has three major periods: from 1951-1968 is the period of romanticism with a gradual transition to realism: from 1968-1985 is the period of realism where the telenovela developed into a genuine Brazilian genre with some of the characteristics I have just described. Finally from 1985/6 and onwards, the period of post-realism developed, within the spirit of democratization and freedom of speech.

3. 1951-1968: Romanticism

Romanticism can be analysed from two perspectives. The first treats romanticism as a basic element that is structural to the genre. This does not only apply to the first period of telenovelas; it has continued: a love story has always been the basic plot in most telenovelas. The other treats romanticism as indicative of the historical origin of the form, with roots in genres dating from the historical Romantic age: especially the *feuilleton*. However, a series of other traces are to be found in the telenovela, deriving from radio, theatre, cinema, circus, *cordel* literature and oral storytelling, as described earlier in this chapter. Both perspectives must be kept in mind.

Telenovelas began in 1951. However, very little research exists on the period prior to the first daily telenovela that appeared in 1963. Most researchers consider 1963 the year of the first telenovela, but this is historically incorrect. More than 255 telenovelas were transmitted in Rio and São Paulo in the period 1951-1963. The most comprehensive study covering this early period was produced by the Brazilian media researchers Martha Klaggsbrun and Beatriz Resende in 1991, dealing with the history of the telenovela in Rio de Janeiro in 1950-1963, and Renato Ortiz in 1988 studying the telenovela of São Paulo. However, the basic problem hampering studies of this period is the lack of archives. No audiovisual archives exist since videotapes only came into use in Brazilian television in 1960, at the inauguration of Brazil's new capital, Brasilia. Klaggsbrun and Resende therefore based their study on interviews with 20 actors, authors, directors and producers of television from this period. Ortiz based his study on the written archives of IDART.

The first telenovela on Brazilian television was *Your Life Belongs to Me* (*Sua Vida Me Pertence*), written by Walter Durst and broadcast on TV Tupi São Paulo in 1951. In these early years the telenovelas were only transmitted two or three times a week; they were very short, about 20 minutes, and characterized by considerable experimentation and improvization in the process of production. Many of the actors, authors and directors came from the radio, and even though they were very aware that they should not simply produce televised radio plays it often ended up like that. The actors were used only to using their voice and not their body.

The content of the telenovelas had its origin in romanticism, a love story entailing dramatic personal conflicts, a hero, an evil character and the woman in between, struggling with her feelings. This universe of feelings, always related to a story of love was inherited from the *feuilleton*, and seen also in theatre and radio from which the telenovelas got a great deal of their initial inspiration. The Brazilian actress Eugenia Levy confirms the romantic predominance: "Love was the theme at all times. It was always around that amorous triangle, the novelas always went in this direction, the theatres as well, I think it is as we say: love is immortal" (Klaggsbrun and Resende, 1991: 68)

The telenovela *Ferra Radical*, Globo 1987.

The telenovela *Ferra Radical,* Globo 1987.

While melodrama and romanticism characterized the first years of the genre, it experienced – especially in São Paulo – a certain decline the mid 1950s, giving way to adaptations of literary classics: Jules Verne, Alexander Dumas, A. J. Cronin, Victor Hugo, Bernard Shaw and Stephan Zweig. It was partly an attempt to compete with the success of theatre at the time, since the potential audience was the privileged few who could afford a television. Another competitor to television and novelas were American films, which started taking a share in the Brazilian market from about 1958.

In Rio the decline and competition were not so evident. Klaggsbrun and Resende attribute this to the arrival of theatre actors and to the work of the writer Ilza Silveira. Ilza Silveira today stands as one of the most important authors in this pioneering phase of the novela. She produced over 30 telenovelas between 1956 and her death in in 1963 in a plane accident, when she was only 31 years old. Unlike many others in the business, she had little experience with radio. After taking a six-month training course in the USA in 1956 she developed into a competent television author and director.

Ilza was one of the first genuine TV professionals. The majority had their origins in radio and theatre; the circus was another source of inspiration. As the Brazilian TV producer and director Walter Avancini puts it:

> Brazilian television was shaped by two influences which are still around today: the radio and the circus. These two popular forms of expression influenced TV to such a degree that it still today contains a certain contradiction. Brazilian television seeks to adapt to a more universal, a more American language, but remains inseparably and excessively rooted in these historical discourses.

Klaggsbrun and Resende, 1991: 15-16

The first daily novela

The first daily telenovela in Brazilian television went on air in July 1963 on TV Excelsior. It was called *25499 occupied* (*25499 Ocupado*) and was written by the scriptwriter Dulce Santucci. The first years of daily telenovelas in Brazil frequently had scripts imported from Argentina, Mexico and Cuba. Many were also old radionovelas adapted for television. The first daily telenovela came after one of the leaders of TV Excelsior visited Argentina and saw a daily telenovela there.

In May 1964 TV Excelsior transmitted the telenovela *The Girl who Came from Far Away* (*A Moca que Veio de Longe*) written by Ivani Ribeiro. It showed the potential of the telenovela for reaching very big audiences. The plot was a love story between a rich man's son and the maid of the house. *The Girl that Came from Far Away* was the first telenovela to be broadcast in prime time, at 8 pm.

In September 1964 TV Tupi transmitted what came to be an extraordinary success with the audience: *The Right to be Born* (*O Direito de Nascer*). It was originally a Cuban radionovela by Félix Caignet, but was adapted for television by Talma de Oliveria and Teixeira Filho. It was adapted and filmed with financial support from a cosmetic company. The plot takes place in Cuba. A single mother, Maria Helena, has a son Albertinho, whom Maria Helena's father, the tyrannical Dom Rafael, will not accept since the child was born outside marriage. Dom Rafael's condemnation of the child causes the black nanny of the family, Dolores, to escape with Albertinho to a secret place, where she brings him up and looks after him until he is a grown man and gets an education as a doctor. Years pass and irony of life later shows that the powerful grandfather Dom Rafael misjudged his daughter's son. Albertinho saves his grandfather from death, and ends up marrying the other grandchild of Dom Rafael, Isabel Christina. The success of *The Right to be Born* was enormous and emphasized the daily telenovela as a new genre in Brazilian television. (Fernandes, 1982).

The Right to be Born became such a success that a huge party was organized in a big football stadium in São Paulo to celebrate the actors, among them Guy Loup who had the leading role of Isabel Cristina. She fainted in the stadium, overwhelmed by the crowd shouting "Isabel Christina", and shortly after changed her real name to Isabel Christina. Fiction merged with reality. Years later she changed back to Guy Loup.

The four major TV networks took up the genre, each showing three to four telenovelas daily by mid 1960s. Different styles were tried; but the most influential author was the Cuban writer Gloria Magadan. She had worked for Colgate in the USA and came to their office in Brazil at the beginning of the 1960s. After having written telenovelas for TV Tupi and TV Excelsior she started working for TV Globo in 1965. She based her melodramatic stories on an unreal world of fantasy, creating spectacular feuilleton-esque melodramas. The Magadan style brought in the Golden Age of this first, romantic period.

Alongside TV Globo's extravagant, large-scale and expensive Magadan melodramas, filmed in exotic places like Morocco, Japan, Spain, the Soviet Union and Mexico, TV Tupi and TV Excelsior experimented in other directions. In 1965, TV Excelsior launched a telenovela *Where the Illusion is Born* (*Onde Nasce a Ilusão*) written by Ivani Riberio. The setting was in a Brazilian circus, where a young circus girl, Lea, promises her mother not to proceed with a circus career. However, she falls in love with the trapeze-artist Rodrigo with whom she does risky performances. The story shows the world of the circus with its joys and sorrows.

It was, however, TV Tupi who gave the genre a new formula for telling love stories. After some years of producing romantic telenovelas, though less extravagant and less expensive than TV Globo could accomplish, TV Tupi tried something new. In July 1968 they launched the novela *Antonio Maria* by Geraldo Vietri. With *Antonio Maria* TV Tupi introduced a language, a content and a setting that anticipated a radical change in the genre and the next era in the history of the Brazilian telenovela: realism.

4. 1968-1986: Realism

The telenovela *Beto Rockfeller* is considered the first realistic telenovela. It was written by Bráulio Pedroso and was broadcast on TV Tupi in 1968. The emergence of this new type of telenovela came at a time where migration was massive: while 40 per cent of the population lived in cities in 1950 this had grown to 65 per cent in 1977 (Kehl, 1986: 286). The transition from romanticism to realism in the telenovela genre reflected the changes occurring in Brazilian society. The urban life of ordinary Brazilians came to play a central role in the telenovelas to come, thematizising many aspects of the tensions, frustrations and difficulties encountered by the migrant recently arrived in town. The clashes between urban and rural values were shown, offering interpretations of how to deal with urban life.

In addition to taking up contemporary urban Brazilian issues, still spun around one or several love stories, the new telenovela brought innovations in language and dramatic form. *Beto Rockfeller* introduced a quicker rhythm, colloquial language and a more relaxed style of acting. The telenovelas became less theatrical and gradually came to resemble reality more and more. Furthermore, the large majority were now telenovelas de autor, written by Brazilian authors, unlike the telenovelas of earlier years which were adaptions of Cuban or other Latin American scripts. Ivani Ribero and Janete Clair were among the first Brazilian authors of telenovelas.

Heroes and anti-heroes

As part of its increased closeness to Brazilian everyday life, Beto Rockfeller also introduced a new hero character. Where the hero in the "Magadan style" novela was inspired by classical theatre – the saviour, the good person, the dream-lover – Beto Rockefeller – the main character and hero of the telenovela – just was an ordinary, simple man, an anti-hero. As Fernandes writes: "..the anti-hero takes over the role so far filled by characters who were sensible, honest, and upright, able to handle any situation to save the heroine from misfortunes of all kinds. The character and virtue of the main role approximates to that of ordinary people" (Fernandes, 1982: 33).

The dichotomy between good and evil was also softened. But why did this change in the role of the hero occur, why did the contrast between good and evil become more blurred? The Brazilian culture researcher Roberto Da Matta conducted in 1979 a study of the leading characters in Brazilian popular literature. He derived three major types of hero characters within Brazilian culture from his analysis: heroes springing from three different social settings. The typical settings were respectively the military-civic parades, carnival and the religious processions. The hero characters he found were the patriot, the marginal type called the malandro, and finally the religious hero who renounces the world to fight the existing society.

The official patriotic hero character is not found as a protagonist in any telenovela. He is too far from everyday life to be a character the viewers would be able to identity with. The religious hero is also rare in telenovelas, while the second type, the *malandro*, is a character who evolves with the emergence of the realistic telenovela, as a popular anti-hero from a favela. The *malandro* type of person has become a well-known character within Brazilian popular culture. Among others, the musician Chico Buarque has contributed to conceptualizing and promulgating knowledge about the *malandro*. In the mid 1970s he released a double LP, *Opera of the Malandro* (*Opera do Malandro*) which was a tribute to this popular character. The Dutch media researcher Nico Vink gives a very precise description of the *malandro*:

> ...he is smooth talking and uses his charm on women to get their money (the typical malandro is male). He is constantly able to invent new tricks and ways to cheat the suckers. He is convinced that in the society he lives in, work is only for suckers, honest work never makes you a rich man. The *malandro* is neither a rebel nor a revolutionary who wants to change society and its structures. No, he is a specialist in finding his "way" (jeito) to escape the law and all its official regulations...he is marginal and/or belongs to the subordinate class.
>
> *Vink, 1990: 174*

Furthermore, the *malandro* is often black or mulatto and is particularly fond of a specific sort of music – samba and *pagode* (see also chapter 3).

In spite of the emergence of an anti-hero, not all heroes were presented as *malandros*. The crucial point in the telenovela was that Brazilians from all social strata could see hero characters who were both human and recognizable.

The Recipe for Success

By creating a plot, a cast and a narrative rhythm and language close to what the ordinary Brazilian knew from his or her everyday life telenovela producers increased the potential for audience identification. Television was in these years getting more and more widespread in the growing peripheries of the cities with their increasing number of low-income urban dwellers. *Beto Rockfeller* lived in many ways a similiar life to theirs. However, the broad social spectrum of Brazilian society was reflected in the realistic telenovelas. You found all types: the industrial manager, the apprentice mechanic and the street seller. They passed through different conflicts and met in lifelike conflict-situations (Mattelart, 1989: 30pp).

The Brazilian TV critic Helena Silveira distinguishes between on one side the melodramatic telenovelas appealing to dreams, fantasy and the irrational – the romantic telenovela – and on the other side the new telenovelas that do not transport the viewer to another world but are rooted in reality: the realistic telenovela. Silveira states: "reality gives higher sales figures than fantasy" (Silveira in Ortiz, 1988). This is part of the explanation of the way the genre developed and the audience success that followed. Viewers clearly loved the telenovelas – the authors and producers had created a genre that struck a cultural chord with them.

103

The telenovela producer Manuel de Barreto, whom I interviewed in February 1991, indicated that the success of the telenovelas in the late 1960s should partly be seen in connection with the political reality of the time. *Beto Rockfeller* broke through in 1968, in one of the darkest years in the political history of Brazil. The military coup was in 1964 but in 1968, with students, artists and intellectuals taking to the streets, and with an emerging urban guerilla war in cities like Recife and Rio, the last constitutional civil rights were put out of function, and for a short while Brazilians lived under curfew. A new military constitution was installed in 1969. The years 1968-74 were the most repressive years of the military regime. The social routine of watching telenovelas every evening, established in these years, was thus rooted in a political reality: repression by the military regime, which influenced everyday life, spreading fear and limiting options for social and cultural activity.

However, Brazil was growing economically, and in this process of growth and "national integration" Rede Globo participated and profited (see also chapter 4). Even though it was TV Tupi that produced *Beto Rockfeller*, Rede Globo became the television network that managed to profit the most from the innovations. Rede Globo established a perfect relation between the new modern style, represented in Beto Rockfeller, and the melodrama and emotional extravagance seen in some of the earlier telenovelas. It was Rede Globo that diversified the genre and that during the 1970s developed different sub-genres linked to a specific transmission-time, sub-genres that were to last for many years to come.

The 6-, 7-, 8- and 10 o'clock novela

Rede Globo was so dominant in the early 1970s on the telenovela market in Brazil, that not only had they created a series of sub-genres, but when people spoke of telenovelas, they referred only to the transmission-time, saying for example the 8-o'clock novela, not even bothering to mention that it was a Rede Globo novela. That was obvious. Even though TV Tupi kept competing until 1979 and Rede Record and Bandeirantes occasionally broadcast telenovelas as well, Globo novelas were the leaders.

TV Tupi however did have one telenovela worth mentioning, following the innovative production of *Beto Rockfeller*: *Nino, the Little Italian* (*Nino, o Italianinho*). It was written, directed and produced by Geraldo Vietri, with Walter Negrao as co-producer and came on air in 1969, based on a story of Italian immigrants living in São Paulo. However, the successes to follow came on Rede Globo, beginning with the 8-o'clock show. Janete Clair had taken over from Gloria Magadan at the head of the telenovela department of Rede Globo, and a series of her telenovelas became the major successes of the 1970s. *Veu da Noiva*, 1969, was Janete Clair's first telenovela after Gloria Magadan had left. It became a great success and brought the actress Regina Duarte to Rede Globo. Regina Duarte was to become the most popular telenovela actress in the history of Brazilian telenovelas.

The year after, Janete Clair wrote another successful story, *The Courage Brothers* (Irmãos Coragem), 1970. Running to 328 episodes, it became the longest telenovela by Janete Clair and among the longest in Brazilian telenovela history (the longest ever was *Redençao*, 1966). *The Courage Brothers* was a western-like story, about *the Courage brothers* and their life in the small town of Coroado, in the rural west of Brazil. *The Courage Brothers* introduced two of the screen couples who were to become most famous in Rede Globo's telenovelas: Regina Duarte and Claudio Marzo, and Glória Menezes and Tarcísio Meira. The fictitious town of Coroado in *The Courage Brothers* was a set built by Rede Globo especially for this telenovela. During a thunderstorm it caught fire and burnt down. The story that Coroada had burnt down was an item on the news. Fiction and reality were again mixed up. However, Coroada was rebuilt and then – as part of the final episode of the telenovela – deliberately set on fire, as part of the fiction. Now fiction had suddenly turned into reality.

Janete Clair continued as one of Brazil's leading authors of telenovelas with some of her major successes being *Stone Jungle* (*Selva de Pedra*) from 1972-73, Capital of Sins (Pecado Capital) from 1975-76 and *Father Hero* (Pai Heroi) from 1979. Janete Clair died in 1983 leaving her telenovelas as the prototype of the 8 o'clock telenovelas in this period of realism. The telenovela *Stone Jungle* became the most popular telenovela in the history of Brazilian telenovelas and consolidated her position as Brazil's telenovela author number one. *Stone Jungle* was a love story between two migrants newly arrived in town. Simone (Regina Duarte) arrives in the city and tries to survive as an artist. She is in love with Cristiano (Franciso Cuoco) who in the meantime gets seduced by the rich girl Fernanda, the fiancé of Simone's cousin. Disillusioned of the betrayal Simone runs away from Cristiano, ending up in a car accident where everybody thinks she has died. However she is still alive and assuming the identity of a long dead sister sets out to reconquer Cristiano. Ratings reached 100 in the chapter where Simone reveals her true identity!

The story of *Stone Jungle* occurred in a period where Brazil was experiencing rapid economic growth, also known as "The Brazilian Miracle". People enjoyed sitting in front of their TV set watching good win over evil in the last chapter of *Stone Jungle*. Ismael Fernandes describes it in the following way: "A miracle occurred in the life of Cristiano and Simone. They managed to re-establish their amorous relationship as it was before, when they got to know each other before migrating to the city. However, they were no longer the same. Now they loved each other, enveloped in money and personal success. This was really the Brazilian miracle" (Fernandes, 1982).

After women had lead the field as authors at the beginning: Ilza Silveira in the 1950s, Ivani Ribeiro from the 1960s, and Janete Clair in the 1970s, men began taking over. Janete Clair's husband Dias Gomes, Aguinaldo Silva, Lauro Cesar Muniz, Walter Negrão and Gilberto Braga became some of the leading telenovela authors in the 1970s, working in different sub-genres.

In 1973 the telenovela *The Beloved* (*O Bem-Amado*), written by Dias Gomes, was the first telenovela to be transmitted in colour, establishing the 10-o'clock novela as a specific sub-genre. *The Beloved* also indicated the first international interest in these genuine Brazilian telenovelas, being sold first to Mexico and later to most of Latin America (Fernandes, 1987: 168).

In 1975 the six-o'clock telenovela becomes established as a sub-genre of literary adaptations of Brazilian authors. Gilberto Braga becomes the most famous author in this sub-genre, writing *Helena* (1975), *Senhora* (1975), *Dona Xepa* (1976) and the international success *The Slave Girl Isaura* (1977). The telenovelas broadcast at 6 pm continued being literary adaptions until 1982, when Rede Globo began orienting this slot towards young people, thus changing the style. The 7 o'clock telenovela has led a mixed life since this transmission time was introduced in the late 1960s. However, continuous experiments with humorous telenovelas at this hour led to it becoming a semi-permanent slot for the comedy sub-genre, with authors like Cassiano Gabus Mendes and Silvio de Abreu.

Silvio de Abreu had his breakthrough in 1983 with the comedy *The Gender War* (*Guerra dos Sexos*).

Alongside these four sub-genres another fiction genre develops in Brazil: the mini-series, that is, stories of 10-20 chapters. They gradually replaced the 10-o'clock telenovela, reaching a more highly educated segment of the audience with more compact stories, often literary adaptations. *Lampião, Tenda dos Milagres, Malu Mulher* and *Teresa Batista* are highlights within this genre and became major export successes. In all these cases, the director was Paulo Grisolli, one of the most accomplished and prominent directors within the mini-series genre.

Meeting the cultural tradition again

The development of a genuine Brazilian fiction genre – the realistic telenovela – was tightly linked to the development of Brazilian society. Rapid industrial development meant, for many people, a direct leap from an oral culture in the rural areas to an electronic culture in the big cities. Illiteracy and semi-illiteracy did not disappear overnight. At the beginning of the 1990s more than 20 per cent still could not read and write. Thus, literary culture – newspapers, books or magazines, apart from fotonovelas, never became part of everyday life for the lowest income groups. They were still solidly rooted in an oral culture and the everyday routines linked to it. Unlike the romantic telenovela, linked very much the feuilleton tradition, the realistic telenovela mixed literary – feuilleton – and oral traditions, thereby inventing a cultural blend that related to the original cultural traditions of the viewers (Pignatari, 1984: 67ff). Basically the realistic telenovela returned to everyday life as the main source of inspiration for storytelling.

The realistic telenovela took its themes from everyday life in the contemporary trends of migration and urbanization, but it also gleaned plots and interesting details from the collective memory of major audience groups. The examples of this are in numerous, but just to give a few: the mini-series *Lampião* (1982) recounts the final days of the Lampião legend from the 1930s in *Nordeste* (explained more in detail in chapter 5); in *A Rose with Love* (*Uma Rosa com Amor*, 1972) the old storyteller Pimpinoni tells stories of the past through a puppet; *O Bofe* (1972) shows the mystical Afro-Brazilian women Gonzaguinha seeking inspiration and help from her Afro-Brazilian gods, while in the same novela the old lady Stanislava dreams about a circus prince. The mini-series *Father Cicero* (*Padre Cicero*, 1984) was based on the true story of a priest who inspired many stories, working miracles in *Nordeste* and later becoming a famous politician (see the beginning of this chapter). These are just a few examples of what characterizes almost all of the telenovelas from around 1970 and onwards. Collective memories as well as contemporary everyday life provide the authors with an infinite selection of very popular stories to adapt as telenovelas.

5. 1986-: Post-realism

> If realism was born out of an authoritarian regime, and reached its maturity in the democratic transition, post-realism is a product of restored civilian power, and the return of democratic institutions. If in romanticism telenovelas are attached to radio, theatre and literature; and in realism telenovelas became a national and popular genre; in post-realism, telenovelas are leaning towards an international aesthetic.
>
> *Belik, 1989: 80*

Two major trends influenced the genre resulting, from 1985 in a fundamental change: the development of the so-called post-realist telenovela. The first trend was the process of democratization in Brazil; the second trend was the international orient-ation of Rede Globo. The opening up of democracy in Brazil, with massive popular participation in the political process and the reinstatement of freedom of speech was reflected at Rede Globo. To explain the overwhelming success of the telenovela *Roque Santeiro*, screened in 1985-86, the director of the production department at Rede Globo, Daniel Filho, said: "Globo itself changed, there is a new spirit within the broadcasting station, resulting in everybody putting a greater effort into it" (Veja, 02.10.85). A new spirit was emerging among Brazilians. There was less fear, popular participation was substantial and there was a cautious optimism about the democratic future of Brazil. A great interest in national affairs was growing. This dynamic process can be seen as a powerful reaction to many years of repression. Obviously this affected the telenovelas and probably also vice-versa. "If before, during the realistic period, television had played the role of legitimating political power, in post-realism, television plays the role of exercising political power"(Belik, 1989: 81).

Together, the trends towards democratization and internationalization resulted in a change in the content, aesthetics and format of telenovelas. Democratization led to an abundance of political criticism. The 8 o'clock telenovelas in the late 1980s and throughout the 1990s contained highly political subtexts reflecting the current situation: criticizing the fight for power, corruption, nepotism, the Catholic Church, the enforced celibacy of priests, etc, etc. These contemporary problems were made into issues discussed by everybody.

Roque Santeiro was the first telenovela of this kind. Written by Dias Gomes and Aguinaldo Silva, *Roque Santeiro* went on air in 1985-86. It became one of the most important novelas in the history of the genre in Brazil, in line with *The Right to be Born* (1964), *Beto Rockfeller* (1968) and *Stone Jungle* (1972). *Roque Santeiro*, 209 chapters, is a story about a small village, Asa Branca, that could have been anywhere in Brazil. *Roque Santeiro* is a man who earns his living making figures of saints. One day, defending his village from some criminal he apparently dies. He quickly turns into an almost mythical figure in Asa Branca because people think he is able to perform miracles. The fame of *Roque Santeiro* spreads and turns Asa Branca into a pilgrimage centre in the region. The mayor, the large landowners, the conservative priest and the large commercial class all profit from this fame. So when *Roque Santeiro* turns up, alive and well, this elite group try to prevent him from revealing his true identity, and a progressive priest trying to do so is not believed by the people. Thus, the story ends without the truth ever being revealed. The myth remains the official story, overcoming the truth: "The remarkable penetration of *Roque Santeiro* into Brazilian habits, with its discussion of religion, popular mysticism and politics, eschewing romanticism in favour of caricatural yet psychologically-based characters, returned to the telenovela its role as a catalyst of the masses"(Fernandes, 1987: 309).

Roque Santeiro was originally a theatre piece, *The Hero's Cradle* (*O Berço do Heroi*), written by Dias Gomes in 1963 and banned two years later. In 1975 Dias Gomes wrote the telenovela, but it was never transmitted. It was completely forbidden by the military censorship. Only 11 years later could *Roque Santeiro* go on air, in an adapted version: "Censorship prohibited all the allusions to the brute reality of the country ... If *Roque Santeiro* had been shown 10 years ago, when it was censored, telenovelas would have developed in another direction"says Aguinaldo Silva who was the co-author of the 1985-86 version (*Veja*, 2.10.85). Several times *Roque Santeiro* reached 100 in the ratings, having an average rating of 80!

Rede Globo did not know how to follow up on this success. They ended up readapting *Stone Jungle*, the old favourite from 1972, but it was less successful than the original. It was only with *Burning Circle (Roda de Fogo)* by Lauro Cesar Muniz that they managed to develop this new political style further, telling a story full of power struggles, corrupt politicians and illegal activities among the middle class. More telenovelas of the same post-realist genre followed in Rede Globo's 8 o'clock slot: *Mandala* (1987),*Worth Everything (Vale Tudo*, 1988) and *Saviour of the Fatherland (Salvador da Patria*, 1989).

These novelas brought satire and humour to the 8 o'clock slot, without preventing the comedy telenovelas from developing their own tradition at 7 o'clock. The parodies of current political events and persons brought a detachment from reality, an ironic distance that is all too comprehensible in the face of a reality that often is more crazy than fiction – for example the absurd inflation rates Brazil experienced for so many years)!

The nostalgic and romantic turn

Around 1990 some changes occurred in the genre. Rede Manchete and TVS each launched some telenovelas that differed from the "Global" telenovela. After two rather successful telenovelas Rede Manchete launched the telenovela *Pantanal* in April 1990, almost simultaneously with Rede Globo's 25th anniversary telenovela, *Rubbish Queen. Pantanal* was very expensive to produce but proved worth the outlay, even surpassing the ratings of Rede Globo.

Pantanal (1990, TV Manchete) was in many ways a trendsetter. It contained many dramaturgical and technical innovations, including hand-held camera, recordings inside cars etc, and many scenes shot on location (ie in the middle of villages and in markets). There were many scenes shot in natural settings, mainly in one of Latin America's most exotic conservation areas, very rich in wild life, the so-called *Pantanal* area, which is a low-lying swamp on the border between Bolivia and Brazil. Both *Pantanal* and *Ana Raio and Ze Trovão* the year after marked a change, using rural settings, a more filmic dramaturgy, a slower and more relaxed "rural" pace and with room for more dialogue and less "urban rhythm", though maintaining a type of behaviour in human relationships, love stories and intrigues, that was closer to the urban than the rural. The year after *Pantanal*, TVS began broadcasting the Mexican telenovela *Carrosel* and soon after that, Venezuelan and Argentinean novelas – with considerable success. Like *Pantanal, Carrossel* threatened Rede Globo, obtaining high ratings. These imported Latin American telenovelas were very different from the familiar Brazilian telenovelas, more along the line of the romantic telenovelas. They reminded the famous Brazilian actress Regina Duarte of her first telenovelas in the mid 1960s in Gloria Magadan's extravagant romantic style: "When I see a part of a Mexican novela it looks as if I am watching one of the novelas I did in the 1960s. The clothes are the same, the hairstyles are the same: its something totally distant from reality" (*Estado de São Paulo*, 21.11.92). This "distance from reality" most possibly explains why they didn't remain so long on Brazilian television. By the late 1990s the "cultural proximity-thesis" (Straubhaar 1998) had demonstrated its validity in the fact that predominantly Brazilian – both nostalgic (*Renascer, Rei do Gado*) and romantic (*Por Amor*) – telenovelas were flowing from the screen.

The multifaceted post-realism

Since the mid 1980s telenovelas have developed in several directions. The political sub-texts in an increasing number of telenovelas reflect Brazil's process of democratization and thus freedom of speech. These subtexts form a sensitive amalgam with other strands within the open structure of the telenovela. This context is linked to a very professional and more international aesthetic in Rede Globo's productions. Simultaneously, the nostalgic trend with rural settings, slower rhythms and beautiful scenery has been very evident. This sub-genre, romanticizing the rural lifestyle, started out with a few of Globo's telenovelas in the 1970s, and was revived with *Pantanal* (Manchete 1990), some imported old-fashioned telenovelas from other Latin American countries. Recent, significant examples are Globo's telenovelas *Born Again* (*Renascer* - 1993) and *The Cattle King* (*Rei do Gado* - 1996/1997).

The *Cattle King* was particularly interesting, linking rural nostalgia with freedom of speech, addressing one of the controversial social problems in Brazil today: the demand for agrarian reform. *The Cattle King* depicted on an epic scale the struggle for land which has been a growing social demand in Brazil over the past 10 years. Through the telenovelas the problem was transformed into an issue of public knowledge and concern. When, in the telenovela, the huts of an illegal occupation by landless people were torn apart and burnt down, close-up pictures showed the Brazilian flag burning. The Brazilian dream, which through the centuries has attracted thousands of immigrants to Brazil, this dream of a piece of land for everybody – symbolized here by the flag – withered away in the flames, provoking strong emotional reactions, but also generating a common knowledge – including among people who had never heard of the issue – about the huge problem of land conflict in contemporary Brazil. A controversial issue was brought to public attention, generating a public national concern, a lot of debate, bringing prominence to the landless peasants' movement and strengthening it considerably in the process, even finally generating political debates in Congress and leading to the passing of two new laws related to the issue of agrarian reform. Although somewhat extraordinary, the public debate articulated by *The Cattle King* illustrates a trend often manifested in the 1990s: a telenovela makes visible an issue of common concern, be it related to ecology, street children, new technology (*Explode Coração*) or the situation of the blacks (*Proxima Vítima*), thereby sparking often very large and profound public debates about the issues. Telenovelas thus become media-based public spheres articulating and promoting debates on issues of common concern (see also Tufte 1999a).

The following is a transcending example of what happened when a controversial mini-series on Rede Globo joined with a real event – a quarrel in the presidential family – and a national economic crisis to stirred up a mood and a social movement among Brazilians which had huge political consequences.

The fall of President Collor

With the coming of freedom of speech, TV fiction – both telenovelas and mini-series – began exercising political power. The mini-series *Rebellious Years* (*Anos*

Rebeldes) is the most expressive example of this, marking a unique event in the history of Brazil, emphasizing the potentially close interrelation between television fiction, culture and civic action.

Rebellious Years was a mini-series written by Gilberto Braga, telling the story of the student movement and their political resistance in the late 1960s and beginning of the 1970s. It showed how young people dared to resist an repressive regime, even using radical methods such as kidnapping an ambassador. The story had many similarities to events that in fact occurred in Brazil in the dark years of 1968-73. As part of the story, some authentic black and white film clips documenting student demonstrations in Brazil in this period were used. They had never been shown on television before.

The overwhelming effect achieved by the programme has to do with the conjuncture under which it was broadcast. It went on air in July 1992, a few weeks after President Collor's brother had denounced the corrupt dealings of the President on Rede Globo's *Jornal Nacional*. Furious about the president's affairs and inspired by the student movement shown in *Rebellious Years*, thousands of students took to the streets. It started with high school students and quickly spread to universities. President Collor reacted by going on to Rede Globo's *Jornal Nacional* encouraging people to mount a counter-demonstration, using the green and yellow colours (his campaign colours as well as the colours of the Brazilian flag) to emphasize their support for him. This became a direct invitation to do the opposite. All strata of society took to the streets on that specific Sunday in the middle of August 1992 all dressed in black, sorrowing over the Collor scandal. In August and September 1992 Brazil experienced the biggest demonstrations seen since the movement for democracy in 1984-1985, with millions taking to the streets. In São Paulo alone, there were several demonstrations with more than a million people each. By 27 September the story came to a head: the Congress decided to set up a committee to investigate the doings of the president. President Collor was impeached. Three months later, on 27 December the council came to a conclusion: sufficient proof has been established to try former President Collor for corruption. He got his political rights withdrawn for a period of eight years. Meanwhile, this final decision in late December 1992 was overtaken on the news by an event announced on that same day: the murder of Daniella Perez, one of the main actors in the 8 o'clock novela, *From Body and Soul* (*De Corpo e Alma*). This story is told in my introduction to this book.

The example of *Rebellious Years* shows how fiction and reality melt together and become an almost transcendant discourse. The example shows that, under certain social and political circumstances, a fictional TV series can interact with the viewers' own attitudes to produce an overriding socio-emotional reaction. In this case the first of these reactions was the train of events that led to the fall of President Collor and the second – as described in the introduction this book – a social movement promoted by sympathy with Daniella Perez and her mother, of which the theme-music was that associated with her character, Yasmin.

Articulating emotion, meaning and social action

Brazilian telenovelas have basically passed through three major phases, and have today reached an increasingly complex and less determined multi-faceted phase, where the different generic styles tend to co-exist. The development of different genres has not prevented the continuing predominance of the realistic telenovela with its colloquial language, relaxed drama, modern discourse and strong authorial voice. The main contribution of the post-realistic phase has been to add elements to the realistic telenovela, such as a more open expression of political themes.

Focusing of the content of the telenovelas, it will be seen that throughout the period, but especially since the breakthrough of realism around 1970, the characteristic subjects are those originating in popular culture. However, over and above the specific theme, and its location in time and place, there has always been a love story and an emphasis on class conflict and social mobility. The main recipe for articulating emotions, meanings and actions among the novela-viewing public has always been the field of tension created in their variable mixture of often dramatic love stories and subtle class conflicts. (See also Chapter 7.)

Another thing is clear; telenovelas are not just American soap operas in Portuguese. The narrative structures happen to be very similar, which often leads to their being treated, erroneously, as if their content, language and role in everyday life were the same. This they are not. The Brazilian telenovela, with its more massive daily presence, has a much larger social and cultural role in the everyday life of Brazilians than soap opera has in the lives of Americans. As the examples of Collor's impeachment and the death of the actress Daniella Perez showed, telenovelas can in extreme situations become almost metaphysical discourses, where the limits between reality and fiction are difficult to draw.

In the following account one specific telenovela, the *Rubbish Queen*, will be presented, providing an insight into this mixture of dramatic love story and subtle class conflict.

6. Introducing *Rubbish Queen*

In April 1990 Rede Globo celebrated its 25th anniversary. That same month Globo launched a jubilee telenovela, *Rubbish Queen* (*Rainha do Sucata*). It was screened on Rede Globo from 2 April to 26 October 1990, a total of 177 chapters. For the occasion, Globo had asked one of the country's best comedy novela authors, Silvio de Abreu, to write a telenovela. Silvio de Abreu was – and still is – regarded as the leading comedy author, writing especially for the 7 o'clock telenovela. All his former telenovelas had been screened at 7 pm obtaining superb ratings of 58-70. It was therefore surprising that the Globo director of production, Boni, asked him to write an 8 o'clock telenovela, because the style is usually different.

However, Silvio de Abreu accepted, and maintained his well-known style, producing a "light" story in an urban São Paulo setting, focusing on humorous and ridiculous stories and events. *Rubbish Queen* broke with the 8 o'clock tradition, promoting the 7 o'clock comedy tradition at a new screening hour. Despite being screened as the 8 o'clock telenovela, *Rubbish Queen* belonged to the traditional comedy sub-genre, though with an increased mixture of genre characteristics than had been seen in Abreu's previous telenovelas.

A series of negative influences from real life did complicate the ambitions of both Silvio de Abreu and Rede Globo: the tough competition from *Pantanal*, the broadcasting of the World Cup and the compulsory screening of the "electoral hour" every evening from August to October, which pushed the scheduled screening time from 8.30 to 9.30 pm. Furthermore, what Silvio de Abreu set out to do was to deviate a little from the traditional comedy sub-genre he had created

Introducing *Rubbish Queen* – here in Portuguese from the TV screen

which apparently confused the expectations of part of the audience. The ratings achieved were a little lower than Abreu's former telenovelas, but this did not call into question the basic success of the telenovela. Like many others before and after it, *Rubbish Queen* became part of the everyday life of approximately 80 million Brazilians for seven months.

Comedy on Brazilian television

Comedy on Brazilian television has a wide-ranging history. Television's origins in circus, radio, theatre and film ensured that comedy appeared in multiple forms on TV from the 1960s onwards. Grotesque scenes and language, satire and slapstick comedy were all on TV. Television comedians made fun of authorities like the police, politicians, lawyers and priests. Following on from circus theatre, the symbolism of all the popular religions became a target for mockery (Magnani, 1984). By the late 1970s Rede Globo's 7 o'clock telenovela had become established as a comedy sub-genre with Cassiano Gabus Mendes and later Silvio de Abreu as the leading authors.

The television predecessors to the 7 o'clock telenovela comedy sub-genre came from TV de Comédia which was screened once a fortnight on TV Tupi from September 1965 to March 1968. This programme was run by Geraldo Vietri, who from 1966 also became a successful telenovela author. With *Os Rebeldes* (1967) Vietri began transferring some of his comedy ideas from TV de Comédia to telenovela, also on TV Tupi. With the telenovela *Antonio Maria* (TV Tupi, 1968) Geraldo Vietri reintroduced 7 pm as a telenovela slot, and simultaneously introduced Sergio Cardoso as an actor (Fernandes, 1982: 110). Cardoso, who was to become a leading actor in comedy telenovelas plays a Portuguese immigrant (Antonio Maria). Brazilians have always tended to hold the Portuguese up to satire ridicule, especially when imitating their gestures and accent.

Alongside TV Tupi's early attempts at comic plays and shows, TV Record was experimenting with comedy telenovelas. Due to lack of resources, TV Record used their comic actors in telenovelas, for example Jo Soares, who later became a well known comedian with his own very popular comedy show (*Ceara contra 007*, TV Record 1965). However, it was Vicente Sesso who in 1970, for TV Tupi, wrote the first successful 7 o'clock telenovela characterized as a "light" comedy: *Pigmalião 70*. After a more romantic telenovela (*Minha Doce Namorada*, Rede Globo, 1971) Vicente Sesso wrote another comedy: *Uma Rosa com Amor*, this time for Rede Globo (1972).

The breakthrough for the comedy sub-genre came, however, with the telenovelas written by Cassiano Gabus Mendes (*Anjo Mau* 1976, *Marron Glacé* 1979, *Plumas e Paetes* 1980 and *Elas por Elas* 1982). *Plumas* and *Paetes* was gradually taken over by Silvio de Abreu, who in the 1980s was to become one of Rede Globo's best telenovela writers, and the most acknowledged writer of comic telenovelas.

Silvio de Abreu

Silvio Eduardo de Abreu, 56 years old, is the son of a pianist, Mozart Abreu, who played in the Circus Piolin. Ever since childhood Abreu has had a passion for the cinema; films are his main interest. He began his career as an actor in the theatre, moved on to telenovelas in the 1960s and acted in five of them before moving on again to the cinema as a producer of light and humorous pornographic films (*pornochanchadas*). In 1977 Abreu wrote his first telenovela.

Abreu is a middle-class man, living in São Paulo, and writing mainly about São Paulo. Although Cassiano Gabus Mendes was the first to launch São Paulo settings in telenovelas, it is mainly thanks to Abreu that the city gained audience-appeal and became widely accepted as the setting of the prime time telenovelas. Traditionally Rio de Janeiro has been the setting for contemporary telenovelas. However, Abreu states that "I can only write about what I know" (Abreu, 2.09.92), which – geographically speaking – is the city of São Paulo.

The telenovelas which Abreu acted in in the late 1960s and early 1970s were not comedies (*O Grande Segredo* 1967, *Os Miseraveis* 1967, *A Muralha* 1969, *Os Estranhos* 1969, *Editora Mango – Bom Dia* 1971). A great deal of his inspiration, and references, come from American film. Abreu has also brought his background in theatre into his writing for telenovelas. He has introduced a considerable number of theatre actors into telenovelas (Paulo Autran, Tonia Carrero, Maria Alice Vergueiro, etc). He even wrote a telenovela in hommage to Brazilian theatre (*Sassaricando*, 1987).

Abreu has written 10 telenovelas and contributed to another three or four. His first telenovela was shown on TV Tupi in 1977 (*Eramos Seis*). The telenovelas Abreu writes are actually a mixture of genres: comedy, musical, tragedy, action, suspense and farce. It is perhaps more precise to call them comedy-like narratives with multiple ingredients. In form and content Silvio de Abreu has developed his own style, and thus his own sub-genre, in close cooperation with the director who has been his partner on seven telenovelas, Jorge Fernando. They started working together on *Jogo de Vida* (Rede Globo, 1981). In addition, Abreu wrote 61 chapters of Cassiano Gabus Mendes' telenovela *Plumas e Paetes* (Rede Globo, 1980), the eight-chapter mini-series *Boca do Lixo* and wrote 20 chapters of Gilberto Braga's telenovela *O Dono do Mundo* (Rede Globo, 1991).

Silvio de Abreu's Telenovelas

Telenovelas:	No. of Chapters
Eramos Seis (TV Tupi, 1977)	169
Pecado Rasgado (Rede Globo,1978/1979)	169
Jogo da Vida (Rede Globo,1981(1982)	166
Guerra dos Sexos (Rede Globo,1983/1984)	185
Vereda Tropical (Rede Globo,1984/1985)	164
Cambalacho (Rede Globo, 1986)	173
Sassaricando (Rede Globo,1987/1988)	184
A Rainha do Sucata (Rede Globo,1990)	177
Deus nos Acuda (Rede Globo, 1992/93)	175
A Proxima Vitima (Rede Globo,1995)	196
Torre de Babel (Rede Globo,1998)	176

Abreu's telenovelas are always full of surprises, action and effects. To Abreu, telenovelas are basically a question of entertaining an audience. This means providing the viewers with new stories: "Novela is always the same story of somebody wanting to marry, and somebody not allowing this marriage take place. Thus, I think it is necessary to present novelties, something people have not seen before"(Abreu, Feb. 1990).

The style which Abreu has adopted from *Jogo da Vida* (1981) onwards is to create not funny characters but funny situations. "Each scene has its universe. The key is the sincerity, through which the essence of the scene is transmitted. This is how people are moved... The cast should not be worried about playing comedy. Nobody is a caricature. The secret of the story is the fun of the situations" (Abreu, 1.04.90). In recent years the characteristics of first Gabus Mendes' and then Abreu's São Paulo style of telenovelas has been taken up by a new generation of authors, with Carlos Lombardi being the most prominent example. He began as Silvio de Abreu's assistant and wrote 3 telenovelas together with Abreu.

Silvio de Abreu mixes many narrative conventions, draws on film history, mixes the tradition of sugary romance with grotesque situations, creating very funny moments: "In Brazil people like to define and label everything. I've been labelled an author of farces, which, in reality, I don't think I ever wrote. My works have always turned out to be comedies, but I like to make a big mixture, arousing different feelings with each speech, so that the audience is surprised in each scene, is moved, laughs, in other words: is entertained" (Abreu in *O Globo*, 1.04.90).

Abreu's telenovelas have, like any telenovela, a basic narrative: a love story. However, there are comic elements scattered throughout the whole narrative, and the main story and the multiple sub-stories develop a great deal as the novela goes on. The openness of the narrative gives ample opportunity to incorporate the audience's response. As Abreu states:

> Everything can be incorporated into the narrative: an accident seen in the street, a fight, a piece of gossip you just heard, a protest against the situation in the country, a reflection on society. Everything is of interest. The dramatic structure of a telenovela is so ample that it allows you to go in any direction at all, as long as it is accepted by the public, without this necessarily representing a concession.

Abreu in Elle, *February 1990*

Silvio de Abreu characterizes *Rubbish Queen*, in terms of North American sub-genres, as a screwball comedy, rather than a slapstick comedy. (Abreu in *Elle*, Feb. 1990).

Plot, characters and setting

> Who has the power in society? Those who have money or those who cultivate their family name? Who is most important in a society? A businesswoman who made her fortune by working in a small second hand shop and who is the owner of many shops and employs hundreds of people, or a society woman, who figures daily in the gossip section of the newspapers and who accepts numerous invitations to dinner, just to be able to eat at least one decent meal a day? One has money but no social prestige. The other, a big name, but not a penny.

With this secondary media text – part of a 25-page press release – Rede Globo launched *Rubbish Queen* to the press on 31 March 1990. A look through the major Brazilian newspapers of 1 April 1990 show that this press release was widely used – most of the articles are lengthy extracts from the press release. None of the newspapers added any substantial information that was not in the press release (*Jornal do Brasil, Folha de São Paulo, Estado de São Paulo* and *O Globo*, all 1 April 1990).

The main conflict takes its point of departure in the confrontation between two women, the nouveau riche *Rubbish Queen* Maria do Carmo Pereira (Regina Duarte) and the society woman Laurinha Albuquerque Fiqueroa (Gloria Menezes). The plot unfolds in São Paulo around the lives of Maria do Carmo and Laurinha, their families, friends and colleagues. The cast consists of 26 people with Maria do Carmo, Laurinha and Edu (Toni Ramos), Laurinha's stepson, as the main characters. Laurinha and Maria do Carmo have a mutual point of reference in Edu. In addition to being Laurinha's stepson, Edu is Maria do Carmo's old class-mate from school. Both women fight ferociously for the good opinion and love of Edu.

There are two main themes in the narrative. One is the love story, with the rivalry between Laurinha and Maria do Carmo. The other is the constant power struggle between the two social classes. On one side is the threatened São Paulo elite, the traditional upper class society of the coffee barons. They live in their own world, cultivate their European roots and customs, dress in European style and practice their expensive hobbies. On the other side are the nouveaux riches, the new rich who have earned and not inherited their money. They are families of poor origin that have done well. They are people like Maria do Carmo, who do not deny their roots among the poor. One of my respondents speaks of the class dimension in *Rubbish Queen* in the following way:

> It was the story about a woman who was very poor. She managed to become "somebody" in life here, gain status in society because she worked a lot. She began by selling old iron and other second-hand materials with her father, until they succeeded in achieving everything they had. She was very sad about her father spending so much money on paying her school fees. She went to school with children from a higher level, so they made fun of her. They called her the *Rubbish Queen*. They bullied her a lot. She kept all this in her mind and sought constantly to "rise in life", always upwards in life, and always with this wound in her heart.
>
> *Eva, 32, Santa Operaria*

115

After this, Eva talks about the love story; Maria do Carmo's old love towards Edu and about how she again and again tries to win his love. Eva's account, and most of the other women's résumés, indicate that they consider Maria do Carmo the main character. It is her story they tell, it is her fight to rise in the world in spite of her poor background, and it is her hopeless love for a rich man they talk about.

Identification and recognition is obvious among all the women interviewed, no matter if they come from Calabar, Vila Nitro Operaria or Santa Operaria. They are all from lower social levels and all take the same side in both aspects of the plot: the women's rivalry over the man, and the conflict and tension between the old São Paulo oligarchy and the newly rich Maria do Carmo.

If we take a look at the cast, the 26 people of the narrative are centered around two women, Maria do Carmo (who is the *Rubbish Queen*) and Laurinha:

The people around Maria do Carmo

Maria do Carmo lives with her parents in the old workers' suburb Santana[5] in the north of São Paulo. Maria do Carmo is rich, beautiful, intelligent and a competent businesswoman. She originates from a poor family but has built up a big business with her father, dealing in second-hand materials found on dumps and in slum dwellings. Over the years it has become a big enterprise including a car-sales business and a nightclub called Sucata (the Portuguese word for second-hand material). When her father dies – early on in the story – she inherits the company.

Maria do Carmo could easily afford to live in the upper class suburb Jardins, but prefers to live among her friends in Santana. After the death of her father she stays living with her mother in their nice house in what is supposed to be a workers' suburb, although it gives more the impression of being a middle-class area. In the upper class to which Laurinha belongs, Maria do Carmo is constantly humiliated because she does not belong to their class. They often make fun of the fact that she makes her money dealing in second-hand materials like scrap iron. This, linked with her different social background, is the main obstacle in her attempt to win the man she loves, Edu.

Maria do Carmo's parents are Portuguese, but have lived in Brazil for many years. The father, Onofre (Lima Duarte) made his money chiefly by selling scrap iron, but also in some (too) smart bargains. He is the closest we come to the *malandro* type of man, as described in the beginning of this chapter, the sympathetic smart anti-hero. The mother Neiva (Nicete Bruno) is a solid, old-fashioned worried mother and house-wife.

In the beginning of *Rubbish Queen* Maria do Carmo gets engaged to the neighbour's son Gerson (Gerson Brenner), a rather stupid, foolishly kind bodybuilder type. Gerson lives with his two brothers and his mother Armenia (Aracy Balabanian). Armenia is a widow. She works as the leader of a parachute school. She is from Armenia and thus speaks in very broken Portuguese, making many mistakes and always saying "my daughters" (*minhas filhas*) about her three beloved sons (*meus filhos*). She is very talkative, a real gossip, and always funny, noisy and not the least timid.

---

5   Both Maria do Carmo's Santana street and Laurinha's luxury mansion in the exclusive suburb of Jardins have been constructed in Globo's huge studio-city in Rio.

Across the road to Maria do Carmo lives the rather clumsy, timid, stammering university teacher Caio (Antonio Fagundes). His parents were Polish but he was born in São Paulo. He is an archaeologist and always wears glasses that are far to big. He has a girlfriend, Nicinha (Marisa Orth). She is a rather spoilt girl, a daughter of the biggest greengrocers of Santana, and a rather demanding womsn. They have been a couple since they were very young. Nicinha is sexually very attracted to Caio who happens to be more interested in his archeological findings than in her. Her character develops and she becomes the mistress of a series of men, which does not, however, cause her to leave Caio.

Caio lives with his timid sister, the librarian Mariana (Renata Sorrah), who is obviously a boring type. Mariana is secretly in love with Maria do Carmo's business partner Renato, and always throws long loving glances at him every time he visits Maria do Carmo across the street. A passionate love story develops between Mariana and Renato later in the story. Finally, Renato (Daniel Filho, who at the time normally worked as the director-general of Globo's production company- Central Globo de Produção) is in charge of the car-sales arm of Maria do Carmo's enterprise. He shares an office with Maria do Carmo. He is a dishonest, cynical and sinister type, who uses whatever method necessary to obtain what he desires.

The story around Maria do Carmo takes place in a broad social space partly around her home, both inside the house (living room, bedroom, kitchen), but also outside in the front garden, on the pavement, in the street, inside the neighbours' houses and at the grocery store, as well as at her workplace.

The people around Laurinha

Laurinha lives in an elegant villa in the fashionable suburb of Jardins in the south of São Paulo, and is a well-known figure in São Paulo high society. It is she who organizes everyday life in her family's luxurious home. She is very elegant in everything she says and does. She is married to an aristocrat, Beto (Paulo Gracindo) who is very much older than her and rather old-fashioned. Due to the difference in age, she is not much older than Beto's son, Edu, in whom she has fallen madly, though secretly, in love.

Beto's passion is horse-breeding. He does not work but lives off his fortune. However, when the story begins he has just gone broke. He is a funny character because he lives in his own unreal world. Laurinha and Beto live with Edu, who as mentioned is Beto's son by a former marriage. They have three servants: the strange chauffeur Jonas, the domestics Lena (Colita Rodrigues) and her daughter, the politically committed Alaíde (Patricia Pillar).

Edu is handsome, elegant, internationally-minded. He goes in for expensive habits like horse-racing, and like his father he does not work. Despite the bankruptcy of his family he seeks to maintain his aristocratic lifestyle. He is the same age as the *Rubbish Queen* Maria do Carmo. He is sometimes comic, other times tragic, but always charming.

Laurinha and Beto have two other children who no longer live at home: Rafael (Mauricio Mattos) and Adriana (Claudia Raia). Rafael is the irresponsible charmer; he is a pilot and parachute instructor, and teaches many young beautiful girls. At one moment he and the maid Alaide fall in love with each other, but the force of social convention renders their love impossible. Both Rafael's father as well as Alaide's mother advise them against the relationship, virtually forbidding it.

117

Adriana is the beautiful but very clumsy and foolishly kind daugther. She works in Maria do Carmo's nightclub Sucata (Rubbish), but dreams of a career on Broadway. She is depicted as a slightly ridiculous person. However, she becomes quite a central figure as the narrative unfolds and the polemical fact of her showing herself topless in one scene created a lot of discussion in the Brazilian media. This was part of Globo's drive to reconquer the ratings they were losing to the competing channel, TV Manchete. The story of Laurinha's upper class family mainly takes place in the elegant living room of the villa, with Greek marble statues, French chandeliers and antique European furniture. Other scenes occur in Laurinha's bedroom, at the race-course and at extravagant upper class parties.

Setting

The thematic setting for the story and the actual popularity of *Rubbish Queen* can best be understood if a number of specific socio-cultural conditions, characterizing Brazil and São Paulo in 1990, are explained:

The recognition of the rubbish story

"The sucateira... ooh yes, Maria do Carmo was her name" – this is how most of the women remember Maria do Carmo when I ask about her in my interviews. First they remember her main activity, secondly her name. Gildete (Vila Nitro Operaria, 63) explained to me what Maria do Carmo actually worked with: "It is litter, she works with litter, empty cans, these things people do not use any more. This she buys and resells to companies. It is similar to those who work over on the dump"

This story about a poor family getting rich by working with rubbish touched on an issue of current concern in Brazil. Throughout the 1980s social and economic marginalization grew, with the consequence that a growing number of people had to survive in the informal economy and in untraditional jobs. The theme of *Rubbish Queen* could hardly have been launched in Brazil of the 1970s. At that time there was economic optimism, at least in the political and economic elite, and development was praised. The elite was vulnerable in face of criticism.

In the Brazil of the 1990s the economic crisis is massive, and the optimism has vanished. Thus, the theme of *Rubbish Queen* fits better into the contemporary debate. *Rubbish Queen* is not negative, but actually the contrary. It gives an example of how people who are poor at the moment should not despair. The moral seems to be that by working hard, enduring a great deal, only believing in one's nearest relations and following one's own dream, one will succeed. A neo-liberal recipe for success. Just look at the *Rubbish Queen* herself – she made it!

With *Rubbish Queen*, Silvio de Abreu touched a responsive chord in many work-worn people, by creating a story out of the depressing fact that an increasing amount of Brazilians are forced to survive collecting litter and reselling what can be resold. It is undoubtedly a story that many recognized from life. By producing a comedy telenovela about a woman earning money this way, Rede Globo benefited from something which is a growing social problem.

The topicality of the story – part of realism

Not only does *Rubbish Queen* fit the overall socio-economic trends and the political climate. It also reflects very recent events from real life. *Rubbish Queen* was launched on 2 April 1990. Two weeks before, on 16 March, Brazil's newly elected president, the right-wing populist Fernando Collor de Melo had taken a series of initiatives to try and get the country's chaotic economic situation under control. One of the initiatives was to freeze all savings in bank accounts, making it impossible for everybody to withdraw their savings from the bank; this hit people on all social levels. These economic shock-tactics resulted in a thorough review of the first 30 chapters of *Rubbish Queen*, modifying and changing scenes and dialogue. The fact was that the political climate and not least the themes of the everyday gossip had suddenly changed. Silvio de Abreu wanted to include this situation of common concern and interest in his story. So he integrated references to the situation in the dialogue, for example when Laurinha says: "Our money is gone, and everyone we knows is in the same situation, because their money is locked in the banks, with this "economic rescue plan"" (Laurinha in chapter 2 of *Rubbish Queen*). The event is described in more detail in chapter 6.

Historical background

A third socio-cultural condition upon which the narrative of *Rubbish Queen* is based is the social stratification in Brazil, and especially in São Paulo which is Silvio de Abreu's home ground. The "local" class differences and class characteristics possess a significant drive, and thus potential for entertainment, in the story of *Rubbish Queen*. The São Paulo class situation is briefly as follows: The city of São Paulo was for many decades economically based on the coffee trade. This trade was – and is still – controlled by the local coffee barons, great landowners with significant fortunes. For a large part of this century they have been the economic and cultural elite of São Paulo. Politically, as well as economically, the industrial bourgisie gained importance in the process of modernization, described in chapter 3 of this book. Nevertheless, it is the traditional upper class of São Paulo, an almost aristocratic bourgoisie to which Laurinha belongs.

This elite has, despite having lived for centuries in Brazil, always maintained a strong cultural orientation towards Europe, especially towards France. This European orientation has been expressed in their aesthetics and thus in their lifestyle: their clothes, their speech, the interior decoration of their villas, their gastronomic taste, their hobbies and travelling customs. This cultural orientation away from Brazil, towards their roots, often centuries ago, in Europe, has resulted in what today seems like a decontextualized and somewhat artificial cultural orientation having very little to do with contemporary Brazil. It is comparable with – and is in fact a historical continuation of – the cultural trends among the wealthiest cariocas (inhabitants of Rio) in the *fin du siecle* period around 1900 (see chapter 5). It is not a product of the social reality in which they live, rather an escape from it.

On the other side we find the cultural identity, the aesthetics and the life-style which Mario do Carmo represents. Where Laurinha's life-style, language and general way of relating to the world are far from real life, the norms, aesthetics and lifestyle of Maria do Carmo are a classic example of the realist style. Maria do Carmo's cultural stance springs from the traditions among the lower social strata: the working class and other low-income groups. Maria do Carmo recognizes her roots in the Brazilian working class and thus in Brazilian popular culture. This despite the fact that she is only a second generation Brazilian. Her parents are/were Portuguese.

The conflict between Laurinha and Maria do Carmo reflects this contradiction in cultural orientation, where the traditional ruling class in São Paulo has followed

European elite cultural traditions, especially French traditions, while the lower social strata have not had any interest in this kind of high culture. Ultimately, the contrast between Laurinha and Maria do Carmo largely reflects existing differences between high and low cultural life-styles in Brazil.

Nevertheless, in *Rubbish Queen*, Silvio de Abreu seeks to destroy the traditional view about who actually possesses the biggest cultural and economic capital. He seeks to upset the pre-established idea that all the rich are chic and were born in "golden cradles" (a popular expression used about rich people having a privileged situation right from birth):

> It is a new way of reflecting a change which is already happening, the telenovela in itself won't change anything. The rich person, in the novelas, is still the type of person like Jorge Andrade who speaks French and is well-educated. On the contrary, the rich are today less "fine". The rich are no longer interested in the people who compose high society. What they want is to buy the high society, which has less and less importance in itself – the "casts" are smaller and smaller... I think I can say, without having major sociological pretensions, that *Rubbish Queen* is a novela about a new society being formed, in which the people who have more money are not the most refined, cool and European.
>
> *Abreu in* O Globo, *1.04.90*

According to Silvio de Abreu, the nouveaux riches are imposing new codes of conduct, not giving so much priority to the traditional aristocratic values but instead just buying what money can buy, no matter what: fine names, fashions, traditions, etc: "This new rich class wants what they like and can buy promptly with their money, no matter if what they buy is considered chic or not. My novela is a game (*brincadeira*) circling around this possibility" (Abreu in *Elle*, February 1990).

To a certain degree I agree with Silvio de Abreu in his description of *Rubbish Queen* as a telenovela about a society in formation. He touches upon some of the conflicts of the process of modernization in Brazilian society. His observations about the noveaux riches are obviously correct. However, I would say that this is exactly one of the characteristics of Brazilian telenovelas. They catch many of the contradicting phenomena of time, space and social relations that form the social reality of contemporary Brazil.

What has not changed other than for the worse – and which is not reflected in *Rubbish Queen*, or any other telenovela for that matter – are the living conditions among the very many low-income urban dwellers who have not managed to become nouveaux riches. The potential for identification in the narrative, and thus success among the audience, lies largely in Maria do Carmo having roots in low-income strata more than in the in-depth – and humorous – description of the living conditions of the nouveaux riches.

6. A queen is born: Producing the *Rubbish Queen*

> Telling stories is not at all just the work of the voice. In the authentic act of storytelling, the activity of the hand intervenes. With gestures involved in the work, the hand supports what is being said in a hundred different ways.
>
> *Benjamin, 1977: 74*

Telling a story is a complex matter, especially when told as a telenovela. In the stories told in Brazilian serial television fiction, Benjamin's "hundred different ways" are represented by technical elements such as music, sound, camera positions and film techniques as well as by the whole process of acting, directing and producing the telenovela. The many elements together constitute the narrative. Thus, many creative workers (Vink, 1988) influence the artistic process of producing a telenovela. Vink focuses on the creative worker's influence on the production process, though combining this with an analysis of telenovelas seen as an industrial product.

The artistic production of the narrative is deeply intertwined with industrial, commercial and organizational factors, all exerting an influence on the production process. Meanwhile, there have only a been a limited number of analyses of the actual production process of films or TV, so there is only a limited theoretical tradition to relate to. Researchers such as James E. Ettama (1982), Todd Gitlin (1985), Michael Bruun Andersen (1988) and Horace M. Newcomb (1991) have all approached production analysis from different perspectives. The Danish media researcher Poul Erik Nielsen (Nielsen, 1992) has tried to link their different approaches, creating an analytical synthesis outlining the general framework of production. He operates with four levels of analysis: (1) the inter-institutional; (2) the institutional; (3) the organization of the production process, and (4) the individual level in production.

Following this framework of analysis, the production of Globo telenovelas must be placed in the context of the Globo institution and the relation between Rede Globo and other institutions like TV networks (and telenovelas producers) as well as

Globo's relation to the state and other institutions of society. Thus, analysing the production of telenovelas must include an analysis of the interaction of individuals and institutions involved in the concrete process, seen in relation to the social, cultural and economic context in which they operate. Since the institutional and inter-institutional perspectives have been analysed in chapters 3, 4 and 5, the concrete production process and individuals' role will be analysed here, both as regards production in general and more specifically in the case of the *Rubbish Queen*.

This analysis must emphasize the fact that Globo telenovelas are the product of a well-organized private enterprise, where the telenovelas function as a means of reaching large markets. However, the telenovela form also constitutes a creative and artistic challenge whereby authors, actors and directors can reach a large audience. Thus, the commercial incentive behind the economic organization of a telenovela interrelates with artistic creation in the daily production scheme of the television networks. It is not possible to argue that telenovelas are either a commercial product or an artistic creation. They are both.

1. Central Globo de Produção

> Central Globo de Produção is the biggest producer of serial fiction in the world.
>
> *Manuel de Barreto, 1991*

When the first daily telenovelas were produced in the 1960s they were sponsored by major private enterprises such as Procter and Gamble, Colgate-Palmolive and Unilever. However, as described in chapter 4, production was gradually taken over by the TV networks themselves, who kept the production within their own organization as was the custom in the old Hollywood film studios in the 1930s. Comparing Globo's quantity of production today, it is significantly higher than in for example Italy, France or Australia (Mattelart, 1989). Furthermore, while most North American and European TV networks today buy their products from independent producers, Rede Globo have their own production facilities, organized in Central Globo de Produção, CGP. CGP is the body responsible for producing telenovelas.

CGP's production schedule is extremely tight, because telenovelas are open narratives, with later chapters being recorded when the series is already on air. The telenovela director Manuel de Barreto told me in an interview in 1991 that he usually keeps 12-15 chapters ahead of the chapter on air, while in the case of *Pantanal* (TV Manchete, 1990) he was sometimes only two chapters ahead. He has also produced telenovelas that were to go on air the same night. These time-constraints and short deadlines mean that a production has to be very efficient.

Within CGP's production scheme, hundreds of people are involved daily, from the author, director and actors, to the producer, editor, and camera team and all the people working in costume, lighting, set design etc. It is difficult to mark the exact limit between the creative and the industrial workers. Some see their job as a merely automatic, industrial activity, while others see it as a unique creative process, some do both. Among the many individuals involved, the author, the director and the actors are the most important creative workers. As Arraes states it: "The author has to write his 20 pages, the actor has to prepare forty scenes and the director has to direct sixty scenes every day" (Vink,1988: 149).

Central Globo de Produção - the largest producer of serial fiction in the world

The audience also plays a substantial role through the feed-back they provide, whether to the producer, the network, or the individual creative workers. The audience responds to the narrative both through taking part in test groups and on their own initiative by writing letters, making phone calls and commenting directly to the creative workers or the TV network. The individual workers however interact with each other on the terms laid down by of a specific production process, determined by commercial, economic and political constraints. No matter how complex the production process may seem, it follows certain basic lines:

The production process

The production of telenovelas is based on a standard formula which counts for all Rede Globo's telenovelas. This production process can be subdivided into three main phases:

1. From initial idea to approval of a synopsis: This indicates the phase from the birth of the idea for a novela to the decision to initiate production. In this phase the story is formulated, the characters defined and the first concrete reflections on the setting are elaborated.

2. Setting up the production scheme: This covers the period from the approval of the synopsis through the writing of the first 20-40 chapters, to the elaboration of a storyboard and the initial organization of the scenes into interiors and exteriors. It includes the design and creation of sets, for example the construction of a street or some houses in one of Rede Globo's outdoor film lots.

3. Production: The production is divided up into two sub-phases. Firstly the recording of the scenes including the editing of each chapter. Secondly the sound editing, which is a phase in itself.

Starting up the production of a telenovela is a very expensive process. Thus, before entering into a telenovela project, Rede Globo needs to have a high degree of certainty that the story can attract the audience, securing high ratings and thus securing advertisers. In a book on the production of telenovelas (Ortiz and Ramos, 1989), all the telenovela authors interviewed unanimously agreed that telenovelas are always based on a particular story-model – the feuilleton model, telling a story of everyday life, with basic dramatic ingredients such as love, hatred and jealousy. To ensure that this story is told in the best manner, the safest strategy is to let a well-known author write the telenovela, an author that has proven popular among the audience. So Rede Globo has contracts with a series of the best authors, like Gilberto Braga, Lauro Cesar Muniz, Silvio de Abreu, Dias Gomes and Carlos Lombardi. Their contracts with Rede Globo are usually for several years, thereby securing for Rede Globo a resource base with enough flexibility to provide for all the different telenovela sub-genres.

After an author has written a synopsis, it is sent to a series of analysts who judge whether the story and the characters will do or not. Once a story is judged to be of a sufficient qualitative level, it passes through another phase of analysis before finally passing on to the production sector of Globo. The most famous and popular telenovela authors have, despite their popularity, to pass through a considerable process of control, before entering phase two in the production process (Ortiz and Ramos, 1989).

The approval of the synopsis has two major consequences for the telenovela. One is dramaturgical: the story can then be structured, indicating the start, the main lines of development of the narrative and at least a suggestion to how it will end, although since this is an open narrative, the ending might change in the course of the development of the story. The approval of the characters and the selection of the cast are part of the process of decision-making related to the narrative.

The second consequence entailed in the selection of a particular story is of an organizational and budgetary nature. By outlining the characters – typically 25-35 in number – and by noting the sets that will be needed, the executive producer gets an idea of the budget that will be required. Once these two basic factors have been approved, the producer can begin to distribute the resources between actors, set-design and manufacture, costume, sound, directing and shooting, props and equipment. The author writes the first chapters, the storyboard begins to be elaborated, and the organization of interior and exterior scenes for the first chapters begin. Here we are both in the middle of phase two and simultaneously initiating phase three. The recording of scenes using the same sets, although belonging to different chapters, takes place on the same day(s). Interior and exterior recordings go on at the same time.

When a telenovela goes on air it is usual for 30-40 chapters to have been written, and 15-20 to have been recorded. However, these indices vary a lot. When the telenovela begins, the first chapters are carefully monitored to gauge the audience response and adjust characters and story to suit the taste of the audience. After the first critical phase of production, the telenovelas usually get into a more routine phase. A metaphor current among producers illustrates the crucial phase in the production process: "A novela is like a Boeing, the difficulty is getting it into the air. Once it gets to a good altitude you just have to turn on the automatic pilot" (Ortiz and Ramos, 1989: 137).

As the narrative develops, so do its numerous characters, although some in different ways than those originally planned by the author. The ratings may very well show that one character is surprisingly popular, another surprisingly unpopular. This can result in a change in the focus of a narrative. Throughout the development of the story, Globo carries out organized group discussions to test audience response. Depending on that response a certain modification as well as prolongation or restriction of the narrative can occur. If ratings are very low the telenovela might be cut short, or in the case of outstanding popularity, made longer The ending of a telenovela is usually a moment of almost national suspense, especially when it concerns the 7 and 8 o'clock telenovelas, which often obtain ratings above 50, 60 even 70, although average ratings today are around 40, whereas two decades ago the average was 60.

Within the framework of this basic production system multiple slight differences and alternative choices occur. However, given the fact that Central Globo de Produção produces three telenovelas simultaneously, recording about 30-40 minutes a day of each of them – the system must be highly efficient and professional. Therefore the basic framework is essential and practically always followed. It is summarized in the term that Globo uses about their own programmes: they have a *padrão Globo de qualidade* (a global level of quality).

Thus, the production of the global telenovela narrative evolves as a dialectic process, on one side taking shape within an industrial production process and on the other side developing as a living story, continuously integrating current concerns and trends from contemporary Brazilian society. This framework both gives the individual participants the freedom to make a living story evolve, and submits them to tough restrictions, and inflexible conditions in terms of time and space. However, above all, the production process of Globo telenovelas requires a high degree of professionalism from all the participating agents.

The commercial incentive

> Telenovelas are the most profitable products in the world's TV history.
>
> *Zevi Ghivelder, Programme director in*
> *Rede Manchete, 1986 in Mattelart 1989*

The main income for Rede Globo comes from commercials, and especially commercials in telenovelas. Thus, telenovelas have a strong commercial incentive integrated in their *raison d'etre*. The TV networks make money and the advertisers get their messages out to millions of viewers. Alongside advertising in the classic commercial breaks, merchandising is on the increase. The selling of secondary media texts as magazines, music, books and kitsch is a growing source of income for the "Global System of Communications" (*Sistema Globo de Produção*). Finally, an increase in international sales over the past 20 years has increased Globo's income. Summing up there are four main sources of income, which together constitute the commercial incentive for producing telenovelas:

(1) Commercials organized in blocs, interrupting the narrative approximately every 12-15 minutes;

(2) Merchandising, ie. advertising integrated into the narrative either by "merchandise actions" or"merchandise signals", which I will explain further below;

(3) Secondary media texts produced by other companies with the Globo enterprise;

(4) Export of telenovelas to countries all over the world.

Commercials organized in blocs

Telenovela chapters of the most usual length (one hour) include about 15 minutes of advertising organized in four blocs, each lasting 3-4 minutes. Each commercial last between 10-30 seconds. Also integrated into the one hour are a few minutes of self-promotion for the TV network. The blocs appear after every 11-13 minutes of the telenovela.

Compared with other kinds of fiction, telenovelas are relatively cheap to produce. They cost an average of between one and two and a half million dollars per telenovela, and typically contain 120-180 chapters. *Roque Santeiro* (Rede Globo, 1985/86) cost two million dollars, an average of 10-15,000 dollars per chapter (Ortiz et al. 1989). Rede Manchete states that their most expensive telenovelas were *Kananga*, which was made in Japan (1989) costing 8 million dollars, *Pantanal* (1990) costing 10 million dollars and *Ana Raio* and *Ze Trovão* (1991) costing 13 million dollars (Folha de São Paulo, 9.12.91). *Pantanal* was 209 chapters long, giving an average cost of 48,000 dollars a chapter.

Merchandising

Merchandising is understood as direct advertising for a specific product or type of product, integrated into the narrative. Within the past decade it has grown significantly as a way to advertise in telenovelas. However, merchandising is a phenomenon that has scarcely been studied. The TV networks are very sparing in providing information about this sort of advertising. Nevertheless, two things are sure: merchandising is increasing, and the prices differ a lot from product to product and from TV network to TV network. There are two types of merchandising. Firstly, product-endorsement: this is when one or more actors are directly involved in advertising for a product or a special type of action like cycling or sewing on a sewing machine. Secondly, there is product placement: this is when a product appears in a telenovela without the actor being actively involved in advertising for it.

Sistema Globo de Communicação has since 1978 had a company, Apoio, with about 30 employees, working specifically with the aim of investigating how and where merchandising can be integrated without harming the story too much. Rede Globo is very cautious about merchandising and runs related audience tests before implementing merchandising. It is a balance between earning money and delivering a telenovela of a reasonable quality which does not appear like one long advertisement.

Not all actors and authors are willing to accept merchandising. Some reject it completely, thus preventing themselves from participating in many telenovelas. Others are of the opinion that merchandising – as a method of influencing the audience to act in a specific way – should rather be used to promote education, community services and responsible social action, for example showing how to write an address on a letter, or to motivate new habits in hygiene or perhaps stimulate environmental concern. No significant systematic study has yet been carried out into the extent to which this method has been used in this way or what "effect" it may have had. However, it has always been present as an issue in telenovela production as well as in communication research on telenovelas. (For further reading on educative telenovelas, see Fuenzalida 1997, Rogers et al 1992.)

The majority of the actors and authors accept merchandising with a commercial objective. Some think it is quite OK, as for example the late author Janete Clair: "As it has been done so far, I find it OK, it is natural. The telenovela shows everyday scenes, so if a person in a telenovela is standing cooking in a scene, and uses a specific spice in the food, then it is reasonable that somebody pays for it". (*Jornal do Brasil*, 1982 in Mattelart, 1989: 76). With the financial crisis in Brazil in the 1980s Rede Globo experienced a period of recession. In addition, producing telenovelas was becoming more expensive, so new sources of income had to be found. The export market was one possibility, as I shall discuss below. Merchandising was another possible source of income. It does have a huge potential and can be seen as a partial reversion to the financial structure of the first telenovelas in Brazil in the 1960s, where one company sponsored a whole telenovela. This gave their name to the North American soap operas, where companies producing soap financed the day-time serials. With a trend in Brazil towards production of telenovelas aimed at more specific segments of society (see chapter 5), combined with an increased use of merchandising, it seems as though a creeping integration of entertainment and advertising will gradually result. This will demand increased audience attention, ultimately making it difficult to distinguish between what is mere entertainment and what is an attempt to convince the audience to buy, buy, buy.

Secondary media texts

Sistema Globo de Produção is, as described in chapter 4, a huge enterprise with more than 100 companies, among which there is Som Livre selling music, Editora Globo selling books and magazines, O Globo, one of Brazil's largest daily newspapers, Sistema Globo de Radio with more than 20 radio stations, Globo Video, Globosat, NetBrasil (distribution of pay-TV), Globo Cabo (cable), Nec do Brasil (telephone company), etc (Isto E, 19.7.95). Through this series of media companies, telenovela production is closely linked with the making of a long series of secondary products. These media products contribute to strengthening the media event that occurs when a new telenovela flows into everyday life. The flow of the telenovela is thus interwoven with many secondary texts. To illustrate how the media event is constituted by many secondary texts as well as the primary text, let me construct an example which, though fictitious in itself, is composed of elements that I have experienced personally, or read about, or heard of:

Globo is to launch the eight o'clock telenovela *Happy Days* in early April. The telenovela is written by Ivani Ribeiro and has Regina Duarte and Tarcisio Meira as the principal actors. The synopsis of the telenovela was approved by Rede Globo in January, and Ivani Ribeiro has since then been working on the script. The press have been informed about the forthcoming telenovela. In February they begin to write articles about the actors, the director, the author and about the theme which the telenovela is going to approach. Both Globo's radios and O Globo make reportages from the first exterior recordings in the Globo film studio park.

Straight after the synopsis was approved, the famous musician Gilberto Gil was contacted to write the musical theme, which is going to be the opening song of the telenovela. Late February this song is written and recorded by Som Livre. It begins to appear as a jingle on the radio. On television the first commercials advertising the forthcoming telenovela appear early in March, accompanied by the opening song. In late March the CD, LP and cassette with all the songs sung by Brazilian artists in the telenovela appear in shops. Globo's Som Livre has also planned their policy for popular music nationwide, on the expectation that Gilberto Gil's other records will sell more, and the other musicians playing similar music will enjoy a revival. Gilberto Gil plans a tour some months later, including the telenovela song in the repertoire.

Around the time of the launch of the telenovela, magazines, t-shirts, caps, stickers, booklets and videotapes appear with features, images, articles, etc linked to the narrative of the story as well as to the actors.The day before the first chapter is screened a 20-page press release is issued by Rede Globo with everything about the telenovela: the story itself, including long quotations from the actors, the author, the director and the producer. Subsequently, on the first day of the telenovela, the newspapers are full of almost identical articles. The first couple of days after, many more articles follow, with the first reactions and reviews.

Now the radio stations are playing the songs all the time and in the late morning radio shows there are revelations about what is going to happen in the next chapters. In addition, all the major newspapers publish TV editions discussing chapters, interviewing actors and revealing stories from the telenovela. Women's magazines such as *Contigo* and *Amiga* do the same. This continues throughout the run of the telenovela.

Some months after the beginning of the telenovela, Som Livre launches a CD, LP and cassette with all the international songs that appear in the telenovela. Som Livre have bought the rights to sell these songs. With *Happy Days*, the focus is on international rock stars, with songs by Guns and Roses, AC/DC and Bruce Springsteen. Now these begin to appear on the radio. Thus, two different CDs – one with national music and one, some months later, with international music – are linked to the same telenovela. Throughout the period of the telenovela, talk shows, game shows, debate programmes, and many other similar TV and radio programmes include interviews and appearances by the actors of the telenovela.

When finally, 6, 7 or 8 months later, the telenovela *Happy Days* comes to an end, the enormous attention given to the telenovela, reflected in Rede Globo's own spin-offs as well as in the other media entering into the turbulence of the event, suddenly disappears. However, the media do not remain quiet and the viewers, listeners and readers remain far from empty-handed. What happens is that everybody's attention now turns to a new similar media event.

As the example shows, there is a massive presence of secondary media texts thus creating a substantial vertical dimension of intertextuality. It is an almost permanent presence throughout the total screening period of six to eight months, after which it is superseded by the launching of a new telenovela with new actors, other songs, etc, but with the same format in secondary media texts.

These spin-offs together constitute a substantial additional source of income to Rede Globo's other companies, especially the sale of music. The primary and secondary texts thus constitute a veritable media event, a period of keen attention on the story, the characters, the actors, the music, the author and the themes of current telenovelas. This whole event has a significant presence in the everyday life of the audience.

Exporting telenovelas

The fourth source of income from telenovelas is export. Since Globo began exporting they have sold telenovelas to more than 130 countries world-wide (Marques de Melo, 1988). The prices they charge differ substantially. In some cases the programmes are not sold for money but for influence. In Portugal for example, the first private TV network, SIN, opened in the autumn of 1992. Rede Globo owns 15 per cent of the stock. However, they did not pay cash, but provided the network with a certain amount of programmes, especially telenovelas (Grisolli, 1993).

The telenovelas exported by Globo are edited versions of the national ones. The narrative thus undergoes a substantial transformation: the characteristics of the open narrative, which makes it possible to integrate current social, cultural, political and economic Brazilian events are often precisely what is edited out. Thus, reactions to telenovelas in for example Europe, as being stereotypical and simplistic can be partially explained by this re-editing for export.

A complex, first class, profitable narrative

The complexity of the production process has been documented in this chapter. However, my analysis has also shown that telenovelas are far from just being just an entertaining work of art. Obviously, the commercial interest is strong: Globo is interested in producing a popular programme, something of good quality and something entertaining, because this can attract companies that want to advertise, either via ordinary commercials or merchandising. And the higher the ratings, the more Globo charges for advertising, and the more money they make. Furthermore, Globo expanded their production of secondary media texts a great deal of recent years. The production of music, magazines, books and kitsch thus constitute a growing source of income for Rede Globo.

In the midst of these commercial interests we find a long line of creative workers who on the individual level contribute to the artistic creation of the narrative. Some of these have their personal ideological, educational, moral or purely artistic agenda which they seek to transmit. However, this must occur within the commercial, political and economic framework given by Rede Globo and the codes of practice determined by state power – and by the audience.

Summing up, the interaction occurring between artistic and commercial production has for many years resulted in a product which is able to keep 70-80 million Brazilians in front of the television night after night. The increased advertising, not least through merchandising, obviously signifies an increased commercialization of the television industry. Nevertheless, in the midst of these commercial trends, we find a group of creative workers who contribute in their own way to the production of professional and high quality television.

2. Creative workers

When a chapter of a telenovela ends, a list of names, typically 30-50 in number, run across the screen. These are the main participants in the production of this narrative, even though a much larger number participate in the actual process. These individuals are divided into different areas, such as writing, acting, directing, music, costume, set design and construction, lighting and camerawork.

However, some areas obviously play a more significant role in the narrative. The ones I will highlight are: (1) The author (s), who develops his/her (or somebody else's) idea into a written story: (2) The director, who receives the manuscript and is responsible for the daily transformation of the story into recorded chapters of the telenovela; (3)The actors playing characters in the story; (4) The audience, who provide the actors, directors and authors – as well as other individuals in the production process – with feedback in multiple ways. To analyse the extent to which the telenovela is an artistic product, the creative process must thus be examined in terms of individual participation in this process.

Novela de autor

In daily speech, Brazilians often refer to telenovelas like *Roque Santeiro*, by Dias Gomes and Aguinaldo Silva, as being by those authors. In this everyday way, the audience acknowledges the central role of the author, by attributing the work to him/her. As we shall see, several other people have central roles in the artistic process. However, unlike soap operas, theatre, cinema or even TV series, the principal creative worker in telenovelas is the author.

> The cinema is the art of the director, there he is sovereign, like the actor in the theatre. But in the novela, despite all these professionals being indispensable, it is not like that. If the story does not catch on, does not move, if there are no characters that really hook the viewer, the director can only do so much. If the author does not write the scenes, does not focus the story on the points of interest to the audience, the actor won't have a chance to display his skill properly. The novela depends basically on the author.
>
> *Abreu, 1985*

The author participates in the selection of the cast, often determining who is to be chosen. Often, authors even write the stories with specific actors in mind for the main roles. However, the fundamental fact which makes the telenovela so dependent on the author, is that it is an open narrative. Once the synopsis has been approved by the director-general of Globo Production the production process begins, leaving very short deadlines, where the manuscripts written by the author are passed on to the director with only minimal revision.

To assist him or her in the very intensive process of writing an entire chapter (30-40 pages) every day, six days a week, the author often has one or more assistant writers. The author typically meets them once a week to give them the gist of the story for the following chapters, and then leaves it to them to write the dialogue. The author then discusses their dialogue with them, and adapts it to suit his or her own ideas, before handing the manuscript on to the next link in the production chain. After the first chapter the author usually hands over six at a time – equivalent to one week's broadcasting.

The elite of telenovela authors in Brazil today have quite a broad range of backgrounds , reflecting both "high" and "low" cultural origins, and having different ambitions in their writing, but nevertheless following the same basic formula in their stories. Some have a background as actors in radio (Avancini), television (Abreu) and theatre (Abreu), some as playwrights in the theatre (Gomes), some as authors of radionovelas two or three decades ago (Gomes and Ribeiro). Some also have their roots in circus families (Abreu).

Many left-wing creative producers (authors, actors and directors) entered television because the military coup of 1964 and especially the decrees of 1968 put an end to progressive cultural activity in the theatre and the cinema (Cinema Novo), in the very years where TV was expanding. Dias Gomes was one of these. However, the famous producer of Cinema Novo films, the late Glauber Rocha, expressed himself very critically towards the critical creative workers from the former communist party who entered and helped build Rede Globo:

> Once the Communist Party was declared illegal, the intellectuals closely linked to the party, whose names I shall keep to myself, got completely corrupted. The large majority of the actors, directors, writers, etc went to work for Globo, during the dictatorship of General Medici. They became corrupt, both politically speaking and on the aesthetic level: a disaster. They sold themselves to Roberto Marinho for a ridiculous price.
>
> *Rocha, quoted in Mattelart, 1989*

One of these was Dias Gomes, who for more than 30 years was an active member of the communist party. While the general attraction of TV for many of the authors, actors and directors of critical film and theatre lay in the lack of jobs after the closing down of all critical cultural channels of expression, they were also fascinated by the idea of being able to communicate their work to millions of viewers. This, they were not always able to do, if the message was not too critical. Dias Gomes, for example, wrote the telenovela Roque Santeiro in 1975, which was prohibited by the state censorship and was only able to be screened in 1986, in a revised edition, becoming one of the most popular telenovelas in the history of the genre Brazil. The late Dias Gomes considered himself an anarcho-marxist and an intellectual with social responsibilities (Mattelart, 1989 and Vink, 1988).

Other authors, like Dias Gomes' wife Janete Clair, had basically only a telenovela background and a completely different aim in their work, focusing on the emotions of their audience and concerned basically with the ambition of giving the viewers dramatic entertainment passing on moral values at the same time.

Others again do not have any illusions as to what message they can pass on to the viewers. Answering a question on what responsibility he considers the author of a telenovela to have when addressing a potential audience of 80 million people, Silvio de Abreu states:

> I don't think of this, I simply write. I do it for myself, trying to pass on something honest, positive. I think this is what makes people have joy, laugh and become fond of the characters. I never worry about whether they are good or not, and whether I am passing on strange ideas to people. Novelas are something watched very superficially, they do not pass any strange ideas on to anybody. You find all the movement of the living room, people walking by, people asking questions, children

crying, the daughter's boyfriend arriving, the doorbell, the telephone. And every 15 minutes everything stops and somebody appears saying "buy this and buy that". What is passed on via telenovelas is "modismos", a new earring, a different skirt... I think it is a characteristic of television itself. It is not a space for serious things, heavy stuff, like the theatre or the cinema with their dark halls.

Abreu in Elle, *1990*

Authors in general see telenovelas as stories rooted in a basic formula which has to do with emotional drama that obviously catches the audience. However, the context in which it takes place differs. It can deal with public affairs – or not; it can touch upon morally controversial themes, or include politically sensitive dialogue. The aspect of "passing on a message" is prevalent among most authors, recognizing the fact that they are communicating with a massive audience. However, they do not overestimate the transcending effects their telenovela may have. They generally express equal concern about entertaining the audience, creating a high quality story and of reaching as many people as possible. Thus, telenovela authors belong to no uniform category, having very different backgrounds and very different ambitions in their work. While Silvio de Abreu limits his ambition to entertainment Dias Gomes tried – despite the superficial character of the television medium, which he recognized – to maintain a political dimension. Benedito Ruy Barbosa describes the double role between artistic ambition and social responsibility as follows:

> Recognizing that I had a very powerful instrument in my hands penetrating into every home, and that the audience was a very important factor for the enterprise – paying me for writing and the advertisers for selling their products via this medium – I always had in mind that it is necessary to reach the audience. I also wanted to build that audience in order to be valued as an author. But at the same time I did not forget that with such a large audience I had a good opportunity to discuss certain matters which needed to be discussed, e.g. education. As I did in *Pe de Vento* criticizing the Brazilian educational system.
>
> *Ruy Barbosa quoted in* Vink, *1988: 146-147*

When asking authors about the influence of the audience upon their work, several authors – like Gomes, Clair and Andrade – find the role attributed to the audience exaggerated. Others give it a large importance, like Silvio de Abreu talking about "the echo from the streets":

> Through the echo that reaches the author from the streets, from the newspapers, among friends, in the family, from the servants, the doorkeepers, the cleaners, the elevator men, the market workers, and many others, through this echo the work is completed. Like a boomerang, the ideas are thrown into the air, absorbed by the viewers and return as answers to the author who then develops them further. All of this happens in a magic space stretching over seven or eight months,

as if it were a long conversation between this professional and the millions of loyal viewers, who then, the following Monday, forget all about those stories when a new novela appears and a new dialogue begins.

Abreu, 1985

Again, no uniform statement can be made about how much the audience influences the author in his or her writing. This differs from author to author. Some consider the writing of a telenovela as their individual creative process, obviously identifying themselves as unique interpreters of an idea, while others have a more pragmatic attitude, acknowledging that the ratings influence the development of the narrative. However, my impression is clearly that the author, in the process of writing, produces a written narrative that firstly depends of the personal background of the author, thereby giving the story a personal touch, a style – and a message. Secondly it follows some clear guidelines – a basic formula, recognizable in all telenovelas. Thirdly, it is influenced by its context – the views of the Globo executive or producer, the ratings, letters from the audience or trends and events in contemporary Brazilian society.

I will leave it to Silvio de Abreu to conclude this analysis with his remarks emphasizing the fact that the production process is a mixture of industry and art:

Behind that blank page which the author has to fill with dialogue, romance, adventure or whatever, there are more than two hundred employees at a television broadcasting station, depending on those ideas to get something made! It is an industry which has to be kept going with emotion, art, interest, in daily doses without interruption. No matter what happens in the private life of an author, he cannot stop having brilliant ideas, daily.

Abreu, 1985

The Directors

The director in a telenovela is the person who dictates the artistic path of the narrative (Avancini, 1991). It is he who – after having chosen the cast together with the author – transforms the manuscript into a televised story. According to the Brazilian director Paulo Grisolli, who worked for 20 years in Rede Globo, the fundamental challenge as a director is to make the story come alive, to be able to transform the drama in the written text into an emotional experience for the audience (Grisolli, 1992). According to the late Paulo Ubiratan, former director of the main telenovela unit in Rede Globo, the secret of directing telenovelas is to follow the principles of the classic feuilleton: "The novela that functions is the old feuilleton... If you diverge from the feuilleton, then it is not novela" (Ubiratan in *Isto É*, 20.3.91). This is obviously a polemical statement, and has been thoroughly contradicted, or at least substantially nuanced in my analysis of the genre and its historical roots (see chapter 3 and 5). However, if being like a feuilleton means placing a strong emphasis on emotion and drama, and serving it up repetitively over a long period of time, then Ubiratan is obviously right.

The two basic tasks of the director of telenovelas are to direct the actors and to create the language of the telenovela – that is to give the script a televised expression, a televised grammar, with a certain rhythm, a certain combination of characters, with emphasis on drama and stimulating identification. Additionally, if you are able to combine love and tragedy in the right doses the ultimate result should then be a true telenovela. In concrete terms, the director is present in the studio throughout the whole process of recording. In order to get an idea of the language and texture of the narrative being produced, Grisolli considers it important to follow the work on the monitor. Only thereby can he imagine how it will appear in the homes of the audience. The process of creation and the relation between director and actors is a lengthy, very intensive and demanding process. Ubiratan describes it like this:

> Novela, really, is like an eight month marriage, a real marriage where the people love each other, and are able to keep it up for eight months. Imagine being with 30 people with whom you live together professionally (...) and who you see much more than your wife. Its obvious that the quarrels are much more frequent. Every one of them has a problem and the director ends up being the great father for them all.
>
> *Ubiratan in* Isto É, *20.3.91*

In the working process, many of the directors – and especially the experienced ones – emphasize the significance of intuition. Paulo Ubiratan works on "feeling", on intuition (*Isto É*, 20.3.91). Atilio Riccó, Director of TV Drama at Rede Manchete emphasizes this "competence" as a principal one for the director (Riccó, 1991). The director Jorge Fernando, also from Rede Globo, states that he does not have to read the script before arriving in the studio:

> Today my intuition is so refined that I do not even have to read the chapters, not before the moment of recording. I do take a lot of risks – but that's the great fun of creation. Planning, studying and cutting scenes before the process of realization does become very frustrating in the end, because in television it is never possible to realize all you imagined. The important thing is to have the full command of the whole team – cast and technicians – to be able to get an external shoot done anywhere: on the beach, on the square or in the shopping centre. It is important to chose one route forward and keep it until the end.
>
> *Fernando in* Veja, *September 1991*

The basic challenge is thus to get a feeling of the language, the rhythm and the vivacity of the narrative. Although the artistic process does allow the director a creative space even in his work the dichotomy between artistic creation and industrial production remains. The directors are aware of this, and indeed the whole process of production, with its continuous activity and short deadlines combines to emphasize it. Manuel Barreto is very aware of this fact:

> I work with emotion all day long. However, I have to have one thing clear in my mind, to avoid becoming frustrated or romanticizing the situation: I know my skills are being used to create a product. Having just finished a job full of emotion, I know that I have been transmitting my emotion: In the last weeks of *Pantanal* there was a scene of intense emotion every day, with people crying in the scene, and I was very touched while directing, passing on this emotion or taking the emotion out of them. I got deeply touched myself (...)However, I have to understand that this emotion is packaged, put into a machine and sold. It is a product.
>
> *Barreto, 1991*

However, despite having the industry "breathing down their necks" all the time, Barreto and the other directors always have the ambition of creating drama, mobilizing emotions and transmitting them from the director to the actor, making emotions grow in the actor so as to appear genuine on the screen. The widespread ideal among directors is obviously to create a language that is expressed in a way that not only looks real, but is real.

When I asked Barreto about the relation between director and audience, he stated that there was none really. According to him, the ratings gathered by the Globo Network are used and integrated by the leaders of the producing enterprise (CGP) and the author, simply in order to get better ratings next time. However ratings can create a bad spirit among the production-team, giving the director the responsibility of keeping their spirits up.

The directors of telenovelas have a central role in the production process. They have great power, and they are continually on the spot as the narrative takes shape. Nevertheless, they are not well known to the public, often remaining completely unknown. Their central role in the artistic process is not recognized. Nico Vink attributes this fact to their replaceability (Vink, 1988: 147). It is seldom that one person directs an entire telenovela. Often interior and exterior scenes are directed by different people, or you also find quite frequently that one director will direct 40-50 chapters, and then another takes over. This was the case with *Pantanal*, for example, as Barreto explained to me:

> In the beginning we were four. For example, Jaime only did the beginning, he and Roberto did the middle, and I was to going to start at chapter 16, but ended up entering right from the beginning. Roberto was responsible for editing, then he went, and Jaime, Magalhaes and I were left. After chapter 16, Jaime left, and after chapter 30 Roberto came back in again. That way, there was always somebody resting.
>
> *Barreto, 1991*

Their role as intermediaries between the author and the actors clearly works against their getting any public credit. They are not the ones to appear on the screen, neither the ones to write the dialogues, but like in film production, they are nevertheless the ones who interpret the script and lead the process of transforming it into a audio-visual narrative. This often occurs in close cooperation with the author, though leaving the spotlight to shine mainly on the actors.

The actors

Brazilian actors are some of the most popular and well known public figures in Brazil, better known even than the president with some social groups. Many Brazilians follow the private lives of the principal actors in magazines, TV talk shows, newspapers and in radio interviews. Actors thus occupy a substantial part of the public space, the media event, surrounding the screening of a telenovela.

The task of the actor

Unlike soap operas, telenovelas attract the best actors in the country, including Regina Duarte, one of the most well-known actresses in Brazil: "All I want is to be an active member of society through the programmes, to be sensitive and try to express some of the worries I sense around me. By expressing some of these worries I would like to get in contact with the audience. My career is dedicated to them." (*Estado de São Paulo*, 21.11.92).

Regina Duarte has been one of the most popular actresses in the history of Brazilian telenovelas. Some years ago she said that early in her career Walter Avancini taught her the power of the look, the expression, on television (*Imprensa*, July 1990). Avancini commented on this: "I think the actor should be more aware that he/she seduces the viewer via the essential part of the person. If you are not seductive, the viewer will not relate to you. Thus, looking is fundamental. If you go on a stage you have your body to express yourself with, however on television it is your look you give the viewer" (Avancini in *Imprensa*, July 1990).

The actor Tarcisio Meira, one of the most popular male actors, argues that playing a role in a telenovela is more challenging than a role in a film or a play: "It is more difficult. In the theatre and in the cinema, the characters have a beginning, a middle and an ending – they are closed characters. On television you only know the character as he takes shape in the course of the development of the telenovela. This is a challenge to any actor" (*Veja*, 11.03.87). So the character can grow as the narrative develops. The task of the telenovela actor is to deliver a contribution to a product for immediate consumption (Lima Duarte in *Vink*, 1988: 152) keeping in mind the continuity of the character for months and months.

The crucial phase for the character, as for the telenovela as a whole, is at the beginning. That is when the main features of the planned character are outlined. Walter Avancini – seeing the artistic process of the actor from the perspective of the director – seeks to make the actor leave the external aspects of the character and move towards the interior aspects, the personality:

> The actor should first of all seek the essential element of the personality. Every character has a central element, his nucleus, his deepest ego, which gives him identity in any circumstance, dramatic or happy, unhappy or not. We are all like that. We have a personality that determines our gestures, what we sound like, all the ways we manifest ourselves. Thus, I like to choose this essential element of the character and gradually get into it, only later seeking the external aspects. You construct a pyramid with the other elements. This gives the characters more substance, you work/mould the actors with more density. It is in the course of this process that the personalities of the characters develop, their way of walking, their body-language.
>
> *Avancini in* Imprensa, *July 1990*

136

The actor's position in the novela industry

Working as an actor in the Brazilian television industry is a hard job. First of all it demands careful preparation by the actor. The director Walter Avancini, a former actor himself, always spends at least a month with the cast prior to production. They have to work hard, getting into their role, developing their character, learning the lines. According to Tarcisio Meira, his role as the main character in *Burning Circle*, comes to about 2000 pages, or about the size of a book (Meira in *Veja*, 11.03.87). Once the production is going, and as they produce 6 chapters a week, working Monday to Saturday, this often leaves very little time to study their role beforehand.

In addition to working hard, the actors are badly remunerated. In1987 there was a conflict, when the actors in Globo wanted a shorter work week. Tarcisio Meira backed it up: "The campaign was more than just. The workload was inhuman... The salaries payed to the actors are very low, even for the actors of the so-called first team... The profits generated by our work at Globo are very badly distributed. The percentage paid to the actors when a novela is sold for export is absolutely nothing, it's really ridiculous" (*Veja*, 11.03.87).

There are a number of factors which make it easy for Globo to keep wages low: (1) the magnitude of the pool of unemployed actors; (2) the weakness of the artistic workers' trade union, which cannot negotiate properly; (3) the actors' own attraction to a mass medium, which can bring them national and even international fame.

Artistic creation vis-à-vis industrial production

Among the actors in television there is a clear awareness of the industrial process of production in which they are participating. The actor Antonio Calmon states: "It is good to remember that television is an electronic commodity whose place in your living room ensures that it fulfills its function of transmitting commercials and other propaganda. The programmes exist to keep the attention of the viewer on the commercials." (Calmon in *Estado de São Paulo*, 21.11.92). Nevertheless, Calmon is very pleased to have a job in the TV business. As a former film producer of the Cinema Novo tradition, and having worked with Glauber Rocha, Calmon obviously comes from a critical, left-wing cultural avant garde. However, contrary to Rocha (see Rocha-quotation earlier in this chapter), he speaks favourably of the possibilities television has given him (Calmon in *Estado de São Paulo*, 21.11.92).

Many actors have a background in theatre and many work in the theatre alongside their jobs in television. However, television does have a strong attraction for them, because it is, after all, a bigger market and thus offers the potential for stable employment. For many professional actors, theatre has a higher cultural esteem. However, José Wilker points out that it is thanks to television that the acting profession has gained public approval. It was through his jobs on TV, and not in the theatre, that he became widely recognised as an actor.

The influence of the audience

The influence of the audience is, when seen from the TV network's point of view, substantial. Media researchers and creative workers in the telenovela industry mean rather different things when they talk about audience influence. The audience themselves, for example the women in my case study, cannot imagine that they have any influence at all. However, since telenovelas are very dependent on income from advertisers, the audience plays a fundamental role. Consequently, Rede Globo puts significant effort into trying to find out what the audiences likes and dislikes about their programmes. There are three main methods by which Rede Globo obtains information about the audience:

a. Measuring ratings

Along with the other major TV networks, Globo has a contract with the public bureau of polls, Ibope. Ibope carries out all their surveys. Since 1990 they have had a TV-meter installed in São Paulo covering 1000 households. The TV networks can also order specific surveys from Ibope.

b. Audience tests every 20 chapters, once a month

Rede Globo has its own unit dedicated to systematically assessing audience response. This is a combination of quantitative surveys, which ask questions about telenovela content, and group interviews with a representative section of the mass audience who are invited to Globo for the purpose. Somebody from the Globo production unit is always present, and the authors of telenovelas are also invited to listen in to the audience's comments, unseen from a room next door. Some accept this invitation, but many others don't.

c. Occasional feed-back to the networks

A third category of feedback is the individual responses which the networks receive from viewers in the form of letters, phone calls, comments in the street and in newspapers and magazines. Often, the letters are addressed to the actors, sometimes to the network, and from time to time also to the authors of telenovelas.

The director Manuel de Barreto, the media researcher João Luiz Van Tilburg, and the author Silvio de Abreu all have different opinions as to what extent the audience really influences the process of producing telenovelas. Barreto warns against romanticizing the influence of the audience. He compares TV networks with any other industry, and emphasizes that market analysis is a central element in any industry: knowing the needs and interests of the consumers. He thus acknowledges the need for a systematic collection of data and surveys, but equates it to other industries's efforts in this direction. This response is then integrated in the overall planning of the novela by the author and the production unit. Once Barreto as a director receives the script the possible response has been integrated into the script. Thus, he does not – in his position in the production process – sense any influence from the audience.

João Luiz van Tilburg argues, on the basis of a reception analysis he did of 3000 letters sent by viewers to Rede Globo – and especially to the leading actress in *Rubbish Queen* – that there is strong interaction between the viewers and the TV network.

The author Silvio de Abreu is probably the most positive of the three in judging the influence of the audience. As Barreto says, the author happens to be the most centrally placed in terms of receiving audience response. It is fundamental in the production process that the authors become aware of the nature of that response. If they do not study the actual response, they still receive production priorities dictated by the executive producer, so on this overall level the audience certainly does have an influence. Silvio de Abreu's statement below polemically emphasizes the strong influence of the audience, as least upon some authors:

> No will within the area of telenovela is stronger than the will of the audience. Nothing intervenes more than the people. As a rule, the author has to be aware of this, has to have the capacity of capturing their sovereign will. This is why telenovelas are unconquerable in Brazil:even in the darkest years they were always democratic. In contrast to what happens in the political world, where the deepest worries of the people are only seldom satisfied, the telenovela always meets their desires. What a pity this is only fiction.
>
> *Abreu, 1985*

Three characteristics

If we summarize the general production scheme for telenovelas, especially Globo-novelas, three main characteristics are clear:

a. Telenovelas are media events: the strategic planning and vigorous marketing of a telenovela results in a strong impact on society. The combination of the text with the production of many secondary texts creates a media environment in which Brazilians cannot avoid knowing that a new telenovela is about to begin and acquiring some knowledge about it. The media flow is substantial. It becomes an everyday event in society that is sustained for six to eight months.

b. Telenovelas are industrial products: telenovelas are commodities produced efficiently and on industrial terms. Probably they have the shortest deadlines in the world for the production of fiction serials, which demands a very tight and well organized production process. Every individual has well defined roles. Furthermore, telenovelas have strong and very apparent commercial incentives. The advertisers reach huge markets and the network often makes a large profit.

c. Telenovelas are, simultaneously, artistic productions: The individuals in the production process are responsible for this. Obviously, well defined ingredients must be included in the narrative, in the acting and in the whole language of the telenovela, but this does leave room for creative processes.

The large majority of the creative workers have an artistic ambition: to express themselves precisely and well in their role, to write a very entertaining story or to create a language and a texture which challenges the traditional televisual style: each creative worker has his or her artistic ambition. However, some also operate with ideological and political ambitions – expressed in subtexts laid into the story by the author, or in a new focus or perspective in the work of the director, or in the acting.

However, artistic creativity, subversive agendas and other individual ambitions and ideas are ultimately determined by the owner of the medium: Globo. Barreto states it polemically: "During the period of dictatorship a scene could be cut out, but now our heads are cut off". If the creative workers cross the invisible lines of ethics, morality and especially politics, they most probably lose their jobs.

3. Producing *Rubbish Queen*

> ... the ideas come to me as they came to Fellini: one signs a contract and is then obliged to write.
>
> *Abreu in* Elle, *February 1990*

Silvio de Abreu got the idea for *Rubbish Queen*, among other sources of inspiration, from a study carried out by the research enterprise "Saldiva e Associados Propaganda" in São Paulo. It stated that the nouveau riches had gained substantial influence on the São Paulo economy, and that the traditional families, considered the haute bourgoisie of São Paulo, were losing influence, though trying to keep up the prestige of their names, and maintain their extravagant life styles.

What follows is an analysis of the process of producing a specific telenovela: *Rubbish Queen*. It has a swift tempo. The first chapter has 62 scenes, of with only eight are in a studio. There are an average of 34 scenes per chapter, which is a very high dramatic tempo, compared with for example *Que Rei Sou Eu* by Dias Gomes (Rede Globo, 1986) which was also directed by Jorge Fernando. It had 19 scenes per chapter. The number of employees credited in the press release of *Rubbish Queen* is 76, spread over categories like: directing, production, costume, sets, etc. However, as in most telenovelas, the author had a very significant role to play as will be analysed below.

The author

The offer to write the telenovela came to Abreu from Globo director Boni in October 1989. Officially it was not Abreu's turn to write a telenovela for Globo. It was Dias Gomes' turn to write the 8 o'clock telenovela, but he had other commitments. Abreu was offered the job, and in one month he wrote a detailed synopsis outlining the plot, setting, characters and principal scenes. Normally Abreu takes four to five months over this process. All elements had to be accepted by Globo productions, among them the choice of director and cast. Abreu wanted to work with Jorge Fernando as his director. They had worked together on almost all Abreu's telenovelas. Abreu also wanted to choose the cast himself, and openly admitted writing the script for specific actors: "I wrote thinking of Regina Duarte and Glória Menezes. Because they are perfect for the characters, but also because it is something new having them working together. This has not happened since the 1960s in *Deusa Vencida*, which also was Regina's first starring role on television" (Abreu in *Elle*, February 1990). Tony Ramos' role as Edu was also written for him.

Abreu succeeded in getting the cast he wanted, consisting of many old colleagues and friends. However, it was the first time Regina Duarte had acted in one of his novelas – an old wish of his which was finally fulfilled. He also brought new names to television, among them Marisa Orth as Nicinha, which came to be one of the most popular characters of *Rubbish Queen*. Abreu brought Marisa Orth from the theatre to television, as he had done with many other actors before her.

Rubbish Queen was the first time that Rede Globo screened an 8 o'clock telenovela set in from São Paulo. Usually, Rede Globo set the main narrative in Rio de Janeiro. However, if they wanted Silvio de Abreu, he set the condition of having full freedom:

> I only accepted on condition of having the same freedom as I have with 7 o'clock telenovelas. I have twice said 'no thank you' to offers of writing novelas for the "noble hour" exactly because the invitation came with the restriction that there was not to be too much comedy. I've written telenovelas for 10 years, I think I have marked a style. Furthermore, if they want drama, there are authors who can write it better than Silvio de Abreu.
>
> *Abreu in* Elle, *February 1990*

Writing the script is a routine work process. Silvio gets up at 6am and begins writing at 8. He then works for 10-12 hours and produces approximately one chapter a day. He sits at home writing. His computer is on-line with the television network to facilitate quick communication. When in the process of writing, he has a series of consultants and researchers assisting him, as well as one or more co-authors. In the first 36 chapters of *Rubbish Queen* Abreu had the society-lady Danusa Leão as an assistant (registered as co-author in the credits). She is part of the haute bourgeoisie in São Paulo and could thus assist by providing him with stories and situations and by correcting Abreu's understanding of their life. Later on José Antonio de Souza took over. In the middle of the telenovela, Silvio de Abreu's brother died, which resulted in Abreu asking Gilberto Braga to step in and take over for him for a while. Throughout the process, Silvio de Abreu maintained the overall supervision of how the narrative was to unfold, even when others where doing the actual scriptwriting.

Due to sudden political and economic changes in Brazil, the initial part of the script suddenly had to be revised and partially rewritten. On 16 March 1990, 17 days before the first chapter was to go on air, president Collor initiated the economic Plano Collor. This Collor Plan had a huge effect on the economy of Brazilian society. Thus, it had to be integrated into the story: "When the package came, I stopped writing for two days until I understood the consequences of it. Then I had to rewrite the first 700 pages, because if I hadn't done that, the novela, which unfolds around the life of a businesswoman, would risk becoming a "story of an era" (name given to the historical telenovelas screened at 6 o'clock for many years)" (Abreu in *Jornal do Brasil*,1.4.90).

It lies in the nature of the more realistic 8 o'clock telenovelas that they reflect contemporary concerns and integrate references to major events occurring in Brazilian society. What happened with the Collor Plan was that all the savings in bank accounts were frozen, people were prohibited from taking out their money. This came as a shock and struck all social classes hard. For the decadent haute bourgeoisie living on their interest rates from the 'over', a form of lucrative short-term investment,[1] it was a catastrophe. As Abreu stated:

> The decadence of Laurinha, an aristocrat living off interest, became much more real after she had her money on the "over" confiscated. What could have been the story of a person became the story of a class; the idea of the novela prefigured exactly the period that was to come.
>
> *Abreu in* Veja, *02.09.92*

Abreu's inspiration for the script came not only from contemporary real life but also, as for many of his earlier scripts, from film history. The first chapter had scenes that were a mixture of the films *Peggy Sue Got Married* and *Carrie*. Like in *Peggy Sue*, Maria do Carmo returns to the 1960s, a period where her parents earned their money selling old steel. As they gradually make some money, they dream of

---

1   The "over" was the short version name given to the"overnight" bank account known in Brazil during high inflation periods. It is a bank account where you could deposit your money one day and redraw it the day after, gaining a rather favourable interest rate, lying a little over the inflation rate. Many wealthy people used to do this. With monthly inflation rates between 20-80 per cent the first months of 1990, the "over" is an attractive bank account.

a better future for their daughter and put her in an expensive high school in the suburb, Higienópolis, where all the haute bourgoisie live. They themselves live in the low-income working class area of Santana, in the Northern outskirts of town. The first chapter also recalls *Carrie* in that when Mario do Carmo is taking part in a high school ball something falls from the roof upon her: it is a huge amount of rubbish. In *Carrie* an identical scene occurred, but pig's blood fell instead of rubbish. Abreu also has references to the film *Imitation of Life* as well as to Frank Capra, Bette Davis, Howard Hawks, The Marx Brothers and to a song sung by Marilyn Monroe (*O Globo*, 1.4.90).

Suicide was until then a taboo in prime time television. In telenovelas you might have heard a shot or just found the person who committed suicide. In *Rubbish Queen* Abreu transcends this taboo and shows the entire act of suicide, including the fall from a skyscraper. This was the first time in Brazilian TV-history.

The apparition the final chapter of the telenovela is a public moment of suspense. All the newspapers and magazines try to discover what will happen in the last chapter. However, Silvio de Abreu has always been very keen on keeping it a secret: "Why conceal the ending of a novela?... The fact is that the press keep on writing about what is going to happen for months and months, anticipating all the chapters for the viewer. As the author I cannot say I find this right, very much on the contrary, but on the other hand I also believe that without this gossip, without speculation, the novela will not end up being a mass phenomenon"(Abreu in *O Globo*, 21.10.90).

As he has done often, Sivio de Abreu wrote three final chapters, with the same number of scenes, cast and setting, but with totally different dialogue. All were produced. He even wrote some extra scenes. His intention was to maintain the suspense until the last moment.

In an article in Globo, on the last Sunday before the end, Abreu confused people a lot, dropping hints about different resolutions to the narrative. For example, nine chapters before the end, Laurinha committed suicide making it look like a murder, performed by the *Rubbish Queen*, Maria do Carmo. In the *Globo* article, 4 days later, Abreu insinuated that she perhaps did not die, and was to return alive (which she did not). Thus, by taking many precautions, Abreu managed to keep the final story unknown to the hungry horde of journalists and thus to the audience.

Other creative workers

In addition to Silvio de Abreu, who is a very influential author, perhaps more influential than other telenovela authors, a series of other creative workers contributed to the production of the final narrative. First, there is the director. Jorge Fernando was, together with Jodele Larcher, the executive director responsible for *Rubbish Queen*. He had been the executive director in all of Silvio de Abreu's telenovelas since *Jogo da Vida* (*Guerra dos Sexos* 1983, *Vereda Tropical* 1984, *Cambalacho* 1986 and *Brega e Chic* 1987). Jorge Fernando is an expert in special effects and musical arrangement. His understanding of musicals makes it possible to include characters like Adriana. He is a at master at filming the many events that are typical for Silvio de Abreu's telenovelas, like for example car-accidents, parties and dramas on top of skyscrapers. Abreu and Fernando speak on the phone for 20-30 minutes each evening, sometimes even hours, discussing the chapter that has just been screened.

Then there are the actors. The three main roles were given to Regina Duarte, Gloria Menezes and Edu Ramos. Regina Duarte is probably the most famous telenovela actress in Brazil, widely respected and very popular. She started her career in television in 1965, participating in *A Deusa Vencida* (TV Excelsior). Since then she has taken part in more than 20 telenovelas (see Appendix 1: her curriculum vitae) having had the main female role in numerous 8 o'clock telenovelas.

Regina Duarte's role as Maria do Carmo was her first in a telenovela written by Silvio de Abreu. She was satisfied playing a "light" role. However, Regina Duarte faced a great challenge after the enormous success of *Roque Santeiro* (Rede Globo, 1986) where she had one of the most popular roles playing the main character Porcina. However, she states: "The difficult part is not having a success but surviving a success like Porcina" (Duarte in *Jornal do Brasil*, 1.04.90).

Two of the characters (and the people playing them) had a surprisingly big impact on the audience. These were two women, both minor characters who were so popular that they gained increased space in the narrative as it developed. These were Dona Armenia (Aracy Balabanian) and Nicinha (Marisa Orth). Dona Armenia was, as mentioned earlier, Maria do Carmo's neighbour, an amusing, noisy character. Aracy Balabanian had until then mainly played melodramatic roles as unhappy, oppressed, worried and concerned women in telenovelas, while also maintaining a theatrical career.

This changed with *Rubbish Queen*. In real life Aracy Balabanian is actually the daughter of Armenian immigrants who fled the massacre in Turkey in the beginning of this century. She thus built up her character as Dona Armenia by drawing on her personal memories, not least as regards speech as for instance Armenians' tendency to mix masculine and feminine words when speaking Portuguese, which brought her huge success in *Rubbish Queen*, where she became a somewhat laughable but highly entertaining character. Her popularity became so big that Silvio de Abreu let Aracy Balabanian as Dona Armenia become one of the characters in his next telenovela (*Deus nos Acuda*, Rede Globo 1991). Globo found the idea interesting, and so it was that, for the first time in the Brazilian telenovela history, a character moved on from one telenovela to another with a totally different story.

Marisa Orth as Nicinha experienced a similar popularity. However, this was a more gradual transformation. Coming from theatre and singing to telenovela production, she was inexperienced as a telenovela actress. She was chosen because Silvio de Abreu had seen her acting in the theatre. Her role was initially rather insignificant, though with a rather controversial theme, being sexually very attracted to her boyfriend, who preferred his archeological studies. This led her into the arms of many men, becoming the mistress of several. Here, not only did Abreu strike another widespread hidden theme of everyday life, extra-marital affairs, but in such an extreme and humorous manner that Nicinha became very popular. According to many critics, Nicinha and Armenia became the two principal comic characters in *Rubbish Queen*.

The fight for ratings: Competition and audience response

The owner of television is not the advertiser, it is not the TV professional, nor is it the owner of the broadcasting corporation. Based on my experience, I would say that today the real boss of TV is the audience ratings.

Regina Duarte in Estado de São Paulo, *21.11.92*

A factor which turned out to be of fundamental importance for the production of the narrative was the fight for ratings. The fight for ratings became especially tough for *Rubbish Queen*, when Rede Manchete began broadcasting *Pantanal*, a novela which was to become the first serious threat to Rede Globo's unique leading position on the Brazilian telenovela market. *Pantanal* periodically obtained higher ratings than *Rubbish Queen*!

Pantanal became popular for a series of reasons: it took place outdoors, in tropical surroundings, glorifying nature and romanticizing life in the countryside. At the same time the rhythm was slow and peaceful with long conversations. The pulse went straight against the hectic metropolitan pace which usually characterized telenovelas. Here *Pantanal* undoubtedly struck some deep feelings and longings in many people's consciousness, as could be seen in the high ratings. At the same time, it contravened the current moral code for television, showing many nude and semi-nude women, in "daring" scenes which attracted more male viewers.

After just a few weeks on air *Pantanal* went past *Rubbish Queen* in the ratings. This fact sent shock waves into the heart of the Globo enterprise, which reacted strongly. Faced with the threat of severe competition, Globo put more daring scenes into *Rubbish Queen* and thus entered into what became a lengthy battle for the prime time viewers. Though both Claudia Raia and *Rubbish Queen*'s director Jorge Fernando deny the fact, the one semi-nude scene, where Adriana (Claudia Raia) appears topless with a fish in her hand running down a street, was obviously put in to attract more (male) viewers. The fact is it did not. At least, looking at the ratings for 30 May 1990 between 9.50 and 9.52 pm when the scene occurred, one cannot detect an increase (rating was 34). These were two of the four to six crucial minutes where *Rubbish Queen* and *Pantanal* were showing simultaneously – the final minutes of *Rubbish Queen* and the beginning of *Pantanal*. Thus, Claudia Raia's breast was not able to keep the viewers on Rede Globo. Globo later regained part of their ratings. *Pantanal* did however keep significantly high ratings throughout the telenovela thereby showing that Globo's monopoly-like position on the Brazilian telenovela market was not unassailable.

Pantanal became a trend-setter for new narrative and editing rhythms and for rural plots and settings. The very next year, 1991, Rede Manchete launched a new telenovela taking place in a rural setting: *The Story about Ana Raio and Zé Trovão*. While naturalism and ecology were the key words for *Pantanal*, *The Story of Ana Raio and Ze Trovão* was launched under the sales slogan: "See the Brazil that the Brazilians don't know". Later, Globo had huge successes with similar rural telenovelas, *Renascer* (1994) and *Rei do Gado* (1996/1997).

The increased competition and the appearance of a new trend-setter expresses the rupture and new orientations occurring within the telenovela genre. The tendency has continued. *Rubbish Queen*, instead of precipitating new directions within the telenovela genre, is now seen to be a continuation of the classical realistic telenovela. It was *Pantanal* that marked the turning-point of the genre.

The echo of the people

Rubbish Queen is, despite being screened at 8 and not at 7 pm, a typical Abreu telenovela. As characteristically happens with the most famous telenovela authors in Brazil, Abreu managed to get through many of his own ideas and preferences in his negotiations with the production company, in this case CGP. Unlike the situation with soap operas, the author's influence is very manifest and clear. The plot of *Rubbish Queen* has a classic *feuilleton* structure in the sense that it centers around one principal (and many secondary) love stories and a cleary defined situation of class struggle. It is a typical Abreu telenovela because it is very light and entertaining, intended to make people laugh. The comedy is in the situations presented, reminding one of the circus theatrical format. Typical of Abreu is that it is based in São Paulo, where he lives. It was the first 8 o'clock telenovela to have São Paulo as the central location for the plot.

Silvio de Abreu's ambition about *Rubbish Queen*, as with all of his telenovelas, is very clear: he wants to entertain. However, he also wants to reflect ironically upon the contemporary situation in Brazil. Clear cut romance is not his intention, nor does he want to portray past situations in Brazil – he specifically seeks to comment the comtemporary problems affecting the everyday life of Brazilians, he wants his telenovela to become a humorous and thereby hopefully elevating comment to everyday challenges. The issue of gathering rubbish as a way of living, the remarks about the Collor plan and the chosen theme of nouveaux riches are all elements that reflect the present situation in Brazil. *Rubbish Queen* thus adresses, clearly but humorously, issues of popular concern, presented within a well known telenovela format, firmly rooted in the historical matrices of the overall genre, but related more clearly to some rather than others by the characteristics of Abreu's comic sub-genre.

The production of *Rubbish Queen* was heavily influenced by the author who managed to choose the director, the main actors and the style he wanted. The production process is a collective activity with room for creativity on the part of its author, director and actors, however with the biggest "role" belonging to the author. Meanwhile, the creativity of the process is subject to constraints arising from commercial interests and the cost-benefit calculations of Rede Globo. The industrial side of production is placed in professionally qualified hands in the Globo studios, resulting in a product of a high technical standard.

The question that remains is which role the television viewers have played in the production process? First of all, the audience has remained a constant concern to Rede Globo, who has focused its interest on ratings. Ratings have a very large impact on the decisions taken about the length and partly also the content of a telenovela, including *Rubbish Queen*. In this respect, the author's leading role gets overruled by the economic concerns of the producer, as reflected in the ratings. However, in another more qualitative and far less measurable way, the audience has influenced the product. This influence is reflected in Abreu's concern for the contemporary problems of everyday life of the common Brazilian. His choice of theme, his rewriting of numerous early chapters to reflect the high impact of the Collor Plan on everyday life, and his statements about how he seeks the"echo of the street" all indicate that the audience had a significant a role in the production of *Rubbish Queen*.

To understand the opposite process, how telenovelas influence everyday life, we must link the analyses conducted in the past four chapters with a closer look at the real lives of specific people in selected communities. How do these many overall aspects of culture, development and telenovelas in Brazil – together constituting the genre trajectories and strategies – relate to the everyday life of some concrete human beings? This is the core question guiding the next three chapters.

7. Women in their neighbourhood

The *favela* Calabar lies in the middle of the big town of Salvador, in Bahia, in the dry and warm north-eastern region of Brazil: *Nordeste*. Vila Nitro Operaria is an old workers' residential area in the far outskirts of the industrial city of São Paulo in central-southern Brazil. Finally, Santa Operaria is an 18 year-old squatter settlement in the outskirts of the town Canoas, in the southernmost state of Brazil.

In these areas live the 13 women who are the focus of this case study. They are between 13 and 63 years of age, six of them are first-generation migrants and the other seven are second generation migrants from the rural areas of Brazil. Six of them are black or mulattos, while the other seven are white. Officially, they all say they are Catholic, but a number of them are also believers in different Afro-Brazilian religions: Umbanda or Candomble. In their musical taste you find a broad repertoire of Brazil's fascinating variety of music, from Eva in the South who loves the German and Polish inspired polka-like gaucho music, to Crioula up in Bahia who is crazy about the Afro-rhythms of Olodum. When you listen to their language it is easy to identify where in Brazil they come from – their Portuguese has clear regional characteristics. Together, these 13 women represent a broad spectrum of the multicultural society of Brazil, in their language, culture and ethnicity. However, their life-stories have things in common: a recent past in the rural areas, a home in the low-income *periferias* of big Brazilian towns and a shared passion for telenovelas.

My introduction to these women's lives, in three neighbourhood cultures in different regions of Brazil, is supplemented by statistical data from 105 households in their neighbourhoods (see chapter 2).

1. Calabar

When you enter Salvador, coming along the highway into the central parts of town, you drive through some middle-class residential areas, mostly tall apartment blocks, and a big modern shopping centre. Shortly after, you turn right, off the highway, past a gas station, around and behind a big hill, where you finally find and enter Calabar. It is like moving out of one world and into another. From a high-speed urban world full of asphalt and tall buildings, and the noise of traffic, you enter of world without cars, overlooking a series of hills covered with wooden or big red-brick houses. Suddenly you can hear the noise of children playing, people laughing and music and TV-sounds coming out of the open windows. The soil is bright red, the houses low, and at first sight it is almost like entering a village in the countryside. Here in Calabar, Crioula (18), Ana (20), Clara (27), Matilde (40) and Maria (42) all live, with their families.

Calabar is a very crowded residential area, about 15 minutes by bus from the central square of Salvador. It is wedged in between main thoroughfares and tall blocks of middle class flats. A few hundred meters from the entrance to Calabar you pass the shopping centre where the surrounding middle-class families do their shopping, go to the cinema and to cafés and buy clothes of the latest fashion. There is only one little road in the area linking the big road outside the area with Calabar. This little road leads in to a square, where there is a police station, a couple of shops and Calabar's residents'association. From there Calabar spreads into a small valley – to one side encircled by the highway, to the other bounded by the sea.

From the small square, tortuous paths and endless staircases find their way into the area. Most of the houses have TV aerials, bearing witness to the massive presence of television even in such a poor area. Walking through the area, you notice many of the windows and doors into the houses are open. It is possible to look right into many houses. Basically all transport in Calabar is therefore on foot. It is a very closed neighbourhood, surrounded by hills and highways, impossible to enter by car, and invisible – as many favelas are – to the rest of the inhabitants in Salvador – except for the inhabitants in the 15-20 storey high tower blocks in the neighbouring quarters.

Calabar is mostly single storeyed houses, with some two storeyed houses and only a few three storeyed houses. The houses lie extremely close to each other, spreading all over the hills of the valley. Calabar is so densely populated that some people practically live inside the small graveyard, on top of the graves! Many activities take place outdoors, with a lot of people coming and going, women washing clothes in the streets, children running in and out of houses, conversations taking place through windows between people in the street and people inside the houses. It is a neighbourhood whose liveliness you can feel.

History

Calabar is a *favela* – a slum area – in the city of Salvador, which is the capital of the state of Bahia in *Nordeste*. Salvador – today a large modern city – was the first capital in Brazil. It was here that most of the slaves from Africa arrived, who were brought to work in the big cocoa plantations in Bahia. The past is still reflected in the present Bahia: it is the state which has the largest concentration of black Brazilians.

In spite of the abolition of slavery in 1889, the black Brazilians are still socially and economically marginalized. They often form the large majority in *favelas* like Calabar. This is even more pronounced in Bahia than in other parts of Brazil.[1]

Socio-economic marginalization is thus closely linked with the racial aspect, and as we shall see later in this chapter, the struggle for resistance against speculators

---

1   For more information about slum, migration and slum culture in Brazil, see Tufte et al., 1990. See especially chapter 4,5 and 6.

Calabar scene 1

and many others is closely related to the historical struggle for liberation and justice fought by the black Brazilians. However, as analysed in chapter 3, socio-economic injustice in Brazil is not limited to blacks, and should therefore not be locked to the dichotomy: black and suppressed /white and free.

Another characteristic of Bahia is the high degree of migration. Large parts of the state of Bahia are covered by the sertão, which is Brazil's scrubby, very dry plain that stretches out through the nine north-eastern states comprising *Nordeste*. Ownership patterns in the rural areas are feudal with huge estates and lots of small farmers and landless peasants. Through the 1970s and 1980s and to a decreasing extent on into the 1990s, the farmers and landless peasants have been moving to the cities, often compelled to do so by lack of food, work and land, and hoping to find a way to survive. Most of them have settled down in favelas like Calabar. Like in most large cities in Brazil heavy migration – combined with high birth rates – has changed the demographic picture in recent years.

From 1980 to 1990 the population of Salvador increased by 38.2 per cent to 2.1 million (*Veja*, January 1991). Large parts of the outskirts are not included in this figure. The total number of inhabitants in Salvador's capital city and its surrounds is slightly above 3 million. The rapid increase has put a lot of pressure on the city's ability to absorb the many newcomers. This development has resulted in a great expansion of the urban area but also in profound changes to existing areas. The large majority of the *favelas* in the central urban zone have been forcibly demolished by entrepreneurs wanting to use the area for construction. Many of the people living in the *favelas* arrived from rural areas years ago, settled down on an empty spot, and never got any formal and legal right to the piece of land they began living on. Numerous conflicts have occurred in these areas over the past decade. Most often the *favelados* – inhabitants of the *favelas* – have lost. Calabar is one of the few *favelas* left in the central urban zone – resisting substantial economical and political pressure. Thus, the inhabitants live with a constant uncertainty as to whether they will be allowed to stay or not.

In 1984 the number of inhabitants living in Salvador, in poor areas like Calabar, was estimated to 1.5 million, about half of the population of Salvador (Conceicao, 1986:152).

Calabar scene 2

A history of resistance

Calabar has existed since the 1940s when some people occupied the area, which used to be scrub and rain forest. The name Calabar originates from a village in the northern Nigeria: Kalabari. Historical tradition asserts that in the 17th or 18th century a group of slaves escaped from a plantation in Bahia and settled down on exactly the area which is Calabar today. Here they created a *quilombo*, the name given to free societies formed by groups of escaped slaves during the 17th and the 18th centuries. The most famous *quilombo* is Palmares, which existed for more than 100 years as an independent society in Brazil, and which at its most populous periods had many thousands runaway slaves living there.

In the late 1960s and through the 1970s Calabar's population increased a great deal. Many people moved to the area after having been thrown out of other *favelas* in Salvador. The mayor of Salvador constructed roads and hotels in the places where similar illegal housing areas used to be. Furthermore, tower blocks for the upper middle class were built in some of the areas. Threatened by the pressure from politicians and entrepreneurs, the inhabitants began organizing themselves to avoid being forced to move out.

A precarious social situation

In addition to the continuous land conflict and threat of expropriation, Calabar suffered right from day one of its existence from serious social and infrastructural problems: no electricity, no running water, no sewers, no roads. Small houses were built out of whatever materials were available, the area had no school, no health clinic and no recreational areas. Social problems such as unemployment, crime, violence, drug dealing, alcoholism and prostitution were also part of everyday life. A survey done in Calabar in the late 1970s showed that most of the inhabitants lived there, not for pleasure, but out of necessity (Conceição, 1986).

Crime and violence were the most serious social problems. Many younger men made a living out of stealing in the city. Furthermore, gang fights used to take place between young men from Calabar and other neighbourhoods, very often resulting in violence, shooting and death. Police violence was also a serious problem. In just one year, 1981, 24 innocent people were killed by the police, a problem reflecting the severe marginalization of Calabar's and many other favelas' inhabitants from civil society.[2]

All the inhabitants were sick and tired of the situation, but the municipality did nothing about it, thus putting indirect pressure on the inhabitants to leave the centrally placed and potentially attractive area. However, Calabar has survived the pressure so far.

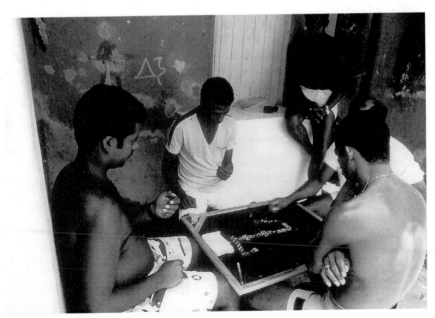

Men's sphere, Calabar

---

2   The massacre in a Rio *favela* in August 1993 where the police entered and killed 15 people, including women and children had world-wide media coverage, leading to a law process against the involved policemen. They were sentenced to prison in 1998. No similar judicial process has ever occurred after the continuous incidents in Calabar.

Men's sphere, Calabar

The Catholic Church stimulates the process of organization

In 1977 the priest Rubens was installed in the parish including Calabar. Not many of Calabar's inhabitants were regular churchgoers, but Padre Rubens managed to make a group of young people from Calabar participate in a competition, a gincana, which the church had arranged. It lasted for several days. For this purpose the young people organized a group, JUC or Jovens Unidas de Calabar, meaning The United Youth of Calabar. JUC happened to win the gincana. It was their first experience of organization. After this occasion they turned into a permanent youth group which – with assistance from the church – began to cope with some of the social problems in Calabar. In 1978 JUC made a statistical survey among the inhabitants. They found out that at that time 1100 families, living in 850 households, lived in Calabar;[3] 70 per cent of the inhabitants were under the age of 17; 90 per cent did not know the name of the mayor of Salvador!

The organization carried out by JUC among the inhabitants became the first step in a long political struggle, which has resulted in many improvements in Calabar. In 1981 JUC was transformed into a residents' association, and throughout the 1980s they organized demonstrations, actions and negotiations with authorities. Many people thereby gained experience of grass-roots organization and mobilization.

Today Calabar is one of the best organized *favelas* in Salvador. They have obtained electricity, water, sewers, paved paths and, not least, a school and a health clinic. The population has also put a huge effort into the work of strengthening the cultural identity of the inhabitants. Given they almost all are black, the task has been centered around the idea of telling the history of the black Brazilians, something seldom done in the official school system, and in promoting old Afro-Brazilian traditions like Capoeira, an old method of self defence, today a combined dance and sport discipline. The Escola Aberta (Open School) in Calabar, where Crioula (18) works, is the centre of all these activities.

---

3   85 per cent of the inhabitants had lived in Calabar in 12-15 years and were in this sense newcomers. Half of this group were newcomers from another occupied area (Conceição, 1986).

Five women

Crioula (18) and Ana (20) are both single, still living with their parents, while Clara (27), Matilde (40) and Maria (42) live with their children and in some cases other relatives. Of these five, the three youngest have lived in Calabar all their life, while the two oldest migrated to Salvador as young women, and came to live in Calabar.

Crioula

Crioula (18) is black. She lives with her parents and five sisters and brothers in a reasonably big house – the boys sharing one bedroom and the girls another. There is a quiet atmosphere in the house – the family spend much of their time in the street. Crioula's father is an unemployed electrician, who now works as a bartender. Her mother is a teacher, president for the residents' association in Calabar and a very busy women. She is an idealist, working all the time in community activities, and Crioula seems to have been socialized into some activities of the same kind. Crioula has lived in Calabar all her life. Her family originally comes from a small village, and she still visits relatives on the sertão (outback) occasionally. Crioula has a job as a kindergarten teacher in the mornings and goes to high-school in the evenings. She is also active in the teachers' association. In the afternoons and weekends, Crioula likes to go out with her best friend. They go to the beach or to discos. Recently she broke up with her boyfriend, Erlando (23), who works as a *Capoeira* teacher at the school (see chapter 3).

Crioula is a relaxed, self-confident girl. She obviously likes her work in the kindergarden, and is very aware of the need to strengthen the (black) cultural identity of the children. She often experiences racism herself. At the time when I did this research Crioula had a plan to migrate to São Paulo and try to get a job as

Crioula

a teacher there. However, in 1998, when I was back on a visit in Salvador, I met her mother who told me that Crioula was now married, had a small daughter, and had moved to another neighbourhood; she was now working in a shop in Salvador.

Ana

Ana (20) is black. She lives with her mother, who is a widow, and her younger brother in a rather small run-down brick house. Obviously it is one of the old houses in Calabar. At present it is Ana's summer holidays, so she has a lot of spare time and watches a lot of TV – she lies on the couch in the light blue living room watching television. She loves it. However, out of holiday time she is a busy woman, with a full-time job as a maid in a private middle-class home and in the evenings she attends school. She is in 6th grade. Since she physically sleeps and works in the house of a middle-class family, I asked her: "So you live there?". She answered: "No, I sleep there, but I don't live there". Home is in Calabar.

Ana has never been active in any kind of grass root work, she finds it very boring. But her mother is quite active in the residents' association. Ana was born and has lived all her life in Calabar. She does not have many friends and says she prefers being alone. She does not have a boyfriend at the moment, but she would very much like to have one. Ana seems like a rather shy, introverted person, with limited social contacts.

Clara

Clara (27) is unmarried, but lives with her boyfriend, their two daughters aged six and two and Clara's sister. Their 85-year old grandmother and their three nephews also live with them, totalling nine people in the small old house, which is built of poor materials: wood and sheet metal. It is very crowded.

Clara has lived all her life in Calabar. She is mostly a housewife, but also has a part time job as a cleaning lady. However, being in charge of the household takes up a lot of her time. Nevertheless she watches a lot of TV all day, and rarely misses the telenovelas. She seems to have an ambivalent relation to the surrounding society: partly she claims that she learns a lot from watching the novelas – that people should be good to each other and that everything is alright. At the same time she voted blank at the last elections and has no confidence in the politicians. She claims that a lot of things could be better. Clara is of the opinion that you should take care of yourself, not interfere in other people's matters, and – if you work hard enough – everything will be all right.

It is very obvious that she does not want to express any discontent about her own life. She feels that watching TV provides her with satisfying entertainment. It is a pleasant escape from her everyday life, where she works hard and where it is difficult for the family to make ends meet. Their household income is among the lowest in Calabar.

Clara is very positive about what the residents' association has accomplished even though she does not participate. She stopped going to school in 5th grade. She used to go to school in the evenings, but one night on her way home at around 11 pm some men tried to rape her. She managed to get away, but since that night she has not dared to go to school again.

Matilde

Matilde (40) is mulatto, married and has four children between 12 and 18. They all live at home, along with a 17 year old nephew. Only two members of the household earn a salary: the nephew, who works as an office boy, and herself. My first visit was on a Sunday in the late morning. Matilde's husband was sitting on the terrace, playing dominoes with a friend and with one of the sons hanging around.

Matilde works in the residents' association's kindergarten, like Crioula. Her husband is a craftsman, who previously worked in construction, but at present is unemployed as are her two sons who are 17 and 18. However, from time to time they contribute to the household with some fish they catch. Matilde and her family have lived in Calabar for 20 years. She is an active women; working full time and also having the main responsibility for the household; cleaning, washing clothes and cooking. However, her 12 year old daughters helps her. Furthermore, she is active in the women's group in the residents' association, and finds it important to help in community work. Matilde is very talkative and extrovert.

Maria Jesús

Maria Jesús (42) is married and has three grown up children. She is a dressmaker and has a sewing machine at home. Her working day is often long and busy. The family has a relatively big brick house, compared to the average houses in Calabar. They have been living in the house for more than 20 years and considerable improvements have been made since they moved in. Maria Jesus is originally from a minor city in the state of Bahia.

Maria used to teach sewing at the school in Calabar, but because of the economic crisis this kind of education could not continue. She feels very positively about the work done by the residents' association in Calabar, and she participates to the extent she finds it possible. At the presidential election in 1989 she voted for the Social Democrat Covas in the first round and for Lula from the Labour Party in the second round.

All of the five women living in Calabar are hard-working women. Four of them have double jobs, working out of the house and also having responsibility for the household (cooking, cleaning, washing clothes and children). Two of them still live at home, and help their mothers. The responsibility for the household, whether domestic chores or money-management, is the women's responsability. Their lives are busy lives.

Many of the women clearly relax with television, it is a distraction and a pause in the rush and struggle of everyday life (see also chapters 8 and 9). However, they also have fun, laugh and joke together in their female networks, either visiting each other at home or in gatherings at the residents' association. The men spend more time outside of the house than the women, and in very different spheres. They frequent the bars, sit on street corners or on the terraces chatting or playing cards or dominoes, or go outside Calabar, looking for jobs, to fish, or to work. The households I visited in Calabar were generally characterized by the continuous coming and going of people, doors and windows always open, a lot of life and sounds around the house – music, television, talking and shouting – an intense experience. A few places, however, especially Ana's, were quite quiet. Despite the crowded environment, there was generally a relaxed and very sociable atmosphere. The contact with neighbours and people passing in the street was continuous, constituting a natural element of everyday life.

155

As a foreigner, I often wondered about how and where Calabar's inhabitants found privacy and intimacy – where could they be alone? Physically, it seemed very difficult. But then again, perhaps here the telenovelas played a role similar to the romance-reading of Radway's subjects, making their "declarations of independence" and finding their moments of privacy in reading romances (Radway 1984).

Living Conditions

That households were crowded was generally confirmed in my survey. The average household in Calabar has six people. However, only 13 per cent of homes include precisely six people. 18 per cent had nine or more people in the house! No one lived alone and only 4 per cent of houses had only two inhabitants. (Table 4, appendix 2). Thus, the household structure is significantly more complex than that of the traditional family structure.

Table 1. Women's matrimonial status (%)

Married	34
Living together	47
Widow	11
Single (not widow)	7
TOTAL	99

Many of the women are living with or have been living with a man. Almost half live in unmarried couples. Many of Calabar's inhabitants thus do not conform with the code of conduct preached by the Catholic church to which 95 per cent of them belong (Table 25, appendix 2).

The women's work- and income situation is characterized by unemployment and badly paid jobs (Table 5 and 6, appendix 2). 43 per cent of the women are housewives or unemployed, and 33 per cent work as maids or cleaners, typically in middle-class homes. The remaining 24 per cent are spread over many different occupations like waitresses, dressmakers and teachers.

Their incomes are generally very low. Almost half of them earn less than half the minimum wage,[4] which corresponds to about 30 dollars a month.

Another 46 per cent of them earn between a half and one minimum wage (30-60 dollars). Thus, 90 per cent of the women have an income of less than the minimum wage. The remaining 10 per cent earn between one and three times the minimum wage (60-180 dollars) a month. This very precarious income situation provides a logical explanation as to why so few women live alone. They have very little possibility of managing financially, if they do not stay in their parents' home while they are still young, or find someone else to support them.

4　In Brazil the income system is by law divided in a system of minimum wages. A minimum wage at the time amounted to about $60 a month (February 1991. In January 1999 it had increased to about $100). Many people working as service personnel as waiters, guards, drivers, secretaries, etc, and as unskilled workers, do not earn more than one minimum wage, whereas skilled workers earn three or five or even eight minimum wages, depending on their seniority. Upper middle class families easily earn 30-40 minimum wages.

The *favela*

Among the women living in married or unmarried couples, their male partner's income situation is generally better. Practically no men earn less than a half the minimum wage, one third earn between a half and one minimum wage, while almost two thirds earn between one and three times the minimum wage. 2.5 per cent earn from five to eight times the minimum wage (Table 8, appendix 2). The men are thus the households' most important providers, but rarely the only ones. Each household in Calabar has an average of 2.2 incomes. One third of the households have three or more incomes (table 9, appendix 2). The men have very different jobs. One third of them work as craftsmen. The rest are skilled or unskilled workers, attendants, waiters, hawkers or drivers.

Children often have incomes too. Most often these children are teenagers, but paid work among the younger children is also frequently found. They work as shoe polishers, paper boys, office boys and have minor jobs in industry. Finally, relatives other than the father, mother and children, often live in the household, be it a cousin who has recently arrived from elsewhere, a sister or a nephew. They also bring money into the household.

Income from prostitution and crime, including drug dealing, can also constitute a significant resource in some households. As mentioned before, Calabar was previously plagued by violence and crime. The violence has almost vanished as a result of the pressure and hard work put om by the residents' association, whereas crime still exists, though it is less visible. The reduction in violence has resulted in the establishment of a little police station on the small square in Calabar.[5]

---

5   Often in *favelas*, the police do not dare patrol because the areas are controlled by gangs. The gangs of mainly young men are often very well organized and have a strict internal hierarchy. They act as guards, protecting the inhabitants, controlling who comes into the area. The police are generally not welcome. Furthermore, the gangs often control the dealing with drugs and stolen goods in *favelas*.

Patrolling in Calabar is however still very limited. The presence of the police has contributed to making crime invisible. Another illegal, but very common source of income is a betting game called *Jogo do Bicho*, which has outlets all over Brazil, mainly in low income areas. People put money on numbers at these outlets, which can be in a bar, a shop or a private home.

Calabar's inhabitants are very marginalized from the rest of society. They live on land without possessing the legal rights to it, despite more than 50 years' residence there. The vast majority are black, many are unemployed. Violence, crime and prostitution have been endemic in the area, and into the late 1990s many of these issues continue to be substantial problems – Crioula's mother had a tired look on her face when she told me about it during my last visit to Salvador, Bahia, in April 1998. Improvements do happen, but at the price of a great drain on the activists' energy. Nevertheless, many activities do demonstrate significant progress in Calabar and illustrate the neighbourhood's impressive ability to survive the pressure from the surrounding society. They are one of the last low-income areas left in the central parts of Salvador – all the others have gradually been pushed out to make way for middle class residential areas.

What enables Calabar's inhabitants to withstand the pressure and move ahead with their integration into civil society? It seems to be a combination of, on one hand, some inner forces and energies, articulated in religious beliefs, historical consciousness and even music, and on the other hand, external forces such as the creation of social networks that have in some cases developed into civic organisations and movements – the residents' association for example. My hypothesis is that telenovelas play a role in this panorama – being an articulator of "inner forces and energies" and also stimulating and articulating the development of the social networks.

The cultural and spiritual forces and energies can be seen as fuel, contributing to keeping spirits high and hopes alive, developing ontological security, meaning and coherence in what otherwise might simply be an exhausting struggle for survival, at best keeping up the socio-economic status quo. As I will describe in the next two chapters, both the social uses of telenovelas as well as the production of meaning through watching telenovelas seem to contribute socializing and socially integrative dynamics to everyday life.

As a civic organisation, Calabar's resident's association is succeeding in enabling its members to resist the strong political and economical powers confronting them. Their work to integrate Calabar into the ordinary spheres of civil society has had positive results in many spheres, ever since the formation of JUC in the late 1970s. Crime has decreased in the neighbourhood, community activities have developed: musical events, carnival, shows, school activities – in addition of the everyday work of organising the community. Furthermore, they have put up their own candidates for the municipal elections and they have even had inhabitants obtaining university degrees.

There are thus a series of positive activities and "inner forces" that contribute to Calabar's continued existence as a neighbourhood in central Salvador where people on a low income can live, though it must be acknowledged that despite multiple and often very creative survival strategies, Calabar's inhabitants are marginalized *vis-à-vis* the organized civil society of their city, Salvador. Nevertheless, it is a neighbourhood with a history of struggle for survival and with a strong cultural profile and identity to which the five women in focus all relate in varying degrees.

2. Vila Nitro Operaria

If Salvador with its 3-4 million inhabitants is a big city, São Paulo with its 12-15 million inhabitants is enormous – the largest city in South America. As with Calabar in Salvador, you see a startling difference when you come from the centre of São Paulo, with its business community, its skyscrapers, its large shopping centers, and travel out to a low-income area, in this case Vila Nitro Operaria. To reach Vila N.O. from the centre is a major undertaking – it takes approximately 2 hours and you travel about 30 kilometers to the East. You take the São Paulo metro on the line going East, travelling for about 45 minutes, until you reach the second to last metro station, Arthur Alvim. From there you take a bus journey of at least an hour, through suburb after suburb until you reach the small town of São Miguel, which has today been swallowed up by the metropolitan area of São Paulo.

Street in Vila Nitro Operaria

Vila Nitro Operaria (Vila N.O.), which in translation means the Nitro Workers' Borough, is an old workers' district in São Miguel. Vila N.O. was founded in the 1930s, and gained its name from a big chemical manufacturing complex, Nitro Quimica, which was built in the 1930s in the outskirts of São Miguel. It became, and is still, the biggest industry in the town. Today São Miguel is considered part of the eastern periphery of São Paulo, while remaining a municipality on its own. East of São Miguel the fields begin, while to the West one can drive through urban areas non-stop for three hours and still be in São Paulo.

This huge area between São Miguel and the centre of São Paulo is called Zona Leste. The large number of working-class people who are employed in São Paulo live largely in Zona Leste, as well as in the northern districts of São Paulo, for example in the Santana area, where the main character of the telenovela *Rubbish Queen*, Maria do Carmo, lives. Most of the 30 kilometre broad Zona Leste consists of single storey and two storey self-built houses, with little or no urban planning. Apart from some large main streets, the infrastructure has developed very slowly and appears chaotic. In recent years however, the image of Zona Leste has been changing. Within the past decade a lot of tower blocks have been built. What was before an endless expanse of one or two storey buildings is now changing, spreading vertically instead of horizontally. Vila Nitro Operaria however, looks physically as it always has, although increasingly run down.

The factory around which the neighbourhood has grown

Vila N.O. lies on the bank of a small and very polluted river in the outskirts of São Miguel at the far east end of Zona Leste. The chemical industry Nitro Quimica lies on the other side, a little further down the river. The neighbourhood comprises approximately 400-600 households. They are situated in between the river on one side and a highway on the other. Vila N.O. is further separated from the neighbouring area by the railway.

In Vila Nitro Operaria live Roberta (13), Elenita (30), Geraldina (38), Ilda (41) and Gildete (63). Roberta lives with her parents and family; Gildete is a widow, and the other three are married and live with their families. Despite all living in the same neighbourhood, their living conditions vary quite significantly, with Elenita clearly having the worst, living in a house close to the river. The houses in Vila N.O. that lie closest to the river – which looks more like a large sewer – are poor, shanty-like buildings, mostly made of wood and corrugated iron, with a few brick houses in between. The river occasionally overflows its banks, as can clearly be seen in these houses closest to the river. Elenita's house is no exception, with walls noticeably affected by dry-rot and damp.

160

The majority of Vila N.O.'s houses are of brick, and were built between the late 1930s and the beginning of the 1950s. Exceptionally for Zona Leste, signs of urban planning can be seen in what was the original infrastructure of this neighbourhood: the roads are wide, paved, and with sidewalks, and there is a normal and reasonable distance between the houses. However, as the years have passed, many lots have been subdivided, with houses built in what used to be the back yards. Vila N.O. is therefore more densely populated than the broad roads might lead one to suppose. Geraldina's house, for example, stands on a lot that used to be twice its size. It was subdivided and her husband's brother built a house on the other half.

The area is generally of a considerable better standard than Calabar, or any other *favela* for that matter. The broad roads function as a playground for children. Also, the majority of the houses are better separated from the streets than was the case in Calabar, so that there is a more limited contact between house and street. The socio-economic standard is clearly higher than in Calabar, and some of the inhabitants also have cars. However, the riverside inhabitants, like Elenita (30), are poor, with living conditions like those in Calabar.

The neighbourhood has a series of shops scattered around it – small grocery stores, a hairdresser, a warehouse and 4 bars. In addition, a series of private homes sell bread, sweets, soda and other products. Vila N.O. also has a school which Roberta (13) attends. Right across the highway there is a large market where the women do a lot of their shopping as well. The houses on that side are of a slightly higher standard than those in Vila N.O.

The Nitro Quimica company has a club for its employees, which has its own facilities in the outskirts of Vila N.O. Some of the men from Vila N.O. work at Nitro Quimica and therefore play football there. Roberta's father used to work at Nitro Quimica, but was fired a month ago. The district also has its own football club, which does not have any facilities of its own, but which has its "headquarters" in a specific bar, where the prizes they have won decorate an entire wall. Geraldina's husband, Servilho, sometimes plays in the club team and occasionally frequents the bar. In the same bar men and women together play a game similar to dominoes. Vila N.O. also has a residents' association, several churches and a local branch of the workers' party, PT. In addition to the two Christian churches: one Catholic and one Protestant, there is also a local Mãe de Santo (a mother of saints), a member of the hierarchy of the Afro-brazilian religion, Umbanda. This woman is Gildete (63). Many people resort to Gildete, and the two churches are well attended.

Another place that is well-attended is a brothel situated in the part of Vila N.O. closest to the centre of São Miguel. The men who visit it are from the whole district, and it is a place the inhabitants clearly dislike, not only because of its business, but because of the drunkeness, violence and noise which go with it.

Vila Nitro Operaria is a less marginalized neighbourhood than Calabar. It has its problems: on the physical level, the infrastructure is old and run down, and there are periodic floods when the river overflows. Violence and prostitution are some of the main social problems, along with poverty, especially in the favela areas on the shore. With the gradual increase in the population of the neighbourhood, the unemployment rate has grown. But social and political movements and organizations exist, as do a variety of religious centres. Whereas Calabar was fighting for proper integration into both the physical urban infrastructure, and the political and social infrastructure of the surrounding society, Vila N.O. is a securely established and integrated suburb, characteristic of Zona Leste of São Paulo. It is, however, affected by the general urban problems of the whole zone, and of São Paulo in general.

São Paulo – Brazil's economical and political dynamo

The city of São Paulo, which is the capital of the state of São Paulo, has a population of about 15 million people: the largest city in Brazil and in South America as a whole. It is also the strongest industrial centre in South America. São Paulo alone produces 70 per cent of Brazil's GNP. There was a great wave of migration to the city in the 1970s and beginning of the 1980s. Industry was growing rapidly at the beginning of the 1970s which attracted farmers and landless peasants from *Nordeste* like a magnet. First Gildete (63) came, then Geraldina (38). In the beginning of the 1980s, when economic growth was decreasing, a fierce drought on the sertao in *Nordeste* kept the migration process to São Paulo going. Elenita (30) came at this time. Migration continued throughout the 1980s, though at a slower rate. São Paulo's population increased by 14.2 per cent from 1980 to 1990 which more or less equals the average annual growth rate for Brazil in the 1980s (IBGE in Veja, January 1991). Compared to Salvador in the same period, the population growth in São Paulo was much lower.

Inside a slum dwelling house in São Paulo

São Paulo was Brazil's centre of social, cultural and political movements in the 1980s. These led in 1985 to the fall of the military regime. The Christian communities in Zona Leste have been many and strong, and Paulo Freire, who lived in São Paulo, was a significant source of inspiration. The organization of the workers is also very strong in São Paulo. It was here the first big strikes in the late

1970s took place, and here the workers party, PT, was founded in 1980 and the national trade union CUT (Central Unica dos Trabalhadores), founded in 1983. Geraldina's husband, Servilho, was extremely active in CUT and PT through the 1980s and 1990s. São Paulo today has Latin America's largest trade union: the Metal Workers, with about 300,000 members. Many of these work in the two major industrial areas in and around the city. One is the ABCD-district, covering four towns just south-east of São Paulo. The other area is Guarulhos in Zona Leste of São Paulo. Ilda's husband works in Guarulhos.

Although the city is the symbol and main agent of economic development and thus "progress" in Brazil, fundamental problems remain unsolved. The municipal administration in São Paulo carried out an investigation in 1990 which revealed that 60 per cent of city zones showed irregularities in the registration of dwellings. 60 per cent – in the largest city in South America (FASE, 1991)! The problem is that the city has not been able to cope with urban development and administer the migration to the city. Although some progress has been seen in recent years, chaotic conditions still exist in large areas of the Zona Leste, with sub-standard living conditions and massive unsolved problems of infrastructure.

Five women

Of the five women I studied in Vila N.O. only two were born in the neighbourhood – Roberta (13) and Ilda (41). The others, Elenita (30), Geraldina (38) and Gildete (63) were all from north-eastern Brazil – and despite many years in the neighbourhood, all maintained a certain nostalgia for their "homeland" up north. As we shall see in the reception analysis in chapter 9, the first generation migrants recognize and enjoy the rural scenes in the telenovelas, through them often cultivating a sort of rural nostalgia. A good example of this is Elenita.

Elenita

Elenita came to São Paulo 8 years ago. She comes from a rural area in the state of Pernambuco in the *Nordeste*. She lived there with her family, but their socio-economic situation became so bad that she migrated to town. Her husband is from Piauí, another state in the *Nordeste*. Elenita misses her family a lot. Watching television makes her forget the 'lousy' life of town, and some programmes even remind her of life back in Pernambuco, for example the telenovelas *Pantanal* and *Ana Raio* and *Ze Trovão*.

Elenita (30) is white and lives with her husband and two children in an old, damp house close to the river. The house has only one large room which is very dark, having only one small light bulb hanging from the ceiling. In one corner there is a large, broad bunk bed which 3 of them sleep in. There is also a plank bed. On the wall of the house it is possible to see how much the river has risen above ground level. About 1.2 meters up there are visible tide-marks. Elenita and her family regularly have to evacuate their most important things and move out, when the river rises. There is nothing they can do, and they have nowhere else to move to.

The TV is situated by the bunk bed. It is turned on most of the day. Elenita used to have a job doing ironing, but lost it three months ago. Her husband works and both her children go to school. Elenita only went to school for one year. She can write her name and read a very little. It is her daughter who writes the letters for her to her family back home in Pernambuco. Elenita's wish is to return to where she came from.

Roberta

Roberta (13) is white and is in the 7th grade at school. She was born and raised in Vila N.O. Roberta lives with her mother (43), her stepfather (38) and her two sisters, one older and one younger. Her stepfather, who is a metal worker, used to work at Nitro Quimica. He lost his job one month ago. Their house is relatively big, built of brick, and with a small front garden. The family runs a small private store, selling sweets and ice-cream from their house to people in the neighbourhood.

Roberta

Roberta goes to school in the mornings, from 8 to 11.20. When she comes home she has lunch with her family. In the afternoons she does her homework and watches a lot of television, often at the same time. When she grows up, she wants to be a model. However, Roberta knows it is not possible because you have to attend a lot of expensive courses. Since she does not want to be dependent on her real father, who is divorced from her mother and who could afford to pay for her, she has decided to become a primary school teacher instead.

Roberta watches both children's TV and telenovelas. In school, she and her friends sometimes make up little plays based on the telenovelas, re-enacting the opening scenes or other scenes. They also talk quite a lot about the telenovelas at break time.

Geraldina

Geraldina (38) is black and married to Servilho. They altogether have 4 children; Geraldina has a boy (14) from a former marriage and Servilho also has a boy (20) from a former marriage. Together they have six year-old twins. They live together with Geraldina's mother in a long but narrow two-storey brick house. It is narrow because the original ground, belonging to Servilho's father, was divided in two.

Thus, Servilho's brother and family have a similar long narrow house right next door, with just two meters separating the houses.

Geraldina's husband Servilho is a metal worker and is very active in politics and especially in union work. He is almost never at home, even at weekends. He is very critical of television, an attitude which Geraldina partly shares. Geraldina's house is often full of guests, mainly at times when Servilho is home: friends, family and especially colleagues who drop by, mainly to have discussions with Servilho.

Geraldina came to São Paulo together with her family when she was 13 years old. She comes from a small village in Bahia, *Nordeste*. Her mother lives with her in the house, and she also has a brother and a sister close by. Geraldina lived in other parts of Zona Leste before she met Servilho.

She has a busy life, looking after her two six year-old children, and shouldering the responsibility for the household. Furthermore, she has recently begun an evening course, aiming to finish the primary school education which she did not get a chance to complete as a child. This has changed her media habits. She used to see more telenovelas in the evenings, but at present she only sees the 6 o'clock novela. Geraldina likes the telenovela *Pantanal* a lot because it reminded her of her childhood in Bahia.

Geraldina is a calm serious woman, but with a strong will, a temper and a sense of humour. She is rather stubborn. Her major concern is her family, and she often gets irritated over how little time her husband spends with the rest of the family.

Ilda

Ilda (41) is white, from São Paulo and married for the second time, like several of the other women. She has three children from her first marriage and one child from her second. The children are between seven and 21 years old. After eight years with her first husband she got divorced. Her new husband is from the state of Pernambuco in *Nordeste*. They have now lived together for 10 years. Ilda herself has lived all of her life in Vila N.O.

Ilda

Ilda works at home, both as a housewife and simultaneously taking care of the family's small grocery store which is right next door to their house. She is also active in the local residents' association. Ilda has the largest and best house of the women in my case study, and her family is the only one with a car. The house is made of brick and has decorative tiles on the floors and walls. Ilda's husband works at Nitro Quimica as a metal worker. He earns a relatively good salary equivalent to almost 400 dollars a month, five times the minimum wage.

Ilda is a smiling open woman, very relaxed and fond of a lot of people around her. Her personal points of view are less profiled than for example Geraldina's but they are well argued.

Gildete

Gildete (63) is white, retired and a widow, having been married twice. Gildete is the *Mae de Santo* of the area, unusual for a white person. She came to São Paulo from the state of Piauí in *Nordeste* at the age of 22. Her husband had left her and two small children and found another woman. That is why she migrated to São Paulo, seeking to start a new life by herself. Initially, she moved in with a sister and later with an aunt, who both lived in São Paulo. She got different jobs here and there, as a maid, in industry, etc. Soon after she found herself a new husband and together they bought a bar which they ran until he died a few years back. She continued with the bar until retiring one year ago.

Gildete has experienced many social ups and downs. Her family in *Nordeste* is quite rich. Her father was a senior official in the municipality and had quite a big farm as well. After her first husband left she had some tough years. Her life with husband number two was fairly stable, though inevitably affected by the fact of living and owning a bar in a low income area as Vila N.O.

Gildete

Gildete and her husband were some of the first people to buy a television set in the area. This was in 1957. Throughout the many years since, she has enjoyed watching telenovelas, and used to watch a lot of television while working in the bar – until the TV set was stolen. Their bar was robbed four times.

Today, Gildete lives with a son and his wife in half of the house she and her husband built many years ago. The other half of the house she rents out to a series of families, who crowd together into single rooms. The house still bears the marks of a major flooding of the river four years ago, which left it damp, and affected by dry rot. Gildete is a very talkative woman and proud of her two sons, who both obtained good educations. One has become an engineer.

These five women in Vila N.O. are generally a little better off than their fellows in Calabar. However, they are just as hardworking, having two jobs in most cases. Their family structures have similar turbulences and ruptures as in Calabar, with divorces, men leaving their women, new marriages, early deaths of husbands, etc. What I experienced in general during my stay, was the close contact between the women in the neighbourhood. These relations tended to be a little more formalized than in Calabar, where the coming and going in each others houses was pronounced and seemed more immediate. There were clearly deliberate patterns, where friends formed part of the social networks and others for particular reasons didn't. However, the networks were there; they seemed to be strong and to work well, though it has to be said that they were frequently also a necessity: everyday life would not have functioned without them.

In socio-economic terms there was a great difference in the living conditions of, for example, Ilda and Elenita, illustrating the socio-economic heterogenity of Vila N.O. – a neighbourhood that on a first inspection hides the harsher aspects of life lived there.

Living conditions

The average household in Vila N.O. is 5 people, of which 3 are children (Table 3 and 4, Appendix 3), thus slightly smaller than the average household in Calabar. However, only 14 per cent of the households actually consist of 5 people, while almost half of them are smaller and 38 per cent are bigger. The principal conclusion must be that there is no "typical" household in Vila N.O.

Like in Calabar only very few women live alone, but many more are married, contrary to the many unmarried couples in Calabar. 54 per cent are married, 14 per cent live in unmarried couples and 28 per cent live alone, either being widowed (16 per cent) or divorced (6 per cent). That leaves only 6 per cent unmarried singles (Table 2, Appendix 3). In other words, the relational status between men and women here is generally more formalized than in Calabar. Part of the explanation might be that the people in Vila N.O. are more oriented towards the formalities and laws linked to their Catholic belief as well as to bourgeois conventions. Therefore they marry.

The general income structure among women in Vila N.O. is slightly better than for the women in Calabar, however it is still in basically the same income categories. 12 per cent have a reasonable salary of over three times the minimum wage, compared to none in Calabar on this level. The table below shows that household incomes in Vila N.O. generally are better than in Calabar. However, a significant number of the women are either unemployed, housewives and/or earn very little. However, 30 per cent of them earn more than the minimum wage, contrary to only 10 per cent in Calabar.

Among the men the differences are more pronounced. In Vila N.O. one third earn more than three times the minimum wage as opposed to only 2.5 per cent in Calabar. The men in Vila N.O. generally earn more than the minimum wage. Earnings can go up to eight times that amount, whereas the general picture in Calabar shows salaries of between a half and three times the minimum wage. Along with this, fewer people per household earn money in Vila N.O. There are 1.7 incomes per household compared with 2.2 in Calabar. Only 18 per cent of the households in Vila N. O have more than 3 incomes compared with 32 per cent in Calabar.

Table 2. Women's income in Vila N.O. and in Calabar (%) and income among their male partners.

Women's income	N.O.	Calabar
Below 1/2 minimum wage	49	44
1/2-1 minimum wage	16	46
1-3 minimum wages	18	10
Over 3 minimum wages	12	0

Male partners' income	N.O.	Calabar
Below 1/2 minimum wage	14	2.5
1/2 – 1 minimum wage	4	30
1 – 3 minimum wages	48	65
over 3 minimum wages	33	2.5

This shows us that the inhabitants in Calabar might have a lower income level per person than in Vila N.O., but relatively more people are involved in earning money to sustain the family. Given the higher income level in Vila N.O. fewer people are needed to provide a reasonable income. There are also fewer people per household in Vila N.O. to sustain.

3. Santa Operaria

Santa Operaria is a squatter settlement. Santa Operaria is also a suburb in Canoas, a medium-sized town right outside Porto Alegre, the capital of the state Rio Grande do Sul. Practically speaking, Canoas and Porto Alegre have grown together and constitute a fairly large urban zone of 1.2-1.4 million inhabitants. The area has a much colder climate than São Paulo's sub-tropical or Calabar's tropical climate. In the winter time it can occasionally fall to below 0°.

The neighbourhood is situated in the middle of a nature reserve along the river Guaiba. Officially it is forbidden to build anything there, but the neighbourhood has remained. The occupation of the land took place in 1980, and since then a substantial infrastructure has been established, in the form of electricity, running water and dirt roads. A gradual improvement of the houses has also been seen.

It was a group of church leaders from the surrounding Christian communities that helped organize the occupation. Today, the church still plays an active role in helping people to get organized: in womens groups, trade unions, residents' associations and Christian communities. The fight with the municipality and with the state government to be able to stay in the area is not over yet. Formally, they are still illegally occupying the area. In practical terms, they have no other place to go to.

The inhabitants are mainly white, descended from Germans, Italians, Spaniards and Portuguese. Three of these inhabitants are Eva (32), Estella (13) and Christiane (14), all of whom are white. Eva and Christiane are decended from German immigrants and Christiane from Italians. There are still many rural zones in Southern Brazil where the population continue to speak the German and Italian dialect their ancestors brought with them to Brazil four or five generations ago. Migration to the towns has been significant here as well, mainly from the rural zones of Rio Grande do Sul to the urban centre of Porto Alegre/Canoas. Eva (32), for example, migrated at the age of 2 with her parents to Porto Alegre, and can, despite 30 years in Porto Alegre, still speak the German dialect of the region from which she originates.

The neighbourhood of Santa Operaria is open and quite green, but also damp and low-lying. Many houses, like for example Eva's, are built on stilts to avoid the periodic floodings. The neighbourhood has more space between the houses than in either Calabar and Vila N.O. Most of the inhabitants have houses with at least two rooms.

Santa Operaria has an active church life and community life in general. Many still do not participate, but they have benefited from the work these grass-roots movements have done to upgrade the area. Minor shops, churches and small scale industry are scattered around in the area. Nobody seriously imagines that the inhabitants today would be forced by the public authorities to move from the area. However, the fact of not being legalized gives the area a formal problem in their continuous struggle to obtain the official right to infrastructural improvements such as roads and drains, and public institutions such as clinics and schools.

Estella

Estella (13) is in the 6th grade at school. She lives with her mother, father and three younger sisters and brothers in a very small house, consisting only of a bedroom and a kitchen. One of her sisters is handicapped, having a bad right arm. Their small house lies on sacred ground, neighbouring the local Catholic church. Her parents function as a kind of caretaker couple for the church. Her family is poor.

Compared with other 13 year-olds – and even with many adults – Estella is very politically conscious. She is also very creative, and generally a inclined to become involved and committed. Both her parents are very active in the residents' association and in one of the Christian communities in Santa Operaria. Her father is also a member of the workers' party and works for one of the members of the municipal council. As was the case with Crioula (18) in Calabar, Estella's parents' activities have integrated her into political, religious and social work at an early age.

Estella likes to watch telenovelas with her sister or mother whenever she has the time. However, her leisure time is packed with activities. She is very active in the children's group at the Catholic church, she sings in the church choir, plays the guitar and writes many poems and stories. When she gets a little older she would like to become a nun and an author. Her greatest dream is to publish a book describing all that she experiences, for others to read.

The telenovela she likes the best is *Top Model* which has an 18 year old girl, a model, as the principal character. Estella is convinced that telenovelas transmit useful things, but they also show many bad things. In *Rubbish Queen* she sees many parallels to the social reality she lives in, where many people live off recycling litter.

Christiane

Christiane (13) is Estella's friend and also goes in 6th grade. Christiane lives with her mother (34), father (43) and her four brothers and sisters. She watches a lot of TV, both in the afternoons and evenings. She watches TV with her brothers and sisters and her mother who is a housewife. Her father, who is an industrial worker in a plant in the municipality, does not like telenovelas.

Apart from watching TV, Christiane spends her leisure time playing. Occasionally she comes to the church, but not as often as Estella. Her mother frequently calls her away to help with the domestic chores. It is her responsibility to clean the house. Her mother and sister take care of the other chores. When Christiane grows up she want to become a maths teacher. Whereas Estella is clearly an opinion leader even when playing games with other young people, Christiane is more of a "follower". She seems a little insecure and shy.

Eva

Eva (32) is, like many other southern Brazilians, of German descent, three to four generations back. She has lived in town since she was 2, when her family migrated to Canoas. She frequently visits her family in Camaquá, the village she comes from. She is still able to speak the German dialect, just like many other first generation migrants in the Porto Alegre region.

Eva is married to a bricklayer, has three small children and is pregnant with the fourth. She has 7 years of education. Eva is in principle a housewife, but is always busy. She is very active in church work and in political work for the workers party. There is no clear distinction between the political and the religious work. For example, together with the mothers' group from the church she participates in political campaigns for specific candidates. She spends a lot of time on all this grass-roots work. She also bakes cakes that she sells in the district to earn some money for the household.

Eva is a very calm but highly motivated woman. She is probably the most committed of all 13 women, reflecting on everything very analytically and possessing a highly developed critical sense. She has many visions about the future, visions that synthesize both her political and religious work. She provides a good example of the committed grass-roots activism growing out of the Theology of Liberation that is to be found in many places in Latin America.

The community of Santa Operaria is poor, without being as marginalized as a favela but with a lower standard of living than Vila Nitro Operaria. There seemed to be close community contact, with a relatively strong social organization involving large groups within the neighbourhood. Most of the inhabitants are of

German descent, including Eva and Christiane. The Catholic faith plays a marked role in Eva's life, as it does in Estella's, though they appear, from the reception analysis, to interpret their belief very differently. In their interpretations of *Rubbish Queen*. described in chapter 9, we shall see how much their religion influences their readings of telenovelas.

4. Socio-emotional characteristics

What do these 13 women have in common? What general characteristics can be found – and what characterizes the neighbourhood culture of which they form a part? Paying due attention to the differences and complexities within the general category of "low-income urban women", let me list some of their main characteristics.

All 13 women are migrants from or have parents who were migrants from rural areas. This is important to note, because it preconditions their lifestyle, and the norms and values that guide them in their everyday lives. The role of telenovelas in everyday life, as will be seen in the next two chapters, is influenced by the rural origin of the viewers. This background has brought in norms and values, ways of socializing and life-styles characteristic of rural communities into the urban centres in Brazil. As we will see, the organization of time and space in these three neighbourhoods, the configuration of private and public spheres, relates a great deal to what happens in rural areas (chapter 8).

When it comes to the organization of social relations, this chapter has shown that many of the women have domestic rifts behind them. However, almost all live in couples, with their children but often also with extra relatives in extended families. The constitution of the households in the survey area are different and more complex than traditional households in the Western societies, and thus also different from the classical unit studied in many reception analyses from Morley's 1986 study onwards. It influences the viewing situations as will be seen in the next chapter, and thereby also influences what Mary Ellen Brown has called "gossip networks", that is the primarily female networks that seem to have a specific function in women's cultures (Brown1994: 30-32). In the area under survey social networks taking in families, friends and neighbours are widespread, function well and are clearly gender specific. They contribute significantly to making ends meet but are also used, as Deborah Jones has pointed out, for house-talk, scandal, bitching and chatting (Jones 1980:197). This is particularly relevant for the reception of telenovelas.

Other significant factors influencing their everyday life are unemployment and a tight budget. The women are either unemployed themselves and/or have husbands, fathers and others who are or have been unemployed for significant periods. The many temporary jobs and coming and going on and off the job market are characteristic of these people's lives. This sometimes makes it difficult to distinguish formal from informal income: the exchange of favours, food and looking after children, the selling of home-baked bread, cakes or sweets, earning a little by sewing, washing or repairing something. All these side-earnings, minor sources of income and/or survival strategies from the informal sector, are widespread. In the poorest families, as for example Clara's family in Calabar and Elenita in Vila N.O. the side-earnings constitute the basic source of income and survival. None of the families could afford anything else than the most essential everyday goods, and some even less.

Female network/neighbourhood culture/social contact

Despite this situation of shortage, TV had a high priority. All 13 had one or more TV sets. The meaning of the TV set in constituting the symbolic order of everyday life will be elaborated on in chapter 8, but, seen in relation to what the families could afford, it is clear that its role is a central one.

The lives of the women introduced in this chapter reflect, on the one hand, social and economic conditions that create the frame within which everyday life takes place. On the other hand their social and cultural practices reflect their life experiences, their religious beliefs and their utopian dreams and hopes for the future. In this interactive process between dream and reality they seek to find themselves, narrating themselves as John B.Thompson would say (Thompson 1995), negotiating and positioning themselves *vis-à-vis* the socio-economic frames that limit their everyday lives and the hopes that are generated. In the course of this process, some norms and values become internalized, others just accepted, but simultaneously, transcending possibilities appear in the forces of everyday life, in the interaction between the emotional mobilization of dreams and beliefs, and rational reflection relating to the social reality they live in. Obviously, the role of telenovelas must be seen in this context.

When it comes to social reality as experienced by the women of the three neighbourhoods described here, five major characteristics must be taken into consideration – all of which influence their reception of TV. First, there is a concern for and and a sense of responsibility towards the extended family, that is, all members of the household, including the elderly, nephews and other relatives living there. The women possess a high degree of loyalty to people they have "blood" ties with, thus to the whole extended family to whom they open their doors. However, from a more pragmatic point of view, the welcome offered to members of the extended family may also result in one more income to assist in

The visibility of religious icons and statues appears in many homes. They relate to both Catholic and Afro-Brazilian beliefs.

covering the daily needs of the family, as in the case of Matilde's nephew. Meanwhile, the ambitions and dreams of education encountered among the women are directed especially towards their children, with the hope that they will obtain higher levels of education than themselves.

The women's pronounced sense of responsibility often results in their having two jobs; one keeping the household in order, which they feel they have the responsibility and the moral duty to do, and another one outside of the house, earning money.

Secondly, the women all have great solidarity with each other, expressed in a strong social network. It is clearly a survival strategy, but also a way of making things easier and more enjoyable. These networks should of course not be idealized, as they have their share of envy and jealousy, conflicts and quarrels. However, this gender specific network – partly a gossip network as Mary Ellen Brown says – makes things work, making sure there is food every day, a clean house, clean clothes, somebody to take care of the children, and whatever else that has to do with fulfilling the minimum needs of each other's families. It also constitutes a principal interpretive community for the women, although they only occasionally share the viewing situation with each other. Telenovelas are mostly, as we shall see in chapter 8, viewed with the family, but the interpretive process continues all next day in the "gossip network", commenting and producing meaning. The residents' associations are also predominantly women's associations, being female social networks with political goals as well the kind of social functions mentioned above.

Thirdly, there is the daily struggle to keep the house decent; getting a beautiful home of their own is a cherished ambition for many. Their dignity as human beings is very much linked to the organization of their household, keeping it clean and orderly. Their wish to be proud of their own home is expressed not just in dreams of modern artifacts such as kitchen appliances, colour television and nice furniture, but also in the daily cleaning, in the decorations on the walls and in the cultivation of small plants and flowers on the little pieces of land in front of their houses. This concern for beauty and decency is also reflected in their treatment of themselves, wishing to look beautiful, wear trendy clothes, use make-up, in other words having an aesthetic concern related to oneself. The stars of the telenovelas may very well play a central role in addressing this concern.

Fourthly, among the black women, and thus especially in Calabar, a racial discourse is constitutive in their personal identity. It was not very explicit in their general conversation, but became very evident when they were asked questions about race (I elaborate on this in chapter 9). Many of the women regularly experience racial discrimination, when shopping, when waiting at the bus stop and when applying for jobs. Discrimination in the representation of blacks was occasionally noted, as for instance in the absence of black people, especially women, as role models in telenovelas. I also return to this in chapter 9.

Finally, when relating to the world around them, a class consciousness and a feeling of marginality is present among all of the women. They know very well they are poor, that they belong to the underprivileged. They are conscious that their chances of obtaining a better life are limited. Some work consciously and politically to change things, others do not. However, most of them clearly have dreams and aspirations for social change, or rather, for a personal change for the better. Many privately dream of the Cinderella story coming true – a clear example is Roberta's current obsession about becoming a top model, just like the characters of a recent telenovela.

8. Living with a TV set

When analysing the role of television in everyday life, I concluded in my theoretical discussion in chapter 2 that it is essential to look in depth at three elements: the organization of time, of space and social relations – and the role of television in this organizational process.

Chapter 7 introduced the 13 women involved in this case study, providing a general insight into the socio-economic conditions these women live under. The chapter concluded by outlining their major socio-emotional concerns, characteristics and survival strategies. The next step is to analyse the social uses of television in their everyday life. In which ways do the television set, the programme flow, and especially the telenovelas interact with the women's organization of time, space and social relations? Let us begin the analysis by outlining the media situation.

1. Media situation

All 13 women have at least one television set at home. In Roberta's (13, Vila N.O.) home they had three, of which two were black and white. Six of the women only had black and white sets. They were all able to indicate quite precisely when they got their first television set, which for most of them was 18-20 years ago. Gildete (63, Vila N.O.) was the first of my respondents to buy a television set. This was in 1957. It was installed in the bar which she and her husband owned where they both worked. The TV was bought to attract customers. Roberta (13, Vila N.O.) and Crioula (18, Calabar) have had television all their lives.

When the first people began to buy television sets it was a social event in the neighbourhood. Ilda's family was the first in her part of Vila N.O. to get a television set. It was installed in her father's shop. When the first daily telenovela was transmitted, *Direito de Nascer* (TV Tupi, 1963) the shop became "loaded with people" (Ilda, 40,Vila N.O.). Ana's family in Calabar was the last to buy a television set. They bought it five years ago, paying in installments over a long period. That was not a social event. Before that time Ana and her family used to watch television at the neighbours'. However, for most of the women television has been an integral part of their everyday lives for many years.

When television appeared in their homes, television viewing gradually re-structured social activities, especially other media habits, like listening to the radio. Geraldina (38) – and her mother, who lives with her – still remember how they listened a lot to radionovelas back in their village in Bahia, before migrating to São

Paulo. They did not have a television there. When they arrived in São Paulo they got their first television. I have no data as to how much listening to radio novelas was superseded by watching telenovelas. However, Matilde gives an idea of the transformation that occurred: "I did it a lot, listening to the radio. I was crazy about it. I almost didn't do anything else but listen to the radio. I almost didn't do anything in the house, I ran around doing things to be able to be in time for broadcast... Now, when it's television time I always watch" (Matilde, 40, Calabar).

Crioula watching TV and combing her sister's hair.

The telenovelas were a novelty arriving simultaneously with the massive purchase of television in the 1960s and 1970s, but were for many a continuation and a replacement of their listening to radionovelas. However, radio did not disappear. Many continued listening to the radio in the mornings, only replacing it by television in the afternoons and evenings. As we shall see elaborated later, the consumption of television is often confined to hearing the sound, thus continuing the tradition of listening to something. We must not forget that radionovelas used to be very popular, and, as analysed in chapter 5, the sound track of the telenovelas is loud and expressive: very radiophonic.

In terms of choice of programming, the habit gradually became linked to one specific television channel, Rede Globo's. When asked if they watch Television Manchete's telenovelas, many answered no. When asked why not, several answered that they were not used to it. Seen from the producers' point of view, several representatives of Television Manchete are convinced that watching Rede Globo's channel is more an expression of social routine than better programming.

Attilio Riccó from Television Manchete relates that Roberto Marinho, the owner of Rede Globo, was against the introduction of remote controls in Brazil. He was very well aware that watching Rede Globo was an institutionalized habit and feared that the remote control would favour his competitors, since it would make it easier to switch channels. However, today remote controls exist in Brazil (Riccó, 1991).

The everyday flow of telenovelas[1]

The continuous, interlinked broadcasting of television programmes throughout an evening was noted by Raymond Williams at the beginning of the 1970s. He labelled it television flow, thereby indicating the lack of clear limits between one programme and the other within an evening's broadcasting (Williams,1975).[2] However, where Williams mainly dealt with the flow characteristic of a 'horizontal' broadcasting policy, I shall argue for the concept of a 'vertical' television flow, based on what I discovered about the everyday lives of low income Brazilians. It is especially linked to the telenovelas. These are transmitted daily, six days a week. The everyday flow of telenovelas transcends the linear time perception, and enters into a cyclical understanding of time, expressed in the repetitive daily routines. Telenovelas are a constant media flow, present every day at the same time, in the same place and space, very recognisable in content, and always having the same characters. The following data support the concept of the everyday flow of telenovelas.

Television sets in most households

Although television today is widespread in Brazil, there are still some who cannot afford it. 84 per cent of my respondents in Calabar do have a television set, but 16 per cent do not. However, only 2 per cent per cent do not watch television at all. Thus, most of the people without their own television set still seek, and obtain, access to television. As Clara describes their experience, before getting their own television set: "My mother came from the rural areas directly to Calabar. There's been television ever since I was little. It was not here in the house, but in the neighbour's house. Later, my sister bought a television set" (Clara, 27, Calabar). In Vila N.O. television sets were more widespread. 90 per cent of the respondents had television in their household. Of the remaining 10 per cent, 4 per cent did not watch television at all. Thus, there were slightly more households in Vila N.O. than in Calabar who deliberately chose not to watch television.

Regarding the women's other media habits, the most used medium was radio: 86 per cent in Calabar and 77 per cent in Vila N.O. have radio (table 21 + 22, appendices 2 and 3). Newspapers were read at least once a week by approximately half of the respondents, while approximately one third of them read magazines (table 21 + 22, appendices 2 and 3). The magazines Contigo, Amiga and Manchete were the most popular, all of which are heavy disseminators of telenovela gossip. Thus, the recorded consumption of written media is limited. However, what is more difficult to measure is the widespread sharing of expensive magazines, which several of the women told me was a common practice among them.

In Calabar, one individual had a central role in the media: the governor of the state of Bahia: Antonio Carlos Magalhães, a very rich and influential man in Brazilian politics. *A Tarde*, the most read newspaper in Calabar, is owned by him. He also

---

1   These data are based on my statistical survey in Calabar and Vila N.O. See questionnaire in Appendix 4.

2   See also chapter 2, where I present Williams' concept of flow.

owns the television-station in Salvador which transmits the Globo programmes. He thus possesses a central influence on the mass media in Bahia, creating something very like a monopoly. This is, however, the case in many places in Brazil. Many politicians are the owners of their own local media empires, which gives them considerable scope for using the media for their own political purposes.

Consumption

A quantitative registration of media consumption is a useful starting point for an analysis of the relational uses of telenovelas. From my data, three points stand out clearly:

1. *There is a very high consumption of telenovelas.* When answering the question: "Which telenovelas do you currently watch?" the respondents indicated that they currently watched an average of 3.4 telenovelas a day in Calabar and 3.2 in Vila N. O! This means, in my interpretation, that they currently follow the story of more than three telenovelas every day (Table 18, appendices 2 and 3).

2. *Watching telenovelas is a prime time activity, covering the period 6-10 pm.* The three principal telenovelas followed were the 6, the 7, and the 8 o'clock telenovelas, which reached average ratings of 55, 51 and 55 in Vila N. O (Table 18, appendices 2 and 3).

3. *The respondents watched telenovelas daily, as a matter of routine.* When asked how often they watched telenovelas, 75 per cent (Vila N.O.) and 80 per cent(Calabar) said they watched them three or more times a week; 61 per cent (Vila N.O.) and 64 per cent (Calabar) watched them every day of the six days a week that telenovelas are broadcast! (Table 14, appendices 2 and 3)

These three findings emphasize the very important fact that the consumption of telenovelas is very high in Brazil. Unlike most other places in the world, apart from some other Latin American countries, prime time television viewing – from 6-10 pm – consists *only* of telenovelas. The evening flow of telenovelas on Rede Globo is only interrupted by 30 minutes of news, from 8-8.30 pm. There are naturally other channels which broadcast other types of programmes, but as showed in chapter 4, their general ratings are minimal compared with the ratings achieved by Globo's prime time telenovelas.

If we further remind ourselves of the massive supplement of secondary media texts, in radio, television and print media – texts that all deal with either the telenovela narrative, telenovela actors and/or telenovela music (see chapter 6) – the total consumption of media reveals a high consumption relating to the telenovelas. Many of the women in my case study listened to the radio programmes in the morning which revealed what was going to happen in the evening chapters. They also listened to the telenovela music on the radio while cleaning their houses. Furthermore, some of them either bought or came across the magazines *Contigo* and *Amiga* in which they could read about the actors' private lives and obtain even more information on how the narrative would unfold in the chapters of the week.

The widespread existence of television sets combined with the regular high rate consumption of telenovelas together constitute the measurable data documenting what I called the vertical dimension of the television flow. Telenovelas are repetitive, linked together across time, occurring at the same hour every day, entering and becoming a constitutive element in the familiar, expected pattern of everyday life. This everyday flow of telenovelas combines both the horizontal flow as described by Raymond Williams and the vertical flow linking yesterday's flow with today's and tomorrow's, thus entering naturally into the cyclical rhythm of the everyday.

Owning a television set was a high priority in most households I visited. Even in homes with a very limited household income I found they had a television set. Even though the people were lacking proper clothes, school equipment, shoes or furniture, somehow they could afford to purchase a television set. The priority of television is further emphasized by the prominent place it gets in the homes, as we shall see below.

Estella watching TV in the bedroom, also the family's TV room

2. Time and space in the household

Analysing the organization of time and space has in recent years become a major exercise in studies of modernity. Obviously, this book can also be characterized as a study of modernity. And it is. However, one must be cautious when talking about modernity in a Brazilian setting. My point with this whole analysis is to generate a broader understanding of the particularities of Latin American types of modernity. Consequently, it is also a critique – including a self critique – of using concepts and theories developed in a European or perhaps North American setting, in a Latin American, and more specifically in a Brazilian context. Therefore, although this study does fall in with the global trend of analysing time and space in modern, mostly urban settings, these particular low-income urban neighbourhoods are confusingly unlike the models we know. Seen from my North European cultural viewpoint, which it is difficult to let go of, these neighbourhoods seem very different in this respect from what I am used to. The further we get in analysing their organization of time and space, the clearer it is that they live with a different organization of time and space than the likewise in Northern Europe. Logically it must be a different modernity.[3]

Both the television set as a material object, as well as the social uses of the everyday flow of telenovelas are integral elements in the organization of time and space in the everyday lives of the viewers. However, analysing the organization of time and space in the households must be based on a more general analysis of time and space in Brazilian society. The Brazilian anthropologist Roberto Da Matta has, in his book *The House and the Street* (Da Matta, 1991), made a thorough analysis of the concepts of time and space in Brazilian everyday life.

Da Matta argues that in Brazilian society, parallel forms of time and space exist. He distinguishes between three different discourses of time and space, linked to three different spheres of signification: casa (house), rua (street) and outro mundo (other world). Each sphere is marked by very different attitudes, gestures, clothes, social roles, language and thus very different frames of reference (Da Matta, 1991: 52). Da Matta argues that any event can be read or interpreted along the lines of three different codes of conduct:

> The code of the house and the family, which stands in opposition to change and history, economy, individualism and progress; the code of the street, which is open to concepts of law and jurisdiction, to the market, to linear history and individualist progress; the code of the other world, which focuses on the idea of renunciation of the world with its pains and illusions and in so doing, tries to synthesize the other two.
>
> *Da Matta, 1991: 53-54*

These codes of conduct are not tied physically to houses and streets. The terms are abstract. They are metaphors which seek to illustrate the differences in the spheres of signification. The categories have similarities with other concepts from social theory relating to the spheres of society. Habermas' system – and life-world categories – as well as the classic concept of the public and the private spheres, which goes right back to the Ancient Greek philosophers – are concepts to which Da Matta's categories clearly relate. However, it would be too comprehensive to make a comparative analysis of these sets of concepts, especially of how Da Matta's third category "the other world" fits into the concept of signifying spheres referred to above. What makes Da Matta's concepts the most applicable to my analysis is the following: first, they were developed in the relevant cultural context: that of Brazil, and secondly they deal explicitly and in a concrete way with the organization of the time and space in the social world of everyday life. Even though they are analytical categories, they are closely related to the daily routines, reflecting substantial knowledge and "feeling" about the cultural setting studied.

Each of the categories possesses a specific language. In concrete terms, one code of conduct may very well prevail. Which one dominates, may be conditioned by class level. All the subordinate social groups, be it migrants from the rural areas, maids, workers in the informal sector, women or children, tend to use what

---

3   In Tufte 1997 I elaborate on the problematics of using theoretical concepts developed in one cultural context in another cultural context.

Da Matta calls the language of the house: "Its points of view are notably modest and balanced, often rooted in a really fantastic naturalization of social relations, which are rarely understood of or talked about as being historic and arbitrary but, on the contrary, talked about as though they were part of a cosmic order, a moral given by God (Da Matta, 1991: 54).

This discourse is thus based mainly on moral values, referring to a morality that seems given by a higher power, a God. As I see it, it appears a politically alienated conception of things, relating to values taken to be universal. Da Matta speaks of "translating the world into an issue of preferences, bonds of sympathy, personal loyalties, reciprocal behaviour, compensations and good things or bad things: the space of the house!" (Da Matta, 1991: 55). Da Matta argues that this discourse is the one that can be seen in populist tradition, seeking to maintain a united situation, abstracting from class differences.

Opposed to this discourse is the one of the dominant segments of society, who use the language of the street. They would never use moral references or focus on personal contacts and values in their discourse. To them, laws are the guiding principle, along with the impersonal mechanisms and logic of the capitalist system, modes of production, class struggle and market orientation. According to Da Matta, the "street" is thus a sphere with little security. It is a dangerous place, where the law imposes equality. This might sound strange – depending on the cultural viewpoint with which you read this – but the law signifies something negative. You lose your personal identity, become anonymous.

Finally Da Matta operates with the language of the other world: "it concerns a system which in an intriguing way relates to a superficial equality and which is given in legal codes of foreign inspiration, generally separated from our social practice; it possesses a hierarchical structure, refusing to take one of the codes as its exclusive and dominant one and always preferring a relation between the two"(Da Matta, 1991: 56). It thus has religious connotations, referring to the Catholic history of colonial Brazil, but also to other forms of religious affiliation.

The three spheres are complementary and difficult to separate. This categorization of the social practices of humanity give a particular insight into the way everyday life is lived, including watching television and producing meaning from it. I find them useful for understanding the overall spheres of signification existing in contemporary Brazilian everyday life. Therefore, in my analysis of the social uses and consumption of television I will relate to these spheres of signification, with their differentiated codes of conduct, and different social and aesthetic discourses.

My analysis of the social uses of telenovelas will cover an analysis of both the space and the time in which television viewing takes place. This encompasses an analysis of the following elements:

1. Where the television set is placed in the household.

2. How the viewing of telenovelas interacts with the rituals of the everyday.

3. The concrete time and space in which the television viewing takes place.

Da Matta would argue that the spatial and temporal setting in which television viewing takes place has its specific spheres of signification, that either relate to "the language of the house" or "the language of the street". However, I find the social reality so much more nuanced, that I shall argue that the temporal and spatial sphere in which television is placed is an independent hybrid sphere, embedded in the sphere of the house, but not detached from the sphere of the street. My findings indicate that television viewing and consumption most often constitutes a sphere of its own. This is a hybrid sphere defined by temporal and spatial parameters which have a relationship to DaMatta's concept of social spheres, but which also emphasize some class specificities and posit a social, spatial and temporal autonomy for that hybrid sphere.

Hybrid spheres and the place of the television set

Any private home is organized according to a specific spatial grammar of the house. The television set is also placed according to specific customs and rules that are embedded in both cultural and socio-economic conditions, as we shall see in the following examples.

A typical phenomenon in the Brazilian homes I have visited[4] is that when entering the front door, you step right into the living room. There is never any hall or corridor in between. That is to say, there is a direct connection between the main room people reside in – the living room – and the street, or at least the space outside the house. Furthermore, as long as somebody is at home, the front door is often standing wide open, so the street can be seen from the living room and vice versa. Often, the windows are also open. Often there is no glass in the windows, but only a hole in the wall, covered by shutters. So in the morning, when the shutters are opened, it is not only to let light into the house but also an often unconscious establishment of contact between the life inside and outside.

In *favelas* like Calabar or Viela Santa Rosa[5] the distance between the house and the street is small, mainly because of the very dense and compact building of houses. In spite of the limited space, many *favela* dwellers, especially the women, use the front space for both practical and decorative purposes. They either have some flowers there, an outdoor sink to wash clothes in or just an open space where visitors can stand and talk with the woman of the house, or the children can play. Thus, the contact between the house and the street is very close. The boundary between the public sphere (the street) and the private sphere (the house) becomes blurred.

Often you find a curtain or a little corridor between the kitchen and bedrooms and the living room which clearly indicates that the private sphere is behind this curtain or on the other side of the corridor, in the bedrooms and kitchen. In the smallest homes, with only one room, this distinction between spheres is not possible, with the physical elimination of the private sphere as a consequence. In those situations, the boundary between the street and the house are clearly marked, for example by a more frequent closing of the front door. Thereby a private sphere is established in the house, and the hybrid sphere physically disappears.

The television set is almost always to be found in the living room. Only in one of the 13 homes I frequented, was the television set placed in a bedroom. This was in

---

4   I have paid many visits to low income homes all over Brazil throughout many work and study missions to the country between1983-1998, having also frequented many homes while living almost two years in the country.

5   This is a *favela* in the Eastern Zone of São Paulo that I frequented daily during 3 months in 1987 and have visited again every year from 1989 to 1992.

Gildete's home (Gildete, 63, Vila N. O). In the many other homes I have visited, the television was placed in such a way as to be visible from the street. In none of the homes I visited was it placed on the same wall as the main entrance, so that it could not be seen from the outside. It stood either by the side wall or by the wall opposite the main entrance to the living room. Let me illustrate this with a few examples:

Gildete watching TV in the bedroom

Crioula's home in Calabar lay on a small hill a couple of meters from the narrow path sneaking tortuously through the narrow confines of the *favela*. There was no fence and no real front yard. Both the door and the window shutters were open every time I visited Crioula in her house. From the street one entered right into the living room which was rather long and narrow. There was a sofa on the left side and the television set in a shelf system to the right. The television set could be seen both from the window and the door, as well as from the dining table in the other end of the living room. From the dining room at end of the house you entered the more private quarters. Thus, the entrance area, together with the combined living and dining room, constituted the physical boundaries of the hybrid sphere in Crioula's home.

In Clara's case in Calabar, space was very limited. From the narrow path one entered directly into a very small room, with a sofa on the right hand side, a huge television on the left side, and with the kitchen facilities at the opposite end of the same room. The room made a small turn to the left, where a little table was fitted in. A back door in the room lead out to a very small path, not more than 1 meter wide, a public path where people passed by. Next to the main entrance were two doors, one on each side. They led into the two bedrooms where everybody slept – 9 people. The narrow living and kitchen room, with an entrance at each end, constituted the physical boundaries of the hybrid sphere in Clara's case. Both

Eva seen in the kitchen from the back yard

doors were kept open all day long, also to provide more light into the house. The private sphere was limited to the bedrooms.

In Eva's case in Santa Operaria, the wooden house she lived in was set back four to five meters from the road. It stood on stilts due to occasional flooding from the river nearby. There was a fence and a gate which you had to go through to reach the house. This prevented her children from running out into the street, where cars passed at quite a high speed. Eva always kept her front door open, except when not at home. Likewise with the window shutters (there is no glass). In the house next door her younger sister lived with her family. They often communicated across the wall. From the entrance one could look straight across at the television set. There was not much furniture in the living room; a sofa, a chair and the television set standing on a television table, and a few pictures on the walls. Television viewing went on all day; in the day time it was mainly the children watching, in the evenings the whole family. Sometimes the children sat on the staircase watching television a little and running around playing in between. It was only on the third of my visits to her house that Eva invited me further inside than the living room. I was a visitor, and therefore kept in the living room, the "visitors' lounge". Only by asking permission to follow Eva into the kitchen, did I get to move around the house. From the living room one entered a small hall, from where there were doors into two small bedrooms and a small dining room which lead on to the kitchen and a very small toilet.

The kitchen had a back door, leading out into the back yard. In the yard lived a dog and clothes were washed and dried. Eva's home had a clear frontier between the living room and the rest of the house, with the small hall constituting the invisible division.

In Elenita's case in Vila N.O., the family house had only one room. The entrance was on one side, with the television placed diagonally opposite, to the right hand side. It could thus be watched both from the door, and from their dining table standing next to the door, and could also be watched from their beds placed along two walls. Finally, the left hand corner was the kitchen corner from where Elenita could also watch television. The room had no windows at all, and only one electric bulb in the ceiling. Thus, the room was badly lit, giving it a more intimate and thus "private sphere" atmosphere than some of the other homes.

These examples show clear socio-economic differences between the women in this case study, which also influenced the way they organized their homes and the concrete placement of their television set. The better their economic situation was, the better their houses were – and the more room they had. Ilda and Roberta were the ones with the best conditions. Ilda's house had a carport in front of the house, where their car was parked. The main entrance was through the carport, from where one entered the kitchen; from the kitchen one entered the living room, where the television set stood. The windows between the living room and the outside were dark, so it was not possible to look through them. In addition to that, they were even covered by huge, heavy curtains most of the day. Here, the living room was physically completely detached from the street. Roberta's house was similar, with a massive separation between house and street – a combination of security measures and the desire for more privacy, something people obviously lack in their very collective life (see also Leal, 1986 and Barrios, 1988).

Da Matta discusses spatial grammar in his reflections upon 'sala de visitas' rooms which, in middle class and sometimes even lower middle class houses are specially reserved for receiving visitors. However, in my case study, nobody had a house big enough to have one: they received visitors in their living room. However, in many of my cases, their living rooms had the same function as the one DaMatta attributes to the 'sala de visitas'. The French scientist Saint-Hilaire, who visited Brazil between 1816 and 1822, made the following observation about the space in the houses:

In the houses of the poor, like in those of the rich, there is always a room called the "sala", which has a side facing directly onto the out of doors. It is there one receives strangers and has one's meals, sitting on wooden benches around a long table. After the guests are satisfied, the host has a place for them to sit: a gallery or a veranda in front of his house, formed by the roof reaching out further than the wall and supported by wooden pillars. Generally, one can stay in these galleries in all seasons of the year, breathing fresh air, or sheltered from the rain or the heat of the sun.

Saint-Hilaire 1975(1830): 96

It was a situation similar to this one that I experienced 175 years later, in Calabar, in Matilde's house. Here the men were sitting outside, playing dominoes, while the women – the wife and daughter – were indoors. What was happening in the living room could equally well have taken place on the veranda, and vice versa, as I found out when I was sitting and interviewing Matilde in her living room, with constant comments on our conversation coming from the veranda.

Figure 1. Hybrid sphere of signification

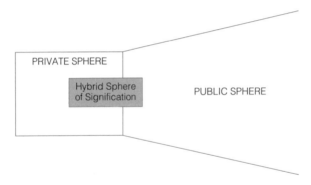

The above description and analysis shows that in low-income urban settings in Brazil there is a close contact between the living rooms and the street, forming the physical boundaries of the hybrid sphere. The fact is that the hybrid sphere is not entirely a part of the private sphere. The demarcation-line between the private and the hybrid sphere is clearly indicated by a boundary between the private quarters, including bedrooms and kitchen on one side, and the living room on the other. The boundary between the hybrid sphere and the public sphere is more blurred, but is always outdoors, between the front yard or the veranda, and the street. However, this physical boundary is just one of several variables which together form the cultural sphere of signification that I have called the hybrid sphere. The further we proceed in the analysis, the more obvious it will become that the traditional concepts of public and private sphere, developed in a very different context, are insufficient and not applicable in analysing the spheres of signification in Brazil. To understand the role of telenovelas in this specific socio-cultural context let us proceed to the next element of the "grammar" of the hybrid sphere: the role of gender in codes of conduct.

The gender difference

The women have their specific spatial and temporal circles in which they move. Within the household the kitchen, the bedrooms and the back yard are predominantly women's areas. The French scientist Saint-Hilaire described how, at the beginning of the 19th century, he experienced the invisible lines of gender sanctuaries:

> The interior of the houses, reserved for the women, is a sanctuary into which the stranger never enters, and people who showed me the greatest confidence never permitted my employees to enter the kitchen in order to dry the paper necessary for conserving my plants; they were obliged to light a fire outside, in the slaves' quarters, or in some porch. The gardens, always situated behind the houses, were a slight compensation to the women for their captivity, and, like the kitchen, were strictly barred to strangers.
>
> *Saint-Hilaire, 1975(1830): 96*

This reminds me a lot of my own experiences, as for instance in the case of Eva's home, described above. Another example was Geraldina's back yard. Although she was the woman I knew best, having visited her regularly for five consecutive years, I was never shown the back yard. Only once did I enter it. To put it differently: it was only on my own initiative that I would get access to the kitchens and back yards in my contact with the women.

The families' everyday life followed these rules for gender conduct, or, in linguistic terms, well defined gender-grammar existed for the organization of space. The women had their domains and the men theirs. The men often sat on the

The hybrid sphere of signification. Estella's mother in Santa Operaria.

Geraldina "listening to TV" whilst cooking.

verandas or on street corners where they assembled to talk and play dominoes or other games. The bars were a domain reserved for them, where women seldom entered. Even in the case of Crioula in Calabar, whose father worked as a bartender in the bar across the path, not more than 10 metres from their house, not once during the week I spent in Calabar did I see her enter the bar. And generally, when I was socializing with the men in bars, I did not see women enter them.

However, in the hybrid sphere, men and women meet and create a mutual space of social interaction. Here a certain power struggle occurs, because the hybrid sphere is not defined as either the woman's or the man's spatial domain. The power struggle can for example relate to what programmes to watch on television or how to combine television viewing with dining – when to do what. While the men and women respect each other's domain, not entering them or interfering much with them, the hybrid sphere of the living room and the veranda/front yard is the main forum for dialogue and mutual decision-making.

Structuring everyday life via television

The programme schedule of television influences the daily routines of everybody, thus influencing the grammar of time. Somebody gets up to see a special programme in the morning, others hurry home from school to see something. Others again plan their day, the cooking or their homework, according to when specific programmes, and especially telenovelas, are scheduled. Watching telenovelas thus contributes to structuring specific rituals within everyday life and becomes itself a ritual – especially – but not uniquely – the 8 o'clock telenovela. Consider some examples of both: Roberta (13, Vila N.O.) describes how she hurries home from school to do her homework before the programme *Mara* begins.

Matilde from Calabar runs home, even from meetings in the women's group or the residents' organization to be able to watch telenovelas:

> Since I like novelas, I do not want to miss them. I may be wherever, I will come running home to watch my novela. The days I miss my novela I go crazy.
>
> *And if you are in a meeting?*
>
> Then I ask to leave early, because I have something to do.
>
> *Matilde, 40, Calabar*

Geraldina (38, Vila N. O) does the cooking in time to see the 7 o'clock telenovela, *Full Moon Love*, and is thus prevented from seeing *Belly for Hire* for that reason: "While I am cooking I listen to *Belly for Hire* and *Full Moon Love*. These I listen to from the kitchen. It isn't possible for me to sit down and watch (...) It is very difficult for me to sit down and watch these two novelas".

Eva (32, Santa Operaria), draws attention to the problem of wanting to watch telenovelas and be active in grass-roots work. She gives priority to the grass-root work herself, but often comes across the problem among the others:

> I know many women who watch television from morning to evening. They even forget their children, house and grass-roots work. We see it in the women's group. We usually tell our women how difficult it makes things. Just because they have to see the 2 o'clock telenovela we cannot put on our meetings until after 3 o'clock, or otherwise they will have to be late. Then we tell them that our meetings obviously mean less to them than watching telenovelas, even though it does not lead to anything. Instead they ought to participate in the meetings and perhaps discuss the same type of problems as those they see in the telenovelas.
>
> *What do they answer to that?*
>
> They answer, "oh, we have got used to telenovelas, we like watching them because we don't have the opportunity to out, we cannot go to the cinema, we cannot afford to dine out. The only thing we have a right to do is to watch television, so if you also take this from us, what will become of us?" This is the answer they give us. The only entertainment the poor man has is television.
>
> *Eva, 32, Calabar*

Eva obviously dislikes this attitude to telenovelas: giving them such a high priority in the everyday. The programme schedule however forces Eva and the other organizers to adapt to their timings to it: the ritual of watching a specific telenovela is stronger than other social activities like participating in grass-roots meetings.

The examples of Roberta (13), Matilde (40) and Geraldina (38) emphasize that television, and especially the viewing of telenovelas has a high priority for many women. It structures their everyday life, both creating rituals and becoming a ritual in itself. In this way television becomes part of the temporal and spatial structure which constitutes the framework of daily social action. Simultaneously, television viewing becomes a structuring element in itself, due to peoples' timing of their other activities to fit round the telenovelas.

Eva and her three children.

The everyday of prime time

Along with a spatial and temporal grammar, the hybrid sphere also has a social grammar. As previously described, the hybrid sphere, with the living room at its heart, is the central spatial and temporal field in what I would call the everyday of prime time. The period between 6 and 10 pm is the principal period of social recreation in most homes. It is when it gets dark outside, people come home from their respective jobs and other activities, dinner is served, the last homework is done and last but not least: telenovelas are on. Finally, many families go to bed after the last telenovela, around 10 pm. The social activity in this period of the day is constituted by many interrelated activities, including television viewing, as my findings will show.

It is very rare that television programmes are watched alone. In Calabar 71 per cent never watch television alone, 14 per cent watch television alone rarely, and only 10 per cent watch television alone regularly (see tables 9 and 12, appendix 2). In Vila N.O. 49 per cent of the women watch television alone, while 45 per cent never see television alone. Thus, television viewing is a very social activity, most of all in Calabar. During the daytime the women often watch television together with their children while in the evenings the whole family is present, including the men.

At the same time as they are watching television more than two thirds of the women both in Calabar and Vila N.O. are busy with other domestic activities (Table 20, appendices 2 and 3): cooking, cleaning, washing clothes, sewing and looking after the children. Several point out that they often listen to television instead of watching television, eg. Geraldina. This means they are often in the room next door, in the kitchen, unable to see the screen, which is why they only hear what is going on on television. Only when the music or other sounds strike a dramatic mood or atmosphere, do they interrupt their activities in the kitchen and go in to see what is happening. Approximately one third of the women say that the television is sometimes turned on without anyone actually watching. (see table 19, appendices 2 and 3). Many in the last category most probably listen to television while doing other things.[6]

Television viewing in the low-income urban areas does in many ways seem similar to the description given by the Italian sociologist Irene Penacchioni when describing the conditions under which television was viewed in the small villages in Nordeste in the beginning of the 1980s:

> Every little town in the north-east of Brazil has its square with a television set on a concrete block which has been specifically constructed for it. In the evening, when the air gets fresher, the television is switched on, and the square starts to fill with the sound of the television, which mixes naturally with the sounds of daily life...with the sounds of children and drunks, with the music from transistor radios, with the rattling and roaring of engines (...), with conversations, which are also continued in front of the television, without anyone asking for silence in order to follow better what's happening on the screen.
>
> *Penacchioni, 1984; 339*

The atmosphere of television viewing on a village square appears to be similar to the atmosphere of the living rooms in Calabar and Vila N.O. The television viewing takes place in a very complex social situation where many people, sounds and surroundings interact in a common sound-space of everyday life. The relations between the many agents in the prime time situation can seem very chaotic. Again, Penacchioni's descriptions from a village in Nordeste give a similar impression as to the situation I found in my survey areas:

> ..television is integrated within a collective sound-space in the midst of almost uninterrupted activity. It is a meeting place, the end of a walk. The television is naturally there, a bit like a trusted Goddess to whom one listens without much respect. But what does one see and hear in point of fact? The picture quality is often poor, and the sound vanishes in the general hubbub. But in spite of that it is likely that the following day one will catch the bus and discuss the story of the telenovela passionately and in detail.
>
> *Penacchioni, 1984: 339*

This social and cultural setting, which I encountered in Calabar, Vila N.O. and in Santa Operaria, is radically different from the setting characterizing television viewing in, for example, Denmark. In Denmark, TV viewing takes place in atmosphere of silence, concentration and attention; the general noise, variety and confusion of everyday life takes place elsewhere. This distinction is non-existent

---

6   It is not so often the women are cleaning while watching television: cleaning is often linked with listening to the radio and taking place in the daytime, due to the fact that many houses are badly lit.

in Brazil; it simply does not fit into a low income Brazilian television setting. Da Matta distinguishes the temporality of cultural spheres in Brazil from the ones in North American families. He argues that the temporality of North American house spheres does not differ from the street sphere. It is linear, individualized, linked to the world out there. Contrasting this he describes the "old order" established in terms of differences in sex, age and "blood" (Da Matta, 1991: 59). The understanding of North American houses can obviously not be generalized in those terms, but it should be subject to just as as thorough anthropological analyses as Brazilian houses and streets. However, what is useful in Da Matta's observation is the dichotomy he formulates between cyclical and linear conceptions of time.

As I interpret Da Matta, the old order acknowledges a communal living space, which allows for the differences in capacities, needs and interests of every individual, as determined by sex, age and family relations. In this order the dominant temporality is cyclical, giving room for family encounters, for coming and going, for repetition and delay. Time and space are structured by rituals which avoid chaos in everyday life. Opposed to this old order, we find the "new order", linked to efficiency, individual-ization, equal rights and obligations. Here the conception of time is linear, cumulative and historic. This is an impersonal cultural setting which does not leave room for going over things again, for yearning, for just "being".

In terms of the social grammar of watching television, the viewing situations I have described above, are clearly oriented towards the cyclical time conception. The existing norms are embedded in the social grammar of the old order, permitting multiple simultaneous activities and a chaotic collective sound-space where television viewing ends up co-existing with talking, sewing, cooking and looking after children.

3. The hybrid sphere of signification

The hybrid sphere of everyday life is a social, cultural and economic construct, an autonomous sphere of signification, defined by the specificity of the organization of time, space and social relations. As I interpret the everyday life of the women in my survey areas, the hybrid sphere is a social and cultural field of everyday practices mediated by the contradictions between urban and rural life, between tradition and modernity, and finally between masculine and feminine norms and values. It thus becomes an important sphere in the development of the hybrid cultures Canclini refers to in his analysis of the development of Latin American modernity (Canclini, 1995a).

The hybrid sphere – the indeterminate zone between the public and the private spheres – is widespread in the urban areas where many first and second generation migrants live, including in the three Brazilian neighbourhoods studied in this book. Although it is a constant element in everyday life, the hybrid sphere is most pronounced, and lived with most intensity, in television prime time, that is between 6 and 10 pm, and at its peak before dinner, which usually means before 8 pm. Television is central to the hybrid sphere, as is physically apparent from the central position of the television set. The hybrid sphere is defined by specificities in the organization of time, space and social relations, in which the everyday flow of telenovelas and the specific viewing situation are substantial interactive agents.

The organization of time

The everyday flow of telenovelas promotes both a linear and a cyclical concept of time. On one hand people adapt their everyday routines to the television programme schedule. Thus, they become very aware of time and get a rational understanding of time, as something concrete which can be abundant or – in the case of a meeting in the residents' association dragging on – very limited. So limited, indeed, that the scheduled telenovela may be missed. An even stronger influence, however, is the rhythm of the telenovela in everyday life. Telenovelas are lengthy; they go on for six to eight months and are broadcast daily. This promotes a more cyclical experience of time. The narrative is produced so that it fits into the rhythm of the everyday, with a lot of repetition, colloquial language, recognizable personal dramas. And it is always scheduled in prime time. Thus, the overall organization of time in terms of a six to eight month coexistence with the same characters is cyclical, but with a linear organization of time as regards one specific chapter.

The hybrid sphere of signification. Calaber (the mixing of public/private sphere).

The organization of space

The hybrid sphere is the place where people watch TV and do a lot else besides. All collective household activities take place here, interlinked with continuous visits from relatives, neighbours, friends and others. It is neither a private not a public sphere, but more of a collective sphere. Physically speaking, it is not private, because it is open to the street, people come by, and finally because there is a sphere which is more private – kitchen and bedrooms – often separated from the living room by a curtain or small hall. It is however not public either, being enclosed within the walls of the house, though extended to just outside. The open windows and doors emphasize this close relationship.

Furthermore, the hybrid sphere is, unlike many other spaces in everyday life, not gender specific. Where men have their bars and specific meeting places on street corners and squares, and where women dominate the kitchen, back yards and market places, the hybrid sphere is a collective space, for both men and women, although the woman's household responsibilities are reflected in her coming and going.

Finally, the hybrid sphere is characterized by being a collective sound-space. The noise of the television, talk, children playing, traffic noise, people coming and going, the sound of cooking in the kitchen all come together to create a specific sound space, in which it is impossible to hear whether you are in a public or private sphere. In terms of sound, the hybrid sphere is both.

Ilda in Vila N.O., São Paulo.

Social relations

The social grammar in the hybrid sphere is very much linked to the old order, being the central sphere of social interaction in the household. When retiring to the bedrooms, people retire to change their clothes, to sleep or take a nap. The social circles of the men and the women, usually very gender specific, meet in the hybrid sphere, while eating, watching television, talking and relaxing. As stated before, it is a collective sphere – where the people of the household meet.

This analysis of the social uses of television has thus provided some explanation as to the way people relate to the everyday flow of telenovelas. The fact is that television is placed in the most social sphere of the household and everyday life. Here people relax and enjoy each other's company. However, they are usually busy with social activities while gathered around the television set to watch a telenovela. If we consider the analysis give in chapter 5, of the historical origin of the telenovela as a genre, we shall see that its popularity resides partly in the fact that this everyday flow of novelas is basically storytelling. It is a new way of enjoying stories and a new way of being together. Seen in this perspective, telenovelas are a continuation of a very old tradition.

The habit of watching telenovelas is so strong in the low-income urban areas that it has even become if not the only, than at least the central structuring activity in everyday life at prime-time. As the word 'living-room' implies, it is a zone of everyday living. It is a sphere of signification with deeps roots in traditional, rural life- styles, but adapted to the contemporary social reality of low-income urban areas like Calabar, Vila Nitro Operaria and Santa Operaria. It has become a mediating sphere, playing an important role in the construction of the symbolic order of everyday life and in the formation of Latin American modernity – a sphere where distinct experiences of times and sociability meet.

9. Telling their own story

If we don't consider the money, then the life in novelas is usually the same as my life: the everyday life is the same, where the daughter has an argument with the mother, the father with the son, the child runs away, comes back later – life is the same.

Ilda, aged 41, Vila N.O.

Ilda's statement expresses the two discourses that construct the thematic frame of any telenovela: the personal discourse and the class discourse. These are analytical distinctions where the keyword of the themes related to the personal discourse is identification and the keyword of the themes related to the class discourse is social difference. The following analysis of a series of themes is structured around these basic discourses, expressed in both the media text and the interpretation of it.

Referring to the personal discourse I explore six sub-themes; the love drama, women's roles, family, community, taboos and the question of humour. The love drama, being central in all telenovelas, invites identification and involvement, and as such is a fundamental aspect of the narrative and its key to success. The other sub- themes are often present in telenovelas, as entry points to establish or reinforce emotional involvement in the narrative and the personal identification of the viewers with the characters of the telenovela. All the sub themes mentioned are explicitly manifest in *Rubbish Queen*.

The class discourse adds social stratification to the categories of emotional involvement and personal identification. Just like in *Cinderella*, the telenovela's classic ancestor, the class discourse adds the dream of rising in society to a story of love and passion. This issue is expressed by all of the women in their characterization of Maria do Carmo (the *Rubbish Queen*) who had been poor but succeeded in becoming rich. The class discourse is however not linked uniquely to the material situation but also to immaterial characteristics: human qualities, aesthetics and taste, social habits. The women's consciousness of a class discourse in the media text differs a lot from one woman to another. However, in their interpretations and their normative valuation of the telenovelas, patterns of class discourse can be seen.

Characteristic for the women's reception of TV is that they all relate normatively and in very moral terms to the telenovelas. They clearly identify with Maria do Carmo because she is honest, modest, hard working, poor and maintains a loyalty to her friends and family, even after getting rich. Opposing categories such as good-evil, life-death, just-unjust, rich-poor, faithful-unfaithful, modest-ambitious and humble-self-asserting are ethical and normative dichotomies which all my respondents relate to in their readings of telenovelas. That is to say, these dichotomies were generally very present in the way the women made sense of the novelas when relating the narrative to me. They become modes and categories of comparison between the telenovela discourse and the women's own life experience. As Gillespie also points out, the soap talk links the world of fiction with the women's personal experiences: "It is the interweaving of fiction and real experience that perhaps most of all characterises the nature of soap talk" (Gillespie1995: 145). The following analysis will elaborate on this characteristic which is very manifest in the "telenovela talk".

The women's talk about telenovelas can further be categorized according to Da Matta's different codes of conduct and spheres of signification. In some situations the code of the house predominates, in other situations it is the code of the street, and finally, some of the women's talk about telenovelas reflects the code of the "other". As the analysis in this chapter will show, very complex and even contrasting codes of conduct appear in the women's discourses, adding complexity albeit also empirical evidence to the assumption that a hybrid sphere of signification does exist, Where chapter 8 elaborated on how this hybrid sphere is constituted in the organization of time, space and social relations, this chapter elaborates on how the telenovela talk reinforces the socio-psychic constitution of this hybrid sphere of signification.

On one hand this hybrid sphere has to do with the relation between the public and the private spheres as elaborated on in chapter 8. The boundaries are not the same as the classical sociological distinctions. Strategic sites of interaction (Murdock 1989: 234pp) contribute to this configuration of boundaries, and a particularly important site of interaction is the "televisive space" that Tilburg speaks about and that this case study has identified empirically. The telenovela talk that springs from these sites contributes to the mestizaje of cultures and traditions. They interact and increasingly melt together within the urban neighbourhoods such as Calabar, Vila N.O. and Santa Operaria. The code of conduct within these spheres expresses both elements of modernity and tradition, rural and urban values and life-styles, and cyclical and linear concepts of time. Canclini talks of a specifically Latin American modernity. This might be it: a sphere of signification, a code of conduct, a production of meaning and thus a way of life that cannot be categorized within traditional sociological concepts. It is hybrid, colourful and expressive and springs from many layers of culture, history and tradition. The socio-emotional characteristics of the women identifed in chapter 7 also reflect this hybrid sphere of signification. Now we can take a closer look at how telenovela talk contributes to the configuration of this hybrid sphere of signification, and ultimately, contributes to the manifestation of a specifically Latin American modernity.

It must be emphasized that the analysis not only relates to *Rubbish Queen*, but generally to the women's experience of watching and interpreting telenovelas. The particular telenovela-characters mentioned below are from *Rubbish Queen*, since this was the guiding thread in my conversations and interviews with the women.

1. Personal discourse

> I liked *Rubbish Queen* because it was an everyday story- a story which is found in my family, and in my friends' families... I was able to identify myself with Maria do Carmo because her life was more or less the same as mine.
>
> *Ilda, 41, Vila N.O.*

As Ilda's quotation demonstrates, the narrative in general relates to aspects of the everyday of her family and friends and Maria do Carmo's story relates to her own life. Thus, the personal discourse on one side related to a concern for the family and the community one belongs to, and on the other hand with a more individualized gender specific identification with the woman Maria do Carmo. However, what often fires the women's interest most is the love drama, and this was the case with *Rubbish Queen*.

Love

When asking the women why they liked a telenovela, most answers related to getting emotionally moved: "Oh, it was full of emotion" (Ana, 20, Calabar), "the novela moved people a lot" (Clara, 27, Calabar) or "it was very moving" (Ilda, 41, Vila N.O.). Ana's example below demonstrates this, when referring to *Pantanal*:

> I liked it, I loved it. It was a great novela. It was a very strong novela, a novela full of emotion. I liked it a lot.
>
> *Could you perhaps explain to me, when you talk about emotion, what do you mean?*
>
> It is something we like, something that makes us feel happy.
>
> *What is it in the novela that makes you feel happy?*
>
> When a couple quarrel and then return and settle down peacefully with each other, kissing, hugging and then they marry. Well, then we feel happy. Or when you are hoping two people get each other. Like in *Ana Raio e Ze Trovão* where I was hoping that Ana Raio and Ze Trovão get each other. Well, then I'm happy.
>
> (...)
>
> *Wouldn't you like a life with emotion like the people in the telenovelas?*
>
> I would like to, of course (laughing a little), right, but sometimes it is very difficult to get. Wanting it, I do. All girls think like this: they want a house, want a husband and want some children. But these days, I think it is so impossible because the men don't want to. They don't want to have a family and sometimes they don't want to have the trouble of having a wife and don't want children. I see many examples around here, where the girls aren't happy in a relationship. They get pregnant and then their boyfriends leave them, saying the child isn't theirs. So, all this happens and they leave the girl pregnant. And she has to have the child. All this leaves me sad. I wish to avoid these things, so I prefer to remain single
>
> *Ana, 20, Calabar*

Thus, the scenes in the novela which touch the viewers most are the love dramas with the main love story being the most moving and emotional experience. As Ana's case illustrates, her attention was focused on stories of couples getting each other. The characters can apparently achieve happiness through love. Ana has no boyfriend herself, and sees many examples of unhappy relationships around her, where young girls end up as single mothers. Similar dramas happened in the telenovelas, however always with predictable happy endings. This makes Ana happy.

The love drama in *Rubbish Queen* is also the central plot, introduced in the first chapter of the telenovela. Maria do Carmo sees an old colleague from high school, whom she used to be very much in love with. This love gets revitalized. However, Edu's stepmother is also – secretly – in love with him, which leads to great dramas. The "drive" in many of Maria do Carmo's actions is her love to Edu – her wish to win his love.

> I learn that we shouldn't hurry with everything – we shouldn't take decisions to quickly, that we must proceed slowly in whatever we try to obtain...
>
> *In what, for example?*
>
> ...(long pause)... In love, yes, that is a good example.
>
> *Ana, 20, Calabar*

Maria do Carmo's strategy is more or less like Ana describes life. One should not hurry in love but give a relationship time to develop. In *Rubbish Queen*, conflicting interests prevent Maria do Carmo from getting Edu. Edu is presented as a macho man who can get any woman he wants. However, his role gradually changes. Before reaching this point, Laurinha and Maria do Carmo pass through a lengthy fight for love. It brings them into complicated dramas where they do everything to win Edu's attention. Laurinha uses her social position as her strongest weapon and attempts to humiliate Mario do Carmo with her "scrap-heap" background, as the daughter of a rag picker. However, as a noveau riche Maria do Carmo can use her money in the struggle to "win" Edu. Actually Edu is most interested in her money. Meanwhile, she wishes to be accepted and respected as the person she is and not because of her money. She finally does succeed, and gets married to him. Through patience, stubbornness and strong will she conquers him, but does not fully gain his love.

After having talked with Matilde about a number of telenovelas, and especially the love dramas in them, I asked her:

> *Don't you think there is too much love in novelas?*
>
> Me? I like it.
>
> *Do you think many women like it?*
>
> I don't know, but I like it (The female neighbour who is present during the interview nods confirmingly and says: "Yes, me to")
>
> *Matilde, 40, Calabar*

The abundance of emotion, manifested first and foremost in the love drama of telenovelas, is a key reason for watching them. It attracts all 13 women of this case study, no matter whether their age is 13 or 63. It is the entry point to identification and involvement in the narrative, confirming Valerio Fuenzalida's thesis of televised language being fundamentally emotional (see chapter 2). The telenovela is probably the best example of this emotional relation between a television genre and its audience. Fuenzalida's intention was to explore the educational potential in telenovelas, and so to a degree was mine. Exploring how the women talk about and reflect upon the love drama illustrates well how both the articulation of pleasure and any process of social learning via television can obviously benefit from centring the narrative on a love drama, which secures identification and emotional involvement.

However, as we shall now see, the women's talk about telenovelas reveals many other layers and dimensions in their interpretation.

Women's roles

Maria do Carmo and Laurinha occupy very different female roles in *Rubbish Queen*. Where Laurinha is a mature lady taking good care of her family, Maria do Carmo is younger, less family minded and independent. She is single, very extrovert and has a career of her own. She leads the big enterprise started by her father with a firm hand. She is strong, sexy and courageous, challenging authorities and given procedures and ways of handling things. Ana admired her very much, as this example shows: "She was a very (mature) person (muito decidida), you know. She was a very strong person. She takes decisions easily (...) she helped people. She was a very friendly person. She was very good" (Ana, 20, Calabar).

Where Maria do Carmo's qualities signify a modern woman's role – as strong, extrovert and independent – Laurinha follows the more traditional female role as a housewife and a mother. Laurinha is the prototype of a high society lady emphasizing traditional female values. She spends most of her time at home with the family, worrying about her children, their education and their future. She is an anxious mother, just like many of the women in this case study, who worry about their own children.

Laurinha and Maria do Carmo thus appeal to different virtues and evoke different feelings among the women. Some express initial sympathy towards Laurinha, but gradually change their attitude as the narrative unfolds. Laurinha becomes so wicked towards Maria do Carmo that many of the women lose all sympathy with her. Matilde is very critical towards Laurinha: "Laurinha Figueiroa only knew how to step on top of others. I did not like her role" (Matilde, 40, Calabar). Laurinha gets so desperate in her attempt to make Edu prefer her to Maria do Carmo that she does dramatic things like organizing accidents, lying and swindling. At last, she loses the fight and ends up committing suicide in the final phase of the telenovela. However, the initial virtues of Laurinha make some of my women describe her positively, but they clearly distance themselves from her when the narrative unfolds and she becomes evil.

Maria do Carmo's strength lies in the fact that she manages to combine traditional virtues with a new strong female type, a modern woman's role. There are thus a series of personal qualities in Maria do Carmo's character, both strong and independent and family-oriented, which most of the women identify with. Virtues such as patience, loyalty and sensitivity are seen as central, and are presented in the novela as being possible for a modern woman like Maria do Carmo too. In spite of the cool courage she manifests on occasions, Maria do Carmo is fundamentally very sensitive, and thus feminine. Sensitivity is the virtue which is interpreted as most gender-specific.

Family

Virtues like loyalty, concern and responsibility are key concepts when analysing how telenovelas treat the issue of family, although in the course of a full 150-180 chapter telenovela narrative many non-traditional social norms are also exposed: family instability, extramarital sex, female empowerment and non traditional family arrangements (Martine 1996: 67). As explained in chapter 5, the narrative usually starts with a position of social harmony, an ideal situation, which is then disturbed and passes through a long series of complications and conflicts to finally reach a new situation of social harmony, including reestablished or reconfigured family relationships. In the course of the narrative many everyday and very recognizable family conflicts are portrayed.

The women in this case study react to the portrayal of family life given in telenovelas in varying ways, from very positive to very negative, and likewise to the impact of telenovelas on their own family life. Ana finds the telenovelas provide good examples of how people should relate to each other: "Telenovelas are good examples. They show how we should treat each other, how we ought to be, what we should do when there are problems in the family, which decision to take" (Ana, 20, Calabar). Maria Jesús also finds the telenovelas instructive as regards family life: "Watching novela and not knowing, we can learn whether something is good or bad for people, like a quarrel within a couple, parents and children, the lack of understanding" (Maria Jesús, 42, Calabar). As described in chapter 7, the women are generally very responsible and concerned about their families, and the fact that telenovelas deal a lot with family issues makes them highly relevant – thus establishing a close relationship between the world of fiction and their everyday life.

Single mothers

When it comes to the family structure *Rubbish Queen* only partially reflects the social reality in which the women live. *Rubbish Queen* shows a majority of broken family relationships and especially single women. This is particularly the case with the group of people around Mariado Carmo. Neiva becomes a widow in chapter 2, Armenia is a widow throughout the telenovela and Mariana who lives across the street to Maria do Carmo is single until chapter 86 where she gets happily married. Finally, but most importantly, Maria do Carmo herself is single, and her struggle to conquer the love of her life is the main narrative in the telenovela.

When comparing these many single women with my survey areas Calabar and Vila N.O., differences appear. In Calabar and Vila N.O. there are only 7 per cent and 12 per cent cent single women, including the divorced women (and widows). However, we must not forget that most of the women have experienced broken relationships. Many "partner conflicts" have occurred in their personal lives and continuously occur within their communities. In *Rubbish Queen*, the broken relationships that have been included in the narrative do not remain broken.

A gradual development is seen, where the narrative progresses from a situation of disharmony to one of harmony, with family happiness and fellowship. As the above examples show, this sense of a move towards family harmony is what many of the women explicitly describe as the principal asset of a telenovela. It is something they also continuously seek in their own lives.

Children

When it comes to children, the family structures in telenovelas also differ substantially from the social reality of this case study. There are for example no children under the age of 18 in *Rubbish Queen*. Roberta, 13, was very dissatisfied with this fact: "There are no children in My good – My bad (8 o'clock pm). There were no children in *Rubbish Queen* either. In *Belly for Hire* (6 o'clock) only one child appeared – a baby. Only *Top Model* has children my age in it" (Roberta, 13, Vila N.O.).[1]

There is no broadcasting time specifically reserved for children or young people. From 1993 onwards a couple of telenovelas have appeared, specifically targeting children and young people. The 6 o'clock telenovela on Globo that started in September 1993, *My Dream*, had a six year-old girl and an old man as the main characters. Both the 7 o'clock telenovelas on Globo in 1993 had teenagers among the main characters. So it appears that Globo have been reformulating their priorities in terms of audience segments and issues in recent years. There has been increased interest in the segment comprising young people and children, coinciding with the increased commercial interest in youth and more recently in children, which has been seen on a global scale, for example with the Disney and Barbie renaissances in multimedia-versions.

Nevertheless, this does not negate the fact that there have, traditionally, been very few telenovelas aiming at these segments, which stands in direct contradiction to the social reality in Brazil, where more than half the population are below 18 years of age. This cannot be explained by telenovelas only being popular among adults, because the three 12-13 year old girls I have included in this case study were all avid consumers of telenovelas.

They not only watch them, but talk about them and relate actively to them: "In school I discuss the telenovelas with my friends. We imitate some of the stories, the opening scenes and some of the characters (Roberta, 13, Vila N.O.)". When I asked Estella whether she thought about telenovelas during the day, part of answer was this: "...sometimes we play "statue" in school, where one has to imitate a person. When I then think of which person to imitate I think of the novelas, and then I choose a person from one of them...and sometimes I think, when I see the paper-collectors that it is like Maria do Carmo, she did that too" (Estella, 13, Santa Operaria).

Childrens' uses and consumption of telenovelas is an unexplored area within media research in Brazil. However, for the first time ever, UNICEF sought to address this question in a seminar held in November 1991 in Rio de Janeiro, where 22 Latin-American scriptwriters gathered to discuss how increased focus could be put on

---

1   This was the case until the mid 1990s when *Malhação* appeared on Rede Globo, a daily Beverly Hills-like telenovela appeared in the 5 o'clock time slot, addressing in particular teenage youth.

children in telenovelas (UNICEF, 1992). The seminar resulted in the "Rio de Janeiro Letter" where the writers declared themselves willing to increase the focus on children's issues in telenovelas. In spite of a positive attitude by scriptwriters and recent examples of Globo-novelas aimed more at children, greater awareness and attention among producers as well as researchers is needed in exploring the relation between telenovelas and children. I can merely put on record that I have met many 12-13 year olds, girls – not boys, who were large scale consumers of telenovelas. Even though children are hardly seen in Brazilian telenovelas, they are clearly among the novela viewers, viewers that relate actively and creatively to what they have seen, using it in their social interaction which other children.

Summing up, concern with and responsibility for the family is central in the everyday lives of many of the women. This is reflected in their identification with the often stormy relations depicted in telenovelas between parents and children, men and women, brothers and sisters. Values like unity, love and mutual understanding are the ones emphasized by the women, when asked to give resumés of favourite telenovelas, and when asked to highlight positive elements. In *Rubbish Queen*, Maria do Carmo had no family nucleus around her, but she did get married, and divorced, during the story. In many ways, the personal complications: disrespect, betrayal, ruptures of all sorts, reflects the social reality of many of the women in this case-study. As was shown in chapter 7, their own backgrounds were often marked by several relationships with men and a series of often tough personal experiences. Thus, telenovelas, although they can seem to be overdramatized and to give a distorted picture of family life, do in fact touch some of the central cores of the women's personal life-experience and their basic worries about everyday family life. Some of the women clearly express their satisfaction with knowing that, unlike what happens in reality, no matter how tough the drama of the telenovela may be, it usually ends with the reestablishment of harmony. This media-created experience of family life enters into their own self-narrative, becoming their inspiration in formulating and articulating the own identity as family members, and often as the de-facto heads of family. Navigating between lived and media-created experience the women formulate their aspirations and dreams for future family life.

Community

Laurinha and Maria do Carmo move in very different social circles and likewise in two different neighbourhood cultures. Laurinha moves in a limited circle of high-society people in her home "up there" the fashionable neighbourhood of Jardins. She is often filmed from a worm's eye view, standing high up on the staircase leading from the living room up to the first floor of her home. Maria do Carmo, by contrast, is mainly seen on street level, in her community in Santana. On some occasions, the two social circles intersect, at parties and social encounters. Maria do Carmo has, to some degree, access to both, being culturally and historically rooted in the working-class neighbourhood of Santana with its particular culture, aesthetics, language and general life-style, while at the same time having access – due to her money and business position – to Laurinha's upper-class circles. Thus, the two different social circles and neighbourhood cultures come up against each other in what might be characterized as a meeting between two cultural fronts – an encounter personified in Maria do Carmo's person and everyday life, although she is obviously rooted in one of these circles. Her story becomes one of constantly negotiating and taking up a position between these cultural fronts, rooted in different trajectories and histories, but intersecting in her everyday life.

What does becomes clear in the reception process is that the respondents identify Maria do Carmo strongly with the neighbourhood in which she lives and the community and class from which she originates. Santana as a community is not dissimilar to those familiar to the women of this case study, although on closer inspection Maria do Carmo's life looks materially affluent. However, her language, life-style and aesthetics all connote a popular cultural background.

Maria do Carmo's relation to the neighbourhood and thus to the neighbours receives quite some attention in the narrative. Her neighbour is Armenia who has three sons, of which one, Gerson, is Maria do Carmo's boyfriend at the beginning of the telenovela. Across the road lives Caio and his sister Mariana, who have been Maria do Carmo's friends for ages. A little up the street lies the grocery store, where they often meet, and the daughter, Nidia, is a girlfriend of Caio. It is a small, limited community, a neighbourhood, with some parallels to the social reality of the women in this case study. They come and go in each other's houses, they meet on a street corner and chat, or they meet in the grocery store.

Estella, who lives in the same area as Eva, says *Rubbish Queen* reminded her of the area she lived in, where many people also made a living by collecting scrap, garbage and litter:

> There are many people who make a living by collecting scrap, even here in this area. Her life is very similar to the life people live here – not all of her life, but a part of it is similar. The scrap workers survive through what they collect. There are even examples of people who managed to collect money to set up a beauty salon just by collecting scrap. So there are many things from this area here that also occur in the novela...
>
> *Estella, 13, Santa Operaria*

The identification with Maria do Carmo's neighbourhood culture is obviously tightly linked to a class-identification, which I discuss further in my analysis of the class discourse, relating particulary to issues of language and life-style. Meanwhile, staying with the concept of community – understood as recognizable ways of living and of organizing time, space and social relations – we shall see that the processes of identification reach back far in time and over a great distance.

Rural Nostalgia

In some cases, the sense of community feeling stretches further than to the immediate neighbourhood, reactivating memories of the women's rural past, their native soil... This was especially the case when I discussed the telenovelas *Pantanal* and *Ana Raio e Ze Trovão* with them. Gildete, 63, left her own area 41 years ago, at an age of 22. She had though been back several times. Some telenovelas reminded her of "home":

> *Pantanal* has similarities with Piauí, so many cattle, riding a horse, lake-shores, alligators, there are a lot of them in Piauí – all this made me remember. And the stones, the small boats passing, I don't even remember what they're called, they go by back home. All this reminds me, it makes me remember a lot. And the old man by the river reminded

me of my father because he liked everything to be correct, all of his things being nicely in order and nothing wrong. This reminded me of my father.

Gildete, 63, Vila N.O.

Elenita, 30, had left her native soil in *Nordeste*, in the state of Pernambuco, 8 years ago, also at the age of 22. She had not been there or seen her family since. When speaking about *Pantanal*, she got very emotional:

The novela was almost like in real life. They had a rural area in it, some sheep...
Did it have similarities...?
It reminded me of the rural areas (a rossa) of Pernambuco.
It brought back good memories (deu para matar saudade)?
Yes, really. It had a very beautiful farm which immediately got me imagining myself on the farm there is close to my home.

Elenita also liked *Ana Raio e Ze Trovao* because if reminded her of "home". It had a rodeo; "and there, close to my home there was a rodeo, and every month when it was there, we went to see it. That is why I watch it"(Elenita, 30, Vila N.O.). Geraldina, who left her home in the rural areas of Bahia 27 years ago, also had memories of the region when watching *Pantanal*.

It was as if, you know, it brought back a little of my origin, of the time when I came from Bahia. Because I was born in a forest area, we stayed there until I was about 5, we lived there in the woods, in the cottage.
So you began remembering this past?
Yes, it had something of me, you know, it made me remember.

Geraldina, 38, Vila N.O.

A village in the Amazon region, illustrating the rural nostalgia many viewers have.

As these examples show, especially the two telenovelas *Pantanal* and *Ana Raio e Ze Trovao*, both screened on TV Manchete evoked associations with the rural homeland of many of the viewers. Six of the 13 women are first generation migrants, the rest second-generation migrants, thus all still carrying a rural past with them in their social and cultural practices. With *Rubbish Queen*, however, the specific "community parallels" between the telenovela narrative and the women's everyday life related mainly to neighbourhood cultures in contemporary urban life.

Taboos

In recent years more and more taboo themes have become key issues in telenovelas, like for example a love affair between a married woman and a priest or a love affair between two people who later in the story turn out to be brother and sister. These issues question the norms and values upon which personal relations in Brazilian society are based. They challenge relational structures and moral codes. However, embedded as they are in identifiable settings and with realistic characters, the issues are not normally rejected, but get debated.

The 6 o'clock telenovela *Belly for Hire* (Barriga de Aluguel, Globo, 1991) touched upon an unfamiliar topic that became a great talking-point. *Belly for Hire* is about two young families and their fight over a baby. *Belly for Hire* was the most popular telenovela among many of the women, especially those who were mothers with young children themselves. The story is about a poor woman who wants to earn some money by giving birth to a child which is to be given to a rich couple, who are unable to have children themselves. Geraldina describes the story like this:

> Because they are rich, the couple believe that they can buy everything and do everything (Geraldina's friend Dora interrupts and says: "even buy themselves a son"). And she, because she is a poor girl who had never seen so much money in her life, she sees all that money and so agrees to be a surrogate mother. But now, when she has given birth to the child, she realizes what she has got into, and then she refuses to deliver the child.
>
> *Why? She will make a lot of money from it?*
>
> No, because on one hand she gives the money back and on the other, there is no sum of money that could make her sell her son.
>
> *Geraldina, 38, Vila N.O.*

Both for Geraldina and her friend Dora and for many of the other women, this was a topic they discussed a great deal. Geraldina and Dora got into an earnest discussion which I sensed they had had many times before. Geraldina's mother, who also was present, did not say anything, perhaps because it was many years ago since she gave birth herself. Geraldina, on the other hand, identified greatly with the dilemma which the surrogate mother was in, because as Geraldina said: "Any woman who is a mother can see herself in this woman's place" (Geraldina, 38, Vila N.O.), whereafter Dora added: "OK, it was another man's seed, but that does not mean a thing" (Dora, Geraldina's friend). The discussion continued, the topic was something that absorbed them, something they had personal attitudes towards. However, they did not imagine it was something that really occurred in Brazil:

"There has been cases like this, but not here in Brazil, have there Dora? (to which Dora answered: "No"), but in USA"(Geraldina, 38, Vila N.O.). Elenita, however, does remember a real case that was similar to the case from *Belly for Hire*:

> It happens, it does happen in real life. I used to live in a part of town where a case like this happened.
>
> *What happened?*
>
> What happened? The real mother got the child.
>
> *Had she received some money?*
>
> No, she hadn't received money. The child was taken away from a hospital. The other woman, who wasn't the mother, went to the hospital and took the child, and the woman who was the mother was left without her child. However, she went to court and managed to get her child back.
>
> *So it was not a case of having been paid to bear a child for another woman?*
>
> No. The real mother had said that when her child was born she would give it to the other woman. However, when the child was born, she regretted it.

This discussion is a good example of how themes from a telenovela are good issues to start a debate among the women. It is an issue which is possible to relate to; it is about the relation between a mother (and father) and child. The "blood" ties, signifying the code of the house (Da Matta 1991), turn out to be the strongest, letting the poor woman keep her child. Many other telenovelas have sparked similar debates when raising other controversial themes. An ideal, the state of harmony, which many telenovelas begin with, is challenged by the introduction of taboo issues. They challenge the relational structures and moral codes that are present in the initial state of harmony, but simultaneously may very well become articulators of debate and "gossip" as Mary Ellen Brown points towards (Brown 1994: 31). *Belly for Hire* is an example of this. In some cases, the controversial intimacy touched upon transgresses the generally accepted codes of conduct, provoking strong feelings and rejection.

Rejecting television as immoral

Worth noting in my statistical data is that 22 per cent in Vila N.O. and 13 per cent in Calabar, consciously choose not to watch telenovelas (Tables 14 in appendices 2 and 3). One of the principal reasons is a moral one – telenovelas show too much sex:

> There are many things I don't think telenovelas should show. For example scenes with sex. An example is a girl who is married, where the mother of the girl is interested in her daughter's husband. They should not show things like that (...) Just imagine: I am married to Servilho and then I leave him and my mother begins to like him and wants to have something to do with him. That's not the way we should go. And these kind of things are on in the 6 o'clock telenovela, *Belly for Hire*, a time when lots of children are watching television. It must not be like that.
>
> *Geraldina, 38, Vila N.O.*

Many others touched on the issue of immoral scenes, especially in terms of "too much sex in telenovelas." They drew my attention to a decline in moral standards which they thought was leading to these new trends in prime-time programming.

> Until a short time ago, it was worth while watching a telenovela on TV, but now it is not possible any more. They are completely shameless. There are certain things a child does not manage to analyse, for example sex which is very visible on TV. It is something children do not understand. It is not because I am an old fashioned mother who does not believe that children should understand, but I mean that we must take the time to teach children these things when they themselves begin to understand a little about life. I mean that these scenes are too shocking to expose children to.
>
> *Eva, 32, Santa Operaria*

The generally strong reaction towards the new trends I believe was rooted in two issues: on one side the women were concerned about their children but on the other side they also felt personally provoked by the liberal attitude on television, something they were not accustomed to. However, in spite of antipathy and indignation, many of the women lived with this ambivalence and chose to watch telenovelas. Other viewing options were limited and also telenovelas were and continue to be firmly-rooted social routines.

The reason for these new trends was the increased competition between Rede Globo and other television channels, which led them into a fierce fight for ratings (see also chapter 4). Additionally, the process of democratization had liberalized both censorship and self censorship, which was reflected in the themes touched upon in telenovelas. Limits on what could be said and shown changed.

A more fundamental opposition to television was also to be found, especially in the case of Eva's mother, who had a very aggressive attitude towards the effect of television in general on family life. She interrupted my interview with Eva, saying: "I dislike TV, because TV has come to destroy people's unity" (Eva's mother, Santa Operaria). This old woman had lived much of her life in Southern Brazil, in a little village with no electricity, near the border to Uruguay. She came to the city of Porto Alegre 30 years ago together with her family, including her daughter Eva. It was very clear that her very spontaneous reaction, interrupting my interview, was caused by an antipathy towards TV; she experienced it as a repellant phenomenon closely connected with the alienating city. The enormous size and complexity of the city compared with a very different way of living in the country can create an antipathy towards anything that is new and different, anything that you do not understand, or whose workings are a mystery to you.

Humour

The comedy in *Rubbish Queen* is mainly of a mild slapstick kind, as when Adriana dances around messing up everything in a night-club show on the inaugural evening of Maria do Carmo's club "Rubbish". There are also comic elements in the use of language and in the dialogue. Maria do Carmo appears comical, especially in the way she talks, often a little too loud. Estella says about Maria do Carmo:

"I find her funny because of the way she – the woman who plays Maria do Carmo, Regina Duarte – acts. It's funny the way she shouts. I find it very funny, and very real as well" (Estella, 13, Santa Operaria). Thus, despite being comic, Maria do Carmo remains believable.

The woman Armenia is probably the most humorous character, for example in the way she speaks – extremely bad Portuguese – and calling her three grown up macho sons "my daughters", which causes a lot of laughter. Armenia's role was extended during the series, due to her popularity. Some of the things she said became popular expressions among the viewers. Estella said about Armenia: "I found her funny" (Estella, 13, Santa Operaria).

Armenia's huge success may very well be due to the fact that Brazil is full of immigrants. By speaking bad Portuguese and demonstrating a lack of comprehension of the general code of conduct, she obviously struck some common cultural chords among the many, many Brazilians that have experienced similiar situations, especially when migrating away from their rural communites of Italian, German, Polish, Japanese, Armenian, Syrian, Lebanese or Russian immigrants who had preserved their language and cultural traditions for generations. Armenia pushes the 'meeting of cultures' situation to the verge of the ridiculous.

Thus, in the vase of *Rubbish Queen* it is largely the slapstick comedy tradition that gave this telenovela its humorous stamp, combined with traditions from the circus, which has a sort of slapstick comedy of its own

Wishing for happy endings

Navigating between many cultural discourses and possible sources of identification as mothers, migrants, immigrants, women or poor people, the women identify in varying ways with the personal dramas of the narrative. *Rubbish Queen* allows many possible articulations of identity, taking up issues relating closely to the everyday life of the women:

* The love drama is obviously central for catching and retaining the women's attention. Many of them emphasized that they liked the telenovela because of the abundance of emotion. The emotional involvement arises from the drama between Maria do Carmo, Edu and Laurinha but is also present in the many subdramas. However, the women emphasize Maria do Carmo's drama when describing the story.

* In addition to her personal love drama, Maria do Carmo's role as a woman is a source of identification. She expresses the ambivalence many of the low-income women in Calabar, Vila N.O.and Santa Operaria live with in their everyday lives, being both mothers and heads of their households with economic responsibility for the family's survival. Maria do Carmo is clearly an example of an empowered woman, being strong, decisive and economically independent. Nevertheless, along with her powerful modern virtues, she maintains more traditional female virtues, linked to motherhood, housewifely qualities and the classic behaviour a "good wife", being loving, caring and above all sensitive. In *Rubbish Queen*, Maria do Carmo honours the normative demands of both women's roles, though emphasizing the values of empowerment that characterize a modern woman's role. However, these different actions and virtues do not necessarily have to contradict each other – they coexist in modern

life, in the way of life of today's women, as a reality or a potential – a combination of different ways of living.

* The structure of relationships and moral codes of family and community life are core issues in most telenovelas, and *Rubbish Queen* is no exception. The women in this study have generally had turbulence and ruptures in their personal lives: they have had the experience men leaving them because of another woman (Ilda and Gildete), of violence (Ana and Clara), of acquiring a "new" father (Roberta), etc. They also have strong feelings of longing because many of them have migrated to the cities earlier in their lives. A powerful longing for their original community, expressed as rural nostalgia in their statements, is thus quite widespread. Many of them express a wish for happiness in both love life and family life. In their attitude to family and community life, they are seeking a state of harmony similar to what Maria do Carmo is searching for in the telenovela. Telenovelas become popular because they always reach a happy ending in which personal dramas are cleared up – often thereby articulating a desire, a dream of similar happy endings in real life – a desire or dream that, as illustrated above, help many women in their own lives.

* In recent years taboo issues have found their way into telenovela narratives, reflecting the network competition and the political liberalization in Brazil. Sex was very open in prime time telenovelas at the beginning of the 1990s, provoking strong reactions. Many other issues of an intimate kind have been presented. They have become issues of discussion among many women, but in some cases they have transgressed the moral codes of conduct held by the viewers, leading to rejection and condemnation. Others, like *Belly for Hire*, have promoted debate, including public debate in the media.

It is fundamental to analyse the personal discourse when seeking the explanation of the telenovela's success with viewers. Among the different ways in which the viewers' personal experience of love and family life influenced their interpretations two elements stand out:

– the search for more harmonious personal relations, reflecting the fact that many of the viewers obviously have had – and continue to have – harsh personal experiences in everyday life. These experiences are obviously widespread, especially in Calabar, with extensive violence, alcoholism, crime and other social problems.

– the popularity of melodrama, or as they say: emoção. The women are very fond of melodrama and emphasize the abundance of emotion as a major reason for their liking the narratives. Expressive emotion seems to be an integral element of the women's personal identities and characters.

Although an analysis of the personal discourse in telenovelas can provide substantial perspectives on the women's interpretations of telenovelas, the class discourse is also essential, especially in a society as class-divided as the Brazilian.

2. Class discourse

As described in chapter 5, the social mobility of the principal female character is often a central element in the narrative. This also occurs in *Rubbish Queen*, as expressed in Matilde's resumé of the story:

> I don't remember any more how it was....(I give her a few key words and she suddenly remembers the story)... She managed to rise in position

selling scrap. Then she got poor once again and managed to rise again. What was actually her name? (Her daughter remembers the name: "Maria do Carmo").

How did you like it?

It was good, I really liked it. When she was about to fall she managed to rise. Ah yes, it was really great.

What was great about it?

The "drive" (garra) she had, her strong will. When she saw that she was descending, she did everything to get there, you see. She didn't show that she was falling. Ah yes, it was really great. She married Edu, and after marrying Edu, the...(female neighbour helping Matilde remember: "the stepmother")..yes, Edu's mother in law did not want it, she didn't like Maria do Carmo because she talked very much like this...she shouted, she didn't like her way of being (neighbour lady interrupting: "and of her being poor"), yes, she believed she was poor (from the veranda, Matilde's husband shouting, helping to remember the name of Edu's stepmother "Laurinha!"). They then got divorced, she returned to her mother's house, but now she was poor. However, she fought immediately, took the car, went, sold scrap, bought, resold, and in a short while she rose again. That's it. She became the *Rubbish Queen* again. It was good, really good. But Laurinha Figueiroa was not worth anything in the novela. She only knew how to massacre the others and step on top of others.

Matilde, 40, Calabar

After being given some key words, and helped a little by her neighbour and husband, Matilde quickly remembered the story of *Rubbish Queen*. As her resumé above indicates, Matilde's main focus is on the social rise and fall of Maria do Carmo, ending with her social rehabilitation. This social mobility is the central thematic focus in Matilde's very emotional summary of the story. She gets angry at Laurinha, Edu's wicked stepmother, who dislikes Maria do Carmo and does everything to destroy her, humiliating Maria do Carmo, and using nasty tricks to destroy her marriage with Edu. However, Matilde places emphasis on the pride, perseverance and hard working attitude of Maria do Carmo which enables her to become rich again selling scrap (junk iron, etc). Once again she becomes the *Rubbish Queen*.

Gildete, 63, from Vila N.O. has a more relaxed attitude to the social mobility of Maria do Carmo. Having a long life experience of social ups and downs herself she knows that material wealth in itself does not make anybody happy:

To me, it does not have any importance, because I have already risen many times, and fallen. I always remain like this, balancing (...) I have risen, been well off in life, we lived well. I had a nice and comfortable house. Look, I had a cook, I had a maid and I had a washing woman, so you see? The neighbour here knows about all this.

I bought nice clothes, clothes in boutiques. Even today I have clothes bought in boutiques. However, to me this does not make any difference.

> If I have to go and live in a hut, I will go and live in it. If I lived in a beautiful mansion and was happy, its fine. But, if I had to live in a small house, really small, look, I have lived in a smaller house, and been happy.
>
> *Gildete, 63, Vila N.O.*

Gildete's statement gives an idea of what is understood by belonging to the higher social strata. It is the style of life – obviously only possible if you have money – but reflected in social habits and life-style: having servants, being able to buy your clothes in fancy shops and living in a nice house. However, I sensed an ambivalence in Gildete's statements: on one hand a bitterness, having experienced how much easier and sweeter life can be when one has enough money, but on the other hand emphasizing that she had been happy even when very poor.

Most of the women possessed this ambivalence between dreaming about an easier life, envying the telenovela characters, their houses, cars and clothes, but on the other hand focusing on the positive elements among themselves and their equals. Eva is the one who formulates it most clearly, talking about the values, the love and the unity found in "the people" (o povo), referring to the broad masses of low-income Brazilians:

> We are all aware that we haven't chosen life ourselves. We have been put in it, and it is obvious that we fight the best we can to obtain a better life than this. We always try to improve our life, but the powers we are up against are too strong. We have accustomed ourselves to living a plain life, and then we are also happier with a simple life. We have a greater mutual understanding, more harmony. We know that those who have all that wealth, they do not have what we have.
>
> *What is that?*
>
> It is this love, this fellowship, this mutual understanding, the fact of being able to tackle problems and come through them without creating ruptures. We have care, we have fathers, children and mothers, we have the love that we know they do not have. They only think of obtaining power, becoming richer, getting a name. We want something plainer, because it has more value to us.
>
> *Eva, 32, Santa Operaria*

In spite of a tough daily struggle for survival along with a struggle for social change, Eva apparently finds comfort in the strong norms of unity and love found in her social stratum. In her analysis of the rich, Eva characterizes them as unhappy people, struggling for power, prestige and a social status which only can be obtained through a constant, dishonest fight for money. Their basic values differ fundamentally from the ones Eva argues that she and her fellow low-income citizens possess. However, this analysis is surely an idealization of their own norms and values, a simplification of the other's norms as a way to find an explanation for – or a least a means of enduring – the everyday struggle for survival.

The story of impossible love between one of Laurinha's stepsons, Rafael, and one of the maids in the house, Alaide, shows him willing to give up his name, his job

213

and thus his social position to be able to have his beloved, but he is forced to give her up. Both the maid Alaide and Rafael himself want to break the system of masters and servants by coming together as lovers, but class-bound social relations overrule their wishes.

The beautiful poor

In telenovelas, the class differences are not as physically explicit as they are in real life in Brazil. For example, slums are never seen in telenovelas, and workers' areas, especially in Globo telenovelas, are always beautified almost beyond recognition – they are always cleaner, more beautiful, richer and with more amenities than in real life. Geraldina gives an example of this:

> Telenovela is telenovela, real life is something else. For me, there is no comparison, and do you know why? It is because in telenovelas the poor get up in the morning and sit down to a well-provided table (...) and in the telenovela you see poor people driving around in nice cars and living in beautiful houses. In real life it is not like that. Our life is a struggle for survival and in the telenovela it is completely different.
>
> *Geraldina, 38, Vila N.O.*

Fiction is thus one thing, reality something very different, at least when it comes to portraying lower social strata. Thus, there is often no pronounced material difference in everyday life "up there" compared to "down here", as interpreted by the low- income women. A significant part of the class difference is coded in aesthetics, language and in lifestyle in general.

Language connotating class

The language which the women use about the characters and the narrative in general indicates that they put a social interpretation upon it. All of them use expressions as "to rise in life", "up there-down here", "fight to get there", "rise-fall" and "ascend-descend". The social ups and downs Maria do Carmo experiences throughout the telenovela are described by means of these expressions. Laurinha is "born in a golden cradle", meaning born to a life in luxury, a life "up there".

Other expressions are proverbial, like for example "wealth is lucky for those who are wealthy" (implicitly saying it's tough luck for those who are poor). Or: "You must not let anything drag you backwards, you must continue forwards", or "you must fight with belief/trust, to be able to obtain something". There are many other similar expressions, and what they all have in common is to underline and emphasize a simplified life philosophy among the low income women – internalized proverbs saying that you must not give up, keep your head up high, there is a reason for it all, keep going. Not only do these expressions constitute a simplified life philosophy, they also contribute to maintaining status quo. If some more politicized person preaches social change, organization and mobilization, the less politicized often reject participation saying that life might be tough, but "vai fazer o que?" (what can we do about it?), implicitly saying it is impossible to change or better the situation. What may look and perhaps be social apathy can also be interpreted as a survival strategy – to endure and keep hope alive.

Thus, in this conflicting social situation, where some believe in social change and others are resigned and stick to explanatory proverbs like the ones quoted above, the telenovelas enter into everyday life, following two main discourses:

* Providing a "GLOBOvised" interpretation of the tough life of the poor: their struggle to survive and rise in the world, often conflicting with the interests of the rich and resulting in humiliation and feeling trodden upon. The suffering of the principal character from a poor milieu becomes a key in the reading of this discourse.

* The telenovelas present almost identical material conditions for everybody. However the social habits of rich and the poor differ substantially and are clearly interpreted as very different life-styles, partly because of marginal differences in their circumstances but chiefly because of the language the characters speak, their attitude to work, and their taste and aesthetics reflected in clothes and houses.

Humiliation and suffering

> ...the poor are very humiliated, very stepped upon. We are not considered anything, we are considered animals. Society does not accept us, that is why we suffer as much as we do, you see. Her story was like ours (Maria do Carmo's story, ed). She rose thanks to a lot of suffering, renunciation and everything. But before, when she was still poor, she was bullied in school, like my children...
>
> *Eva, 32, Santa Operaria*

As Eva's statement clearly expresses. for her as for most of the women, one of the worst elements of suffering is the experience of humiliation. Human dignity and pride is the last thing a person possesses, when everything else is lost. Eva proceeds: "Generally, those who fight, those who raise their voice here in the world are us, us that suffer most. Meanwhile, we don't have anything to lose, we have lost everything already. The only thing we haven't lost is our struggle, our dignity (Eva, 32, Santa Operaria)". A person may be poor, but she ought to be treated with respect and dignity like any other citizen of society. Matilde sees Maria do Carmo's story as a "beautiful" lesson in the survival strategy of everyday life:

> It was really good, superb. It was a novela that taught people a lot. The people that are losing, they must not collapse, they have to hold up their heads to be able to... We must never bow our heads, must always go with our heads held high.
>
> *Does that provide a solution?*
>
> It provides a solution in our lives, telling us never to bow our heads.
>
> *But what does that mean?*
>
> Because, it means that if you bow your head it's finished, over (laugh!). You must raise your head, because if people don't raise their heads, how will they be able to go out and work, and fight for life? They will stay with heads bowed. So if people hold their heads up, they will find a solution to things.
>
> *Matilde, 40, Calabar*

The struggle to maintain your personal pride becomes essential, in real life as well as in the telenovelas. This struggle leads you through a lot of suffering. Roberta, 13, emphasizes that the story of a suffering woman is essential in the telenovelas. It is the suffering that makes people get involved in the story. However, the suffering of a telenovela's character is far from as harsh as the suffering of the poor in real life:

> *Don't you find it strange when you see the same actor or actress in one novela and later in another and yet another?*
>
> No, I don't find it strange. Because, in the case of Regina Duarte, she only plays the suffering person.
>
> *Why?*
>
> Because in all the novelas she acts in, she suffers, except as Viuva Porcina (in *Roque Santeiro*, Rede Globo 1986, ed). In *Vale Tudo* she suffered, in *Rubbish Queen* as well...
>
> *There is a lot of suffering in novelas?*
>
> Yes, there is a lot.
>
> *Do you like this?*
>
> No. It is not that I like it, but that is what makes people watch the novelas. It is the suffering that attracts people to novelas.
>
> *Why?*
>
> Because, the next day she (the suffering woman, ed) will always get over the next obstacle, be able to lift her head again and recover from what she was feeling.
>
> (...)
>
> *And in real life – is there as much suffering as in novelas?*
>
> There is a lot more.
>
> *What kind of suffering?*
>
> Many people starve, some suffer because of their husbands, the husbands beat them, leaves them, are unemployed. A son or daughter dies, a daughter is raped, these things, of this kind.
>
> *Is there a lot of this?*
>
> Yes, a lot.
>
> *Also in this neighbourhood?*
>
> Unemployment there is a lot of, fights among men and women as well, and also children that have died.
>
> *Roberta, 13, Vila N.O.*

These examples touch upon the fundamental issue of human dignity, respect and pride, all circling around the constant struggle, the suffering they experience in their everyday lives. Eva formulates the problem as a question of not possessing the basic human rights that any citizen of society has a right to expect. Matilde's and Roberta's examples show that a lot of social humiliation, struggle and violence takes place among themselves. Here we are at the core of one of Brazil's basic problems: that many inhabitants in areas like Calabar, Vila N.O. and Santa Operaria are socially, economically and culturally so marginalized that they in practical terms lack a lot of the fundamental rights of citizens of society.

It is no coincidence that the struggle for citizen's rights has been the most important struggle mounted by the social movements in Brazil in recent years. It relates to the right to a decent life, with access to housing, education, work, transport, social services and legal protection no matter what your social status, gender and colour. It is this fundamental struggle for citizen's rights that Matilde, Eva and most of the other women relate to when they identify strongly with the struggle of Maria do Carmo.

The telenovela in no way formulates Maria de Carmo's struggle politically or as a polemical social issue. However, when she is "stepped on", "massacred" and made fun of and humiliated in multiple ways, her suffering lies in both the human and the social humiliation and marginalization. The women often relate very much in moral terms to the way Maria do Carmo is treated by the others, for example Laurinha and Renato. They are incensed by the humiliation she experiences. No punishment can be too tough for their treatment of her. Referring to Renato's treatment of Maria do Carmo, Eva formulates it bluntly by saying: "For someone who has done so much injustice (towards Maria do Carmo, ed), death is not justice enough (Eva, 32, Santa Operaria).

Meanwhile, the women seem willing to put up with the suffering, as long as there is a long term perspective, with the prospect of that suffering coming to an end. Eva gives a religious interpretation as to what the pain of the everyday struggle will lead to. She says: "the true objective is to create God's kingdom" (Eva, 32, Santa Operaria). Like many activists in the Brazilian social movements, Eva is strongly inspired by the Theology of Liberation and merges her religious and political visions into one, expressed in the everyday struggle for survival.

Estella's religious interpretation seems less inspired by the Theology of Liberation, accepting that salvation and paradise might not come until after dying. However, her example is thought-provoking, touching on the central core of what I think many seek in their religious belief: a salvation, a bettering in their conditions, maybe sooner but quite possibly only later:

> Some time ago there was a young man, his body was laid out here in our (residents', ed) association. He had gone to prison because of having joined a gang of criminals (marginais) and had sold drugs with them at CEASA. He was seen and caught together with the others. The policemen beat him a lot. Then his father, who works here in our (Christian) community went to the prison and asked them like this:"why don't you pray to be able to leave prison?" They said they didn't know how to pray, so he taught them "Our Father" and "Ave Maria". And then they prayed. After 5 days he died and he left a letter with the following message in it: "The day a painter paints the sun on a tear I will stop loving my family." However, a painter will never be able to paint the beauty of a tear on a person's (face), never. He might paint it, but never perfectly, as it is. So, what he writes means that he will never stop loving his family. Well, I went to the association the day his body was there and I started thinking: there are so many people like him who suffer like he

suffered, but at last they learn something and end up winning, isn't it so? In the novela it's like that as well. There is always somebody who suffers throughout the novela and who in the end of the novela ends up winning – like the *Rubbish Queen* did.

Estella, 13, Santa Operaria

Estella's example is first of all a very harsh description of a violent experience from her own everyday life. A son of one of the members of the Christian community gets involved in criminal affairs, ends up being caught and dies due to police violence, still while in police custody. However, he became a Christian before dying and declared an infinite love for his family. The moral is depressing, seen from a social or sociological point of view. In a religious interpretation it is perhaps less depressing, though not so liberating as what the Theology of Liberation would preach. However, Estella's story gives an idea of how some of the women in this case study seek energy, perspectives, and explanations to their daily suffering in the Catholic belief. Others, like Gildete, are both Catholic and practise Afro-Brazilian spiritism, thus providing other interpretations of why people suffer. The point is that this discourse of humiliation and suffering is explicit and clearly present in most telenovelas, including the *Rubbish Queen*, making identification and emotional involvement in it easy and obvious for low-income, often religious, women like the ones in Calabar, Vila N.O. and Santa Operaria.

Lifestyle

Maria do Carmo is, in spite of her material wealth, "like us poor", some of the women say. Even though she has a nice house, servants, a car and lots of money, her life-style is similar to theirs. Her background and present way of life prevents her from full recognition among the traditional haute bourgoisie, no matter how much money she has. As Eva explains:

Maria do Carmo managed to become part of the nice bourgoisie, getting everything she wanted, going nicely dressed, eating well, coming and going among people who acknowledged her as one of theirs. However, it was not really like that, because even though they knew she was rich and well-known, she was considered a flop, because she messed up so many things. Poor thing, even though she had all that money she did not succeed in healing the wound in the soul she got as a young student (referring to a scene in the first chapter of the telenovelas) – she was still considered as an uneducated person, an upstart, just because she rose by collecting scrap.

Eva, 32, Santa Operaria

The differentiation in life-style was reflected in many of her social actions: Her language and behaviour: Maria do Carmo speaks loudly, is very direct, can sound vulgar, and has a much less sophisticated vocabulary than the haute bourgoisie. She is very emotional in her reasoning, does not care much about good manners. She is, however, very conscious of her attraction to the opposite sex. Matilde identifies with Maria do Carmo because of some of these similarities between Maria do Carmo and herself:

You found yourself similar to her?

In some aspects yes. Even in the way she spoke and shouted, I found myself similar to her (laugh).

Do you think many people felt like this?

Ah, I don't know. I felt like that, right, because the same things she was doing on television I found myself doing at home, like talking loudly to people. Because she was talking like that, right?

* *Way of dressing*: Even though Laurinha and Maria do Carmo both wear beautiful clothes, their style differ substantially. Laurinha is dressed in long gowns, pearl necklaces and in a classical European style. Maria do Carmo dresses more simply, in mini skirts and a blouse. Her style is fashionable but less ostentatious.

* *Class consciousness*: This is expressed in their relation to work and in their personal relation to servants and employees in general. Unlike Laurinha, Maria do Carmo has a job and is often seen at work, while Laurinha is most often seen at home or on her way to, at, or coming back from grand parties. Furthermore, they have very different attitudes in their relation to their servants at home. Laurinha has three servants and she commands them in a traditional "upstairs" manner. Maria do Carmo only has a maid. She speaks to her in a proper and respectful manner and even seeks her advice occasionally.

* *Leisure activities*: Laurinha loves attending gala parties among her haute bourgoisie friends in São Paulo, and being the centre of attention.The men around her also have expensive habits like motor racing, horse riding and parachuting. Maria do Carmo's former fiancé practices the more popular and less expensive sport of body-building. Maria do Carmo has no leisure activities herself.

To conclude: a clear bipolar class discourse can be identified, both in the telenovela text itself and also in the talk about telenovelas. Although there are material similarities, the characters' way of speaking, dressing, relating to others, their aesthetic sense and taste differ substantially according to their class. Seen with the eyes of the haute bourgoisie, Maria do Carmo is not only from a poor background, but she is uneducated, has bad manners, is vulgar and irrational and in general has bad taste. However, the low-income women like her way of speaking, they respect her way of treating maids (many have worked as maids themselves) and they admire her clothes and her taste in general.

Opposed to Maria do Carmo, Laurinha's lifestyle is generally more difficult to identify with. She has been exposed to a totally different socialization process, resulting in totally different behaviour, different taste and aesthetics. She is sophisticated, favours European (especially French) culture and has a traditional, aristocratic, old-fashioned taste. Everything about her signifies "different class". The women of this case study, low-income urban women, clearly identify with the life-style represented by Maria do Carmo.

Silvio de Abreu, who wrote *Rubbish Queen*, had the intention of casting a spotlight on the lives of the nouveaux riches – like Maria do Carmo – contrasting their success with the decadence of the traditional haute bourgoisie of São Paulo. This intention was fulfilled.

Race

Despite the official cultural discourse of national identity characterized as *mestizo* identity (see chapter 3), most telenovelas lack this recognition of *mestizo* identity. In the majority of telenovelas there exists a clear sub-theme of race within the class discourse. As discussed in chapter 3 Gilberto Freire largely contributed to the recognition of Brazil as a multiracial society – his concept of *mestizo* identity accurately reflected the multiple racial origin of Brazilians. However, the representation of blacks in telenovelas shows very little sign of this *mestizo* identity. While this is a clear case of racial discrimination, it also largely represents the *de facto* situation of blacks in Brazil.

When discussing the issue with the women in Calabar and Vila N.O. I became aware that they were conscious of the place of blacks, not least black women, in telenovelas: they always got cast as servants or other people in an inferior social role. As Ana explains when asked about blacks in telenovelas: "There are a few, very few. When people of dark skin appear in a novela, the large majority get roles as servants. You never see an actress, very rarely a black actress becoming successful. Until today I've only seen one novela where a negro actress worked and became a success. Only one novela. It was in *Body to Body*. It was Zézé Motta, she was a success" (Ana, 20, Calabar). Matilde confirms this tendency:

> When there is a negro in the novela she is a maid, a cook, a waitress. It is like that. I have never seen a negro getting good jobs in novelas.
>
> *Why not?*
>
> I think it's the prejudices they have.
>
> *Who has?*
>
> Those who actually film the novela. They have prejudices against the negroes, because if they didn't have, it wouldn't be like that, would it? And it's the same with poor people. You mostly see rich people in novelas. Why don't they use some poor, some favela people to make a novela? Why haven't they ever done that? It's prejudice against poverty, against the negro, or whatever. In my opinion there is still racism.
>
> *Matilde, 40, Calabar*

Maria Jesús, who, like both Ana and Matilde, is mulatto, confirms the inferior social positions given to blacks in telenovelas. Maria Jesús states further: "I think the blacks have the same talent as the whites, it is a question of getting the opportunity. It wouldn't hurt them (the novela producers, ed) if they gave the blacks a chance as well. But it is difficult. That is the situation as it is" (Maria Jesús, 40, Calabar).

Thus, despite the official discourse about recognizing *mestizo* identity and the ethnic and racial multiplicity of Brazilian society, the blacks generally have an inferior social and economic position compared with the descendants of Europeans. Very few blacks and mulattos obtain high positions in public life. It is a mark left by history – that of slavery – on today's Brazilian society. So, even though Brazil boasts of peaceful coexistence between races in the multi-ethnic melting pot of society, the fact is that segregation still occurs. The telenovelas reflect this situation, where blacks only seldom get significant roles. Always being placed in inferior roles contributes to uphold a certain picture of the role of black Brazilians in contemporary society.

> There are only whites. You never see a dark person, you never see a negro. Why? Because many people are racists, many are descendants of racism, they like to humiliate. I find this very wrong, I think a role should be given to anybody (no matter what colour, ed). There are many negros who would like to be somebody in life, but how would it be possible? (...) Life is good, but nevertheless there isn't anything to push blacks in this direction, to help blacks to get there, into television, radio or something else.
>
> *Have you felt discrimination yourself?*
>
> Yes, I have. Sometimes, here in Salvador, when you go to the market place (...) there I was in the queue when a woman said "Ugh, look at that negro" (and then Clara tells about how she reacted and how she felt about this experience).
>
> *Clara, 27, Calabar*

Dreams of rising in the world

Class consciousness is not equally present among the women of this survey. However, my analysis of their readings of telenovelas reveals a significant class discourse in their talk about telenovelas. In my discussions with them, the class discourse was apparent: both in their opinion on racial aspects, their focus on the suffering of Maria do Carmo and in their descriptions and interpretations of the life-styles of the principle characters. In others words, the class discourse is key when searching for an explanation for the huge success of telenovelas in Brazil. Three elements in particular signify class: racial segregation, emphasis on suffering and difference in life-styles.

Firstly, the examples from Calabar illustrate how racial differences are related to class differences. As I concluded in chapter 3, the description of Brazilian identity as a *mestizo* identity in the process of modernization in Brazil, has contributed to the internalization of the racial *status quo*. By this I mean, the social practices of Brazilian everyday life, as the examples in this study illustrate, follow traditional patterns of racial discrimination. It is difficult for blacks to obtain jobs when competing with whites. Racial discrimination exists in the everyday. The representation of race in telenovelas confirms this.

It might not be a conscious racial discrimination that we see in telenovelas, but it is *de facto* occurring. It is a heritage of the days of slavery in Brazil that is still reflected in social practices. It is so internalized in the norms and values of the women that it has become a self-evident part of everyday life. Blacks are always portrayed in inferior roles in telenovelas. The women's interpretation of telenovelas do not include comments about the racial aspect unless they are directly asked to comment on it. The women most often focused on other aspects of the class discourse, thus emphasizing that racial discrimination is not an isolated problem, but, as I pointed out in chapter 3 and earlier in this chapter, is closely interlinked with the problem of social polarization and marginalization in Brazil.

Secondly, all of the women in the survey focus on the suffering experienced by Maria do Carmo and other principal characters in telenovelas.. The suffering is of course linked to the love drama they are involved in, but then again closely intermixed with a more class oriented suffering. Not only do the novela characters have difficulties in winning the love of their beloved, but they are also struggling against poverty and for social mobility and social recognition. Their main challenge in the class oriented suffering is their experience of humiliation. Maria do Carmo experiences this a great deal, from both her colleague at work, Renato, and from Edu's stepmother, Laurinha.

If we look specifically at the discourse of suffering in the telenovelas, we can see that they rarely focus on material suffering, on an explicit struggle for survival. It is more abstract, more sophisticated, focusing on emotional suffering, as for instance when a (once) poor woman experiences severe "social harassment", when representatives of the haute bourgoisie practise class discrimination against her or people like her, attacking their human dignity and respect. This is seen when the rich make fun of the poor due to their lack of academic knowledge, clumsy performance or simple language. This was the cause of Maria do Carmo's suffering. It does not signify material suffering, because Maria do Carmo lives in a nice house and has a comfortable life, not comparable with the life of poor women in Calabar or Vila N.O. Nevertheless, these women identify strongly with Maria do Carmo, some of them so much that Maria do Carmo's emotional suffering, in love and humiliation, becomes conflated with their own material suffering. They become convinced that Maria do Carmo experiences something similar.

Furthermore, some of them relate to suffering as an almost compulsory – or at least naturally given – phase of life, giving a religious interpretation to their reading. As the telenovelas show: even tough people suffer a lot, but they end up obtaining what they sought to obtain. They find an explanation to their harsh daily struggle for survival in a religious – mainly Christian but also Afro-Brazilian – interpretation of the logic or lack of logic of everyday life,

Thirdly and finally, the bipolarity of lifestyles, as exemplified by Laurinha and Maria do Carmo, is expressed in social practices, social habits and in language and aesthetics. They have different ways of speaking and dressing, and they differ substantially in attitudes to class (to servants) and in attitudes to work and leisure time. Also, their women's roles, as described in the analysis of the personal discourse, signify class differences.

Two elements thus characterize the class discourse in telenovela texts and readings: on one hand the women have been born into one of the socially most polarized societies of the world, on the lowest step of the social pyramid; on the other, every day they watch telenovelas showing a standard of living that is at the very least rather better then theirs, with a narrative that ends happily, every time. It is in this dichotomy between a harsh class polarization experienced in everyday life and their personal dreams of social mobility and change that we find a significant part of the explanation as to why so many low-income women watch three to four telenovelas every day.

3. Telling their own story

As one of the last questions in my interviews with the women, I asked them: "Imagine if you were able to write your own telenovlea, tell a story yourself, any story at all that could be made into a novela. Which story would you tell?" Some of them had difficulties answering the question; some simply began retelling a favourite telenovela while others were unable to think of any specific story, or would not reveal intimate dreams or visions to me. However, the majority did answer the question, revealing a broad variety of stories. As I interpret them, they reflect visions and dreams of social and emotional change in their everyday lives, some touching upon themes which they obviously feel are not sufficiently treated in the telenovelas that are broadcast.

Roberta, who was complaining the lack of children in telenovelas, would like to focus on children in a novela: "It would be a novela about children, about the life of a Brazilian. And also, the novela I would like to do would be with children playing. A dream I have is that the best of everything happens, not thinking about money, but just thinking of love and happiness. This is what I would do in a novela" (Roberta, 13, Vila N.O.). Discussing it further, she says she would like her 11-year-old cousin to act as the main character.

Gildete – the oldest women in my survey and furthermore a women of status in the Afro-Brazilian spiritual hierarchy, declaring herself a Catholic at the same time – would like to focus on love and good behaviour: "I would make a novela with a lot of love and teaching. I would teach religion, I would teach people to do good deeds and to educate themselves, for today people don't even say 'please' anymore" (Gildete, 63, Vila N.O.).

Estella had two clear ideas. One reflected her religious belief, her identification with the Virgin Mary and her ambition to become a nun. The other was on a more concrete level, being the story of a girl her own age, and the life she experiences. Her religious story was based on some texts from the Bible:

> The texts I talk about are not just fiction. They represent everything that I experience inside myself. What I think I always write down. It would be a story about a nun, Agnes of God. She became pregnant by the Holy Spirit, like Mary. I found the story very beautiful, because she was in a convent and got pregnant. She didn't know by whom she had become pregnant. And when "a mada" made her confess, blood began flowing from her body, even though she hadn't cut herself. Then she began crying and the more she cried the more blood flowed out. So, I would like to make a novela about this text and also about a text which is very similar to my life, you know. It is about a girl who lived as I did. She lived some of the time with the children, some of the time with the young people and the elderly, in the Christian community, and then she travelled all over the country. She wrote down something about everything she saw, writing a whole book. You see, I would also like to write a book like that.
>
> *Estella, 13, Santa Operaria*

Eva, 32, saw a clear mission in raising awareness among the rich, showing in a telenovela how the poor live, what it actually is like to live as people in her own community do. She touched upon the very characteristic situation in Brazil: the almost total lack of contact between social classes, the polarization and not least the invisibility of the huge low-income urban peripheries lying around all Brazilian towns, but never seen or frequented by the people of higher social strata. It was very similar to my personal experiences while living as an exchange student in Brazil in 1983/84.

> Ah, if I could, it would be a story about the whole question of an underprivileged people, like our class really is. I would show the reality, show what it is to suffer, show what it is to be poor, show what it is to eat small bits of warmed-food every day at work, things that for these "big people" don't happen. They don't know what it is, they just eat well and eat the best. Don't know what it is like to put out a small rationed portion of food, because if we don't take care there won't be anything to give to our children tomorrow. I would show the reality, because, as you know, throughout the nine years of living here in this community, I have seen many people from other social classes who don't know that this class exists. I have had the opportunity to visit schools attended by children from other social levels. We have told them about the poor children, and they have been shocked. They are born and live in a closed world, in a world where they do not see the reality a few meters away from the place where they live.
>
> *Eva, 32, Santa Operaria*

Maria Jesús touched upon the same issue of showing how the underprivileged live, or rather how they struggle for survival: "I would tell a very real story, you see, about children that do not study, about the people who starve, about the beggars – there are so many unhappy things around which really should be shown, not only in Brazil but in the whole world. Who knows, perhaps somebody would become more aware of things?" (Maria Jesús, 42, Calabar). Obviously, Maria Jesús hopes for better social conditions, and attributes part of the problem to people's lack of knowledge and the invisibility of the poor in the everyday life of the more privileged.

The dreams, wishes and ambitions reflected in the women's ideas for telenovela narratives contain the same variety and breadth that is seen in their interpretation of telenovelas. Some are very oriented towards success in love, some focus on happiness in their personal life in the broader sense, some on more political issues relating to the miserable social conditions of many Brazilians. And then Estella has a very religious dream, closely related to the big questions in her personal life – her dream of becoming a nun. However, something which all the ideas presented have in common is that they are based on the women's personal experience and life situation, reflecting real life events and reflecting their very different concerns and priorities. What they all aspire to do is to tell their own story.

4. Complexity in para-social relationships

Living with the *Rubbish Queen* and other telenovela-characters is a complex matter – it may very well enrich your life and even change your life. It seldom leaves your life unchanged, just as little as any other process of social interaction.

While chapter 8 provided insights into the social uses of television and telenovelas in particular by showing how telenovelas contribute to the configuration of time, space and social interaction in a hybrid sphere of signification, this chapter has provided a series of insights into what meaning is produced about and by telenovelas.

The telenovelas articulate feelings and identities, give an incentive to dialogue within social networks, and in some instances promote social action. Through the analysis of talk about telenovelas – interviews and conversation with the 13 women in this case study – this chapter has provided insights into how these processes of emotional involvement, identification, dialogue and social action occur. It has provided empirical evidence as to the ways in which telenovelas influence the socio-psychic configuration of hybrid spheres of signification. Ultimately – and fundamentally – it has provided insights into some of the "raw material" constituting everyday life – feelings and relations which are increasingly linked to the mass media – from which Latin American modernity is spun.

First and foremost, the telenovelas lead to a high degree of emotional involvement: being moved, touched, provoked and entertained. Although a love story is central to the narrative in most telenovelas, it is the overall melodramatic character of the telenovelas that catches the viewers' attention. The telenovelas are – precisely as Fuenzalida states – based largely on an emotional relation with their audience, enabling the articulation of a broad variety of feelings and identities.

In many of the cases, the processes of identification also leads to a mingling of reality and fiction. That is, the telenovelas obtain a central place in the consciousness of the viewers not only in the everyday life of prime time, but throughout the everyday. All the women are aware of the fact that telenovelas are fiction, but the strong emotional involvement which the story evokes often gives the lives of telenovela characters a central place in the everyday life of the viewers, articulating feelings, stimulating conversation and thus influencing the production of meaning and the articulation and formation of identity.

A significant part of the telenovelas' popularity lies in making the dream of rising in society come true: a dramatic narrative with social conflict, most often leading to social mobility for a principal character. Telenovelas thus reflect a central characteristic in Brazilian society- as in Latin America in general – that of class polarization and social conflict, in some cases stimulating social action among the viewers. Thus, the production of meaning resulting from watching telenovelas promotes different social processes – deriving from the fact that they are entertainment of a particularly gossip-promoting kind. These processes of entertainment and gossip are enriching aspects of everyday life, considering the lack of other opportunities, as many of the women argue. Often, this "gossip" implies social learning: about family relations, gender characteristics, urban life etc – thus proving useful, enriching and often awareness-raising and thought-provoking for the audience. This chapter has provided many such examples, from involvement in the passionate emotions of a love-drama, through admiration of female role models like Maria do Carmo, to the discussion of taboo issues occurring in everyday life All these issues reflect what are significant concerns for many people, confirming the thesis that telenovelas are meaningful programmes, often more meaningful for the audience than news programmes dealing with issues far from the daily concerns of the audience (elaborated further in chapter 1). The above processes of production of meaning are at the same time what constitutes the socio-psychic configuration of the hybrid sphere of signification. That is to say, the processes of emotional involvement, identification, dialogue and social action articulated through the use of telenovelas in everyday life constitute the socio-psychic "material" which feeds into the configuration of time, space and social interaction of the hybrid sphere of signification and, in last instance, into the configuration of Latin American modernity.

Thus, the hybrid sphere of signification encountered in my analysis constitutes a special organization of time, space and social relations, possessing a special code of conduct which is central in the configuration of Latin America modernity and central in the articulation of Latin American identity – carried largely by emotion, and with the telenovelas as central agents.

Analysing the hybrid sphere of signification demands an intellectual framework that takes the specific Latin American process of development into consideration: a framework that relates the organization of time, space and social relations to aspects of tradition and modernity, rural and urban, narrative traditions, gender, religion and individual biography. The explanatory value of traditional sociological categories, developed in other contexts, prove insufficient in this analysis. Some social researchers will obviously argue that classical sociological concepts are perfectly applicable to contemporary ethnographic studies in Latin America. They might argue that the process of integration into modern society is just slower in this region of the world. This media ethnographic study has, it is hoped, shown that what is occurring in Latin America, and more specifically in the Brazilian urban areas studied, is not a slower process of development towards a modern society, but another process of development.

By identifying, analysing and seeking to understand the characteristics of this other development process one finds the key to the success of telenovelas in Brazil. Telenovelas both reflect and articulate a way of life which has deep roots in the history of narration, in the history of the Latin American process of modernization and not least in the personal life histories, current circumstances, and normative, moral and religious attitudes and beliefs of the telenovela viewers. It can be very difficult to grasp the characteristics of these social and cultural practices, as these concluding reflections illustrate.

Characteristic of Latin American art and literature is 'magic realism', an emotionally highly-charged form of expression. In the everyday life of the urban neighbourhood cultures of Vila N.O., Calabar and Santa Operaria, my North European eyes have also seen a magic and fantastic realism expressed in the actual and real role TV fiction has obtained in the everyday life of many viewers. A fascinating universe of stories entering and affecting the lives of the viewers, sometimes with narratives which to my North European sensibility appear incredible. However, as Mexican culture researcher Jorge Gonzalez once said to me while discussing this issue of magic realism in telenovelas, and whether it wasn't too far-fetched: "It's ethnography, it is everyday life".

As with the Trancoso-stories told at Cariri in the Northeastern state of Ceará (see chapter 5), it does not really matter what is fiction or reality, and what representation is found in the story, or the telenovela. What ultimately counts is the talk about and the social use of telenovelas, and thus the process of integration of the story into the social and cultural practices of everyday life.

10. Fictions with power: Making happy ends happen

Can the success of melodramatic television narratives in Latin America – the telenovelas – be related to the people's struggle to be recognized socially, culturally and politically? And is there, as Jesús Martín-Barbero argues, "a secret thread" linking the melodrama and the history of Latin America, say a "cultural connection" that emphasizes "the weight that the other primordial society of relatives, neighbourhoods and friendships holds for those who recognize themselves in the melodrama" (Martín-Barbero, 1993: 225-226)? This concluding chapter emphasizes that there is such a link, arguing for the social and political significance of television fiction, especially in Latin American societies. In some cases television fiction becomes politically more influential than news broadcasts.

In substantiating this argument, three findings from this book will be emphasized. Firstly, I have shown the significant role played by media-generated experience in the social organisation of everyday life and in the articulation of identity. Secondly, I have argued, on the basis of this case-study, that there is a hybrid sphere of signification, and that telenovelas have a pivotal role in the symbolic construct of this sphere. Thirdly, I have assessed that, on a macro-sociological level, television fiction influences the construction and articulation of cultural citizenship and the socio-cultural and symbolic construction of modern and democratic societies.

I wish to argue that television fiction is an important player in the processes of constructing and articulating cultural citizenship. I do take note of the comments of British scholars Nancy Morris and Philip Schlesinger to the effect that cultural citizenship seems to have become one of the new "buzz words" of social theory (Morris and Schlesinger 1997: 12). However, as they also suggest, cultural citizenship may be a valid political project with which to replace "the obsolescent project of a national communication policy, which has been outflanked by the new international relations of communication" (ibid). By describing through my book how television fiction can construct and articulate cultural citizenship, I argue for cultural citizenship as a political project.

Following this line of thought it is relevant to refer to the Dutch media researcher Joke Hermes who remarks, a propos of cultural citizenship, on "the crucial and positive potential of popular fiction genres and the domain of the cultural in general for the interpretative frameworks and community-building of many subordinate groups" (Hermes 1998: 159). Citizenship concerns much broader relations than merely the citizens' relationship to democratic government. As the Swedish sociologist Peter Dahlgren has also argued: "For citizenship to be a living force within a democratic society, it must be internalized – as a value system, as a horizon, as a form of identity – and anchored within the life-world of civil society. Citizenship must be a part of the democratic culture of civil society" (Dahlgren 1995: 141). Thus, cultural citizenship emphasizes the potential of culture, including cultural forms and expressions like television fiction, in articulating what might be described as a "citizen identity". This chapter describes how television fiction, as an - albeit commercially exploited - expression of popular culture, constitutes a space for different social groups to be recognized and to feel recognized, thereby contributing to the articulation of a citizen identity among subordinate groups in society.

The media in life

As this book has shown, alongside with lived experiences, media experiences obtained by watching television and by consuming other media, can be fundamental in the formation and articulation of identity, and in the organisation of time, space and social relations. The massive use of telenovelas in everyday life by Brazilians plays a fundamental role in these processes. They are of course a source of entertainment, but the recognition and relevance that the audience accords to the narratives reveal the meaningful social, cultural and even political functions that can be attributed to telenovelas. In many cases, television fiction proves more relevant and thus more meaningful than the evening news, addressing more issues of concern and articulating what Mary Ellen Brown has called active and re-active pleasures (Brown, 1994: 173ff).

Active pleasure, she argues, is similar to Barthes' (1975) notion of *plaisir*, in which one's sense of identity is confirmed:"active pleasure for women in soap opera groups affirms their connection to a women's culture that operates in subtle opposition to the dominant culture. It is this culture of the home and of women's concerns, recognized but devalued in patriarchal terms, that provides a notion of identity that values women's traditional expertise" (p.173). On the other hand reactive pleasure also recognizes that these concerns often arise out of women's inability to completely control their own lives. Thus they are able to recognize and to feel at an emotional level the price of oppression. The social mobilization leading to the impeachment case against Brazil's corrupt President Collor in 1992 (described in chapter 5) was partly rooted in a felt oppression articulated from the television fiction series *Rebellious Years* (*Anos Rebeldes*, Globo 1992).

In the everyday use of telenovelas, as described in chapters 7-9, ontological security is produced through a series of mechanisms relating to the recognition of plots, persons, issues and their relevance to the public's own concerns in everyday life. Normative debates are conducted firstly in the narratives and secondly in the discussions among the public, a process by which social norms are affirmed, adapted and revised. The 'true life' character of telenovelas, emphasized by Fuenzalida (chapter 2), and empirically documented in this book (chapter 9), validates the viewers' daily life, making them recognize themselves as actors in their daily story. Thus, despite often portraying a material world far from the viewers' own lives, the telenovelas touch some everyday experiences which are highly recognizable for them, thereby setting in motion identification and feelings of satisfaction and pleasure, promoting a sense of social and cultural membership of a variety of different communities, counter-balancing the many processes of socio-cultural and political-economic marginalization experienced by many low-income citizens of Brazil. It becomes an important way of exercising cultural citizenship in the sense of finding a recognition of everyday concerns and to some degree experiencing that these concerns are shared by others.

However, it is important to warn against the celebration of reactive pleasure as a socially and politically elevating activity *per se*. The point I wish to make is that there are a variety of ways in which the experience of pleasure does lead to activity in society. As for example Fuenzalida has emphasized in his work (Fuenzalida 1992, 1997) we all fundamentally relate emotionally to our television use, and obviously seek pleasure. Obtaining pleasure is involving, and can thus stimulate discussions and even social action, in addition to the pleasure of feeling represented on the screen. The point is to take one's analysis of popular culture in the media, of which TV fiction is a prime example, beyond the questions of the active reception and articulation of pleasure, and explore the questions of cultural change, citizenship and the democratic functioning of the genre.

Arguments for such perspectives on television fiction and its use are increasingly being advanced in empirical reception studies and media ethnography, like for example Marie Gillespie's work of 1995 on the relation between television, ethnicity and cultural change. James Curran emphasizes the point very well when discussing why it is unusual to link television fiction to analyses of media's democratic functioning:

> ...entertainment is usually omitted from conventional analysis of the media's democratic functioning because it does not conform to a classic liberal conception of rational exchange. But, in fact, media entertainment is one means by which people engage at an intuitive and expressive level in a public dialogue about the direction of society. (...)More generally, media fiction provides cognitive maps that structure and interpret reality, and provide a commentary upon our common social processes. It is in this sense an integral part of the media's "informational" role.
>
> *Curran 1996: 102*

The case of the telenovela *The Cattle King* (Globo 1996/1997), elaborated upon below, illustrates this argument very well. The point is that with the increased participation of the media in the public sphere, the television flow becomes an important agent in articulating citizenship, and television fiction is able to address a broad variety of issues - often better and more frequently than news programmes - in a form that is relevant to and recognizable by its public.

The media as public forum

In the case of Brazil, the telenovelas – especially since the development of the post-realist telenovela from the mid-1980s onwards - have increasingly won a

229

place in the process of re-democratization and articulation of citizenship. In a time where the constitution of society is undergoing profound changes, new technology and mass communication is playing an increasingly important role. Everyday life is saturated by the media, leading to new forms of sociability and communication, challenging the traditional organization of life in public and private spheres and resulting in reconceptualized notions of politics and power. These conditions, linked with the popularity of the telenovelas, have favoured the telenovelas' growing role in the exercising of political power.

While the classical representative democracy was symbolized by the market-place and by the public assemblies of Ancient Greece, democracy at the beginning of the 21st century has developed within an information society and is characterized by passing through the public forum of the media. This forum, according to the English-American sociologist John B. Thompson, is a "non-localized, non-dialogical, open-ended space of the visible in which symbolic forms can be expressed and received by a plurality of non-present others" (Thompson 1995; 245). Face-to-face communication as the central dynamic in politics and power struggles is being challenged by a new public forum where the struggle for visibility in the media is becoming the core issue. Participation in the democratic debate in society becomes increasingly dependant on being visible in the media.

It is here – in the interconnection between the reconstitution of public and private spheres on one hand, and the reconceptualization of politics and power on the other – that the televised genre of telenovelas, in Latin America, enters as a central player in today's main public forum; that of the media. Given the massive presence of nationally produced telenovelas in the everyday lives of the Latin American audiences, these nationally produced fiction programmes have an enormous potential for promoting public debates and articulating an identity as a citizen.

Viewers recognize in the telenovelas the themes of striving to belong and participate as members of different communities, whether national, local or relating to gender or profession, transforming their use of telenovelas into a process that promotes "belongingness" or rather: citizenship. *The Cattle King* (Globo 1996/97) is a good example of this. It was a telenovela where the author deliberately chose to set the issue of agrarian reform in Brazil on the agenda, leading to an increased awareness and discussion of the issue, social mobilization among the landless, visibility of the issue in the media in general and finally to the passing of two new laws in Brazil. The sympathy for the fictional senator in *The Cattle King* who fought for agrarian reform was so strong in Brazil that when he was killed – in the fiction – by the gunmen of some large land-owners, some real senators from the Brazilian Workers Party, PT, participated, as themselves, in the fictional funeral!

Taken upon its initial premise, *The Cattle King* looks very like a typical Cinderella-story. The poor landless woman, whose shelter is burnt to the ground, gets married to a rich landowner, This is the overall plot, which appeals to the audience's hopeful aspirations social change and upward mobility for themselves. However, telenovelas like *The Cattle King* also make visible and take account of day to day problems and pleasures, problems that everybody has to deal with in their everyday lives – problems involving relations with family and friends, economic problems, personal dramas, etc.

Thus, despite portraying a material world often far from the viewers' own lives, the telenovela touches some everyday experiences which are very recognizable for the viewers, thereby inducing identification and feelings of satisfaction and pleasure, promoting a sense of social and cultural membership, counterbalancing the many processes of socio-cultural and political-economic marginalization experienced by many low-income citizens of Brazil.

It is also a fact that telenovelas like, for example, *The Cattle King* have played a fundamental role in the symbolic construct of Brazil as a nation, creating a social and cultural imaginary dimension that everybody in the huge nation of Brazil could and still can relate to and identify with. It is an imaginary dimension that reflects the social problems and questions characteristic of Brazil – whether it be migration and urbanization or social inequality, problems of crime, environmental damage, particular social taboos, etc. For example, the national problem of not having implemented an agrarian reform, thus generating constant migration to the cities, conflicts and violence in the rural areas and constant rural poverty, is a problem which was made visible in *The Cattle King*. When the huts of an illegal occupation by the landless in the telenovela were torn apart and burnt down, close-up pictures showed the Brazilian flag burning. The Brazilian dream, the old image that has attracted millions of immigrants to Brazil over the centuries, this dream of a piece of land for everybody withered away in the flames, bringing tears to the eyes of many viewers, but also generating a common knowledge – for some the first knowledge acquired at all – about the whole problem of land conflict in contemporary Brazil. A dimension of the symbolic construct of Brazil was brought to public attention generating a public national concern to this issue. With *The Cattle King* , this issue explicitly became a referent in the question of "Who are we, the Brazilians"?

As the case study in this book has shown, Brazilian telenovelas also reflect characteristics in the relations between men and women, between rich and poor, between parents and children. Questions of religion, syncretism and mysticism typical of Brazil are also dealt with, along with many other issues. Altogether, the social and cultural particularities of the roles and relationships in the narrative are often very recognizable for the Brazilian public. They are a product of, and a referent to a particular history, culture, and socio-economic situation that the whole public has in common. These processes of recognition and identification with persons, problems and situations that viewers have in common contribute to and generate a common sense of belonging, often a sense of national belonging. By producing this sense of belonging the use of telenovelas is central in the construction of cultural citizenship among Brazilians.

Hybrid Spheres

My concept of "hybrid spheres of signification", developed in chapter 7-9, should be seen as a way of understanding some of the current forms of socio-cultural and socio-spatial organisation of everyday life, emphasizing the processes of media use within it. The case study in this book has revealed the existence of a hybrid sphere of signification, an intermediary zone, neither private nor public. It implies a special organisation of time and space, linked with a special code of conduct, which together create a sphere that is central in the formation of self, of identity, underpinned by emotion, and with the telenovelas as central agents.

In this specific reality, the hybrid sphere of signification is a collective zone in which the television plays a fundamental constitutive role. The hybrid sphere is the symbolic construct from which the processes of cultural hybridisation and interaction with the mass media make their way out into the innumerable practices of everyday life.

The hybrid sphere of signification demands a conceptual framework that takes account of particular local development processes, a conceptual framework that relates the organisation of time, space and social relations to aspects of tradition and modernity, rural and urban discourses, narrative traditions, gender, religion and life histories. The explanatory value of sociological categories developed in other contexts is considerable, but their conceptualization of social reality and thus their analytical and theoretical approach has often proved inadequate in empirical analyses carried out in other contexts than those in which, and on the basis of which, they were developed.

The case study in this book has shown how a recognition of the growing interaction of the mass media with everyday life, and of the importance of cultural difference, challenges the classic sociological notions of public and private spheres, and demands that social theory become more media-sensitive and culture-sensitive. The point is that a lot of social theory, media theory included, has an ethnocentric bias, as is revealed when they are tried out empirically in other cultural contexts than their own.

I discussed this point in an article (Tufte 1997) using the case of Roger Silverstone's book *Television and everyday life* (Silverstone 1994). I analyzed this book in terms of its applicability to other cultural contexts than Britain. Fortunately Silverstone's concepts and analytical framework turned out to be widely applicable to other cultural realities than his own, as a series of points and observations revealed. For example when Silverstone quotes Morse's description of hybridisation as a non-space (a cultural vacuum, as Silverstone puts it), he argues it is a hybrid space, within which individuals, families and neighbourhoods can, in different ways, create something of their own culture and their own identities: "spaces for dreaming as well as spaces for action" (Silverstone 1994: 62). This is very similar to my discovery of what I called hybrid spheres of signification in the low-income urban reality of Brazil.

I am also reminded of my hybrid sphere of signification when Silverstone observes that such spaces are a "product of technological and social changes, but also continuously reconstructed in the daily activities of those who attend to them – distracted maybe, but nevertheless committed participants in the ongoing struggles of everyday life" (62-63). Finally, Silverstone speaks of "a new kind of fused and fusing reality, in which boundaries; between nature and culture; the country and the city; and perhaps also between fantasy and reality, become indistinct and inadequate. Here, the suburb represents a useful hybridisation... (172)". Silverstone ends up concluding that a new kind of public sphere has emerged – an emergence which he analyses and describes as a suburbanisation of the public sphere.

Despite many such observations which I do consider insightful, useful and "culturally convertible" my conclusion is: be cautious in generalizing. Universalism is difficult to handle. Focus on the reality at stake, carry out the relevant historical analyses, be loyal to the richness of detailed descriptions – in them is hidden the cultural diversity, the nuances.

Other types of modernity

Some social researchers will obviously argue that classic (mostly European) sociological concepts are perfectly applicable to contemporary ethnographic studies in Latin America. They might argue that the process of integration into modern society is just slower in this region of the world. My point, referring to my own Brazilian case story as well as to several other media ethnographical studies from Latin America, is that it is not a slower process of development towards a modern society, but simply another process of development. One should speak of a different type of modernity. However, to say that one should be cautious about generalizing is not an argument for cultural relativism. It is simply an argument for contextualization, without which one runs the risks Silverstone mentions himself: historical inaccuracy, universalism and reductionism.

Qualitative empirical media studies are more necessary than ever in order to understand the society we live in, of which the mass media are an ever-more integral part. Although the number of empirical reception studies is constantly growing, the number of comprehensive media ethnographies is still very limited and with the academic agenda largely set by Anglo-Saxon scholars. In 1996 James Lull launched a polemical critique of the British cultural studies tradition, saying that the "cultural myopia of cultural studies has inadvertently produced an imperialistic intellectual discourse and academic practice" (Lull 1996: 10). He also criticised the lack of methodological competence in many such ethnographical studies.

Most work around media use remains theoretical or very limited in empirical scope. Lull's critique may be somewhat extreme, but it is a fact that in recent years there has been (1) a very limited number of truly ethnographical studies about the use of media and (2) a boom in the international activity of British and American scholars, including in Latin America. With regard to this second point, what is often overlooked or insufficiently reflected upon, is the conceptual confusion and limited applicability of much British and American theory and analysis in qualitative empirical media studies, when carried out in other cultural settings. Such inadequacies are generated by the different realities upon which the (media) theory is tried out, which again is an argument for a larger degree of contextualization when producing sociological knowledge. It is an argument which is increasingly recognized, although not sufficiently, within media studies.

The need to do more anthropological studies of the TV audience argued for by Silverstone in 1990 must be addressed by many more scholars throughout the world. In order to generate greater understanding of the role of television in our everyday lives there must be critical, culturally sensitive, media aware, socio-historically contextualized and methodologically well elaborated media ethnographic studies of these issues. William Rowe and Vivian Shelling argue in similar terms when they call for further investigation of popular urban cultures, such as the mass culture of telenovelas. They emphasize the need for investigating (a) the traces of what came before, (b) the active recipients, and finally (c) the popular as a space of resignification (Rowe and Shelling 1991: 107pp).

The North American geographer Edward Soja's call for further research is more general. He argues for an ontologically, epistemologically and theoretically balanced meta-philosophy, taking account of what he calls 'historicality', 'spatiality' and 'sociality'. The nucleus of Silverstone, Rowe & Schelling and Soja's demands corresponds very much, to the argument I have been developing.

The demand for increasingly contextualized media ethnographies should, in its final and ideal version, aim for the"trialectics" advocated by Soja (Soja 1996), it should focus on a popular cultural genre as proposed by Rowe and Schelling, and should generate the anthropological insights about the public implied by Silverstone's argument.

Some media researchers, like Schrøder, have put forward the criticism that one loses the media focus when carrying out excessively comprehensive context analyses. However, I have argued that text and context should not and cannot be separated, even analytically. The de-contextualization of media analysis limits the focus and thus the scientific, social and political perspective of the analysis. My aim has been, on the contrary, to seek to build scientific bridges, broaden the perspective and seek to meet the empirical constraints this would require. Unlike Schrøder I am convinced that media theory must be loosened from the grip of literary traditions that demand a clear separation of text and context. The challenge for me has rather been to determine the relation between the text and its context. The concept of genre as deployed in this book has consequently been much broadly defined than what is expressed in a text.

The notion of hybrid spheres of signification should be further developed, remaining a central empirical focus of the proposed three-dimensional media analyses, looking at media use *vis-à-vis* the organization of time (historicality), space (spatiality) and social relations (spatiality), where the public and the popular, and the private and the public, instead of being disentangled and rationalized into individual boxes or binary sets should remain melting pots of lived life in which the media are an integral part. It is from here that the dynamics of agency, late (or post) modernity and domesticity merge to create new hybrids in our organisation of time, space and social relations, and create new hybrids in our formation of selves and collectivities.

Appendix 1

The telenovelas and mini-series in which Regina Duarte has appeared.

NAME:	AUTHOR	TV-STATION	YEAR
A Deusa Vencida	I. Ribeiro	Excelsior	1965
A Grande Viagem	I. Ribeiro	Excelsior	1965-66
Anjo Marcado	I. Ribeiro	Excelsior	1966
As Minas de Prata	I. Ribeiro	Excelsior	1966-67
Os Fantoches	I. Ribeiro	Excelsior	1967-68
O Terceiro Pecado	I. Riberio	Excelsior	1968
Legião dos Esquecidos	R. Lopes	Excelsior	1968-69
Os Estranhos	I. Ribeiro	Excelsior	1969
Véu de Noiva	J. Clair	Globo	1969-70
Irmãos Coragem	J. Clair	Globo	1970-71
Minha Doce Namorada	V. Sesso	Globo	1971-72
Selva de Pedra	J. Clair	Globo	1972-75 1986
Carinhoso	L. César Muniz	Globo	1973-74
Fogo Sobre Terra	J. Clair	Globo	1974-75
Nina	W. G. Durst	Globo	1977-78
Sétimo Sentido	J. Clair	Globo	1982
Roque Santeiro	D. Gomes	Globo	1985-86
Rainha do Sucata	S.de Abreu	Globo	1990
Por Amor		Globo	1996-1997
Juana (miniseria)		Globo	
Malu Mulher (miniseria)		Globo	

Appendix 2

The statistical results of the questionnaire survey in Calabar - 56 respondents.

PART 1. The socio-economic conditions of the household

Table 1. Age distribution
See Appendix 4, table 1.

Table 2. Matrimonial status

Married	19
Living together	26
Widow	6
Single, but not widow	5
Not answered, because young under the age of 14	0

Table 3. Number of children

0	1
1	6
2	13
I3	9
4	9
5	4
6	5
More than 6	7
Not informed	2

216 children among the 56, that is an average of 4 children per respondent.

Table 4. The size of the household

1	0
2	2
3	6
4	11
5	6
6	6
7	4
8	4
9	4
10	2

Average size of an household: 5.9 persons.

Table 5. Employment

Working at home	22
Unemployed	1
Maids	15
Cleaner	3
Teacher	3
Street trader	2
Lawyer	0
Employed in a shop	0
Waiter	4
Sewer	1
Pensioner	1
Other	2
Not informed	2

Table 6. Income per month (in Cruzados)

Less than a 0.5 minimum wage, 0-8,500	24
0.5 - 1 minimum wage, 17,000	25
1 - 1.5 minimum wages, 17-25,000	3
1.5 - 3 minimum wages, 51,000	3
3 - 5 minimum wages, 85,000	0
5 - 8 minimum wages, 136,000	0
More than 8 minimum wages	0
Not informed	1

Table 7. Employment of the partner

Street trader	2
Driver (bus/taxi/truck/ticket collector)	4
Architect, drawer or similar	0
Employed in a shop	1
Tradesman	18
Unskilled worker	5
Skilled worker	2
Attendant	6
Waiter, piccolo	1
Self-employed	0
Unemployed	1
Pensioner	2
Has no partner	10
Not informed	2
Other	2

Table 8. Income per month of the partner (in Cruzados)

Less than a 0.5 minimum wage, 0-8,500	1
0.5 - 1 minimum wage, 17,000	12
1 - 1.5 minimum wages, 17-25,000	14
1.5 - 3 minimum wages, 51,000	12
3 - 5 minimum wages, 85,000	0
5 - 8 minimum wages, 136,000	1
More than 8 minimum wages	0

Table 9. Number of incomes per household

0	0
1	18
2	16
3	9
4	3
More than 4	4
Not informed	6

An average of 2.2 incomes per household.

PART 2. TV habits

Table 10. *Do you have a TV set at home?*

Yes	47
No	9

Table 11. *If not, do you watch TV anyway?*

Yes	9
No	

Table 12. *Do you watch TV alone?*

Yes	14
No	40
Do not watch TV	-
Not informed	2

Table 13. *Which novela do you watch most?*

Ana Raio (9.30 pm)	3
Meu bem meu mal (8 pm)	10
Barriga de aluguel (6 pm)	10
Lua Cheia de Amor (7 pm)	6
Watch All Globo-novelas	5
Watch 3-4 Globo-novelas	7
Do not watch novelas	8
Do not watch tv	4
Not informed	3

Table 14. *How many times per week do you watch novelas?*

0	7
1-2	2
3-5	9
Every day (that is 6 times)	36
Not informed	2

Table 15. Did you watch **Pantanal?**

Yes	21
No	29
Not informed	6

If no, why not?

Was being shown too late	1
Saw another/did not like it	16
Cannot watch TV Manchete	-
Other	2
Not informed	10

Table 16. Did you watch **Rainha do Sucata?**

Yes	45
No	6
Not informed	5

If no, why not?

Was being shown too late	3
Saw another/did not like it	-
Other/not informed	3

Table 17. Did you see **Ana Raio?**

Yes	7
No	44

If no, why not?

Was being shown too late	2
Saw another/did not like it	22
Cannot watch TV Manchete	-
Other	2
Not Informed	17

Table 18. Which novelas do you watch at present?

GLOBO -All	10
Barriga de Aluguel	32
Lua Cheia de Amor	36
Meu Bem Meu Mal	33
Araponga	37
Top Model	10
SBT	
Brasileiros e Brasileiras	-
MANCHETE	
Ana Raio e Ze Trovão	4
Others	6
None	7
Not Informed	2

Average number of novelas per person (excluding the persons who watch 0 novelas): 3,4 novelas

Average number of novelas per person: 3.0 novelas

Table 19. Is the TV ever turned on, when noone is watching?

Yes	14
No	35
Do not have TV	6
Not informed	1

Table 20. Do you do other things while the TV is turned on?

Yes	42
No	7
Not informed	2

Has no television: 5.

If yes, what (some have mentioned more than one thing)

Cook	9
Do the dishes	-
Clean	4
Wash the clothes	3
Sew	2
Some of the work in house	30
Have dinner	2
Other	2

PART 3. Other Media Habits

Table 21. Do you have radio at home?

Yes	48
No	8

Table 22. Do you read newspapers?

Yes	31
No	22
Not Informed	3

If yes, which?

A Tarde	28
Jornal da Bahia	1
Tribuna	2
Correio do Povo	2
Other	-
Not Informed	3

Table 23. How many times a week?

0	22
1	9
2-6	6
7	2
Not informed	13

Table 24. Do you read magazines?

Yes	18
No	38

If yes, which?

Contigo	4
Amiga	1
Veja/Isto É or similar	1
Manchete	3
Mulher Manequin	1
Nova Saude	1
Cartoons	6
Horoscope Magazines	1
Fotonovelas	4

Table 25. Religious belief

Catholic	38
Deus e Amor	2
Not informed	16

Appendix 3

The statistical results of the questionnaire survey in Vilo Nitro Opereria - 49 respondents.

PART 1. The socio-economic conditions of the household

Table 1. Age distribution

	Vilo N. O.	Calabar	Total	Men
Under 20	3	0	3	4
20-29	12	14	26	3
30-39	23	18	41	2
40-49	8	12	20	0
More than 50	5	12	17	1
Total	51	56	107	10

Table 2. Matrimonial status

Married	27
Living together	7
Widow	8
Single, but not widow	3
Divorced	3
Not answered, because young under the age of 14	2

Table 3. Number of children

0	3
1	9
2	9
3	8
4	9
5	4
6	2
More than 6	2
Not informed	0

An average of 3,08 children

Table 4. The size of the household

1	1
2	6
3	7
4	10
5	7
6	10
7	2
8	1
9	2
10	3
More than 10	3

Average size of an household: 5 persons.

Table 5. Employment

Working at home	14
Unemployed	8
Maids	3
Cleaner	4
Teacher	2
Street trader	1
Lawyer	1
Employed in a shop	2
Waiter	2
Sewer	2
Self-employed	1
Fabric	2
Pupil	2
Pensioner	4
Other	2
Not informed	0

Table 6. Income per month (in Cruzados)

Less than a 0.5 minimum wage, 0-8,500	2
0.5 - 1 minimum wage, 17,000	8
1 - 1.5 minimum wages, 17-25,000	6
1.5 - 3 minimum wages, 51,000	3
3 - 5 minimum wages, 85,000	3
5 - 8 minimum wages, 136,000	2
More than 8 minimum wages	1
Not informed	2

Table 7. Employment of the partner

Streettrader	2
Driver (bus/taxi/truck/ticket collector)	3
Architect, drawer or similar	4
Employed in a shop	2
Tradesman	6
Unskilled worker	2
Skilled worker	5
Attendant	0
Waiter, piccolo	2
Self-employed	6
Unemployed	3
Pensioner	1
Has no partner	13
Not informed	0
Other	0

Table 8. Income per month of the partner (in Cruzados)

Less than a 0.5 minimum wage, 0-8,500	1
0.5 - 1 minimum wage, 17,000	1
1 - 1.5 minimum wages, 17-25,000	2
1.5 - 3 minimum wages, 51,000	11
3 - 5 minimum wages, 85,000	5
5 - 8 minimum wages, 136,000	3
More than 8 minimum wages	1
Not informed	9

Table 9. *Number of incomes per household*

0	0
1	25
2	15
3	6
4	3
More than 4	0
Not informed	0

PART 2. TV Habits

Table 10. *Do you have a TV set at home?*

Yes	44
No	5

Table 11. *If not, do you watch TV anyway?*

Yes	3
No	2

Table 12. *Do you watch TV alone?*

Yes	24
No	22
Do not watch tv	3

Table 13. *Which novela do you watch most?*

Ana Raio (9.30 pm)	9
Meu bem meu mal (8 pm)	11
Barriga de aluguel (6 pm)	12
Lua Cheia de Amor (7 pm)	1
Araponga (9.30 pm)	3
Others	2
Do not watch novelas	10
Do not watch TV	1

Table 14. How many times per week do you watch novelas?

0	11
1-2	1
3-5	7
Every day (that is 6 times)	30

Table 15. Did you watch **Pantanal**?

Yes	26
No	23

If no, why not?

Was being shown too late	1
Saw another/did not like it	9
Cannot watch TV Manchete	3
Other	9
Not informed	2

Table 16. Did you watch **Rainha do Sucata**?

Yes	41
No	8

If no, why not?

Was being shown too late	0
Saw another/did not like it	2
Other/not informed	6

Table 17. Did you see **Ana Raio**?

Yes	18
No	31

If no, why not?

Was being shown too late	3
Saw another/did not like it	14
Cannot watch TV Manchete	3
Missed the first chapters	2
Other	9

Table 18. Which novelas do you watch at present?

GLOBO

Barriga de Aluguel	27
Lua Cheia de Amor	25
Meu Bem Meu Mal	27
Araponga	15
Top Model	6

SBT

Brasileiros e Brasileiras	2

MANCHETE

Ana Raio e Ze Trovao	14
Others	2
None	11

NUMBER OF NOVELAS	%
0	22
1	12
2	8
3	18
4	29
5	10

Average number of novelas per person (excluding the persons who watch 0 novelas): 3.2 novelas

Average number of novelas per person: 2.4 novelas

Table 19. Is the TV ever turned on, when no-one is watching?

Yes	17
No	28
Do not have TV	4

Table 20. Do you do other things while the TV is turned on?

Yes	13
No	32

If yes, what (some have mentioned more than one thing)

Cook	6
Do the dishes	5
Clean	3
Wash the clothes	3
Sew	1
Some of the work in house	11
Have dinner	9
Other	2

PART 3. Other Media Habits

Table 21. Do you have radio at home?

Yes	38
No	11

Table 22. Do you read newspapers?

Yes	20
No	29

If yes, which?

Noticia Popular	13
Folha da Tarde	2
O Estado	2
A Folha de Sao Paolo	1
Jornal da Tarde	1
Other	3

Table 23. How many times a week?

0	26
1	6
2-6	9
7	6
Not informed	2

Table 24. Do you read magazines?

Yes	14
No	35

If yes, which?

Contigo	3
Amiga	1
Veja/ Isto é or similar	4
Manchete	2
Religious magazins	2
Others	8

Table 25. Religious belief

Catholic	40 (11passively)
Spiritualist	2
Jehova's witness	1
Non-believer	3
Fundamentalist (Crente)	2
Other religion	2

Appendix 4

Questionnaire

Part 1

Age:

Marital status:

No. of children:

Age of children:

Your job:

Your salary:

Husband's job:

His salary:

Other salaries in the household?

Who's?

Amount:

Part 2

Do you have TV in your home?

If no, do you still watch TV?

If yes, where?

Do you watch TV alone?

Never alone?

With whom?

What does your husband watch most?

What do your children watch most?

Part 2 (continued)

What do you watch? When? How many hours?

Hour	Programme	No. of hours	Sundays
6-12			
12-18			
18-			

What telenovelas do you watch at present?

Which one do you watch most?

How many times a week?

Do you watch *The story of Ana Raio and Ze Trovao*?

If no, why not?

Did you watch *Pantanal*?

If no, why not?

Did you watch *Rubbish Queen*? (Globo, 1990)

If no, why not?

Is the TV set ever turned on in your home without anybody watching?

Do you do other things while the TV set in turned on?

What?   Cooking, washing clothes, cleaning, dish washing, sewing, other

Underline the indicated ones.

Part 3

Do you have radio in your house?

What do you listen to? When? How many hours?

Hour	Programme	No. of hours	Sundays
6-12			
12-18			
18-			

Do you read (a) newspaper(s)?

If yes, which one(s)?

How many times a week?

Do you read (a) magazine(s)?

If yes, which one(s)?

How many times a week?

Do you read anything else?

If yes, what?

What is your religion?

Appendix 5

Interview guide for the qualitative interviews

Most of the persons have been asked the questions in the questionnaire prior to the in-depth interview. In some cases the questions of the questionnaire have been part of the in-depth interview.

Introduction

Name, age, family members, place of origin, number of years in this area.

Preferred telenovela

Which programmes do you prefer to watch on TV?
Why?
Which novelas do you watch?
What is the story of your preferred novela? Tell the story.
What do you like in it?
Do you recognize anything from your everyday in the novela?
What?
Does the story seem realistic?
Why/ why not?
What is realistic/ what is not realistic?
Do you find neighbourhoods like your own in the novelas?
If no, why not, do you think?
Do black people appear in the novelas?
Which characters do they act?

Identifcation

Why do you like to watch novelas?
Who do you like best in the current novela?/in *A Rainha do Sucata*?
Why?
Do you recognize anything of yourself in the characters of the novela?/in your preferred character?
What do you recognize?
Would you like to live like the main characters of the novela?
Why/ why not?
Would you like to have a house/ clothes like they have?

Traces in the everyday

Do you daily think of the novelas/ the characters/ the story?
What do you think about?
Do you talk to friends/ colleagues about the novelas?
Do you use the story of the novela *vis-à-vis* problems in your everydaylife?
How?

Do the novela give inspiration to solutions of problems in your everyday life? Which?

Production - music/commercials

Do you notice the music in the novela?
Do you like it?
Why/ why not?
Commercials - do you watch them?
If yes, do you do something else, while they are on? What?
Is it possible for you to follow the story of the novela, if you miss some chapters?
If yes, how do you do that?

Your own novela?

If you could make your own novela - imagine you could tell a story in a novela - which story would you like to tell?
Why?

Bibliography

Abreu, Silvio de. 1990. *Elle*, February 1990.

Abreu, Silvio de. 1990. In: *Folha de São Paulo*, 1.4.90.

Abreu, Silvio de. 1990. In: *O Globo*, 1.4.90.

Abreu, Silvio de. 1990. In: *Jornal do Brasil*, 1.4.90.

Abreu, Silvio de. 1990. In: *O Globo*, 21.10.90.

Abreu, Silvio de. 1992. In: *Veja*, 2.9.92.

Allen, Robert C. 1985. *Speaking of soap operas*. Chapel Hill and London: The University of North Carolina Press.

Allen, Robert C. (ed). 1987. *Channels of Discourse: Television and Contemporary Criticism*. London: Methuen.

Allen, Robert C. (ed). 1995. *to be continued...Soap Operas Around the World*. London: Routledge.

Amin, Samir. 1976. *L'Imperialisme et de developpement Inegal*. Paris: Les Editions de Minuit.

Amin, Samir. 1979. *Den ulige udvikling. Studier af samfundsformationer i kapitalismens periferi*. Copenhagen: Aurora.

Andersen, Michael B. "Kan man planlægge kreativitet? om tv-produktionsanalyse". In: *Mediekultur No. 8*, July 1988. 6-25.

Ang, Ien. 1985. *Watching Dallas*. London: Methuen.

Ang, Ien. 1989. "Wanted: audiences". In: E. Seiter, H. Borchers, G. Kreutzner, and E. Warth (eds). *Remote Control: Television, Audiences, and Cultural Power*. London: Routledge.

Ang, Ien. 1990. "Culture and Communication: towards an Ethnographic Critique of Media Consumption in the Transnational Media System". *European Journal of Communication* 5, 23: 239-60.

Ang, Ien. 1991. *Desperately Seeking the Audience*. London: Routledge.

Antola, Livia and Everett M. Rogers. 1985. "Telenovelas: A Latin American Success Story". *Journal of Communication* Vol. 35, No. 4:24-35.

Araújo, Inácio. 1991. "O trabalho da crítica." In: Adauto Novaes. *Rede Imaginária: Televisao e democracia*. São Paulo: Compania das Letras, Secretaria Municipal da Cultura.

Atkinson, Paul and Martyn Hammersley. 1983. *Ethnography: Principles in Practice*. London and New York: Tavistock Publications.

Atwood, Rita and Emile McAnany. 1986. *Communication and Latin American Society. Trends in Critical Research, 1960-1985*. The Universityof Wisconsin Press.

Avancini, Walter. 1988. "Estética na Televisao." In: Claudia Macedo, Angela Falcao, Candido J.M. De Almeida (eds). *Tv ao Vivo: Depoimentos*. São Paulo: Editora Brasiliense.

Avancini, Walter. 1990. In: *Imprensa*, July 1990.

Barthes, Roland. 1975. *The Pleasure of the Text*. New York: Hill & Wang.

Barreto, Marcelo. 1991. Personal Interview by Thomas Tufte. Rio de Janeiro, February 1991.

Barrios, L. 1988. "Television, Telenovelas, and Family Life in Venezuela". In: Lull, J. *World Families watch Television*. Newbury Park: Sage.

Barrios, L. 1992. *Familia y Television*. Venezuela: Monte Ávila. Editores Latinoamericana.

Bausinger, Herman. 1984. "Media, technology and daily life". In: *Media, Culture & Society*, 6: 343-352.

Bech-Jørgensen, Birte. 1994. *Når hver dag bliver hverdag*. Copenhagen: Akademisk Forlag.

Becker, Beatriz. 1992. *O sucesso da novela Pantanal: Um fenomeno de mídia*. Rio de Janeiro: UFRJ.

Belik, Helio. 1989. *Reading Brazilian Telenovelas: From Romanticism to Post-Realism*. Queens College, USA.

Beltran, Luiz Ramiro. 1975. "Research Ideologies in Conflict". In: *Journal of Communication*, 25, 2, pp. 187-192.

Beltran, Luis Ramiro. 1977. "TV Etchings in the Minds of Latin Americans: Conservatism, Materialism and Conformism". *Gazette* 24:61-85.

Benjamin, W. 1977. "The Work of Art in an Age of Mechanical Reproduction". In: Curran, J. et al. *Mass Communication and Society*, pp.384-408. London: Edward Arnold.

Bennet, T. and Janet Woollacott. 1987. *Bond and Beyond*. London: Methuen.

Biltereyst, Daniel and Philippe Meers. 1998. Reverse Cultural Imperialism? The case of the flow of telenovelas to Europe. Paper presented to the 21st Scientific Conference of the IAMCR, 26th-30th July 1998. Glasgow, UK.

Bondebjerg, Ib. 1988. "Kritisk teori, æstetik og receptionsforskning". *Mediekultur 7*. Aalborg.

Bondebjerg, Ib. 1989. "Tekst, reception og samfund: argumenter for et kritisk helhedsperspektiv". In: Lennart Højberg (ed). *Reception af levende billeder*. Copenhagen: Akademisk Forlag.

Bondebjerg, Ib. 1993. *TV som fortællende medie*. Copenhagen: Borgens Forlag.

Borelli, Silvia H.S, Ortiz, R & Ramos J.M.O. 1989. Telenovela, historia e produçáo. São Paulo: Brasiliense.

Borelli, Silvia H.S. 1993. "Fictional Genres in Mass Culture". In: Jose Marques de Melo (ed). *Communication for a new world: Brazilian perspectives*. São Paulo: ECA/USP.

Bouquillion, P. 1992. "La Reception des Telenovelas Bresiliennes en France". *Intercom*, 15 (1): 98-117. São Paulo.

Bourdieu, Pierre and Jean-Claude Passeron. 1977. *Reproduction in Education, Society and Culture*. London: Sage.

Bovin, Mette. 1988. "On Provocation Anthropology". In: *Drama Review* Vol. 32, No. 1. London.

Braga, Nice. 1989. "Oral traditions in Brazil - popular communication in rural areas". *Media Development* 4: 37-38. London: WACC.

Brown, Mary Ellen. *Soap Opera and Women's Talk. The Pleasure of Resistance.* London: Sage.

Brundsdon, Charlotte. 1981. "*Crossroads*: Notes on soap opera". *Screen* 22, 4: 32-37.

Brundsdon, Charlotte and David Morley. 1978. *Everyday Television: "Nationwide"*. London: British Film Institute.

Bryce, Jennifer. 1987. "Family time and television use". In: T.Lindlof (ed). *Natural Audiences, Norwood*, New Jersey: Abex.

Caceres, Jesus Galindo. 1990. "Buscando un rostro, encontrando una mirada: cultura y movimiento social". *Estudios sobre las Culturas Contemporaneas* Vol IV, No. 10: 11-40. Colima/Mexico: Universidad de Colima.

Calmon. Antonio. 1992. In: *Estado de São Paulo*, 21.11.92.

Canclini, Néstor García. 1987a. *Politicas Culturales en America Latina*. Mexico: Editora Grijalbo.

Canclini, Néstor García. 1987b. "Ni folklorico ni masivo: Que es lo Popular?". *Dialogos* 17: 4-11. Lima: Felafacs.

Canclini, Néstor García. 1988. "Culture and power: the state of research". *Media, Culture and Society*. Vol. 10, No. 4: 467-498.

Canclini, Néstor García. 1989. *Culturas Hibridas*. Mexico: Editorial Grijalbo.

Canclini, Néstor García. 1990a. "El Consumo Sirve para Pensar". *Dialogos* 30: 6-9. Lima: Felafacs.

Canclini, Néstor García. 1990b. "Los estudios culturales de los 80 a los 90: perspectivas antropológicas y sociológicas en America Latina". *Punto de Vista*: 41-48.

Canclini, Néstor García. 1993. *El Consumo Cultural en México*. Grijalbo/ Consejo Nacional para la Cultura y las Artes. México.

Canclini, Néstor García. 1995a. *Hybrid Cultures*. Minneapolis: University of Minnesota Press.

Canclini, Néstor García. 1995b. *Consumidores y Ciudadanos*. Mexico City: Grijalbo.

Canclini, Néstor García. 1997. "Hybrid Cultures and Communicative Strategies". In: *Media Development 1/1997*, pp. 22-29. London, WACC.

Cantor, Muriel G. and Suzanne Pingree. 1983. *The Soap Opera*. London: Sage.

Cardoso, Fernando. 1972. "Dependency and Development in Latin America". *New Left Review*, no. 74.

Cardoso, Fernando and E. Faletto. 1979. *Dependency and Development in Latin America*. Berkeley: University of California Press. (Original in Spanish 1969/Mexico).

Chavez Mendez, Lupita. 1992. *La producción de telenovelas mexicanas y su forma moderna y racional de operar*. Universidad Iberoamericana, Mexico.

Clark, Walter. 1991. *O Campeão de Audiencia: uma autobiografia*. São Paulo: Editora Best Seller.

Clifford, James & George Marcus (eds). 1986. *Writing Culture. The Poetics and Politics of Ethnography*. Berkeley: University of California Press.

Conceicao, Fernando. 1986. *Cala a boca, Calabar: a luta politica dos favelados.* Petrópolis: Vozes.

Corner, John. 1991. "Meaning, Genre and Context: the Problematics of "Public Knowledge" in the New Audience Studies". In: James Curran and Michael Gurevitch (eds). *Mass Media and Society.* London: Edward Arnold.

Covarrubias, Karla Y., Angélica Bautista & Bertha A. Uribe. *Cuéntame en Qué se Quedó. La Telenovela como fenómeno social.* 1994. Mexico: Trillas/Felafacs.

Covarribuas, Karla Y. & Ana. B. Uribe Alvarado. "Hacia una nueva cultura televisiva: analisis de los públicos de la telenovela Mirada de Mujer". In: *Estudios sobre las Culturas Contemporaneas.* Época II/ Volumen IV/ Numero 7/ Junio 1998, pp. 137-152.

Curran, James. 1996. "Mass Media and Democracy Revisited". In: J. Curran & M. Gurevitch (eds). 1996. *Mass Media and Society.* London: Arnold.

Da Costa, Alcir Henrique. 1986. "Rio e Excelsior: projectos fracassados?" In: Inimá Simões, Alcir Henrique da Costa and Maria Rita Kehl. *Um Pais no Ar: Historia da TV Brasileira em tres canais.* São Paulo: Brasiliense.

Dahlgren, Peter. 1995. *Television and the Public Sphere. Citizenship, Democracy and the Media.* London: Sage.

DaMatta, Roberto. 1981. *Carnavais, Malandros e Herois.* Rio de Janeiro: Zahar.

DaMatta, Roberto. 1991. *A Casa e A Rua.* Rio de Janeiro: Editora Guanabara Koogan S.A.

Da Silva, Carlos Eduardo Lins. 1985. *Muito alem do Jardim Botanico: Um estudo sobre a audiéncia do Jornal Nacional da Globo entre trabalhadores.* São Paulo: Summus Editorial.

Da Tavola, Arthur. 1988. "Televisao e Sociedade". In: Claudia Macedo, Angela Falcao, Candido J.M. De Almeida (eds). *Tv ao Vivo: Depoimentos.* São Paulo: Editora Brasiliense.

De Certeau. 1984. *The practice of everyday life.* Berkeley and London: University of California Press.

De Moragas Spa, Miguel (ed). 1985. *Sociología de la Comunicación de Masas.* Barcelona: Gustavo Gili.

Dorfman, A. and A. Mattelart. 1972. *Para Leer al Pato Donald: Comunicacion de Masa y Colonialismo.* Mexico City: Siglo Veintiuno Editores.

Drotner, Kirsten. 1993a. "Media Ethnography: an Other Story?" In: Ulla Carlsson (ed). *Nordisk forskning om kvinder och medier,* pp 25-40. Göteborg: Nordicom.

Drotner, Kirsten. 1993b. "Medieetnografiske problemstillinger - en oversigt". *Mediekultur 21*: 5-22. Aalborg.

Drotner, Kirsten. 1994. "Ethnographic Enigmas: "The Everyday" in Recent Media Studies". *Cultural Studies* 2: 208-25.

Drotner, Kirsten, 1996. "Less is More: Media Ethnography and its Limits", in *The Construction of the Viewer: Media Ethnography and the Anthropology of Audiences.* Højbjerg: Intervention Press.

Duarte, Regina. 1990. In: *Jornal do Brasil,* 1.4.90.

Duarte, Regina. 1992. In: *O Estado de São Paulo.* 21.11.92.

Eco, Umberto. 1981a. "Læserens rolle". In: Olsen, M. (ed).

Eco, U. 1981b. *The Role of the Reader. Explorations in the Semiotics of texts.* London: Hutchinson.

Ellen, R.F. (ed). 1984. *Ethnographic research: A guide to general conduct.* London and New York: Academic Press.

Elsaesser, Thomas. 1987. "Tales of Sound and Fury: Observations on the Family Melodrama". In: Christine, Gledhill (ed). *Home is where the heart is: Studies in melodrama and the woman's film.* London: BFI.

Ettama, J.F. 1982. *The Organisational Context of Creativity: A Case Study for Public Television.* Beverly Hills: Sage.

Fadul, Anamaria. 1989. "Cultura e comunicação: a teoria necessária". In: Margarida M. Kunsch and Francisco Assis Fernandes: *Comunicaçáo, Democracia e Cultura.* São Paulo: Intercom and Loyola.

Fadul, Anamaria. 1993. *Serial Fiction in Tv. The Latin American Telenovelas.* São Paulo: USP.

Fadul, Anamaria, Emile McAnany and Ofelia Torres Morales. 1996. "Telenovela and Demography in Brazil". Work Paper. Presented in Gender Section at 20th Scientific Conference of the IAMCR, Sydney, Australia, 18-22 August 1996.

Fair, Ellen. 1989. "29 years of theory and research on media and development: the dominant paradigm impact". *Gazette 44:* 129-150.

Fernandes, Florestan. 1975. *A Revolução Burguesa no Brasil.* Rio de Janeiro: Zahar.

Fernandes, Ismael. 1982. *Memoria da Telenovela Brasileira.* São Paulo: Proposta.

Fernandes, Ismael. 1987. *Memoria da Telenovela Brasileira.* São Paulo: Editora Brasiliense.

Fernandes, Ismael. 1994. *Memoria da Telenovela Brasileira.* São Paulo: Editora Brasiliense.

Fernando, Jorge. 1988. "Teledramaturgia II - A Direcao". In: Claudia Macedo, Angela Falcao, Candido J.M. De Almeida (eds). *TV ao Vivo: Depoimentos.* São Paulo: Editora Brasiliense.

Fernando, Jorge. In: Veja, September 1991.

Feuer, Jane. 1987. "Genre Study and Television". In: Robert C. Allen (ed). *Channels of Discource: Television and Contemporary Criticism.* London: Routledge.

Filho, Daniel. In: *Veja,* 2.10.1985.

Fish, Stanley. 1979. *Is there a Text in this Class? The Authority of Interpretive Communities.* Cambridge, MA: Harvard University Press.

Fiske, John. 1987a. *Television Culture.* London: Methuen.

Fiske, John. 1987b. "British Cultural Studies and Television". In: Robert C. Allen (ed). *Channels of Discource: Television and Contemporary Criticism.* London: Methuen.

Fiske, John. 1989. *Understanding Popular Culture.* Boston: Unwin Hyman.

Fiske, John. 1991. "Postmodernism and Television". In: James Curran and Michael Gurevitch (eds). *Mass Media and Society.* London: Edward Arnold.

263

Folha de São Paulo. 9.2.91. *Ilustrada*: "Marinho vê excesso de novelas na Globo". Interview with Roberto Marinho.

Folha de São Paulo. 9.12.91. "Manchete assume estilo *Pantanal* e estreia um novela sem história". *Televisáo*.

Folha de São Paulo. 9.5.95. "Globo nomina mercado e caminha para monopolio na exploracao da tv a cabo." *Televisáo*.

Fox, Elisabeth. 1988. *Media and Politics in Latin America: The Struggle for Democracy*. London: Sage.

Fox, Elisabeth. 1994. "Kulturel afhængighed: tre dimensioner". In: *Mediekultur, Special Issue on Media, Culture and Development*. Århus: SMID. pp 11-17.

Fox, Elisabeth. 1997. *Latin American Broadcasting: From Tango to Telenovela*. University of Luton Press/John Libbey Media.

Frank, A.G. 1970. *Kapitalism och underutveckling i Latinamerika. Historiska studier över Chile och Brasilien*. Steffanstorp, Sweden.

Freire, Paulo. 1972. *Pedagogy of the Oppressed*. Harmondsworth: Penguin.

Fuenzalida, Valerio and P. Edwards. 1985. *TV y Recepcion Activa*. Santiago: CENECA.

Fuenzalida, Valerio. 1987a. "La Gente es lo mas importante". *Communicacion America Latina* 17: 31-35.

Fuenzalida, Valerio. 1987b. "La influencia cultural de la television". *Dialogos* 17: 20-29. Lima: Felafacs.

Fuenzalida, Valerio. 1988. "El Programa CENECA en recepcion activa de la TV". *Dialogos 19:* 81-96. Lima: Felafacs.

Fuenzalida, Valerio. 1991. *Television, pobreza y desarrollo*. Santiago: CPU.

Fuenzalida, Valerio. 1992a. "Investigacion". *Paper solicitated for UNICEF conference,* Rio de Janeiro: November 1991. Published in *Dialogos 33* (1992): 36-40. Lima: Felafacs.

Fuenzalida, Valerio. 1992b. "Tv Broadcasting for Grassroot Development". *Paper presented at the conference "TV and Video in Latin America"*. Denmark, November 1992: Danchurchaid.

Fuenzalida, Valerio. 1994. *La apropriacion educativa de la telenovela*. (forth-coming). Santiago.

Fuenzalida, Valerio. 1997. *Television y Cultura Cotidiana. La influencia social de la TV percibida desde la cultura cotidiana de la audiencia*. Santiago: CPU.

Fuenzalida, Valerio and María Elena Hermosilla. 1989. *Visiones y Ambiciones del Televidente: Estudios de Recepcion Televisiva*. Santiago: CENECA.

Furtado, Rubens. 1988. "Programacao I - Da Rede Tupi á Rede Manchete." In: Claudia Macedo, Angela Falcao, Candido J.M. De Almeida (eds). *TV ao Vivo: Depoimentos*. São Paulo: Editora Brasiliense.

Garfinkel, H. 1967. *Studies in Ethnomethodology*. Englewood Cliffs, NJ: Prentice-Hall.

Geertz, Clifford. 1973. *The Interpretation of Cultures*. New York: Basic Books.

Gerbner, George, Larry Gross, Michael Morgan and Nancy Signorielli. 1986. "Living with Television: The Dynamics of the Cultivation Process. In: Jennings

Bryant and Dolf Zillmann (eds). *Perspectives on Media Effects*. Hillsdale, NJ: Lawrence Erlbaum Associates.

Giersing, Morten. 1982. *TV i USA*. Copenhagen: Gyldendal.

Giddens, Anthony. 1987. *Social Theory and Modern Sociology*. Cambridge: Polity Press.

Gillespie, Marie. 1995. *Television, Ethnicity and Cultural Change*. London: Routledge.

Gilroy, Paul. 1993. "Between Afro-Centrism and Eurocentrism: Youth Culture and the problem of Hybridity." *Young*, Vol.1, No.2. 2-12. Uppsala: Swedish Science Press.

Gitlin, Tod. 1985. *Inside Prime Time*. New York: Pantheon Books.

Gledhill, Christine. 1987a. "The Melodramatic Field: An Investigation". In: Christine Gledhill (ed). *Home is where the heart is: Studies in melodrama and the woman's film*. London: BFI.

Gledhill, Christine (ed). 1987b. *Home is where the heart is: Studies in melodrama and the woman's film*. London: BFI.

Goffman, Erving. 1975. *Stigma*. Copenhagen: Gyldendal.

González, Jorge A. 1987. "Los frentes culturales: culturas, mapas poderes y luchas por las definiciones legitimas de los sentidos sociales de la vida". *Dialogos* 26: 33-47.

Gonzalez, Jorge. A. 1988. La Cofradia de las Emociones (In)Terminables. In: *Estudios sobre las culturas contemporáneas*, Vol. II, No. 4-5, Universidad de Colima. Published in English in 1992: "The Cofraternity of (Un)Finishable Emotions: Constructing Mexican Telenovelas". In: *Studies in Latin American Popular Culture*. Volume Eleven 1992.

Gonzalez, Jorge. A. 1994a. *Más(+) cultura(s). Ensayos sobre realidades plurales*, México, CNCA.

Gonzalez, Jorge. A. 1994b. "La formación de las ofertas culturales y sus públicos en México". In: *Estudios sobre las culturas contemporáneas*, Vol. VI, No. 18, Universidad de Colima.

Gonzalez, Jorge. A. 1997. "The willingness to weave: cultural analysis, Cultural Fronts and networks of the future". In: *Media Development* 1/1997, Vol. XLIV. London: WACC.

Gonzalez, Jorge. A. 1998 (ed). *La cofradía de las emociones (in)terminables. Miradas sobre telenovelas en Mexico*. Guadalajara: Universidad de Guadalajara.

Gripsrud, Jostein. 1995. *The Dynasty Years. Hollywood Television and Critical Media Studies*. London: Routledge

Grisolli, Paulo. 1992. Personal interview by Thomas Tufte. Denmark, November 1992.

Grisolli, Paulo. 1993. Personal interview by Thomas Tufte. Algarve, Portugal, August 1994.

Grisolli, Paulo. 1994. "Drømmefabrikken". *Mediekultur* Special Issue on Tv, Culture and Development in Latin America. First presented as a paper at a conference of Danchurchaid, Denmark, November 1992.

Habermas, Jürgen. 1961. *Borgerlig Offentlighet*. Oslo: Gyldendal.

Habermas, Jürgen. 1981. *Theorie des kommunikativen Handelns.* Frankfurt AM.

Halbwachs, Maurice. 1968. *La Memoire Collective.* Paris: PUF.

Hall, Stuart. 1973. "Encoding and decoding in the television discourse". Occasional Paper No. 7. Birmingham: CCCS.

Hall, Stuart. 1980. "Encoding/decoding". In: Stuart Hall, Dorothy Hobson, Andrew Lowe and Paul Willis (eds). 1980. *Culture, Media, Language.* London: Unwin Hyman.

Hall, Stuart. 1982. "The rediscovery of "ideology": return of the repressed in media studies". In: Michael Gurevitch, Tony Bennet, James Curran and Janet Woollacott (eds). *Culture, Society and the Media.* London and New York: Routledge.

Hall, Stuart, Dorothy Hobson, Andrew Lowe and Paul Willis (eds). 1980. *Culture, Media, Language.* London: Unwin Hyman.

Hannerz, Ulf. 1992. *Cultural Complexity - Studies in the Social Organization of Meaning.* New York: Columbia University Press.

Hastrup, Kirsten. 1986. "Veracity and visibility: The problem of authenticity in anthropology". In: *FOLK.*

Hermes, Joke. 1997. "Gender and Media Studies: No Woman, No Cry". In: John Corner, Philip Schlesinger and Roger Silverstone(eds). *International Media Research.* London: Routledge.

Hermes, Joke. 1998. "Cultural Citizenship and Popular Fiction". In: Kees Brants, Joke Hermes and Liesbet van Zoonen (eds). *The Media in Question. Popular Cultures and Public Interests.*

Herz, Daniel. 1989. *A historia secreta da REDE GLOBO.* Porto Alegre: Ortiz.

Hobson, D. 1982. *Crossroads: the Drama of a Soap Opera.* London: Methuen.

Hoggart, Richard. 1958. *The Uses of Literacy.* London: Penguin.

Horton, D. & R.R. Wohl. 1986 (1956). "Mass Communication and para-social interaction: observation on intimacy at a distance". In: Gumpert, G & Cathcart, R. (eds). *Inter/Media. Interpersonal communication in a media world.* Third Edition, New York: Oxford University Press.

Højberg, Lennart (ed). 1989. *Reception af levende billeder.* Copenhagen: Akademisk Forlag.

IBGE. In: *Veja*, January 1991.

Intercom. No. 15. 1992. São Paulo: INTERCOM.

Iser, W. 1978. *The Act of Reading.* John Hopkins University Press.

Isto é . 20.3.1991. "Viva o folhetim".

Isto é. 19.7.95. "Imperios Contracatacam", p. 108-109.

Isto é. 3.4.96. "Sai de Baixo", p. 124-129.

Jacks, Nilda A. (In Press). *Querencia. Cultura, Identidade e Mediação.* Porto Alegre: Editora da Universidade.

Jacks, Nilda A. and Thomas Tufte. 1997. "Televisao, identidade e cotidiano". In: Antonio Albino C. Rubim et al (eds). *Produçáo e Recepção dos Sentidos Midiáticos.* Petropolis: Editora Vozes/COMPOS.

Jensen, Klaus Bruhn. 1986. *Making Sense of the News.* Aarhus: Aarhus University Press.

Jensen, Klaus Bruhn. 1987. *Seernes tv-avis*. Copenhagen: Danmarks Radio.

Jensen, Klaus Bruhn. 1988. "News as a social resource: a qualitative empirical study of the reception of Danish television news". *European Journal of Communication* 3 (3): 275-301.

Jensen, Klaus Bruun. 1989. "Discourses of interviewing: validating qualitative research findings through textual analysis". In: S. Kvale (ed) *Issues of Validity in Qualitative Research*. Lund: Studentlitteratur.

Jensen, Klaus Bruhn. 1991. "Reception analysis: mass communication as the social production of meaning". In: Klaus Bruhn Jensen and Nicholas Jankowski (eds). *A Handbook of Qualitative Methodologies for Mass Communication Research*. London: Routledge.

Jensen, Klaus Bruhn. 1991. "Humanistic scholarship as qualitative science: contributions to mass communication research". In: Klaus Bruhn Jensen and Nicholas Jankowski (eds). *A Handbook of Qualitative Methodologies for Mass Communication Research*. London: Routledge.

Jensen, Klaus Bruhn. 1992. *Mimeo*. Nordic Seminar on Ethnography and reception studies. Vipperød, Denmark.

Jensen, Klaus Bruhn and Nicholas Jankowski (eds). 1991. *A Handbook of Qualitative Methodologies for Mass Communication Research*. London: Routledge.

Jensen, Klaus Bruhn et al. 1993. *Når danskerne ser TV: En undersøgelse af danske seeres brug og oplevelse af TV som flow*. Copenhagen: Samfundslitteratur.

Jensen, Solveig, Finn Rasmussen and Thomas Tufte. 1989. *Oplysningsarbejdets Dialektik*. Copenhagen: Kultursociologis Reproserie.

Jones, Debora. 1980. "Gossip: Notes on women's oral culture". *Women's Studies International Quarterly*, 3, 193-198.

Katz, Elihu and Tamar Liebes. 1987. "Decoding *Dallas*: Notes from a cross-cultural study". In: Horace Newcomb (ed). *Television: The Critical View*. Oxford: Oxford University Press.

Kehl, Maria Rita. 1986. "Eu vi um Brasil na Tv". In: Inimá Simões, Alcir Henrique da Costa and Maria Rita Kehl. *Um Pais no Ar: Historia da TV brasileira em tres canais*. São Paulo: Brasiliense.

Kjørup, Søren. 1992. "Faktion - en farlig blanding". In: *Mediekultur* 18-19. 62-72.

Klagsbrunn, Marta and Beatriz Resende. 1991. "A Telenovela no Rio de Janeiro 1950-1963". *Quase Catálogo* 4. Rio de Janeiro: CIEC Escolade Comunicação UFRJ.

Kottak. Conrad Phillip. 1990. *Prime-Time Society. An Anthropological Analysis of Television and Culture*. Belmont: Wadsworth Publishing Company.

Kvale, Steinar. 1996. *InterViews. An Introduction to Quatitative Research Interviewing*. London: Sage.

Lasswell, H. 1948. "The structure and function of communication in society". In: B. Berelson and M. Janowitz (eds). *Reader in Public Opinion and Communication*, Glencoe, IL: The Press.

Leal, Ondina Fachel. 1985. *Mass Communication: Culture and Ideology. A field statement*. Berkeley: University of Califomia.

Leal, Ondina Fachel. 1986. *A Leitura Social da Novela das Oito*. Petrópolis: Editora Vozes.

Leal, Ondina Fachel. 1990. "Popular Taste and Erudite Repetoire: The Place and Space of Television in Brazil". In: *Cultural Studies*.

Leal, Ondina Fachel and Ruben Oliven. 1988. "Class Interpretations of a Soap Opera Narrative: the Case of the Brazilian Novela Summer Sun". *Theory, Culture and Society*. Vol 5, pp. 81-89.

Lewis, Oscar. 1968 (1959). *Dagligt Liv i Mexico. En skildring af fem familier*. København: Samleren.

Lima, Francisco Assis de Sousa. 1985. *Conto popular e comunidade narrativa*. Rio de Janeiro: FUNARTE.

Lindlof, Thomas and Timothy Meyer. 1987. "Mediated Communication as Ways of Seeing, Acting, and Constructing Culture: The Tools and Foundations of Qualitative Research". *In: Mediated Communication ad Culture*.

Livingstone, Sonia. 1998. "Audience Research at the crossroads: the 'implied audience' in media and cultural theory". In: *European Journal of Cultural Studies*. Vol.1 No.2, May 1998. 193-218.

Livingstone, Sonia M. & P. K. Lunt. 1994. *Talk on Television: The Critical Reception of Audience Discussion Programmes*. London: Routledge.

Lloyd, Peter. 1979. *Slums of Hope. Shanty Towns of the Third World*. London: Hammondsworth.

Lopes, Maria Immacolata V. 1993. "Communication Research in Brazil". In: Jose Marques de Melo (ed). *Communication for a new world: Brazilian perspectives*. São Paulo: ECA/USA *Intercom*, No. 62/63. 1993. Special Issue on Brazilian telenovelas.

Lull, James. 1980. "The Social Uses of Television". *Human Communication Research* Vol 6, No. 3: 195-209.

Lull, James. 1988a. *World Families Watch Television*. Newbury Park: Sage.

Lull, James. 1988b. "Critical response: the audience as nuisance". *Critical Studies in Mass Communication* 4: 318-22.

Lull, James. 1990. *Inside Family Viewing: Ethnographic Research on Television's Audiences*. London: Routledge.

Lull, James. 1991. *China Turned On: Television, Reform, and Resistance*. London: Routledge.

Lull, James. 1995. *Media, communication, culture. A Global Approach*. Cambridge: Polity Press.

Lull, James. 1997. La "vericidad" política de Estudios Culturales". In: *Comunicación y Sociedad* 29: 55-72. Universidad de Gualajara, Mexico.

Lull, James. 1998. Interviewed by Nilda Jacks and Thomas Tufte. "En los Estudios Culturales, el sur también existe". Buenos Aires. *Causas y Azares*. No 7. 145-153.

Løngren, Hanne and Birgitte Holm Sørensen. 1993. "Deltagerobservation - tv: det elektroniske familiemedlem". *Mediekultur* 21: 58-69. Aalborg.

MacBride, Sean (ed). 1980. *Many Voices, One World: Towards a New More Just and More Efficient World Information and Communication Order*. London: Kogan Page.

Macedo, Claudia, Angela Falção, Candido J.M. De Almeida (eds). 1988. *TV ao Vivo: Depoimentos.* São Paulo: Editora Brasiliense.

Machado, Romero C. 1988. *A fundaçáo Roberto Marinho.* Porto Alegre: tche.

Marcondes Filho, Ciro. 1991. *Quem manipula quem?* Petrópolis: Vozes.

Marinho, Roberto. 1985. In: *Newsweek*, 23.9.85.

Marques de Melo, Jose (ed). 1985. *Comunicação e transição democrática.* Porto Alegre: Mercado Aberto.

Marques de Melo et al. 1971. *Folkcomunicacao.* São Paulo: ECA-USP.

Marques de Melo. 1973. *Comunicacao Social: teoria e pesquisa.* Petrópolis: Vozes.

Marques de Melo, Jose. 1988. "Communication theory and research in Latin America; a preliminary balance of the past twenty-five years". *Media, Culture and Society.* Vol. 10, No. 4: 405-418.

Marques de Melo, Jose (ed). 1989. *Comunicação na America Latina.* São Paulo: Papirus.

Marques de Melo, Jose. 1992. "Mass Media and politics in Brazil. The Collor phenomenon". In: Jose Marques de Melo (ed). *Brazilian Communicahon Research Yearbook 1* pp 122-139. São Paulo: University of São Paulo.

Marques de Melo, Jose (ed). 1996. *Identidades Culturais LatinoAmericanas em tempos de comunicacao global.* São Bernardo: Editora Edims/Catedra UNESCO.

Marques de Melo, Jose (ed). *Teoria da Comunicação. Paradigmas Latino-Americanos.* Petropolis: Editora Vozes.

Marques de Melo, Jose and Jucara Gorski Brittes (eds). 1998. A Trajetoria Comunicacional de Luiz Ramiro Beltrán. Sao Bernardo do Campo, São Paulo: UNESCO/UMESP.

Martín-Barbero, Jesús. 1987. *De los medios a las mediaciones: Communicación, cultura y hegemonia.* Barcelona: Gustavo Gili.

Martín-Barbero, Jesús. 1988. "Communication from culture: the crisis of the national and the emergence of the popular". *Media, Culture and Society.* Vol. 10, No. 4: 447-466.

Martín-Barbero, Jesús. 1989. "A comunicacao no projeto de uma nova cultura política". In: Jose Marques de Melo (ed). *Comunicacao na America Latina.* São Paulo: Papirus.

Martín-Barbero, Jesús. 1991. "Pensar la sociedad desde la comunicación: un lugar strategico para el debate a la modernidad". *Diagolos* 32: 28-33.

Martín-Barbero, Jesús. 1993a. *Communication, Culture and Hegmony.* London: Sage.

Martín-Barbero, Jesús. 1993b. "La Telenovela en columbia. Television, melodrama y vida cotidiana". In: Nora Mazziotti (ed). *El espectáculo de la pasion: Las telenovelas latinoamericanas.* Buenos Aires: Colihue.

Martín-Barbero, Jesús. 1996. "La Ciudad Virtual - transformaciones de la sensibilidad y nuevos escenarios de comunicación". *Revista de la Universidad del Valle* No. 14, August 1996. 26-38.

Martín-Barbero, Jesús. 1997. "Globalización communicacional y descentramiento cultural". In: *Dialogos*, No. 50, Okt. 1997. Lima, Peru: Felafacs. 27-42.

Martín-Barbero, Jesús y Sonia Munoz (eds). 1992. *Television y Melodrama.* Colombia: Tercer Mundo Editores.

Martine, George. 1996. "Brazil's Fertility Decline, 1965-95: A Fresh Look at Key Factors". In: *Population and Development Review 22* (1): 47-75. March 1996.

Mattelart, Armand. 1974. *La cultura como empresa multinacional.* Mexico: Ediciones Era.

Mattelart, Armand. 1976. *As Multinacionais da Cultura.* Rio: Civilizacao.

Mattelart, Armand and Michele. 1989. *O Carnaval das Imagens.* São Paulo: Editora Brasiliense.

Mattelart, Armand and Michele. 1991. "La recepción: el retorno al sujeto". *Dialogos* 30:10-18.

Mattelart, Armand, Michele Mattelart and Xavier Delcourt. 1987. *A cultura contra a democracia?* São Paulo: Brasiliense.

Mattelart, Michele. 1986. *Women, Media and Crisis: Femininity and Disorder.* London: Comedia.

Mattos, Sergio. 1990. *Um perfil da TV brasileira: 40 años de historia: 1950-1990.* Salvador: A TARDE.

Mazziotti, Nora. 1983. "Migraciones internas y recomposición de la cultura popular urbana (1935-1950)". Mimeo. Buenos Aires.

Mazziotti, Nora. 1993a. "Intertextualidades en la telenovela Argentina: Melodrama y Costumbrismo". In: Nora Mazziotti (ed). *El espectáculo de la pasion: Las telenovelas latinoamericanas.* Buenos Aires: Colihue.

Mazziotti, Nora (ed). 1993. *El espectáculo de la pasion: Las telenovelas latinoamericanas.* Buenos Aires: Colihue.

Mazziotti, Nora. 1996. *La industria de la telenovela. La producción de ficción en America Latina.* Buenos Aires: Editora Paidós.

Mazziotti, Nora. 1998. "All that ratings allow. Fiction and market in Argentina TV". Paper presented at International Conference, Tel Aviv. June 1998.

McAnany, E. & La Pastina, A.C. (1994). "Telenovela Audience".In: *Communication Research*, 21 (6): 828-49.

Media Development. Cultural Boundaries: Identities and Communication in Latin America. No. 1/97 Vol XLIV. London: WACC.

Media, Culture and Society Vol. 10 No. 4. 1988. Special Issue on Latin American Perspectives. SAGE.

Media, Culture and Society Vol. 13 No. 2. 1991. Special Issue on The Analysis of "Culture".

Mead, Margaret. "Visual Anthropology in a Discipline of Words". In: Paul Hockings (ed). *Principles of Visual Anthropology.* The Hague/Paris: Mouton Publishers.

Mediekultur 7. 1988. Special Issue on Reception Analysis. Aarhus: SMID.

Meers, Ph. & Biltereyst, D. 1997. *Telenovelas through Europe.* (report) Leuven: Department of Communication.

Meira, Tarcisio. In: *Veja*, 11.03.87.

Meyrowitz, Joshua. 1985. *No Sense of Place: The impact of electronic media on social behaviour.* New York: Oxford University Press.

Miceli, Sergio. 1972. *A noite da madrinha*. São Paulo: Editora Perspectiva.

Midgley, J., Anthony Hall, Margeret Hardiman and Dhanpaul Narine. 1986. *Community Participation, Social Development and the State*. London: Methuen.

Milanesi, Luiz Augusto. 1978. *O Paraíso via Embratel*. Rio de Janeiro: Paz e Terra.

Modleski, Tania. 1982. *Loving with a vengeance*. New York: Routledge.

Monsivais, C. 1978. "Notas sobre la cultura popular in Mexico". In: *Latin American Perspectives*, No. 5 (1).

Moores, Shaun. 1993. *Interpreting Audiences - the ethnography of Media Consumption*. London: Sage.

Moores, Shaun. 1996. *Satellite Television and Everyday Life - articulating technology*. London: University of Luton Press.

Morley, David. 1980. *The "Nationwide" Audience*. London: British Film Institute.

Morley, David. 1986. *Family Television*. London: Comedia.

Morley, David. 1989. "Changing paradigms in audience studies". In: E. Seiter, H. Borchers, G. Kreutzner and E. Warth (eds). *Remote Control: Television, Audiences, and Cultural Power*. London: Routledge.

Morley, David. 1992. *Television, Audiences and Cultural Studies*. London: Routledge.

Morley, David and Robins, Kevin. 1995. *Spaces of Identity. Global Media, Electronic Landscapes and Cultural Boundaries*. London: Routledge.

Morley, David and Roger Silverstone. 1991. "Communication and context: ethnographic perspectives on the media audience". In: Klaus Bruhn Jensen and Nicholas Jankowski (eds). *A Handbook of Qualitative Methodologies for Mass Communication Research*. London: Routledge.

Morris, Nancy & Philip Schlesinger. "Cultural Boundaries: identity and communication in Latin America". In: *Media Development 1/1997*. London: WACC. 5-17.

Murdock, Graham. 1989. "Critical Inquiry and Audience Activity". In: B. Dervin et al. (eds). *Rethinking Communications*. London: Sage.

Negt, O. and, A. Kluge. 1963. *Offentlighet og Erfaring*. Nordisk Sommeruniversitet.

Newcomb, Horace (ed). 1987. *Television: The critical view*. Oxford: Oxford University Press.

Newcomb, Horace. 1991. "The Creation of Television Drama". In: Klaus Bruhn Jensen and Nicholas Jankowski (eds). *A Handbook of Qualitative Methodologies for Mass Communication Research*. London: Routledge.

Nielsen, Poul Erik. 1992. *Bag Holleywoods drømmefabrik: Tv-system og produktionsforhold i amerikansk TV*. Aarhus: Aarhus University. Ph.D Dissertation. 360p.

Nogueira, Armando. 1988. "Telejornalismo I - A Experiencia da Rede Globo". In: C. Macedo, A. Falcao and C.J. Mendes de Almeida (eds). 1988. *TV ao Vivo. Depoimentos*. São Paulo: Editora Brasiliense. 81-92.

Nogueira, Lisandro. 1993. "O diálogo de Gilberto Braga com Machado de Assis, Jose de Alencar, Pedro Bloch e Bernado Guimaraes". Paper presented September 1993 at Intercom Annual Conference. Vitoria, Brazil.

Novaes, Adauto. 1991. *Rede Imaginária: Televisão e democracia.* São Paulo: Compania das Letras, Secretaria Municipal da Cultura.

O'Connor, Alan. 1991. "The Emergence of Cultural Studies in Latin America". In: *Critical Studies in Mass Communication* 8 (1991), 60-73.

Olodum. 1991. *Olodum News Bulletin.* Salvador, Bahia.

ORBICOM. 1998. *ORBICOM Newsletter*, Spring 1998. Quebec, Canada.

Orozco Gomez, Guillermo. 1990. *No hay una sola manera de "hacer" televidentes.* No. 10. Vol.4.

Orozco Gomez, Guillermo. 1992. "La Audiencia Frente a la Pantalla". *Dialogos* 30: 54-63.

Orozco Gomez, Guillermo. 1993. "Television Publica y Participación Social: Al Rescate Cultural de la Pantalla". *Dialogos* 33: 4-10.

Orozco Gomez, Guillermo. 1996. *Televisión y Audiencias, Un Enfoque Cualitativo.* Madrid: Ediciones de la Torre.

Orozco Gomez, Guillermo. 1997. *La Investigación de la Comunicación Dentro y Fuera da América Latina. Tendencias, Perspectivas y Desafíos del Estudio de los Medios.* Buenos Aires: Ediciones de Periodismo y Comunicación. Universidad Nacional de la Plata.

Ortiz, Renato. 1984. "Cultura Popular no Brasil: Iluminados e Alienados". *Intercom* 49/50: 43-55.

Ortiz, Renato. 1985. *Cultura Brasileira e Identidade Nacional.* São Paulo.

Ortiz, Renato. 1986. *Cultura Brasileira & Identidade Nacional.* São Paulo: Brasiliense.

Ortiz, Renato. 1988. *A Moderna Tradicao Brasileira.* São Paulo: Editora Brasiliense.

Ortiz, Renato. 1989. "Evolucao histórica da telenovela". In: Renato, Ortiz, Silvia H.S. Borelli and José Mário Ortiz Ramos (eds). *Telenovela: Historia e Produção.*

Ortiz, Renato. 1994. *Mundialização e Cultura.* São Paulo: Editora Brasiliense.

Ortiz, Renato. 1997. "World Modernity and Identities". In: *Media Development 1/1997*, Vol. XLIV. London: WACC. 37-40.

Ortiz, Renato and Jose Mário Ortiz Ramos. 1989. "A produção industrial e cultural da telenovela". In: Renato, Ortiz, Silvia H.S. Borelli and Jose Mário Ortiz Ramos (eds). *Telenovela: Historia e Produção.*

Ortiz, Renato, Silvia H.S. Borelli and Jose Mário Ortiz Ramos (eds). 1989. *Telenovela: Historia e Produção.*

Palmer, Jerry. 1987. *The logic of the absurd: on film and television comedy.* London: British Film Institute.

Palmer, Jerry. 1990. "Genrer og medier - et kort overblik". In: *Mediekultur* 14: S-17.

Pasquali, A. 1963. *Communicación y Cultura de Masas.* Caracas: Universidad Central de Venezuela.

Penacchioni, Irene. 1984. "The reception of popular television in Northeast Brazil". *Media, Culture and Society 6:* 337-341.

Peruzzo, Cicilia M. K. 1993. "Community communication, culture and citizenship". In: Jose Marques de Melo (ed). *Communication for a new world: Brazilian perspectives.* São Paulo: ECA/USP.

Petraglia, Claúdio G. 1988. "Programação II - Definição de um Projeto: Rede Bandeirantes". In: C. Macedo, A. Falcão and C.J. Mendes de Almeida (eds). 1988. *TV ao Vivo. Depoimentos.* São Paulo: Editora Brasiliense. 71-80.

Pignatari, Decio. 1984. *Signagem da televisão.* São Paulo: Brasiliense.

Pike, K. 1966 "Etic and Emic Standpoints for the Description of Behaviour". In: A. Smith (ed). *Communication and Culture.* New York: Holt, Rinehart & Winston. pp. 152-163

Ramos, Roberto. 1987. *Grã-finos na Globo: Cultura e merchandising nas novelas.* Petropolis: Vozes.

Ramos, Jose Mário Ortiz and Silvia H.S. Borelli. 1989. "A telenovela diária". In: Renato, Ortiz, Silvia H.S. Borelli and Jose Mário Ortiz Ramos (eds). *Telenovela: Historia e Produçáo.*

Rasmussen, Tove Arendt and Peter Kofoed. 1986. *Dallas.* Århus.

Radway, J.A. 1983. "Women Read the Romance: An interaction of Text and Context". In: *Feminist Studies* 9, no.1.

Radway, J.A. 1984. *Reading the Romance. Women, Patriarchy and Popular Literature.* London: Verso.

Radway, J.A. 1988. "Reception study: Ethnography and the Problems of Dispersed Audiences and Nomadic Subjects". In: *Cultural Studies* 2, 3: 359-76.

Reeves, Geoffrey. 1993. *Communications and the "Third World".* London: Routledge.

Riccó, Atílio. 1991. *Personal Interview* by Thomas Tufte. Rio de Janeiro, February 1991.

Ridell, Seija. 1996. "Resistance Through Routines. Flow Theory and the Power of Metaphors". In: *European Journal of Communication.* SAGE/London. Vol. 11(4): 557-582.

Ridell, Seija. 1998. "Audience as Concept in Cultural Media Studies". Paper presented at the *Crossroads in Cultural Studies Conference*: Tampere, Finland, June 28-July 1 1998.

Rivera, J.B. 1980. *La Forja del Escritor Profesional.* Buenos Aires. CE de AL.

Rogers, et al. 1992. Paper presented at the IAMCR Conference in Guaruja, Brazil.

Romero, L.A. 1984. "Una empresa cultural para los sectores populares: Editoriales y libros en Buenos Aires en la entreguerra". *Mimeo.* Buenos Aires.

Rostow, W.W. 1960. *The Stages of Economic Growth: A Non-Communist Manifesto.* Cambridge: Cambridge University Press.

Rowe, William and Vivian Schelling. 1991. *Memory and Modernity. Popular Culture in Latin America.* London: Verso.

Sainte-Hilaire, Auguste de. 1975 (1830). *Viagem pelas províncias do Rio de Janeiro e Minas Gerais.* Editora da Universidade de São Paulo/Itatiaia.

Salles, Mauro. 1988. "A Televisão no Brasil e no Mundo". In: C. Macedo, A. Falcao and C.J. Mendes de Almeida (eds). 1988. *TV ao Vivo. Depoimentos.* São Paulo: Editora Brasiliense. 11-24.

Salles, Vicente. 1985. *Repente & Cordel.* Rio de Janeiro: FUNARTE.

Santoro, Luiz Fernando. 1989. *A Imagem Nas Maos.* São Paulo: Summus Editorial.

Scannell, Paddy. 1991. Introduction: "The Relevance of Talk". In: Paddy Scannell (ed). *Broadcast Talk.* London: Sage.

Scannell, Paddy. 1993. "Communication as Social Interaction". *Mimeo.* Annual Conference of SMID 1993. Ebeltoft, Denmark.

Scannell, Paddy. 1994. "Communicative Intentionality in Broadcasting". *Mediekultur* 22.

Schrøder, Kim. 1984. "Et måleinstruments anvendelighed: Om "den ideologiske seismograf"". *Massekultur & Medier* 12: 8-35.

Schrøder, Kim. 1988. "Oplevelsens Kvalitet". *Mediekultur 7:*101-118.

Schrøder, Kim. 1993. "Den etnografiske bølge og receptionsforskningen". *Mediekultur* 21.

Schwarz, Christina and Oscar Jaramillo. 1986. "Hispanic American Critical Communication Research in Its Historical Context". In: Atwood, Rita and Emile McAnany. *Communication and Latin American Society. Trends in Critical Research, 1960-1985.* The University of Wisconsin Press.

Seiter, E., H. Borchers, G. Kreutzner, and E. Warth (eds). 1989. *Remote Control: Television, Audiences, and Cultural Power.* London: Routledge.

Silverstone, Roger. 1991. "From Audiences to Consumers: Household and the Consumpdon of Communication and Information". *European Journal of Communication* Vol. 6 No. 2: 135-155.

Silverstone, Roger. 1994. *Television and Everyday Life.* London. Routledge.

Silverstone, Roger. 1997. Introduction. In: Silverstone, Roger (ed).*Visions of Suburbia.* London: Routledge. 1-25.

Simões, Inimá, F. 1986. "TV á Chateaubriand". In: Inimá Simões, Alcir Henrique da Costa and Maria Rita Kehl. *Um Pais no Ar: Historia da TV brasileira em tres canais.* São Paulo: Brasiliense.

Simões, Inimá F., Alcir Henrique da Costa and Maria Rita Kehl.1986. *Um Pais no Ar: Historia da TV brasileira em tres canais.* São Paulo: Brasiliense.

Sinclair, John, Elisabeth Jacka and Stuart Cunningham. 1996. "Peripheral vision: world regional television markets in the satellite age". In: *Intercom.* Vol. XIX. No. 2 1996. São Paulo: Intercom.

Sinclair, John. 1998. "Geolinguistic Region as Global Space. The Case of Latin America". Paper presented to the Working Group on Regional Communication and Cultural Diversity at IAMCRs 21st Conference, Glasgow, July 26-30.

Sjørslev, Inger. 1983. "Ritual magt og social undertrykkelse i Brasilien". In: *Den Ny Verden,* No.4.

Skovmand, Michael. 1990. "Raymond Williams - et overblik". *Mediekultur* 13: 55-58.

Slater, Candace. 1987. "Literatura de Cordel (Folk - Popular Poetry)and the Mass Media in Today's Brazil". *Hispanic American Historical Review* 1987.

Sodré, Muniz. 1977. *0 Monopolio da Fala.* São Paulo: Vozes.

Sodré, Muniz. 1991. *0 Brasil simulado e o real: ensaio sobre o quotidiano nacional.* Rio de Janeiro: Rio Fundo Editora Ltda.

Soja, Edward. 1996. *ThirdSpace. Journeys to Los Angeles and other real-and-imagined places*. Malden/Oxford. Blackwell.

Straubhaar, Joseph. 1982. "The development of the telenovela as the pre-eminent form of popular culture in Brazil". In: *Studies in Latin American Popular Culture*, pp. 138-150. Tucson.

Straubhaar, Joseph. 1983. "The Wane of Brazilian Show de Auditorio Television Programs: Popular Culture, Industry, and Censorship". In: *Studies in Latin American Popular Culture*, Vol.2.

Straubhaar, Joseph. 1998. "Cultural Capital, Language, Travel and Cultural Proximity in the Globalization of Television". Paper presented at *Crossroads in Cultural Studies*, June/July 1998, Tampere, Finland.

Thompson, John B. 1995. *The Media and Modernity - a social theory of the media*. Cambridge: Polity Press.

Tufte, Thomas et al. 1986. *Brasilianske basismenigheder - konkretutopiske implikationer*. Department of Cultural Sociology, University of Copenhagen.

Tufte, Thomas et al. 1990. *Jurema & Co. i Brasilien: Selvfølgelig gør de modstand! Hverdagsliv og udvikling, slum ogbevægelse*. Copenhagen: Kultursociologisk Reproserie, No. 4.

Tufte, Thomas. 1993a. "Everyday life, women and telenovelas in Brazil". In: Anamaria Fadul (ed). *Serial Fiction in TV: the Latin American telenovelas with an annotated bibliography of Brazilian telenovelas*. São Paulo: USP.

Tufte, Thomas. 1993b. "Hverdagsliv og telenovelaer". *Mediekultur* 21: 45-57

Tufte, Thomas. 1994. "Telenovela'en - introduktion til en genre". *Mediekultur*. Special Issue on TV, Culture and Development in Latin America.

Tufte, Thomas. 1995. "How do telenovelas serve to articulate hybrid cultures in contemporary Brazil?". In: *The Nordicom Review of Nordic Research on Media and Communication*. No.2/1995. Nordicom, Göteborg University.

Tufte, Thomas. 1996a. "La Televisión como un mediador cultural - el caso de las telenovelas Brasilenas". In: Jose Marques de Melo (ed). *Identidades Latinoamericanos em Tempos de Comunicação Global*. IMS/UNESCO, São Paulo, Brazil.

Tufte, Thomas. 1996b. "Estudos de Midia na America Latina". In: *Comunicação e Sociedade* No. 25. São Paulo, Brazil. 21-49. Special Issue on "O pensamento latinoamericano em comunicacao".

Tufte, Thomas. 1997a. "Televisión, Modernidad y Vida Cotidiana. Un Análisis sobre la obra de Roger Silverstone desde contextos culturales diferentes". In: *Comunicacion y Sociedad*. Universidad de Guadalajara, Mexico. 65-96.

Tufte, Thomas. 1997b. "Questoes a serem estudadas em estudos etnograficos de mídia: mediacoes e hibridizacao cultural na vida cotidiana" (Questions to be studied in media ethnography: mediation and cultural hybridity in everyday life). In Maria Immacolata V. de Lopes (ed). *Contemporary Issues in Communication*, INTERCOM/EDICON, São Paulo, Brazil.

Tufte, Thomas. 1998. "Local Lives, Global Media, Multiple Identities". In: Hjarvard & Tufte (Eds). *Audio-Visual Media in Transition, Sekvens 1998*. Yearbook of Dept. of Film and Media Studies. University of Copenhagen, Denmark.

Tufte, Thomas (1999). "The Popular Forms of Hope - tv-fiction, audience consumption and social change in Brazil: a media ethnographical approach". In Ingunn Hagen and Janet Vasco: *Consuming Audiences? Production and Reception in Audience Research* . New York: Hampton Press.

Tufte, Thomas. (1999). "Television Fiction, National Identity and Democracy - the role of national television fiction in modern societies". In: Durousseau, Isabelle (ed). *Reception de la Television*. L'Institut Francais, Copenhagen, Denmark.

Tulloch, John. 1989. *Television Drama: Agency, Audience and Myth.* London: Routledge.

Tunstall, Jeremy. 1977. *The media are Amercian.* London: Constable.

Turner, Graeme. 1990. *British Cultural Studies: An Introduction.* Boston: Unwin Hyman.

UNDP. 1996. *Human Development Report.* UNDP: New York.

UNDP. 1997. *Human Development Report.* UNDP: New York.

UNESCO. 1998. *World Culture Report. Culture, Creativity and Markets.* Paris: UNESCO Publishing.

UNICEF. 1991. First Latin American Tv Scriptwriters' Workshop. UNICEF Bogotá: Regional Office for Latin America and the Carribbean.

Uribe, Ana. 1993. "La telenovela en la vida familiar cotidiana en Mexico". In: Anamaria Fadul. *Serial Fiction in TV. The Latin American Telenovelas.* São Paulo: USP.

Van Tilburg, Joao Luiz. 1979/1980. *A Telenovela Instrumento de Educacao Permanente.* Petropolis.

Van Tilburg, Joao Luiz. 1989. "A Televisao no Brasil". *Mimeo.* Rio de Janeiro.

Van Tilburg, Joao Luis. 1990. *A televisao e o mundo de trabalho: o poder de barganha do cidadao-telespectador.* São Paulo: Paulinas.

Van Tilburg, Joao Luiz. 1990. "Ecologia e Telenovela". *Mimeo.* Rio de Janeiro.

Van Tilburg, Joao Luiz. 1991a. "A Estrutura da Televisao Brasileira: Fator de Integracao". *Mimeo.* Rio de Janeiro.

Van Tilburg, Joao Luiz. 1991b. "A especificidade da TV Brasileira: alguns prolegomenos." *Mimeo.* Rio de Janeiro.

Van Tilburg, Joáo Luiz. 1993. "A Leitura de um texto televisivo". Paper presented September 1993 at Intercom Annual Conference. Vitoria, Brazil.

Varis, Tapio. 1985. *International Flow of Television Programmes.* Reports and Papers on Mass Communication. No. 100, Paris: UNESCO Publishing.

Verón, Eliseo. 1977 (1963). *Ideologia, estrutura, comunicacao.* São Paulo: Editora Cultrix.

Verón, Eliseo. 1993. Relato televisivo e imaginario social. In: Nora Mazziotti (ed). *El espectáculo de la pasion: Las telenovelas latinoamericanas.* Buenos Aires: Colihue.

Vink, Nico. 1988. *The Telenovela and Emancipation: a study on tv and social change in Brazil.* Amsterdam: Royal Tropical Institute.

Vink, Nico. 1990. "A subcultura da classe trabalhadora e a decodificação da novela brasileira". In: *Intercom. Revista Brasileira de Comunicação.* V. 13, No. 62/63, pp.97-118. São Paulo.

Werlen, Benno. 1993. *Society, Action and Space. An Alternative Human Geography.* London: Routledge.

Wildermuth, Norbert. 1998. "Global going local: Fighting for the Indian Tv Audiences". In: Hjarvard & Tufte (eds). *Audio-Visual Media in Transition, Sekvens 1998.* Yearbook of Dept. of Film and Media Studies. University of Copenhagen, Denmark.

Williams, Raymond. 1966. *Communications.* London.

Williams, Raymond. 1977 (1990). *Marxism and Literature.* London: Oxford University Press.

Williams, Raymond. 1975 (1990). *Television: technology and cultural form.* London: Routledge.

Williams, Raymond. 1981. *Culture.* London: Fontana Press.

Williams, Raymond. 1988. "Kulturen og Teknologien". In: *Mediekultur* 13: 59-81.

Willis, Paul. 1980. "Notes on method". In: Stuart Hall, Dorothy Hobson, Andrew Lowe and Paul Willis (eds). *Culture, Media, Language.* London: Unwin Hyman.

Willis, Paul. 1986. "Deltagerobservation som metode". In: Bai and Drotner (eds). *Ungdom. En stil, et liv.* Copenhagen: Tiderne Skifter.